THE STONES

'Compulsively readable'
*New Statesman*

'A book which I found every bit as riveting as SHOUT.
If you want to know what makes the world's number
one group tick, then this is the book to read'
*Manchester Evening News*

'Wonderfully unravels the social history of that
extraordinary time, and does not pull any punches'
*Daily Telegraph*

'A wide-ranging book . . . an excellent piece of research
and a good read'
*The Journal, Newcastle-upon-Tyne*

'The book is well worth reading. Mr Norman is that
rarity among chroniclers of rock: beady-eyed without
being either sensationalistic or unsympathetic . . . It
makes salutary reading'
*Dublin Evening Press*

'His account of the group's early years is excellent, and
his penetrating sketches of individual members'
personalities reveal a novelist's searching eye'
*Publishers Weekly*

Philip Norman travelled extensively as a correspondent for *The Sunday Times*, writing profiles of figures as diverse as Indira Gandhi, Elizabeth Taylor and P.G. Wodehouse. He has written widely about rock and blues music for *The Times* and *The Sunday Times*, and a collection of these articles, *The Road Goes On Forever*, was published by Corgi in 1984. He has won critical acclaim for his novels *Slip on a Fat Lady*, *Plumridge* and *The Skaters' Waltz*, and particularly for his bestselling biography of the Beatles, *Shout!*

Also by Philip Norman

THE SKATERS' WALTZ
SHOUT! THE TRUE STORY OF THE BEATLES
THE ROAD GOES ON FOREVER

and published by Corgi Books

# The Stones

## Philip Norman

**CORGI BOOKS**

# THE STONES

## A CORGI BOOK 0 552 12487 7

Originally published in Great Britain by Elm Tree
Books/Hamish Hamilton Ltd.

PRINTING HISTORY
Elm Tree/Hamish Hamilton edition published 1984
Corgi edition published 1985

This book is set in 10/11 Baskerville

Corgi Books are published by Transworld Publishers Ltd.,
Century House, 61–63 Uxbridge Road, Ealing,
London W5 5SA, in Australia by Transworld Publishers
(Aust.) Pty. Ltd., 26 Harley Crescent, Condell Park,
NSW 2200, and in New Zealand by Transworld Publishers
(N.Z.) Ltd., Cnr. Moselle and Waipareira Avenues,
Henderson, Auckland.

Made and printed in Great Britain by the
Guernsey Press Co. Ltd., Guernsey, Channel Islands.

To Angela Miller

# *Contents*

# Acknowledgements

The author and publisher would like to thank the following for permission to use copyright photographs in this book:

Adam Cooper for photographs by the late Michael Cooper: p. 3 (Andrew Oldham); p. 4 (bottom picture); p. 5 (bottom picture); p. 6 (bottom picture); p. 7 (bottom picture); p. 11 (both pictures)

Ken Llewellyn: p. 1 (all pictures)

Rex Features Ltd: p. 2 (line-up with Ian Stewart – photo by Dezo Hoffmann); p. 3 (Battersea Park – photo by Dezo Hoffmann); p. 10 (Rock 'n' Roll Circus – photo by David Magnus); p. 16 (top picture – photo by Richard Young)

Pictorial Press Ltd: p. 2 (concert poster)

EPS Bent rej: p. 3 (Eric Easton)

Popperfoto: p. 4 (top picture); p. 13 (top picture)

Gered Mankowitz: p. 5 (top picture)

Syndication International: p. 7 (top picture); p. 8 (top picture); p. 10 (Beggars Banquet); p. 13 (bottom picture)

Granada Television Ltd: p. 8 (bottom picture); p. 9 (both pictures); p. 12 (top picture)

James Barraclough: p. 12 (bottom picture)

Keystone Press Agency Ltd: p. 10 (Brian and Anita); p. 16 (bottom picture)

Christopher Sykes: pp. 14 and 15 (all pictures)

The extract from *The Cecil Beaton Diaries: The Parting Years* is reproduced courtesy of George Weidenfeld & Nicolson Ltd; the extract from William Rees-Mogg's *Times* leader of July 1, 1967 courtesy of Times Newspapers Ltd; and the extract from the *World in Action* programme of July 31, 1967, 'Off the Hook', courtesy of Granada Television Ltd. Thanks also to *New Musical Express* and *Record Mirror* for permission to quote extracts from these publications.

The title of Chapter 2 is taken from 'Round and Around' and Chapter 3 from 'Come On', © Arc Music, UK publisher Jewel Music. Chapter 1 is from 'Jumpin' Jack Flash', Chapter 7 from 'Under My Thumb'; Chapter 10 from 'Sing This All Together' and Chapter 11 from 'Street Fighting Man', all © Abkco Music Inc./Westminster Music.

Every effort has been made to contact the copyright holders of material used in this book. Should any omission have been made, we apologise and will be pleased to make the appropriate acknowledgements in any future editions.

# 'God Speed the Rolling Stones'

The John F. Kennedy Stadium, Philadelphia, is built of reddish stone embellished with turrets, loophole windows and irregular battlements reminiscent of a British fort in nineteenth century India. Today, September 25, 1981, it has the appearance of such a fort long breached and overrun by mutineers. On the outside, all is eerily quiet. A pallid sun beats down on the steel mesh fences, the raw concrete approaches and the white helmets of mistrustful police, left to guard a mass of parked cars that surrounds JFK Stadium for approximately five square miles. Decrepit gas-guzzlers, garish Dodge pickups, old Volkswagen buses with 'Philly or bust' scratched among mouldering graffiti, stand row on row, block after block, sullenly yielding up their last pigments to the heat. Youth is on the move again in America, leaving behind, as is customary, promiscuous deposits of food wrappers, bottles, cans, fried chicken tubs and foot-crunched paper cups.

Close to, JFK Stadium emits a steady roar, as if huge amounts of wet shingle are seething under a tide which its red battlements can barely keep in check. This afternoon, the Rolling Stones give the first concert in their twentieth anniversary tour of America and Europe. Ninety thousand people are waiting to welcome back the World's Greatest Rock 'n' Roll Band.

The stadium doors lead to long sub-Gothic cloisters, lined with stalls purveying the T-shirts, sweatshirts and other merchandise which the Rolling Stones have authorised to be sold at venues along the route of their twentieth anniversary tour. T-shirts, hung up like Neapolitan laundry lines, bear the Stones' name in gold, red and black mid-Seventies script. On the reverse, a cartoon dragon rears over North America, its thick red lips parted to hang out a sagging and lascivious tongue. The sweatshirts cost $12.50 each, the T-shirts $10.50. Almost every boy and girl in the lower concourse wears a T-shirt or sweatshirt, carries a poster or sports a

11

badge or button or pocket patch imprinted with that same unmistakable mouth and lolling tongue. Here and there among the pillars are roped-off enclosures with rows of stretchers, ready for the casualties which will occur when the owner of the mouth eventually shows himself.

Dirty stairs, through unfinished concrete cross-beams, lead to the terraces where people have paid fifteen dollars to see the Rolling Stones from no more than a quarter of a mile away. It is like emerging suddenly in the midst of downtown Calcutta. Boys and girls, crushed together on shallow stone ledges, extend upwards and downwards, in a great, seething human tenement of blue denim and brown skin, as far as the eye can see. Many are already drunk, many more semi-comatose with the marijuana that can be smoked almost openly in America nowadays. The attention of all is fixed on that far curve of the stadium where a pink, purple and faint yellow stage stands between two scaffolding towers, moored in place by bunches of multi-coloured balloons. The sky is full of small aircraft, towing indecipherable messages or relaying reports to local radio stations. From time to time, a police helicopter swoops down low, casting a shadow like a giant bee over the shirtless multitude furthest out in the sun.

Habits peculiar to the Stones fifteen years ago have evolved through their countless imitators, into time-honoured Rock concert tradition. It has long been acknowledged that no band which aspires to greatness ever begins playing on time. With the World's Greatest Rock 'n' Roll Band, lateness is naturally expected on an heroic scale. The crowd in JFK Stadium has waited four hours already, at the mercy of heat and hot dog vendors, with no entertainment save an obscure 'support band' and occasional records booming over the PA. It bears its vigil, not merely with patience, but with an enjoyment divorced from anything seen or heard so far today. This is the first young generation for whom nostalgia is more powerful than hope. Nostalgia for a past never experienced, and a youth never savoured, keeps them almost happy as one tedious, sticky hour follows another. This, surely, must be how it felt at Woodstock or in Hyde Park, back when young people ruled the world and gathered so often in exaltation under the brilliant, strange-scented Sixties sun.

*    *    *

The stage that will accompany the Stones across America – and, later, Europe – squats on its end curve of the stadium, straining gently under its rainbow barrage of balloons. Each 70-foot high side panel is a swirl of dim blue and yellow Japanese shapes, incorporating Mick Jagger's mouth and an American flag, zigzagged instead of striped. The performing area is a pink and purple apron, stretched into a pair of purple catwalks extending almost to the nearest spectator blocks. Above the left-hand catwalk, a 'cherry-picker' crane waits on its 30-foot stem, close to the well-guarded scaffolding.

Empty of music as the stage still is, it nonetheless exhibits multifarious life. On the broad ramp from the backstage 'VIP enclosure', figures toil ceaselessly up into the proscenium, carrying clean towels, drinking water, guitars, cartons of cigarettes and boxes of long-stemmed carnations. Launching the five Stones into performance is an operation that involves approximately a hundred people, onstage and in the area behind, hurrying to and fro with a sense of keen urgency that does not seem to bring the concert any nearer to beginning. The black towered amplifiers give off huge gusts of unused power as a technician re-checks the computer which regulates them. There is always the chance that a local taxi company using the same frequency might interpolate a radio call gigantically into the middle of Jumping Jack Flash.

In the backstage enclosure, and a single block of empty seats behind it, some 200 journalists and photographers wait to file stories about the World's Greatest Rock 'n' Roll Band to newspapers, magazines, wire-services, radio and TV stations throughout America, Europe, Australasia and Japan. Though fifteen years have passed since the peak of their notoriety, the Rolling Stones remain indestructibly notorious, a sure-fire circulation boost in however loose a conjunction with sex, drugs and unbridled behaviour. Press interest has naturally increased with the realisation that on this present tour, the Stones reach their twentieth year together; that the ban once denounced as a risk to health as well as morals has acquired the status of an institution; that – extraordinary as it may seem – Mick Jagger is approaching his fortieth birthday.

A band whose press coverage in the past has contributed to the imprisonment of its two leading members could not be expected to treat journalists with pure naive goodwill. Even so, the delay, frustration and downright humiliation inflicted on reporters and photographers covering any Stones tour have been raised to something like an art. At Philadelphia, they are penned into an open lean-to with duckboards, reminiscent of The Camp on Blood Island. Every few minutes, in their long, uncomfortable, unrefreshed wait, some new manoeuvre is devised for herding them into a different place, even further from where they would like to be, and in general reducing their self-esteem to dust.

Such a manoeuvre, in the past few minutes, has raised a low, crooked barrier of metal equipment boxes across the enclosure, and put the press remorselessly on the uninteresting side of it. Leaning over this barrier, half-way along, is a bulky, grey-bearded man whose bald head seems half retracted into his plump shoulders, by innate caution or habitual humility. Before him, clustered with all the fervour of Russian housewives at a meat counter, half a dozen photographers and correspondents jostle to catch his dark-shaded eye. The man is Paul Wasserman, the Rolling Stones' chief American publicist. He is engaged in telling a reporter that the one permitted vantage-point for reporters is the stadium's far distant press box. Only photographers are to be allowed into the stage-front pit, for a sacramental few minutes at the very start of the performance. The overseas press accept this with resignation. The American press argue the point in affronted fury. One by one they thrust themselves before Paul Wasserman to plead, cajole, exhort, even threaten. The publicist, whom nothing can alarm more than his clients alarm him, stares back through dark glasses with all the indifference of some assistant on the sausage counter at the Gum department store.

The other conspicuous backstage figure is an immensely tall black woman, dressed in an abbreviated French sailor suit, with hair dangling round her face in tightly-coiled ethnic plaits. This is Paul Wasserman's assistant, Alvinia Bridges. When, from time to time, a journalist's pleas stir Wasserman, he directs Alvinia Bridges to exchange the plaintiff's adhesive silk PRESS pass for what seems – but is not – a superior pass, lettered GUEST. A 'guest' of the Rolling Stones in this so-called VIP enclosure fares no better in human rights than a journalist. It is noticed that Wasserman and his assistant both wear yellow metal identity tags which allow

14

them, and a few others, free access into the tunnel by which, ordinarily, baseball teams come out to play. Behind a black bodyguard's arm, somewhere down that tunnel, the Stones and their real guests and VIPs are believed to be foregathering.

The heavy metal gate from the exterior parking lot now swings open. A column of some 30 youths, black mixed with white, in uniform yellow T-shirts and scuffed shoes, crosses the enclosure in ragged march-time, swinging arms of irregular length. They are 'security' guards, charged with protecting the stage and its environs from attack during the Stones' performance. They halt, right wheel, stand easy to receive brief instructions from their leader, then disperse under the stage to reappear on the crash barriers beyond, surveying the murmurous throng around them with expressions as patient and reasonable as that of Cro-Magnon Man.

The Stones invented such 'security', long before other Rock stars had anything but hugs and kisses to fear from fans. Now the world has changed: it is barely ten months since Mick Jagger's old friend and rival, John Lennon, was gunned down in New York by a boy with an LP record under one arm. Jagger, with his own vastly greater backwash of enemies, reportedly lives in constant terror of assassination. That is why, at JFK Stadium, yellow-shirted teenage thugs glower down in long lines at inoffensive paying customers; why huge black men block thoroughfares with their whole bodies; why huge white men in crumpled safari jackets whisper devoutly into walkie-talkies or dash to and fro on miniature motor cycles. That is why naked paranoia rages, under the balloon-skin veneer of one great, carefree garden party.

As well as the visible and the undercover security, there is a guard of a special sort, posted alone on the staircase by which the Rolling Stones will eventually make their way up to the stage. The guard is a bearded young man, upwards of seven feet tall. He is dressed as for college athletics in a navy blue sweatshirt, shorts and white jogging shoes. On his head he wears a blue baseball cap bearing the gold-wreathed inscription TULSA POLICE. His face, made as expressionless by sunglasses as the face of a praying mantis, promises something very different to anyone without authority who should try to climb that staircase. You could not wish a more perfect evocation of the kill-or-be-killed industry which – as Mick Jagger characteristically reminds us – is 'only Rock 'n' Roll'.

\* \* \*

The real VIP enclosure, at the inner end of the players' tunnel, is a little portable garden, surrounded by pink and purple Japanese screens, and containing all that, it is hoped, will keep the World's Greatest Rock 'n' Roll Band happy during their pre-concert rendezvous and conference. There are palm trees in pots and flower baskets and somnolent caged parrots and, for more advanced aesthetic stimulus, lines of Kabuki masks mounted on poles around that perimeter. On either side of the garden, a pink and purple trailer houses the continuous bars and running banquets without which no Rolling Stone is expected to function for ten minutes at a time. About a dozen highly privileged, highly nervous people are seated at tables under sun umbrellas or standing on the artificial grass, glancing this way and that over their shoulders.

At the inner end of the garden, Mick Jagger, swathed in a bright yellow quilted ski-jacket, trots briskly to and fro, lifting his knees in regular drill-instructor's time. He stops, spreads his legs, flexes his torso, touches his toes and rotates each shoulder-blade in turn. It is a warm-up period essential before two hours onstage calculated to be, at least, the equivalent of a twenty-mile run. Jagger goes through it with the half-closed eyes and muttered counting of a trained athlete whose life, these past weeks, has been virtually non-stop circuit exercise.

From a distance, he seems miraculously unchanged. There is the same boyish, girlish haircut; the same build, so unexpectedly small and slight for all the fantasy it has unleashed. Mick Jagger, at almost 40, somehow still has the body of a gawky, self-aware sixteen-year-old. His pre-performance bends and stretches separate his skimpy red T-shirt from his white knickerbockers, the way Jagger's clothes always did come apart sooner or later. There is a glimpse of the torso which, as Cecil Beaton noted, is smooth and quite hairless, like a eunuch's. The visible rib-cage, the tiny, budded navel, are unencumbered by even a millimetre of mid-life paunch.

The difference is all in the face. Once, before going onstage, Jagger would make himself up like a drag queen with silver and rouge. Nowadays, he uses ordinary orange powder to soften the creases round his eyes, the deep grooves which plunge downward through either cheek. The lips, that always hung out like wet bolsters of lust, seem thinner and paler under their pancake camouflage. It is not a young god we see, but an old pro, getting ready to go through the whole thing again.

On the threshold of middle age, unchallenged in his towering eminence as a performer, wealthy beyond even his dreams, Mick Jagger remains chiefly intent on disowning all outward and visible marks of his incalculable celebrity. It was always his best weapon against a hostile world to become this utter antithesis of his public self in private: to become disarmingly and disconcertingly modest, even shy. So he still makes himself today, before an admiring, ogling world. So he can appear even at JFK Stadium, surrounded by his employees, advisers, servants and courtiers, in earshot of the first 90,000 among millions waiting to see him, hear him and use him in multitudinous dreams. He is distant, self-absorbed, quiet, unassuming. His quietness and unassumingness hold the garden in a thrall as absolute as the Sun King at Versailles.

He speaks in a level, pleasant, accentless voice, unlike any of those he uses onstage and at press conferences. His smile is frequent, dissolving his whole face into dimples and revealing, embedded in one upper front tooth, a tiny diamond, sparkling like frost. One feels taken into his confidence until one notices that irony never absent from the wide, narrow, endlessly ambiguous eyes.

The multimillionaire, with his New York mansion and his French château, takes pleasure in small economies. The breeches he will wear throughout his tour are standard American football issue, of chalky doeskin with a rigid front gusset replacing codpieces of former days. 'Fifteen dollars a pair,' Jagger says, in unaffected pride. 'You can get 'em down on Canal Street. I've got the knee-guards, too. I need 'em for when I 'it the deck in a 'urry.' The letter h has been dispensed with for symbolic simplicity; there is probably no less simple person on the face of the earth.

Dressed somewhat like an eighteenth century ship's cabin boy, the outwardly simple, modest, guileless being continues preparing himself for his eternally juvenile profession. Only the palpable dread adoration round him spoils the picture – and the succession of people who sidle up to him and whisper interrogatively in his ear. Paul Wasserman the publicist, Bill Graham the tour-promoter, Alan Dunn the monarch's factotum, regularly interrupt what might seem an essential period of psychological as well as physical limbering-up. So does a burly Englishman with a boxer's face and

17

thinning hair, dressed in a crumpled green Chinese smock. This is Jim Callaghan, the Stones' chief of security and the most powerful man on the tour, bar one. Even Jim Callaghan's power is limited to the potency with which he can say 'No'. Only one person on the Rolling Stones' twentieth anniversary tour has the absolute, irrevocable power to say 'Yes'. His name is Michael Philip Jagger.

Two of the four remaining Stones, Bill Wyman and Charlie Watts, also wait in the garden, each at the centre of a small, tenaciously jovial group. Tour life for a Rolling Stone may once have been perpetual sex, drugs and madness. Now it seems little more than an unremitting cocktail party.

With this Bill Wyman, at least, seems content. The palely sullen second rank Stone of former days has metamorphosed into a neat, quiet, orderly man in a conservative yellow suit, a blue bandanna wound through his dark – or, conceivably, darkened – hair. At 44, Bill Wyman, too, still has the Sixties Rock star physique of match-thin body and collar-stud buttocks, a waist drawn tight just underneath his arms. He is talking, in his measured, genteel Cockney voice, about the computer he uses, as the Stones' official archivist, to file away all material pertaining to the past twenty years. Ever and again, one hears the words 'floppy disc'. Bill Wyman, waiting to go onstage, epitomizes the agreeable life of the bit-part megastar. He has nothing to do but drink, smoke, chat and be patient until the giant, gentle forces that look after him gather him up and transport him to another place a few yards away.

Charlie Watts, by contrast, paces up and down uneasily with hands sunk deep in the pockets of his grey pantaloons. His hair is now fully grey, with a bald patch behind. Charlie, of course, never did look young. At 40, his face wears the same look that has always floated among high hat cymbals in the Stones' hinterland – a look of gentle glumness and resignation. It amuses Mick especially that Charlie even now cannot believe his ill luck at finding himself in the World's Greatest Rock 'n' Roll Band; that, wherever he is with the Stones, he lives in constant hope of being allowed to catch the next plane home.

It is many years since the Stones faced their audience as a simple guitar band. Both in the recording studio and on tour, they employ numerous auxiliary musicians, some of whom are celebrated in the music business for fatal attempts to become extra Stones offstage as well as on. For the Philadelphia concert, there are two background keyboard-players. One is Ian McLagen, a waif-like man in a Sixties waistcoat. The other is a massive, long-jawed, grey-haired Scot named Ian Stewart who carries around, without apparent resentment, the memory of having once been as much a Rolling Stone as Mick Jagger. 'Stew' was the one fired by their original manager for looking 'too normal'. As their faithful roadie and session pianist, he remains uncompromisingly so; part of that inner core of normality, embodied by Charlie Watts, which has held the Stones together somehow through their frantic generation of life.

That part of the Rolling Stones is always punctual and conscientious. Charlie looks at his watch and grimaces lugubriously. ''alf past four,' he says. 'We should have been on at two-fifteen. I *hate* keeping people waiting.'

A stir down the players' tunnel announces that the final two Stones have run out of excuses to postpone their arrival. Into the garden first comes a girl of about sixteen, wearing a long black ball gown and black crocheted shawl, carrying a half-empty bottle of Southern Comfort in the attitude of some ceremonial mace. After her comes Ronnie Wood, a creature hatched and bred in the Rock music swarm from his spiked black hair and cheese-pale, pointed face to his spindly legs, swaying and staggering on vermilion boot-heels with almost obligatory mirth. 'Woody', as lead guitarist Stone, survives in the niche where Brian Jones and Mick Taylor could not, chiefly through being this ideally complete and recognizable Rock star parody, a cartoon trailer, as it were, to his friend and confederate, Keith Richards. For Keith is just a few paces behind.

Even in broad daylight, he manages to look fairly frightening. His skin is corpse-white as if, in his battles with heroin, all the blood truly has been pumped out of him. His eyes, under the draggled pompadour, are smudges of leering black. His mouth is a grimace of rotted teeth, held in suspense by lines nicked out of his face like duelling cuts. He is half naked in his bare-chested jerkin, cracked jeans tucked into ankle boots, a mangy white silk scarf wound many times around his neck. His gait is unsteady and sidelong as if he is only just now arisen from his vampire's casket. And yet, for all the gipsy squalor and reek of suicidal decadence, there is something about Keith Richards strangely and resiliently alive. He seems, within his own ghastly parameters, a happy, even healthy man.

Staggering across the garden, he bites the cap from a beer bottle. He lurches up against a member of Bill Wyman's party, throws his dead white arms around someone else and says, 'Why is everyone making such a fuss about a bunch of middle-aged madmen on tour?' The vampire speaks in the boozy, affectionate tones of some old-time actor-manager.

He swigs from his beer bottle, follows Woody up the steps to the right-hand trailer and disappears through a purple door marked 'Tuning'. Jagger, across the garden, has not yet acknowledged his presence. Evidently this is one of the days when Mick and Keith affect to have nothing in common.

After a few more moments, Bill Wyman puts out his cigarette, flexes his yellow cuffs and strolls towards the trailer on the opposite side. 'This is a bit like getting ready to go off with the family to the seaside,' he says. 'You have to be sure to have a wee, first.'

The Stones are ready at last. The stadium, by some vast animal instinct, has divined it even before the little group of blonde womenfolk, business aides and record company executives are shepherded out through the players' tunnel, across a VIP enclosure swept clean of all press, and up the narrow staircase to their privileged places on the stage. The seven-foot TULSA POLICE giant stands respectfully aside. Now the roar changes to uproar. The Stones themselves are issuing from the tunnel-mouth.

The World's Greatest Rock 'n' Roll Band, being all so small and thin, seem, rather, like the last tiny herd of some nearly extinct gazelle. Jagger goes first as always, in his yellow jacket, pumping his knickerbockered knees in a final exercise. The figure of Keith staggering after him holding two guitars, smoking a long, droopy cigarette, brings from afar a cry filled with desperate would-be brotherhood:

'He-e-e-e-ey . . . *Keith*!'

The five little beings flee up to the safety of their gigantic proscenium and the horizonless humanity beyond. Ninety thousand people are about to learn the secret of careless, unstoppable youth from men, in most cases, old enough to be their fathers.

It was Keith Richards who almost put an end to the Stones in 1977. And it is Keith who has persuaded them to go back on the road yet again in 1981. Without him, the other four would still be comfortably enmired in their wealth, their millionaire hobbies and their illimitable freewill. Keith is the Stone who has most to fear when he has nothing in particular to do.

At intervals early in 1981, therefore, he visited Charlie Watts, the English landowner and antique silver expert, and Bill Wyman, the photographer, composer and friend of Marc Chagall, and proposed that they turn themselves back into teenage Rock stars. Most assiduously did he visit the childhood friend who has, at times, seemed more like a lover, who can resemble a nagging wife and yet maintains an inimicably opposite existence within their indestructible partnership. All Keith's persuasion was needed to entice Mick away from the life, floated on silk clouds between New York, the Caribbean and the Loire Valley, which he likes to characterize as that of 'a dilettante Englishman'.

Jagger almost never wants to go on tour. The passing years have required more and more punishing effort to whip his body into the condition needed for a Mick Jagger performance. Mere mention of another tour would be enough to make his face go into the well-known Jagger put-down look: 'Not *that* old thing again!' Or he would produce one of the epigrams he polishes so carefully against his next press conference. 'Performing's like sex. You might like it but you don't wanna do it all the time.'

What decided him in the end was not so much Keith's enthusiasm as the figures prepared by the Austrian prince who supervises his and the Stones' financial affairs. Jagger has a persuasive way of insisting that he cares nothing for money. His close friends – certainly his ex-wife – are equally convinced he cares for nothing else.

The band which had ruled pop music style in the Sixties and half the Seventies could not be sure, for all their heaped-up fame, that the Eighties would not laugh them into extinction. Their classic work aside, the fact was that they had not achieved a significant new success in almost a decade. They had remained on their treadmill of monster tours and monster money while pop music was undergoing its most radical change since its most radical change was themselves. Punk Rock had become New Wave, splitting off into Two Tone and the New Romantics. Each was a jolt of reactive energy from new kinds of young musician against the encrusted and cynical Rock establishment personified by the Stones. Together they had set up a force field of contempt for all the old rockbiz glamour and conceit which the Stones both invented and apotheosized.

In the summer of 1981, a new Rolling Stones album on their eponymous label was released, as Stones albums had continued to be every year or so. Its title was *Tattoo You* – like that of its predecessor, *Emotional Rescue*, a vague, unrepentant swipe of male chauvinism. *Tattoo You* contained a track called Start Me Up, sung by a voice as snarlingly adolescent as if the past decade had never been, set about by plain guitar chords of dark, lazy malignity. Among the prevailing aural high-tech, its effect was that of a cave painting, lit by primitive fire. All that was new and current could not suppress its Neolithic growl. For the first time since Angie in 1973, the Stones were top of the American singles charts.

A familiar seismic shudder, midway between joy and terror, spread across the United States in August when it was confirmed that the Stones would be giving concerts in 26 cities throughout October, November and December. Long years have not dimmed memories of outrage, real or imagined, which the wild young Stones visited on Middle America, and which to this day cause parents to blanch, hotel clerks to cower and sheriffs to reach for city ordinances whenever their name is mentioned. Enormous stone structures and wide open spaces have likewise learned to be afraid of the Stones. In New York it is a tradition always to keep the name of their final and climactic tour venue a secret for as long as possible, lest its audience surround it prematurely and rend it brick from brick.

The response to that frisson down North America's spine was bigger than in 1978, 1975 or even 1972. Within 48 hours of the tour's announcement, almost three and a half million people had applied for tickets. The string of sports arenas and concert bowls long battered into accepting the Stones box-office percentage would, this time, yield some $15 million. Then there were the proceeds from 'authorised' merchandise, T-shirts, buttons, badges, posters. There were the proceeds from TV, video and film rights, to say nothing of record sales. There was the wholly unlooked for dividend arising from an agreement with Jovan Perfumes Inc. to allow its name – merely its name – to be printed above the Stones' on concert admission tickets. With an expected total gross of $40 million, the 'old men of Rock', as one recent critic called them, were rolling the biggest moneymaking snowball the music industry had ever seen.

The build-up continued with consummate artfulness during the Stones' seven weeks of rehearsal at a secluded farm-cum-studio in rural Massachusetts. It was announced that, as well as playing their high-gross stadium dates, they hoped to make spontaneous, unscheduled appearances at 'small clubs' along the tour-route. Lords and superstars as they were, they wanted to re-establish contact with the kind of places and audiences which had given them their earliest foothold and fame. All across America for the next three months, groups of kids would gather, eyeing their local juke joint and wondering raptly if, some night soon, they would see the Rolling Stones there.

Mick and Keith meanwhile, thumbed through the Jagger-Richard song-book, reminding themselves of the words and basic chords of its approximately one hundred titles. Between rehearsals, Mick exercised with weights and barbells, played squash and practised karate with his black bodyguard and ran seven miles daily through the autumnal woods. Far from provoking horror in the district, the visitation was accounted a positive blessing. A church in the neighbouring village of North Brookfield rearranged the letters on its announcement-board to say GOD SPEED THE ROLLING STONES.

Most of the pre-tour publicity, as always, centred on Mick. There were stories about his new passion for physical fitness; his apparently happy life with the model Jerry Hall; the eternal possibility of his appearing in a film – would it be Werner Hertzog's *Fitzcarraldo*, or *Annie*? Mick can keep such stories coming when he does nothing for eighteen months at a time. But there was a growing interest in Keith, as evidenced by a *Rolling Stone* cover story. 'The Human Riff' is receiving his due, belatedly, as the true soul and mainspring of the Stones as well as the one incorrigibly bad boy among them. The difference in interviews with Keith is that – even when asked about heroin or his breakup with Anita Pallenberg, and her terrible deterioration – he answers candidly.

One last little charge remained, to set off the main explosion at its best. Early in September, in the small town of Worcester,

Massachusetts, 300 people made their furtive way towards a club called Sir Morgan's Cave to hear a band whose identity could be only half guessed from its obvious pseudonym, Little Boy Blue and the Cockroaches. The 300 had been selected by a local radio station under an oath of strict secrecy and all would have gone well had not a rival station got wind of the plot and begun announcing, at ten minute intervals, that the Rolling Stones were about to play in Worcester. Eleven thousand people instantly descended on Sir Morgan's Cave. A riot was averted only by throwing open all the club doors. The Stones gave their first performance in the Eighties from a sort of sweating gazebo, with Mick Jagger stripped to the waist, lathered like a steeplechaser and grinning like an eight-year-old Kentish schoolboy.

Next day, half a dozen other small towns in North Massachusetts hastily issued pre-emptive ordinances, banning the Stones from all clubs, bar rooms and billiard halls within their precincts. Overnight, the dilettante Englishman, the connoisseur of silver, the friend of Chagall and the two ageing plutocrats were transformed back into outlaws, vagrants and fire hazards. Now they were ready to go on tour.

Out across the blue distances of JFK Stadium roll giant bass notes, circling downwards in register and backwards fifteen years. The song is Under My Thumb, from the 1966 *Aftermath* album. The Stones have launched their assault on the Eighties by starting almost at the beginning.

The world since 1966 may have changed beyond recognition. But the voice, blown forth by giant speaker-mouths, has not changed or aged a day. It is the voice which, for all its owner's vast sophistication, can still utter sentiments of child-chauvinist triumph over some luckless dolly bird: not a voice, indeed, so much as a scowl, or perhaps a pout made audible. The voice is so much the same, one forgets how surprising the song was originally – the muted undertow of melody Brian Jones gave to it with his African xylophone.

Behind the stage, reporters stand staring desperately upwards, trying to see the source of the thunder rolling back past Charlie Watts's bald patch. Paul Wasserman the publicist, clutching his briefcase of passes to him, beckons the first chosen photographers under the stage, to its frontal pit. Each has five minutes only, shooting upward at a fixed angle of 70 degrees. Should any photographer exceed his allotted time, or be otherwise recalcitrant, a man named Jerry Pompini will touch his camera with a long metal wand like a cattle-prod, instantly destroying the film inside.

Others, suspended above in helicopters and small aircraft, train telescopic lenses down on the figure, now shucked from its yellow jacket and prancing, over shallow pink steps, to the edge of a wild human sea. Tiny and contourless as that figure is, it has ignited its most distant watchers into the same self-contorting frenzy as those around its feet. Only Mick Jagger has ever projected sex so unerringly over so huge an outdoor distance. That girlish toss of his head is a challenge issued impartially to all 90,000, female and male. That strutting elbow-pumping walk carries its innuendo over the whole expanse of heads and arms and waving banners. They can see the glare on his face, the very pout of his lips, from a quarter of a mile away.

As the first great wave of clapping rolls round the stadium, mingled with cheers and whistles, Jagger bends double like an old-fashioned maestro at the podium, then flings his head back so that the cords stand taut in his neck. 'Good aftahnoon, JFK,' he says in that well-known public voice, part English lord, part Cockney errand-boy and part Southern black mammy. 'Are you feelin' awright? Yeah . . . it's nice to be back 'ere in Philadelphia . . .' And, apparently euphoric, he looks at Keith, then shuffles backward on his toes like a little boy unbearably excited. 'Okay – we're gonna 'ave a good time.'

The first half-dozen songs do not need to be announced. It has always seemed miraculous that the Stones, unlike the Beatles, never succumbed to amnesiac loathing of their early work, but were always prepared to do their oldies, affectionately unrevised. The cheer given to each is as much for the epoch it summons up. Under My Thumb awakens vague memories of Courrèges boots, Op-Art dresses, boutiques and bistros in candlelight. You Can't Always Get What You Want reincarnates the Chelsea Drug Store, that neon-lit folly of tubular glass which perished almost as soon as Jagger left the neighbourhood. A song grown almost quaintly innocent by modern standards still brings a whiff of its old indolent wickedness. There is an excited murmur as Jagger

25

bleats the 'na-na-na-na' phrase that unloosed so many bans and prohibitions. Is he really going to dare sing Let's Spend the Night Together?

The energy taken for granted even three years ago, now seems nothing less than phenomenal. Energy has replaced outrage, just as peacock robes have yielded to practical athletics kit. There are moments when Jagger, in his white breeches and knee-guards, seems less like a Rock star than a PT instructor, exhorting his huge class to follow his example. Each song is a piece of circuit-training, packed tight with every pose he has ever struck. In a single verse he can change from street-corner tough to primping aesthete, from bitchy old harridan to high-kicking, beaming Tiller Girl. In the space of a line, he will march, mince, strut, chassé, kneel, implore, roll over, and suddenly be airborne like the Nureyev he has sometimes wished he was. And all the time, the same rather unfriendly, callow voice is singing about chasing women, or being chased by them.

Behind the Jagger show, to left and right, the World's Greatest Rock 'n' Roll Band are meanwhile playing like so many learners on pneumatic drills. Seven weeks' intensive rehearsal have left Keith and Woody still apparently only half familiar with the chosen programme; nor has their arrival in the rapt eye of the spectators aroused any lively notion that it matters. Both move asymmetrically round the mauve middle ground, cranking at their guitar faces as if the only question is which can produce the more expressionless metal din. Two backup keyboards, pacing them steadfastly, serve as a reminder of what is not happening. The Stones today are still essentially what Brian Jones designed – a 'two guitar band' whose mesmeric effects never came from any tricksy, egocentric soloist. It is no accident that the most volatile, insecure – even dangerous – role among them has always been that of lead guitarist. Woody thrives in it from temperament rather than original talent. For Woody can accept that whatever he plays is no more than elaborate descant. The sound of the Rolling Stones is the sound of chords. It is the chords only Keith Richards can shape, and only he can strike with an evil elegance that plunges the song into the brain before Mick has opened his mouth.

Woody is on impish form as usual, in his red leather blouson and streetwalker boot-heels, gambolling back and forth with the freedom his cordless guitar allows; crossing behind Bill Wyman to nudge the stoic bass-player in the ribs, then skipping up to peer at Charlie Watts, at work like a blacksmith among his cymbals and drum silverware. Keith, meanwhile, has come to a halt on the left hand promontory, against the declining sun. His draggled head peers down at his oscillating white arm, as if still unable to comprehend what it is doing. More than anything, he resembles a haggard charwoman, half heartedly washing out socks. The intro to Miss You begins and expires on a five-string chord in which barely two fingers seem to have been awake.

The Rock concert audience is almost infinitely forgiving. It requires to see and hear only the vaguest approximation of the dreams it has acquired through the engineered illusion of records. Just the same, after 40 minutes or so of gigantically botched intros and hopelessly tangled-up solos, it is borne upon JFK Stadium that – Mick Jagger aside – the Rolling Stones are not trying. The applause is still vast: it can be nothing else. But it is an ebbing vastness. Jagger shows uneasy awareness of the fact. 'Aw-*right*!' he shouts, the Rock star's wild response to a wild ovation, not yet detectable. 'Aw-*ri-ight*!' Several times he inquires anxiously, 'Can you 'ear at the back awright?' It is what the rawest teenage beginner might say to an audience at a church hall social. 'Okay – Shadoobie!' The intro begins at breakneck speed, then topples over in a great crash of mangled, molten uproar. Jagger looks back and, briefly, buries his face in his hands.

Next – as if their names might not be generally familiar – he 'introduces' each member of the band in turn. ' . . . on drums, Mistah Charlie Watts!' It is Mick's humour always to pretend that Charlie is the big star onstage. Bill Wyman in his yellow suit – despite not yet having exerted himself sufficiently to remove the cigarette from his mouth – receives a special little burst. He has just written his first film score, and has a solo single in the British and US charts. It is a witty song, based on the pidgin French Bill has spoken for the past ten years in the villa next to Chagall's. 'Si si, je suis un rock star,' Jagger says indulgently – for he, of course, speaks immaculate French. His indulgence does not, however, extend to letting Bill do the number here.

Black Cadillac goes better, being just a long, chromium-plated

27

version of the Blues which Keith and Mick used to drive around the Surrey back-streets twenty years ago. Twenty Flight Rock is bedlam – but interesting. For all their undisputed sobriquet, the World's Greatest Rock 'n' Roll band have rarely attempted genuine Fifties bass-slapping Rock 'n' Roll. Jagger plays rhythm guitar, as he has done on studio sessions since the late Sixties. Some people around the Stones consider this deeply revealing. Despite his mastery of his own unique milieu, what Mick has always seemed to want most is to be a *real* musician, like Keith.

Similarly in Keith, the Stones once had a quite possible alternative vocalist. You can hear him, back in Come On days, before tobacco, and worse, spoiled the perfect pitch of an angelic English choirboy. There are private tapes by Keith which hint at what the band has lost through Jagger's pre-eminence, and his own odd, unexpected self-effacement. Lost for good and all, it now seems. His performance of his song Little T and A, from *Tattoo You*, is such a mess of thunderous chords and steel wool syllables that Jagger actually walks offstage, back to the place, behind Charlie Watts's drums, where a urinal is discreetly positioned. The stadium, by contrast, demurs less than in the preceding half-hour. Mick is an idol, but Keith is a hero. From his tattered head to his tattered boots, with all his tattered life in between, they love him.

In the backstage enclosure, conditions have slightly relaxed. The press, and those who have passed themselves off as press, stand unmolested under the rear apron, gazing avidly up at the noise through the proscenium, in some cases showing their kinship with the Stones, and the principle of wildness, by doing self-consciously frantic little solo dances. The intro to Start Me Up acts like a sudden air raid warning. A line of security guards, the seven-foot TULSA POLICE frighteneer among them, moves across slantwise, pushing and jabbing all superfluous onlookers back into the empty rear grandstand. Four identical yellow minibuses with blackened windows have appeared below the stage-ramp, their side doors slid back wide. Subdued panic and paranoia once more take hold. Only an hour remains before the Stones must make their getaway.

This final hour is an unbroken run of the malign two-minute classics whose opening chords, heard in however modern a disco, still bring the whole clientèle boogieing out under the lights.

Street Fighting Man, from dear old cosy, militant '68; Honky Tonk Women, with its clopping cowbell, from Hyde Park '69. Tumbling Dice, Brown Sugar: sex in a gambler's throw, a sweet tooth. To stir up memories of two countries' conjoined outrage, Jagger has wrapped himself in a big robe made of the British and the American flag. '. . . Ah laid a divorc-ay in New Yawk Cit-a-ay . . .' The difference is that in the wings, his ten-year-old daughter, Jade, is watching him. '. . . Ah just can't get that drinkin' off ma-ah mind . . .' Jade looks bored but tries to hide it, as ten-year-olds do on formal grown-up occasions.

The stadium roars louder as the golden oldies keep coming: there are sirens in the distance, mixed up with police car whirligigs. Backstage, the condition is Red Alert. A dozen or so guards plunge amid the stage supports to reinforce their colleagues on the frontal barrier-system. Four of them return, carrying a boy who has managed to climb over. The boy, aged about fourteen, looks draggled and exhausted, as if just rescued from the surf at Malibu. The guards carry him off, restraining him by the arms, legs and windpipe.

The finale – there can be no other – is Jumping Jack Flash. The anthem to the Stones as Devil agents, the vicious black midnight of the sunshiny Sixties, summons its dancing demon even on an overcast afternoon near Philadelphia. Jagger is still enough of a Blues man to know that if you hit a groove, you stay there. This version lasts twenty minutes and takes him writhing and rotating down both catwalks. He runs back to the right-hand tower, climbs into the cab of the cherry picker, is cranked up and swung out, 30 feet above the crowd, still hunched like a hag, singing, 'Jumpin' Jack Flash, it's a gas . . . Jumpin' Jack Flash, it's a gas . . .' Rock 'n' Roll can have produced no stranger sight, nor one more removed from its origins, than this figure in knee-breeches, suspended before a huge blue and yellow Japanese mural, repeating 'It's a gas' in a 10,000-watt whisper, and pelting the faces below with long-stemmed carnations.

One encore – a perfunctory Satisfaction – and it is over. The Stones, swaddled in white towels, flee down the backstage ramp to their four waiting yellow trucks. Behind them, the acclaim is unmistakably tinged with reproach. Jade and Jerry Hall are already in the lead vehicle when Jagger reaches it. Out in the stadium, his voice continues to agree and exhort, 'Aw-*right*! Aw-*ri-i-ight!*' He is speaking through a radio-controlled microphone. He has no intention of going back on stage.

The heavy compound gate swings open. The motorcade bumps through in clouds of dust. Beyond the balloons, a $12,000 firework display cracks and rackets in the disappointed sky. Stage-hands fall on the Japanese garden, flattening it like a cardhouse, rolling up the artificial grass, packing into hampers the sodden T-shirts and towels which Jagger, in less careful days, might have tossed out among his audience.

The *New York Times* speaks for all in comparing the Stones' performance to that of 'a teenage garage band'. Not even *Rolling Stone*, with all its special privileges at stake, can pretend that the JFK Stadium show, and another the following day, have been anything more than tortuous tuning up. *Time*, mixing metaphors as usual, calls the tour 'a floating World's Series', calculatedly fobbing off its public with empty spectacle instead of the excitement for which some $15 million has already been paid. The 'major financial involvement' of Jovan Perfumes is sarcastically noted – a whiff of cheap scent replacing what once smelled only raw and sulphurous. 'For anyone interested in resisting the social pressures when the Stones pass through town,' *Time* continues acidly, 'the following reasons are offered as a public service . . .'

At the Amherst-Marriott hotel, near Buffalo, NY, an under-manager picks up a telephone which has just rung in the brown, scarlet and orange, fairground-lit front lobby. On the line, by prior arrangement, is the host of Buffalo's most listened-to morning radio show. He asks his contact at the Marriott to hold, then addresses his rush-hour, car-bound audience in tones of conspiratorial excitement:

'Okay – right after this, we'll be going across live to the hotel . . . I can only say it's in the Buffalo area . . . where the Rolling Stones checked in late last night. And I'll be talking to our special contact there, who's anonymous, naturally – security, right? – who'll be talking to us, live, about just what's going down as of now – uh – in the Stones' hotel. Hello . . . hello, this is the Rush Hour Show. Am I talking to the Rolling Stones' hotel?'

'Yeah – hi,' the under-manager answers.

'Hi there . . . And you're talking to Rush Hour from the hotel where the Stones are checked in.'

'Yes, Sir!'

'They checked in late last night, huh?'

'Yes, Sir, they checked in real late.'

'And they're still in their rooms as of now?'

'Yes, Sir – all still in their rooms.'

'Not moving about the public areas at all?'

'No, Sir.'

'Just staying real quiet in their rooms, huh?'

'Yes, Sir, it's been real quiet.'

A pause: of palpable disappointment.

'Real quiet, huh?'

'Yes, Sir.'

'No screaming groupies – nothing like that?'

'No, *Sir.*'

'So the Stones can come back?'

'They sure can!'

Buffalo is the nearest the Stones can get to Canada since 1977, when Keith Richards was arrested for heroin smuggling in Toronto, and Mick Jagger featured in an erotic scandal with the Prime Minister's wife. It was the note on which the world took leave of them: older-looking, outmoded but still searching for new definitions of the phrase persona non grata.

Buffalo's chief autumn feature is a dishmop-grey sky which, for all its apparent listlessness, harbours sudden rain squalls and gales of eccentric ferocity. There is such a sky today as the cars and pickups and plastered microbuses come streaming across the Canadian border, past clumps and pickets of police in broad-brimmed Mountie hats, and the numerous misty slip-roads to Niagara Falls.

Behind the Amherst-Marriott, the four yellow vans that fled JFK Stadium three days ago, stand innocently in an almost empty parking lot. Beside the first van, half a dozen teenage boys squat on the grass verge, gazing up at a top floor picture window whose brown, red and orange curtains have yet to be drawn back. From time to time, the same boy advances, cups his hands and bellows,

31

'C'mon *out*, Jagger!'

At Rich Stadium, 25 miles away, the wind scuds down the empty stands at a steady 40 mph. The Stones' pink and purple stage set takes shape at the westerly end, in conditions that force its scaffolders to cling on aloft like sailors working an Indiaman round Cape Horn. By noon, the wind has almost toppled the right-hand tower backwards, and buffeted both Japanese side-screens to colourless shreds. There is, even so, no question of cancelling the afternoon's concert. Printed on each fifteen dollar ticket under the Stones' name, and that of Jovan Perfumes, is the blithe assurance that it is an 'all weather' show.

The wind rises to gale force as Rich Stadium fills with its audience of 65,000. The Canadian contingent gather round the stage with red and white national flags and old fashioned hippy hair which from a distance, en masse, has the look of good quality manure. The support band plays almost inaudibly, amid a skirl of balloons and orange frisbees, bobbing on capricious up-draughts. To the rear, in an arc of empty stands, photographers queue up to bellow against the wind into Paul Wasserman's ear. His black assistant, Alvinia, dressed today in plaids and earmuffs like an elongated Dutch doll, trips among tip-up seats, exchanging impotent PRESS passes for equally impotent GUEST passes. Wasserman, within his raised coat-collar, endlessly shakes his Russian shop assistant's head. The Stones are even more remote than at JFK Stadium; bunkered deep under the back bleachers with their banquets and their bars. When the press sees them, it is for the briefest instant, running to the stage across an elevated drawbridge. Big and important as the Stones are, their servants do not always tell them everything. They clearly had no idea before this moment that a storm was in progress.

The headwind hits Jagger first, catching the radio-controlled mike in his hand and whirling it up to bump his mouth with such force, it loosens the diamond in his top front tooth. The others, less hale and well-protected, battle their way out into the applause, gripping guitars like imperilled umbrellas, their trouser cuffs flapping madly around their built-up heels. Jagger's voice comes only in patches through the juddering breeze.' . . . under ma thumb . . . gurl . . . just changed her ways . . . ' The stage gives no protection from the head-on-squalls. The shredded side-panels flap insanely. It is too windy for Woody to sky-lark, or Bill to hold a cigarette in his mouth. The only thing they can do is stand there. They cannot hear their audience, and can hardly hear themselves. The wind gulps that vast kilowattage, carrying it off with balloons and frisbees, up over the stadium-rim and away to vanish in the fogs and white uproar that hang eternally above Niagara Falls.

For all that, the five fragile little remnants of an endangered species, panoramically revealed by their half destroyed set, have suddenly begun playing like the Rolling Stones of old. They are playing, in the teeth of this ludicrous gale, like the band of young tearaways who could wreck a circuit cinema or transfix a half-million hippies; the band which could affront and disappoint its public just as enormously by a flicker of this same unfathomable whim. They are playing with percussion of inspired lawlessness, smashing the high hats and policemen's helmets; a bass-line below it, groping up the little girls' skirts. They are playing with one heartless heart, one vicious voice, one thin, bare arm pumping a pale driftwood guitar with renewing force as light streams back into the vampire's red-rimmed eyes. 'The Human Riff' is awake at last. The World's Greatest Rock 'n' Roll Band is in business again. The Rolling Stones are back in the bloodstream.

As for Jagger, the sprawling pink stage and two long catwalks now seem too small to contain him. He dances down to the left, high-kicking like a drum majorette, taunting and beckoning all 20,000 along that curve. He sprints back up the right-hand catwalk, leaps the scaffolding, climbs six feet and hangs there, leaning out as far as his fingertips will reach. Before Rich Stadium can touch hands with him, he jumps down, rolls over, struts to the front and stands there, yellow ski jacket slanted into the storm as his body beats time with each syllable. 'Yuh can't always *git* what yuh want. No, yuh can't always *git* what yuh wa-hant . . .

'Okay . . . ' his voice says among the wind-swallowed cheers. 'Good aftahnoon, Buffalo . . . Yeah . . . it's nice to be back. We're gonna 'ave a good time, awright? Aw-*ri-i-ight*!'

# PART ONE

# 1

## 'I was schooled with a strap right across my back'

When the black man was alone and destitute, he played the Blues. With a roof over his head, however leaky, he played Rhythm and Blues. The difference is as great as between the country and the city; between Southern cotton fields and Eastern ghettoes; between fatalistic old age and vigorous, upwardly mobile youth. It is the difference between a guitar powered only by its own mournful echo, and a guitar belligerently amplified, played with aggressive slides and swoops along the fretboard by a switchblade knife or broken bottle neck. It is the difference between bleak, dusty, desperate noontide and pulsating, pleasure-seeking night.

While the Blues stretch back into vague infinities of work gangs and prison cells, Rhythm and Blues can be given an approximate time and place of genesis. It grew up first during and just after the Second World War, amid the mass redistribution of American blacks into their country's war machine. Its sound was of newly explored streets and unfamiliar alleys; of cheap neon, soda-fountain sugar and wafting gasoline; of the old, sleepy twelve-bar Blues reacting in astonishment, delight – and sometimes fury – to all the varied stimuli of big-city life.

Nowadays, there are expensively illustrated books to familiarize us with R & B's golden postwar age. There are the photographs of Muddy Waters, Jimmy Reed, Otis Rush or T-Bone Walker, in their white shirts and enormous gabardine trousers, singing against heavy silver microphones, perspiring over huge guitars with pearled fretboards, in clubs, bar lounges or juke joints, some tropic Forties night below the Mason-Dixon line. There are the show bills – usually from the Apollo Theatre in Harlem – which depict the young B. B. King, Bo Diddley or Fats Domino, wearing demure tuxedos and tiny bow ties, and smiling with a strained, reassuring politeness.

The smile of an R & B artist circa 1949 was the smile of someone expecting to be beaten up at any moment. The Blues – stigmatized since the Twenties as 'race' or 'specialty' music – had been generally too esoteric for whites to understand. Rhythm and Blues, with its flash suits, flaunted saxes and unrepressed sexuality, seemed to offer the most blatant threat to respectable – that is to say, all-white – Society. It was denounced as lewd, ungodly, demented, a corrupter of children. Its clubs were raided and wrecked by white vigilantes; its performers attacked and, in not a few cases, lynched. Up to 1956 or so, every Blues band travelling in its own country was a band on the run.

Throughout the Forties and early Fifties, its greatest creative period, the music remained segregated and submerged. Though R & B songs often appeared in the American hit parade, they were bowdlerized versions, purged of their sexual content by all-white crooners and dance bands. Roll With Me, Henry, an overt sexual challenge, for instance, became Dance With Me, Henry, an invitation to foxtrot. The original artists, with a few exceptions, were unknown to the general record-buying public. They could perform only in black clubs, record only on obscure black-owned labels, have their discs played only by the handful of radio stations controlled by blacks. When Bo Diddley finally got a booking on nationwide TV in 1958, it was stipulated that, to preserve decency, he must perform completely motionless. On camera, Diddley forgot his promise, lapsed into a shuffling *pas seul* and was docked his entire fee.

'Help save the youth of America!' – so ran one anti-R & B pamphlet of the early Fifties. 'Don't let your children buy or listen to these Negro records. The screaming, idiotic words and savage music are undermining the morals of our white American youth . . .'

A prophecy of things to come if ever there was one.

It is a journey further than any Bluesman could imagine from Beale Street, Memphis, to Bexley in deepest Kent and the playground of Maypole infants' school, where, one sunny day in 1950, Ken Llewellyn called a group of his favourite pupils together for an informal photograph. The boys who assembled were the brightest and liveliest in Mr Llewellyn's class. They included Robert Wallis and John Spinks and Michael Jagger, the least likely of all to stand still for a photograph. The others reined him in with arms around his shoulders, neck and waist. They stood together in their flannel shorts, their elastic school belts with metal S-clasps, English schoolboys at their apotheosis, laughing into the warm, safe, unchanging Fifties sky.

Kent as a county begins in London, south-east of the Thames, in ranks of suburbs barely distinguishable from one another, crossed by railway bridges, whose names are synonyms for dullness and decorum – Bexley, Bromley, Beckenham, Dartford, Sidcup, Sevenoaks and the rest. One must travel far on grubby trains, crossing many bridges, to discover what is still called 'the Garden of England', with its apple orchards, hop fields and oast-houses. It is a large and bewilderingly imprecise county, ranging from the miles of drab dockland around Chatham and Rochester to the Regency splendours of Royal Tunbridge Wells; from the medieval majesty of Canterbury Cathedral to the faded Victorian seaside of Margate and Broadstairs, where Charles Dickens wrote *Bleak House*. Somewhere in that sprawling landscape is the field in which Mr Pickwick lost his hat while watching military man-oeuvres, the bucolic landscape, bespoken by Alfred Jingle, of 'apples, hops, cherries, women'. You will not see it from the window of your train. You will see only 'shopping centres' and squat terraced streets, the commuter stations, glimpsed in an unreadable sign, a flash of faces turned hopefully back down the line towards London's main rail termini.

Least romantic of all Kentish suburbs is Dartford, 30 minutes from Victoria Station, where, on December 7, 1940, Basil Joseph Jagger married Eva Scutts. The bridegroom was a slight, quiet-looking man whose wiry frame betrayed his calling as physical-training teacher. The bride was a pretty young woman with a wide smile and that air of determined gentility which sometimes goes with slight foreignness. Eva, in fact, had been born in Australia and had emigrated to Britain with her family in her early teens. The best man was Basil's more ebullient brother, Albert. Afterwards, there was a reception for 50 guests at the Coneybeare Hall.

Basil – known as Joe to his family and friends – was not merely a drill sergeant in white singlet and gym shoes, exhorting local schoolchildren to lift up their knees and swing their arms. He subsequently became a lecturer in physical education at Strawberry Hill College, Twickenham. Horace Walpole's sumptuous mock-Gothic mansion was – and still is – the nucleus of this teacher-training institute, run by a Catholic order, the Vincentians, to supply Catholic schools all over the world. Joe Jagger's job was to give a grounding in physical education simple and comprehensive enough to be passed on to student priests or mission children in the wilds of Africa or Asia.

He also worked as a lecturer with the nascent British Sports Council. His speciality was basketball, an American sport not much in vogue in mid-Fifties Britain. Joe Jagger was among the pioneers of the British basketball movement and was the author of what remains the definitive book on the subject, published by Faber and Faber in 1962.

His wife Eva was a lively and energetic person whose vivacity at times seemed to verge on the domineering. Eva had always been secretly rather ashamed of her Australian origin, with its implied stigma of roughness and unsophistication. Marriage to Joe, with his markedly superior social standing and education, increased her determination to show herself the equal of any true 'Brit'. Their small house, in Denver Road, Dartford, was scoured by Eva into a spotless state the equal of any neighbour's. Joe and Eva's whole life as a young married couple was dictated by consideration of what those ever-vigilant neighbours might think.

Their first son, Michael Philip, was born on July 26, 1943. The tide of World War II had long since turned in the Allies' favour, but Britain was still an embattled redoubt of air-raid precautions, white-helmeted wardens, clothing coupons and butcher-shop queues. Though the RAF nightly pounded Hamburg and Essen in 'thousand-bomber raids', attacks by the German Luftwaffe on London continued. The Kent suburbs heard the distant thunder and saw the horizontal flashes as the poor old East End caught it from the sky again.

Michael Jagger was a child of absolutely conventional beauty, with chubby cheeks, guileless eyes and hair that assumed a reddish tinge. As a toddler, he proved amiable and obedient, though prone to boisterous spirits that could sometimes go too far. Once, on holiday at the seaside, his mother remembers, he marched along the beach, deliberately kicking down every other child's sandcastle in his path. His reign as an adored only child lasted until 1947, when Eva presented him with a younger brother, Christopher.

Home life for the Jagger brothers was pervaded by their mother's house-proud fastidiousness and their father's devotion to physical fitness. Their Denver Road neighbours were accustomed to seeing the small back garden of the Jagger house littered with sports equipment – weight-training barbells, cricket stumps and archery targets. Other children asked home to tea by Mike or Chris were somewhat intimidated by the schoolmasterly regimen, which included Grace before meals and a system of fixed penalties and punishments for misbehaviour. Thirty years later, the millionaire rock star would look with astonishment on Joe Jagger's leniency as a grandparent. 'It amazes me what he lets Jade get away with. If I'd done the same things when I was a kid, I'd have got a wallop or a task to do as a punishment.'

Mike's physical prowess showed through early at Maypole infants' school and afterwards at Wentworth County Primary, to which his Maypole teacher, Ken Llewellyn, an expatriate Welshman, had also transferred. Mr Llewellyn remembers him fondly as one of an outstanding junior class whose ascent to grammar school and university seemed assured. 'It was a joy to teach them. They were full of life, full of all sorts of questions. I took them for games as well. Mike was already looking like a useful cricketer. If I remember him at all, it's running in from the playground with both knees grazed and a great big smile on his face.'

John Spinks lived in Heather Drive, Dartford, not far from the Jaggers in Denver Road. He was Mike's playmate in the sandpit that lay between their houses. When Mike accidentally impaled a hand on a spiked metal railing, it was John Spinks who, with praiseworthy coolness, pulled it free. To John, he seemed at times almost too conventionally law-abiding and obedient. 'I always thought he was a bit of a mother's boy. He did *everything* he was told at home. He was an indiarubber character, really. He could bend any way to stay out of trouble.'

Even as a small boy, his other friend Robert Wallis remembers, he had a strangely remote, abstracted quality – a sense of being

41

preoccupied with matters far weightier than their schoolboy games together. Joe Jagger was currently acting as adviser to a commercial TV programme called *Seeing Sport*, designed to promote physical fitness in children. Once a week, he would take his elder son with him to the studios, to act as model for instruction about athletics or camping. 'Mike is going to show you how to light the fire,' the voiceover would say, or: 'Here's Mike, getting into the tent.' 'He became a bit of a star for doing that,' Robert Wallis says. 'He always had some interest outside the ones we had as a group. He gave the idea that he'd sooner be somewhere else than with us, doing far more glamorous things.'

Robert, John and Mike took the Eleven-plus exam together, passing it as effortlessly as Ken Llewellyn had predicted. This crucial step determined whether they would go on to receive a mundane basic education at a 'secondary modern' or be admitted to the far superior privileges of Dartford Grammar. Eva Jagger had every reason to be proud of her boy in his smart new uniform of gold-trimmed maroon blazer and cap.

Dartford Grammar School, when Mike Jagger arrived there in the early Fifties, possessed most features of an English public school – masters in gowns, house captains, societies, ceremonial Speech Days, ritualised athletics and sport. As its school magazine, *The Dartfordian*, attests, scholarship was generally excellent, yielding an unusually large annual export to Britain's redbrick universities. Prominent in the school curriculum was the Army Cadet Force, designed to cushion the shock of the two years' compulsory National Service each boy would face before embarking on his chosen career.

At Dartford Grammar, Mike Jagger's academic promise – and his buoyant enthusiasm – mysteriously evaporated. From the first form to the fifth he merely coasted, doing only enough work to stay out of trouble. It became a sore provocation to the several teachers in whose subjects he was obviously gifted. The senior languages master, Dr Bennett, particularly resented his indifference, for – aided by unusual powers of mimicry – he showed all the signs of a first-class linguist. 'There was one occasion when I spoke to him about his attitude very severely,' Dr Bennett says. 'He was so deliberately insulting that I simply knocked him down.'

42

His apathy extended even to sport. He seemed to lose interest in cricket after discovering he was not the deadly spin bowler he had supposed himself at Wentworth. The only sport he played regularly was basketball, his father's speciality. Joe Jagger, in fact, introduced the sport to Dartford Grammar and helped coach the Basketball Society, of which Mike was Hon. Sec. 'He was most keen on that, I think, because it was American,' Robert Wallis says. 'Mike was the one who had *real* American basketball boots to play in when the rest of us only had gym shoes.'

His appearance, from the age of fourteen onward, seemed to reflect his slack and insubordinate attitude. The chubby, laughing schoolboy of Ken Llewellyn's class had grown into an adolescent whose skinny frame, hovering on the edge of effeteness, caused uniform distaste among his teachers. Likewise his face, with its somnolent eyes, its retroussé nose; most of all, the wide, sagging lips, set in what seemed a permanent grimace of either scorn or dumb insolence.

As he moved higher in the school, he became adept at flouting its dress regulations. Instead of the prescribed black lace-up shoes, he would arrive for class in French slip-on moccasins. In place of his blazer, he acquired a black, gold-threaded 'Teddy Boy' jacket, which, to Dr Bennett's annoyance, he wore even to the annual Founder's Day ceremony.

He was already a source of much discussion at the nearby girls' grammar school, where opinion as to his attractiveness remained sharply divided. In terms of conventional handsomeness he was obviously a non-starter. Yet some of the very girls who dismissed him as 'ugly' or 'a weed' still looked for him in the after-school swarm and made bold attempts to talk to him – since he seemed uninterested in talking to them. It became almost a competition to pierce that scornful reserve and bring forth that rare smile which could split open the sullen face, making him look still the happy schoolboy who had laughed into the sun.

In 1955 came the plague called Rock 'n' Roll. Bill Haley and the Comets invaded Britain's sleepy hit parade with Rock Around the Clock, See You Later, Alligator, Everybody Razzle Dazzle and Rockin' Through the Rye. Britain's regimented teenage boys awoke to the sound of a braying sax, a slapping, spinning double

43

bass, a voice that did not croon but jerked and jogged and hiccupped and jumped. What Haley was in fact playing was Negro Rhythm and Blues, purged of its bite and wit and wrapped in a swing or Country-Western beat. The very phrase 'rock and roll' was Negro slang for energetic fucking. Even in America, its origin had scarcely been realised. In Britain it was simply the most exciting noise that ever confused an adolescent's glands. A British tour by Haley and the Comets in 1956 left a trail of wrecked theatres and slashed cinema seats. Music became, for the first time, a source of conflict between the young, who adored this outrageous new noise, and their parents, who loathed it and strove to extinguish it by every possible means.

A few months earlier, the British Decca label had released a record which, though quieter than Haley's joyous gibberish, was destined to transform many lives more permanently. The record – one of the newfangled 'long playing' kind – was *New Orleans Joys*, by the Chris Barber Jazz Band.

Barber, at 25, led Britain's most commercially successful Dixieland band. He remained, however, principally an archivist, devoted to keeping alive sources and style that might otherwise have been overlooked in the current 'Trad' boom. His *New Orleans Joys* LP included two Blues songs played in the 'skiffle' style evolved in the Depression years, when musicians were often reduced to instruments extemporised from household utensils. The songs, Rock Island Line and John Henry, were performed by a primitive rhythm section of double bass, kitchen washboard and banjo, the last played by a skinny Glaswegian named Tony Donegan who had changed his name to Lonnie in honour of the American Bluesman Lonnie Johnson.

The two songs, released on a single in 1956, became a stupendous British Top Ten hit. Haley and his group, in their plaid jackets and bow ties, owed their appeal to outlandish remoteness. But Donegan, with his nasal whine, his ex-service-man's haircut and backing of mundane domestic implements, made comparably exciting sounds that anyone could reproduce. Within days of Lonnie Donegan's first appearance on national television, acolyte 'skiffle groups' had sprung up all over Britain. The craze centred on London's Soho, its jazz cellars and newly fashionable espresso coffee houses, into whose gloomy recesses record-company talent scouts now plunged in a hectic search for ersatz Lonnie Donegans. For the first time ever, musical talent was held to be of secondary importance to looks. Any boy who played a guitar and wore a plaid shirt with the collar turned up, if he sat around long enough in coffee bars like the Heaven and Hell, the Gyre and Gimble or the 2 I's, could hope to follow the starry path of Lonnie Donegan or 'Britain's First Rock 'n' Roller,' Tommy Steele.

All over Britain, in suburban living rooms, boys crouched together with their matchwood guitars, their mothers' washboards and basses improvised from tea-chests and wire, struggling to learn the Blues songs made popular by Donegan and his successors, grateful for the easy chords and pattered tempo, blissfully unaware that the lyrics, as Woody Guthrie or Huddie Leadbetter had written them, were violent political tracts; that Midnight Special was a cotton slave's suicidal lament or that Lonnie Johnson's plaintively sweet Careless Love was a song about syphilis, ending with murder.

Eva Jagger remembers that even as a very small boy her elder son would stand in front of the family wireless set, singing along to music with words made up in his head. Most of all he seemed to like Latin American rhythms, which he would accompany with a stream of Spanish-sounding nonsense. At the age of ten, on a Spanish holiday with Joe and Eva, he posed for a snapshot in a straw sombrero, playing a toy guitar. Sombrero tipped back, guitar flourished flamenco-style, the pose was, even then, self-consciously theatrical.

The skiffle craze swept through Dartford Grammar as through almost every other British school. Two of Mike's friends, Bob Beckwith and Alan Etherington, acquired guitars and began practising together. But Mike, though he too had a guitar, joined none of the ad hoc classroom skiffle groups that would strum together, perched on desks during break time.

He never really liked Bill Haley, or even Elvis Presley, after the gold-suited, magical lout had superseded Haley as the corrupter of Britain's youth. His first fan worship, significantly, was for Little Richard, the original *black* Rock 'n' Roll star whose R & B beginnings were now camouflaged in a demented scream, a

45

wobbling drape suit and an aura – though few perceived it then – of sexual ambiguity.

He did succumb, as most did, to the charm of Buddy Holly and the Crickets. Holly is blessed by countless guitar demigods for having first showed them the way from skiffle to Rock 'n' Roll, in simple but inventive chord sequences through G and E. As his enormous output shows, he was a stylistic chameleon, equally at home with Texas Rockabilly and black R & B. Soon to die, he visited Britain on tour only once, in March 1958. Mike Jagger went with another Dartford Grammar School friend, Dick Taylor, to see the Holly stage show at the Granada Cinema, Woolwich. Buddy Holly that night played one of the more esoteric items in his repertoire – a song called Not Fade Away, set to a halting, staccato beat invented by the Blues star Bo Diddley. Dick Taylor remembers what an impression that song in particular made on Mike Jagger.

A wispy, amiable boy, son of a plumber in nearby Bexleyheath, Dick Taylor came nearer than most to penetrating the Jagger reserve. For Dick knew about American music far more exotic and exciting than Elvis and Little Richard. What Dick Taylor liked was *real* Blues – the scratched and blurred master sketches that the Rock 'n' Roll industry had turned into glib cartoons. It was at Dick Taylor's house that Mike Jagger listened to Muddy Waters, Jimmy Reed, Howlin' Wolf, giants of the urban Blues with heart-shivering voices, calling and answering their virtuoso guitars, that could change the view beyond the lace curtains from Kentish suburbia to the dark and windy canyons along Chicago's Lake Shore Drive. From then on, the Blues became Mike's consuming passion.

Part of the music's attraction was its sheer unavailability. Simply hearing it was complicated enough. You could not buy Blues records in the Dartford or Bexleyheath record shops. As with all truly worthwhile things, it involved a trip to London. Mike and Dick would spend their Saturday afternoons at the jazz record shops in Charing Cross Road, thumbing through the Blues 'import' stock in sleeves already dog-eared and thumbed in their wandering journey across the cultural hemispheres. The very label logos excited them – not boring British Decca and Philips, but Okeh and Crown and Chess and Sue and Imperial and Delmark.

If listening to Blues was difficult, seeing it was virtually impossible. Though famous Bluesmen like Big Bill Broonzy did perform in Britain during the late Fifties, news of their coming did not percolate down the line to Dartford. The only glimpse given to Dartford Grammar School's secret Blues caucus involved sitting through *Jazz on a Summer's Day*, a film documentary about the American Newport Jazz Festival. Almost at the end, a lanky young black man got up onstage and sang through a derisive grin and played a red guitar that dangled almost to the level of his wildly knocking knees. That, for Dick Taylor, Mike Jagger and countless other British boys, was their first tantalizing sight of Chuck Berry. The film sequence ended with Berry dodging a hail of flashbulbs thrown by photographers in fury that the 'pure' jazz had been so interrupted.

Mike Jagger's earliest attempt at Blues singing was at the house of a boy named David Soames in Wentworth Drive, Dartford. David was trying to form a Rhythm and Blues group with Mike Turner, another ex-pupil of Wentworth County Primary School. Both quickly decided that Mike Jagger sang in far too strange a fashion to be their vocalist. He accepted the decision without rancour and afterwards walked home with Mike Turner, discussing their forthcoming GCE 'O' Level examinations.

Dick Taylor owned a second-hand drum-kit, which gained him admittance to several small amateur groups otherwise top-heavy with guitarists. By his last year at Dartford Grammar, he was practising regularly with Bob Beckwith, Alan Etherington and Mike Jagger. It was hardly a group at all, since they had no equipment – only the Etheringtons' radiogram to amplify the guitars – and because Mike Jagger, their singer, refused to play a guitar himself, as was customary. He just stood or sat there and sang, diffidently until his powers as a mimic came to his aid. 'The first song I remember him doing was Richie Valens's La Bamba,' Dick Taylor says. 'Mick used to come out with this stream of words that sounded just like Spanish. He'd just make them up as he went along.'

The group was called Little Boy Blue and the Blue Boys, in order that there be no mistake concerning their musical intentions. From first to last in their two-year history, Little Boy Blue and the Blue Boys never played to an audience other than Dick Taylor's

47

mum. 'She dug Mick right from the start,' Taylor says. 'She always told him he'd got something special.'

Their repertoire was limited to the precious store of Blues import discs Dick Taylor had collected – Howlin' Wolf's Smokestack Lighting; Don and Bob's Good Morning Little Schoolgirl; Dale Hawkins's Susie Q; and primitive numbers by Jimmy Reed and Ike and Tina Turner. 'We never even *thought* of playing to other people,' Dick Taylor says. 'We thought we were the only people in England who'd ever *heard* of R & B.'

After *Jazz on a Summer's Day*, Chuck Berry dominated their thoughts. It was Mike Jagger who found out you could get Berry records by writing direct to the Chess record company in Chicago. Berry's voice, light and sharp and strangely white-sounding, had a pitch not dissimilar to his own. Singing along with Sweet Little Sixteen or Reelin' and Rockin', he suddenly felt something more than just a mumbling impersonator. And Chuck Berry was the first intimation that Rhythm and Blues might be an expression of youth. Each Berry song was a novel in miniature about American teenage life, teeming with brand-name cars, sassy high school queens and anarchic exhortations to forsake the classroom for just sheer driving, singing and dancing.

Practice sessions took place at Alan Etherington's house – because of the radiogram – or in Dick Taylor's bedroom at Bexleyheath, seated on the bed around a big old-fashioned tape recorder. Dick remembers an anxious moment when Mike turned up to rehearse for the first time after accidentally biting a piece out of his tongue in the school gymnastics class. 'He was terrified it was going to affect the way he sang. We all kept telling him it made no difference. But he did seem to lisp a bit and sound more Bluesy after that.'

His own home, though welcoming to his friends, did not suggest itself as a practice place for Little Boy Blue and the Blue Boys. Eva Jagger was not discouraging. She had nothing against their music, she told them – it was just that the neighbours might mind the noise. Joe Jagger's main concern, as always, was keeping his son up to the mark in physical education. Once, when Mike was going off with Dick Taylor, his father called out, 'Michael – don't forget your weight training.' Mike turned back obediently, went into the garden and exercised with barbells for a conscientious quarter of an hour.

He had passed his GCE 'O' Levels in a respectable enough seven subjects, and had qualified for entry into the Sixth Arts form to do Advanced Level English, History and French. He also became a school prefect, despite the headmaster's manifest disapproval. The head, Mr Hudson, had never quite forgiven him for leading what seemed like an organized insurrection by lower-school boys against compulsory enrolment in the school Army Cadet Force.

He stuck out the two-year 'A' Level course with no idea what he was working for, beyond a vague notion that journalism might be interesting. For a brief time, too, he toyed with the idea of becoming a radio disc jockey. A London record producer named Joe Meek was currently advertising for would-be deejays to submit demonstration tapes. Robert Wallis remembers copying out Meek's address from a newspaper and passing it on to Mike Jagger. But the project languished, apparently under parental discouragement.

His 'A' Level passes in English and History were only mediocre but by then it did not matter. He had already secured himself a place at the London School of Economics in Aldwych, W.C.2, to follow a two-year course in the subject that seemed best suited to his indecisive talents. 'I wanted to do arts but thought I ought to do science,' he says now. 'Economics seemed about halfway in between.'

So, each morning, from the autumn of 1961, Mike Jagger, in his striped student scarf, joined the daily crowd of business people at Dartford station, his face turned towards a future that still seemed to lie only a little way up the commuter line to Victoria.

Each morning, from the top deck of the green Kentish bus, Dick Taylor would see the same thin, slouching figure trailing reluctantly up the long hill to Sidcup Art College. Winter or summer, Keith Richards wore the same tight blue jeans, 'winklepicker' shoes, denim jacket and the violet-coloured shirt that never seemed to be given a rest or a wash. In summer as well as winter, he contrived to look pinched and cold, his bullet head accentuating protuberant ears, his nose red raw, his mouth chapped around with teenage pimples. In one hand, he held a Player's Weights cigarette; in the other, his only possession, a guitar. Dick Taylor knew it would be another day of abandoned study, and of Rock 'n' Roll practice in the college lavatories.

Guitars, and loving them, are among Keith's earliest memories. His mother's father, Theodore Augustus Dupree – the family were originally Huguenots from the Channel Islands – led a small semi-professional dance band in the 1930s and himself played several instruments including saxophone, violin and guitar. The guitar still stood in 'Grandfather Gus's' house, in a corner of the sitting room. Keith remembers with what excitement, even as a tiny boy, he would approach it and draw his hands with a soft thrum across its untuned strings.

'He was a great character, my grandfather Gus. At the time, when I was small, he had a job in some tailoring sweatshop – he'd always be bringing little squares of felt out of his pocket and showing us. He carried on playing music, too, right up to the Sixties – touring the American air force bases with a Country band. He'd got a job as janitor at Highgate School where Yehudi Menuhin's son was a pupil. My grandfather, in the end, got to know Yehudi; they'd even have a bit of a scrape together on their violins. What a fantastic hustler!'

Bert Richards, Keith's father, was a very different character, quiet and cautious with a reserve that – his son thinks now – was created largely by overwork and exhaustion. Bert worked as a supervisor at Osram's light bulb factory in Hammersmith. He got up each day at 5 a.m. and did not come home in the evening until 6. 'He'd have something to eat, watch TV for a couple of hours, then go to bed, absolutely knackered,' Keith says. 'He must have been horrified to see what a thug he'd produced in me.'

The boy born in December 1943 thus grew up closest to his mother, Doris, a warm and jolly woman who had inherited the Dupree fondness for music and romance. Keith remembers how, as Doris did the housework, the radio would constantly pour out American big band music. When he first started school and was too nervous to walk there, Doris carried him all the way, bundled lovingly in her arms. From his earliest childhood, she encouraged him to do, and be, exactly what he wanted.

As a small boy, Keith had a beautiful soprano voice, good

enough to be heard in Westminster Abbey itself. 'Only three of us, in our white surplices, used to be good enough to do the hallelujahs. I was a star then – coming up by coach to London to sing in the inter-schools competition at the Albert Hall. I think that was my first taste of show business: when my voice broke and they didn't want me in the choir any more. Suddenly it was "Don't call us, we'll call you." I think that was when I stopped being a good boy and started to be a yob.'

Doris and Bert Richards lived in Chastillian Road, Dartford, just a street or two away from the Jaggers in Denver Road. Keith attended Wentworth County Primary School and was taught by Ken Llewellyn. He had met Mike Jagger, too, briefly, in the scream and jostle of the infant playground. Jagger, who customarily affects to remember nothing past, can nonetheless recall what a strong impression Keith made on him. 'I asked him what he wanted to do when he grew up. He said he wanted to be a cowboy like Roy Rogers and play a guitar. I wasn't that impressed by Roy Rogers, but the bit about the guitar *did* interest me.'

That first acquaintance was short-lived. Doris and Bert moved soon afterwards from Chastillian Road to a house on a new council estate on the other side of Dartford. Thereafter, Keith Richards became the very last kind of companion Joe and Eva Jagger could have wished for their elder son.

The Richardses lived on the Temple Hill Estate, in a small semi-detached house, No. 6 Spielman Road; the estate was brand new, dumped down on raw new tarmac roads without amusements or amenities. Bert Richards, as before, got up at five each morning to go to work at Osram's in Hammersmith. Doris worked part-time in a Dartford baker's shop. And Keith, between his father's indifference and his mother's over-indulgence, began to go resolutely to the bad.

It was not that he lacked ability – even talent. He could be, Ken Llewellyn remembers, a bright, attentive boy, responsive especially to words and language. He enjoyed cricket, swimming and – most surprisingly – tennis. He was, besides, good-natured and open, with a mischievous wit that made even schoolmasters unbend towards him.

What he could not do was accept discipline in any form. It was a lawlessness partly compounded of running wild on the estate;

51

partly of his mother's soft-hearted pampering. Doris did not mind if he failed to do his homework or went AWOL from cross-country runs or – as increasingly happened – if he failed to turn up for school altogether. She would leave him money at home to buy fish and chips for his lunch. Even when he dumped the fish and chip leavings in the kitchen sink, newspaper and all, Doris cleared up after him without complaint.

By the time he was thirteen, ordinary teachers despaired of educating him. It was decided he should go straight to Dartford Technical School, where his father hoped he might succumb to learning a useful trade.

Now, however, the long-suffering Bert Richards faced an additional vexation. 'Every time the poor guy came in at night,' Keith says, 'he'd find me sitting at the top of the stairs with my guitar, playing and banging on the wall for percussion. He was great about it, really. He'd only mutter, "Stop that bloody noise."'

Doris had bought Keith his first guitar, for seven pounds, from her wages at the baker's shop. 'I never knew what make it was,' Keith says. 'The name had been painted out.' The only stipulation Doris made, supported by Grandfather Gus, was that he must learn to play *properly*. Soon afterwards, she gave him more money for a record player, from Dartford Co-Op shop, so he could learn by listening to the skiffle and Rock 'n' Roll hits.

Now was the time of British Rock 'n' Roll – of Tommy Steele and Terry Dene and the 'cover' versions of American songs put out on a label called Embassy that was sold only at Woolworth's. Embassy records were the first that Keith Richards tried to copy, sitting at the top of the stairs at 6 Spielman Road. 'I always sat on the top stair to practise. You could get the best echo that way – or standing in the bath.'

He soon realized that what made British Rock 'n' Roll so tinny and false was not the vocal so much as the backing – the staid guitars played by bored 'session men', and sounding just as plumply complacent. Better by far to scrape up the full six shillings and fourpence for the original American version with guitars that shrilled and echoed as from a separate universe. Keith's next idol, after his grandfather Gus, was Scotty Moore, Elvis Presley's session guitarist. He still thinks Moore's solo on Presley's I'm Left, You're Right, She's Gone the most exciting thing ever recorded. 'I could never work out how he played it, and I still can't. It's such a wonderful thing that I almost don't *want* to know.'

His guitar, allied with the life of a Dartford Teddy Boy, became the final, irresistible temptation to play truant. In 1958, he was expelled from Dartford Technical School. A sympathetic teacher suggested there might be one last hope in the art college in the neighbouring dormitory town of Sidcup.

Sidcup Art College sounds immeasurably grander than it ever was. It existed, in fact, to give just such last chances to those whose inglorious school careers had fitted them for nothing better than what was then belittlingly called 'commercial art'. Sidcup's art college was remarkably similar to the one in Hope Street, Liverpool, which – also in 1958 – admitted a similar habitual truant named John Lennon.

For Keith, Sidcup Art College was a first introduction to authentic Blues music, never captured on a Woolworth's Embassy label. A group of students – including Dick Taylor – would meet in an empty room next to the principal's office, and play Little Walter and Big Bill Broonzy songs among the drawing boards and paste pots. It was from one of them that Keith acquired his first electric guitar, swapping it for a pile of records in a hasty transaction in the college 'bogs'.

So far as Dick Taylor was concerned, Keith Richards was just an incorrigible and hilarious distraction from the business of studying graphic design. 'When I think of Keith at college, I think of dustbins burning. We used to get these baths of silk-screen wash, throw them over the dustbins and then throw on a match. The dustbins used to explode with a great "woomph".

'We were all popping pills then – to stay awake without sleep more than to get high. We used to buy these nose inhalers called Nostrilene, for the benzedrine, or even take girls' period pills. Opposite the college, there was this little park with an aviary that had a cockatoo in it. Cocky the Cockatoo we used to call it. Keith used to feed it pep pills and make it stagger around on its perch. If ever we were feeling bored, we'd go and give another upper to Cocky the Cockatoo.'

One morning, on his railway journey from Dartford to Sidcup, Keith happened to get into the same dreary commuter carriage as

Mike Jagger, en route to Victoria and LSE. They recognized each other vaguely from Wentworth County Primary School and a subsequent meeting when Mike had a holiday job selling ice cream outside Dartford Library. This meeting might have been as casual as the previous ones were it not that Mike had under his arm a pile of the import Blues albums he had got from America by mail order. Keith noticed the sacred names of Chuck Berry and Little Walter, and, with some incredulity, asked the striped-scarfed LSE student if *he* liked that kind of music, too.

Chatting further, they discovered they had a common friend in Dick Taylor. Dick had already mentioned to Keith that he was rehearsing with a group sworn to play nothing but Blues and R & B. By the time their train reached Sidcup, it was half-arranged that Keith Richards should come along and try rehearsing with Little Boy Blue and the Blue Boys.

He brought with him his semi-solid Hofner cutaway guitar and what seemed to the others a stunning virtuosity. Sitting on the stairs at home, he had managed to master nearly all Chuck Berry's introductions and solos, even the metal swarm of notes running through the Berry classic Johnny B. Goode. He understood that even this complex break, like two guitars in unison, required something more than simply playing notes fast. 'Keith sounded great – but he wasn't *flash*,' Dick Taylor says. 'When he came in, you could feel something holding the band together.'

Keith's arrival, even so, did not advance the fortunes of Little Boy Blue and the Blue Boys. They continued to practise as before, with no thought of any audience beyond Dick Taylor's mum – no inkling that R & B music was a secret vouchsafed to anyone in Britain but themselves. The nearest they came to a public performance was playing together for a snapshot outside the Taylors' back door. The snap shows Dick and Keith with their guitars parodying Chuck Berry's duck walk, and Mike Jagger, in his student's button-up cardigan, striking a dramatic pose against the background of drainpipe and pebbledashed council house wall.

Music in that era forged many friendships between personalities that might otherwise have remained polar opposites. It had happened three years earlier between cynical, trouble-prone John Lennon and cautious, conservative Paul McCartney in Liverpool.

It happened now, when Keith Richards, the 'Ted' from a council flat on the wrong side of Dartford, started to go around with Mike Jagger, the LSE student from middle-class Denver Road,

Though the LSE in 1961 was not the political hotbed it later became, a mild radicalism was as de rigueur among its students as the prevailing 'bohemian' look. For Mike Jagger it was to be little more than a look, expressed in his new leather tie and 'sloppy' knitted cardigan. Just the same, armed with new words like 'capitalism' and 'proletariat', he seemed intent on rejecting his careful upbringing and sliding down to the class his mother so abhorred. At LSE, he dropped the 'Mike', which now seemed redolent of bourgeois young men with sports cars. 'Mike Jagger' would henceforward be a creature only in the memory of his earliest friends. It was Jagger who hung around with Keith Richards, talking in broad Cockney and affecting some of Keith's chaotic nonchalance and street-tough recklessness.

The mimicry was not completely one-sided. Keith on occasion could become thoughtful, self-effacing, even shy. It was as if each provided the other with a role he had desired but never dared assume before. Dick Taylor noticed what was to become a regular interchange of identities. 'One day Mick would become Keith. But then on another day, Keith could go all like Mick. You never knew which way round it would be.

'But from then on, Mick and Keith were together. Whoever else came into the band or left, there'd always be Mick and Keith.'

Before Alexis Korner and his wife Bobbie went to bed in their flat in Moscow Road, Bayswater, they would be careful to leave the kitchenette window slightly ajar at the bottom. Next to the window was a table positioned in such a way that the late-arriving or unexpected guest could enter by rolling sideways across it. When Alexis and Bobbie got up next morning, four or five sleeping figures might be peacefully disposed under the table, against the cooker legs or among the food bowls of the Korners' several cats.

The sleepers were American Blues musicians on tour, for whom Alexis and Bobbie Korner provided refuge and hospitality in an otherwise bewildering land. Big Bill Broonzy, Muddy Waters, T-Bone Walker, the guitar giants so often visualized by Mick

Jagger and Keith Richards in their windy and harsh Chicago heaven, might be sitting barely twenty miles from Dartford in that Bayswater kitchenette, eating the Southern-style ham hocks that Bobbie Korner had learned to cook. Her daughter, Sappho, would sit there unconcerned among the big black men with their strange, shuffling feet and heads tied into red bandannas to hide the curlers with which they eternally tried to straighten their hair.

Alexis Korner's antecedents were as richly cosmopolitan as the syllables of his name suggest. His father was Austrian, a former cavalry officer, and his mother was Greco-Turkish. By his father's first marriage he had a Russian step-grandmother. He himself was born in Paris and spent his early childhood in Switzerland and North Africa. There was something more than a little Moroccan in his dark skin and tightly curled hair, and the vibrant, husky voice which only accidental circumstance was to bend into the brogue of suburban West London.

His father, the former cavalry officer, was an autocratic, distant figure, vaguely connected with high finance and – Alexis later thought – international espionage. 'I know he lost a lot of money in the Twenties, when Britain went off the gold standard, and he couldn't live as well as he had before. He was also supposed to have had something to do with the scandal surrounding the Zinoviev Letter. I'm sure he'd done something pretty major to earn the gratitude of the British government. When war broke out in 1939, we were living in England; my father could have expected to be interned as an enemy alien. Instead, he got his naturalisation papers as a British subject virtually overnight.'

One Saturday in 1940, Alexis, a pupil of St Paul's School, went from his home in Ealing to nearby Shepherd's Bush market to indulge in the boyish pastime of pilfering from the stalls. His haul that morning included a record by the Blues pianist Jimmy Yancey. 'From that moment,' he remembered later, 'I only wanted to do one thing. I wanted to play boogie-woogie piano.'

When he attempted to do so on the family piano, his father would come along in a fury and slam down the lid. Nor was the elder Korner any better pleased when Alexis brought home his first guitar. 'My father used to say the guitar was a "woman's instrument". He imagined it in operettas, tied with pink ribbon.'

Two years' military service brought relief from this parental prejudice. Alexis served with the British Army in West Germany and – as well as playing football for his regiment – became a part-time announcer over the Forces' radio network. He could saturate himself, not only in the music played to British troops, but also in the far more exciting output of AFN, the American Forces Network. As surreptitiously listening German boys already knew, AFN broadcast the very best in jazz and swing and even types of black music not available to civilians back home in the States. So the Blues took root, on NATO bases and, later, in local clubs, amid pornographic bookshops, strip joints and mud-wrestling pits.

Back in London, working in the shipping firm owned by his mother's Greek family, Alexis gravitated naturally to that first postwar 'younger generation', which haunted the Soho cellars, avid for politics and traditional jazz. 'We were elitist – and *highly* political. We used to speak quite seriously in those days of founding a "fourth class". There'd be the upper class, the middle class, the working class and us. That was how the Blues came into it. When we heard a Leadbelly song or a Woody Guthrie song, we knew we were listening to a powerful political protest.'

The principal jazz bandleaders of the period did what they could to bring Blues to the larger Dixieland audience. Humphrey Lyttelton, trumpeter, Old Etonian and friend of Royalty, had brought Big Bill Broonzy to Britain as early as 1953. Ken Colyer, most pure of all the jazz and folk purists, featured some of the greatest American Bluesmen at his London club, Studio 51, just off Leicester Square.

Chris Barber remained the music's most passionate, consistent champion – the only one, in Korner's words, to 'put his money where his mouth was' and plough actual cash into keeping Blues alive. Barber, in the early Fifties, had been the moving spirit behind a formal conservation body, the National Jazz League. The league flourished, acquiring sufficient capital to buy its own Soho club, the Marquee in Wardour Street.

Alexis Korner joined the Barber band as banjoist during Lonnie Donegan's absence on National Service. When Donegan returned and Rock Island Line became a hit, Korner was well placed, had he desired, to participate in the nine days' skiffle wonder. He almost joined another successful skiffle group, the

Vipers, signed up at the 2 I's coffee bar by a then obscure EMI-label executive called George Martin. Instead, he formed his own group, bowing to commercial pressure with the word 'skiffle' only for its first extended-play record. Thereafter, the group was to be known as Alexis Korner's Blues Incorporated.

The first band in Britain to play nothing but Blues was a curious amalgam of fervent fantasy wedded to unlikely and incongruous human shapes. Its chief member, after Korner himself, was Cyril Davies, a fifteen-stone panel beater from South Harrow, a virtuoso on Blues harmonica and twelve-string guitar, whose every waking moment was clouded by chagrin that he had not been born a black man. On saxophone there was Dick Heckstall-Smith, who in aspect and manner bore a passing resemblance to Lenin. On double bass there was the future bass guitar maestro, Jack Bruce. The drummer – when Alexis could persuade him to sit in – was a sad-faced boy called Charlie Watts. 'I'd met Charlie at the Troubadour in Brompton Road, and always liked his playing. I'd said to him, "If I ever form a Blues group, would you come in as drummer?" But he'd only do it part-time. He was too busy, studying commercial art in Harrow.'

It was Korner's plan from the beginning to start his own club, as Ken Colyer and other musicians had, to protect their chosen music from the jibes or hostility of rival factions. Soho cellars or pub backrooms in those days could be hired for a few shillings a night. Alexis Korner's first such venture, grandly styled The London Blues and Barrelhouse Club, was a room at the Round House pub in Wardour Street. The residency was sometimes interrupted by disputes between Korner and Cyril Davies, which led one or other to storm off and play in some rival club like the Troubadour.

As Blues Incorporated became more established, they started to receive bookings further and further outside London. One night, towards the end of 1961, Alexis found himself playing the Blues to a rapturous crowd at a municipal hall in the genteel spa town of Cheltenham, Gloucestershire.

After the performance, a boy came up to Alexis in the pub across the road and talked to him earnestly – but with evident authority – about the Blues and Bluesmen. The boy was short but broadly built, and looked well-to-do in his smart Italian suit,

58

white tab-collar shirt and Slim Jim tie. He spoke in a soft, well-mannered voice, lisping slightly. He said his name was Brian Jones. He was a musician himself, playing saxophone semi-professionally in a Rock group called the Ramrods. What he really wanted to do, he told Alexis, was play Delta-style slide guitar with a band like Blues Incorporated. Alexis said – as Alexis always did – that if Brian Jones ever came to London, he was welcome to sleep on the Korners' kitchen floor.

In March 1962, tired of battling against the prejudice of the Soho jazz crowd, Alexis Korner decided to see how a new Blues club would go in his own West London suburb, Ealing. The venue was a small room under the ABC teashop, just across the road from Ealing Broadway station. The first session, on March 17, was announced by a small display ad in the *New Musical Express*.

The ad caused astonished excitement twenty miles away in Kent, among a self-defeatingly modest group called Little Boy Blue and the Blue Boys, to whom it still had not occurred that anyone else in Britain shared their musical fixation. The following Saturday, crammed into Alan Etherington's father's Riley 'Pathfinder' car, they set out for Ealing to investigate the extraordinary possibility that other people were playing the Blues, to an audience, for money.

## 2

## 'Well, the joint was rockin' . . .'

It truly was happening, in a poky downstairs room between the ABC bakery and a jeweller's shop: their secret music, the contraband repertoire of Muddy Waters, Otis Spann and the Chicago Bluesmen, translated from inconceivable distance to deafening propinquity by the oddest imaginable group of men. Blues Incorporated performed, like jazz musicians, with almost professorial seriousness. Alexis Korner, curly-haired and moustachioed, in a white business shirt and tie, occupied the foreground with his Spanish guitar, seated on a chair. Cyril Davies stood next to him, sucking and coaxing the Blues 'harp' with a breathy passion that made his pleated trousers wobble. Their audience stood around the tiny recessed stage in equal formality, nursing half pints of beer. As 'Squirrel' ended his harp solo, snatched the silver slide from his mouth and mopped his streaming brow, he received a round of polite applause like a speaker at a temperance meeting.

The instant success of the Ealing club proved to Alexis what he had always suspected – that the Blues music, for some reason, had its most devoted following in suburban West London. After the second or third night at Ealing, something even more satisfactory happened. Alexis had brought Blues Incorporated away from Soho partly to escape the hostility of the Traditional Jazz faction. Now, the very clubs that had rejected him were starting to lose business, as more and more of their customers made the long Saturday-night trek to Ealing. Even the purist National Jazz League could not ignore the commercial possibilities implied. Harold Pendleton, manager of the league-owned Marquee Club, came out to Ealing to hear Blues Incorporated, and afterwards offered Korner – whom he had previously not admired – a regular Thursday night engagement at the Marquee.

The band, at that time, had no regular vocalist. 'I'd sing lead – or Squirrel would,' Korner later remembered. 'But we didn't really believe in words. We were *instrumentalists*. The words just got in the way.'

Each Saturday night audience, in any case, was filled with young men, eager to exchange their world of 'Magicoal' fires and Bourn-Vita cocoa for the Blues shouter's world of tin tenements and dance-hall queens. Anyone who wanted to sing with Blues Incorporated was welcome to try, though Alexis knew from long experience that the results were generally terrible. Then one night, a 6' 7", sandy-haired and pink-faced youth got up and sang in a voice so black and raw, it felt like Beale Street there in the room. The boy's name was 'Long' John Baldry. He became Blues Incorporated's first featured singer at the Ealing Club on Saturdays and on Thursdays at the Marquee.

A few days after the first Ealing session, Alexis Korner received a letter with a Dartford postmark enclosing a small spool tape. The letter, from someone called Mick Jagger, solicited Korner's opinion of three songs by a group named Little Boy Blue and the Blue Boys. The material offered was Reelin' and Rockin', Bright Lights Big City, and Around and Around. The tape was subsequently lost; all Korner could ever remember of it was that it sounded 'absolutely terrible'.

The tape served a useful enough purpose, introducing Little Boy Blue himself to an established musician, known for unusual kindness towards musical beginners. Mick Jagger received the same invitation as everyone else to Ealing, to join Blues Incorporated on the bandstand for what singers, too, called a 'blow'. So, the next Saturday, taking all his courage, Jagger stepped on to the little stage, with its grubby tarpaulin canopy, and sang in public for the very first time.

He did so looking every inch the LSE student in his white poplin shirt, half-unknotted tie and chunky 'bohemian' cardigan, glancing nervously behind him as the dignitaries of Blues Incorporated began to vamp the – for them – absurdly simple chords of Chuck Berry's Round and Around. He himself has only a hazy recollection of standing there, half drunk, off key, forgetting his words and almost paralysed with fright. 'The thing I noticed about him wasn't his singing,' Alexis Korner said. 'It was the way he threw his hair around. He only had a short haircut, like everyone else's. But, for a kid in a cardigan, that was moving quite *excessively*.'

The song died into silence. Then – to the singer's vast astonishment – there was a burst of applause. Even tetchy 'Squirrel' Davies was prepared to clap someone whose love of Blues could take him so far beyond the embarrassment barrier. The fact that he had copied Chuck Berry's phrasing note for note was further proof of being a true disciple.

The next time Mick Jagger sang for Alexis Korner, it was for a fee of fifteen shillings, plus beer. Within a month, he had become Blues Incorporated's second-string vocalist, singing with Korner for that same modest stipend whenever Long John Baldry was not available.

On Saturdays, it became a habit for the Dartford boys, Mick, Keith, Alan and Dick, to call at Alexis's flat in Bayswater and spend a couple of hours with the Korners before going on to Ealing together. Bobbie Korner would give them tea while Alexis told them stories of what Muddy and Broonzy had said in that very same kitchen – how Big Bill could never pronounce his fellow Bluesmen's names (he called Fats Waller 'Fat Wallace') or how T-Bone Walker, fuddled by distance and drink, had once seriously inquired, 'Is this Paris, France?'

The Korners both remember Jagger in this period as quiet and polite, though with political pretensions that Alexis found mildly aggravating. 'We were talking about the Blues one day and Mick said, "Why are you playing our working-class music?" I said, "Mick – you're at the *LSE*! What could be more middle class than that?"'

Keith, by contrast, was instantly sociable and engaging. 'He'd sit at the kitchen table and talk to Bobbie for *hours*. I remember how he loved words. I didn't really know him as a musician then – only that he played guitar in that group of theirs in Dartford. He never pushed himself forward as a musician. He just seemed happy to be around Mick.'

By this time, the hospitable Korners had another young visitor regularly sleeping on their kitchenette floor. It was the boy Alexis had talked to in Cheltenham, little realizing how that morsel of encouragement had ignited the boy's fierce desire to be in London, playing Blues. So, late at night in Moscow Road, the kitchenette window would slide up. A dim figure would roll sideways across the table, down to the floor. Like Muddy Waters and Big Bill Broonzy before him, Brian Jones would fall asleep somewhere between the cats' bowls and the legs of the electric cooker.

Hatherley Road, Cheltenham, lies just outside the smugly elegant Gloucestershire spa town which will be ever associated in the English mind with retired Army colonels and colleges for genteel young ladies. Hatherley Road is a long suburban avenue of identical 1930s houses, each with a single bay window, a neat front lawn and a wrought-iron 'sunrise' gate. Here and there, beyond a uniform creosote-covered garage, one can see the terraces of Cheltenham's exclusive district and beyond, the soft green Cotswolds, striding away towards Wales.

That Lewis Jones was a Welshman could not be doubted by his colleagues at Dowty and Co., Cheltenham's aeronautical engineering works. Short, straight-backed, severe in manner, he possessed the inflexible virtues of Welshness in exact measure with its irreproachable faults. He was, in other words, respectable, decent, hard-working, religious, conventional, puritanically intolerant of those less strong-minded than himself. Like many of his countrymen, he regretted the advance of the twentieth century almost on principle. 'Times change but *I* don't,' he would say, adding a heartfelt 'Thank God!'

The Welsh have almost an obligation to be musical. Lewis Jones played the organ at his local parish church for some years, until his dislike of petty ecclesiastical politics led him to resign. His wife Louisa – also Welsh – possessed a more pronounced talent, and supplemented Lewis's income from Dowty's by giving piano lessons to local school-children.

Their first child, Brian Lewis Hopkin Jones, was born on February 28, 1942. Of the two daughters who followed, only one – Barbara, born in 1946 – survived. The other, Pauline, died of leukaemia when Brian was three. Brian thought his parents had given her away and, for a long time afterwards, lived in terror that the same would be done to him.

He was, his father says, a thoroughly normal and happy small boy, healthy but for childhood ailments and an attack of croup which left him prone to bronchitis and chronic asthma. At his first school, Dean Close, he worked well, enjoyed sport – particularly cricket and badminton – and became an excellent swimmer and diver. Sea air aggravated his asthma, however; after a single day at the beach, he would be confined to bed, wheezing and croaking piteously.

Like his parents, and the race from which he sprang, Brian Jones was instinctively musical. Louisa started giving him piano lessons from the age of six; he afterwards took up the recorder and clarinet. Though able to read music, he mastered the reed instruments by ear and intuition, stumbling on melody by means he himself did not fully understand. So marked was his talent as a small boy that Lewis Jones thought he might be destined for a career as a classical musician.

He passed the Eleven-plus exam without effort and went on, as his parents had hoped, to Cheltenham Grammar School, down in the exclusive district of 'The Promenade', the retired generals and the Ladies' College. This exclusive seminary, in fact, stood immediately adjacent to Cheltenham Grammar School and daily provided its senior boys with an unreachable fantasy as the young ladies ran forth, squealing, for their mid-morning break.

Brian began well at Cheltenham Grammar, getting good marks for work, especially science and languages, excelling at cricket and swimming and winning a place as a clarinettist in the school orchestra. 'Then, all of a sudden,' Lewis Jones says bleakly, 'he became very difficult. He started to rebel against everything – mainly me.'

The trouble began when Brian ceased practising classical pieces on piano and clarinet, and began listening to a kind of music that Lewis Jones abhorred. At thirteen, he discovered jazz and, at fourteen, the music of Charlie Parker. The baby-faced Negro with the overweight body, who could make a heavy saxophone sing with the labyrinthine sweetness of a nightingale, became Brian's all-eclipsing passion. He sold the clarinet his parents had bought him and used the proceeds to buy a second-hand alto saxophone. Within a few days, to his parents' horror, the sound of a first, shaky sax solo brayed through the quiet house in Hatherley Road.

He was soon good enough to sit in with local bands playing the Trad Jazz of Chris Barber and Humphrey Lyttelton. Even Cheltenham had its bohemian quarter, centred on the art college, on coffee bars like the Aztec, the Patio and the Waikiki, or pubs like the Wheatsheaf Inn, Leckhampton, where the 66 Jazz Club convened, with Brian Jones as membership secretary.

At Cheltenham Grammar, meanwhile, he became known as a troublemaker, able to disrupt a whole class by his blandly outrageous behaviour. A classmate, Peter Watson, remembers how Brian would sit in class in football boots, claiming they were more comfortable than shoes. 'Brian said it was boring to drink the regulation milk at break time, so he started the fashion of drinking brown ale instead. It became a whole fashion to drink brown ale at break time instead of milk.'

At break, according to immemorial custom, the whole class would crowd at the window and gaze longingly down on the Cheltenham young ladies as they frolicked on the grass below. Brian Jones, it was well known, belonged to the select few Grammar School boys whose sexual adventures had gone beyond mere kissing and 'petting'. It was known, too, that he scorned the Durex contraceptives that other boys carried symbolically in their wallets. 'Bareback' was the best way, he would insist, smiling a smile so lascivious, yet so mischievous, no one knew whether to believe him.

They believed him when, in 1958, a fourteen-year-old pupil at the girls' Grammar School became pregnant and named Brian Jones as the father. The news caused a scandal in Cheltenham and even got into the more lurid national Sunday newspapers as gleeful contradiction of the town's bath-chair image. For Lewis and Louisa Jones, it was an epoch they can hardly bear to mention even now. The baby was born but put out to adoption. All that could be hoped, after bringing such disgrace on his family and himself, was that Brian had well and truly learned his lesson.

The scandal brought about his premature exit from Cheltenham Grammar School, despite nine passes at GCE 'O' Level and Advanced Level passes in Physics and Chemistry. For the next eighteen months, he worked variously as a shop assistant, a coalman and a trainee in the Borough Architect's office of Cheltenham Council. A boyhood passion for buses led him to a brief career on Cheltenham municipal transport, as conductor and driver. He continued to play alto sax in various Trad bands, then in a Rock 'n' Roll combo called the Ramrods, which enjoyed some local fame until its lead singer went away on honeymoon and choked to death while eating a chip.

In 1961, Brian made a second girl pregnant. Her name was Pat

Andrews: she had met Brian at the Aztec coffee bar during one of his spells of unemployment. He had left home by now and was living with a friend named Dick Hattrell at a flat in Cheltenham's art college district. This time, he seemed to accept that there was no alternative but to marry the girl he had put 'in the club': Pat herself was confident of his intentions. After the baby was born, he visited her in hospital, bringing a vast bouquet of flowers he had bought by selling some of his precious LPs. On his insistence, the baby was named Julian, after the jazz musician Julian 'Cannonball' Adderley.

Brian did not marry Pat Andrews. Instead, shortly after his conversation with Alexis Korner, he took off for London suddenly, accompanied by Dick Hattrell, to start a job his father had found for him with a firm of opticians. Lewis and Louisa Jones heard no more from him until he had become nationally notorious.

He continued to write to Pat Andrews, assuring her he still loved her and would be sending for her and the baby soon. Pat grew increasingly restive after learning he had several girlfriends in London. Finally, one day in 1962, she bundled Julian Mark in her arms and, with just one pound note in her purse, set off from Cheltenham by long-distance bus to track the baby's father down.

He had left even his name behind in Cheltenham. It was not Brian Jones but 'Elmo Lewis' who made his first guest appearance with Blues Incorporated at the Ealing Club. He had changed instruments, too, from alto sax to electric guitar, a brand-new, shiny Gibson, bought with money half saved, half stolen, and mastered by his usual blend of intuition, will power and desire.

No greater contrast could have been imagined between the middle-aged, rather beery-looking Blues sideman and the boy who stepped up beside Alexis in his neat Italian suit, holding the shiny new Gibson with one finger pointed stiff across its pearled fretboard. His debut was the Elmore James classic Dust My Blues. In his West London bedsitter, he had taught himself to play it exactly as James did, with a metal 'slide', swooping the metal bar along the guitar neck to lengthen each note into almost a second angry, sarcastic voice. The sudden appearance of Pat Andrews and baby Julian had only temporarily interrupted the transfiguration of Elmore into Elmo.

Even then, Alexis remembered, his stage presence was subtly but unmistakably flavoured with aggression. The fact that he stood absolutely still somehow intensified an air of challenge to all comers, even as his eyes remained studiously downcast, his wide mouth pursed in virginal tranquillity. 'He'd learned how to *bait* an audience, long before anything like that occurred to Mick. You should have seen those kids' reaction when Brian picked up a tambourine and gave it one tiny little shake in their faces.'

Even the Korners, his best London friends, knew almost nothing of Brian beyond what he inadvertently betrayed. He told them nothing of his home or family, and only under gravest sufferance mentioned the detested word 'Cheltenham'. Alexis and Bobbie, as surrogate parents, came to realise in time that frustration and unhappiness of an abnormal depth lay beneath Brian's driving wish to become famous by any means whatever.

He had abandoned his traineeship as an optician by now, and had a job as an electrical-appliance salesman at Whiteley's department store in Queensway, just a block away from the Korners' flat in Moscow Road. Alexis would sometimes see him after work, crossing the road to meet a girl waiting reproachfully for him in the doorway to the Mac Fisheries shop. Though Pat Andrews and the baby had moved into Brian's tiny Notting Hill bedsitter, she saw little more of him now than she had in Cheltenham. Eventually, she was forced to take a part-time job to support the child Brian now scarcely acknowledged as his.

To the Korners and the Ealing Club crowd, he presented the aspect of a young bachelor, interested only in clothes and in forming a Blues band that would take the world by storm. Each time he arrived at the Ealing Club he seemed to have a new suit, a new tab-collar shirt, a new bouffant-haired girlfriend admiringly in tow. The money for both, more often than not, would have come from Pat Andrews's minuscule pay packet or from robbing the till in Whiteley's electrical department.

He stayed always one jump ahead of retribution, buoyed up by belief in his destiny and by that way he had of looking as if butter wouldn't melt in his mouth. When Brian fixed anyone with his big baby eyes and spoke in his soft, lisping, well-brought-up voice, it was impossible to imagine such chaos accumulating behind him. 'He had a way of talking that was all his own,' Alexis Korner said. 'It was a most beautiful mixture of good manners and rudeness.'

Ostensibly still living with Pat, Julian and Dick Hattrell, he contrived to lead a semi-nomadic life in London and outside, travelling from town to town, reconnoitring the music clubs, sitting in with local groups in the hope of finding musicians for a band of his own. One of his regular haunts was Guildford, where he would play at the Wooden Bridge Hotel with a scratch band called Rhode Island Red and the Roosters, featuring a pale and – it then seemed – deeply unpromising guitarist named Eric Clapton.

In Oxford, a city catacombed with student-run jazz and Blues clubs, he became friends with an English undergraduate named Paul Pond who led a Blues group called Thunder Odin's Big Secret. Paul Pond subsequently became Paul Jones, singer with the Manfred Mann group. 'Brian was *terribly* smart in those days,' Jones says. 'Italian box jacket, winklepicker shoes, never a hair out of place. Whenever he passed through Oxford, he'd sleep on my couch. I remember waking up one morning to hear this awful wheezing and snorting from the next room. Brian was lying on the couch, hardly able to breathe. He gasped out that he'd got asthma and had left his inhaler at the party we'd both been to the night before. I had to jump on my bike and go dashing off to get it back for him.'

After sitting in with Thunder Odin's Big Secret a few times, Brian decided that 'P. P. Pond' was the Blues partner he needed. The two made a tape which impressed Alexis Korner so much he gave them the job of 'interval band' at the Ealing Club. It happened that P. P. Pond was singing Dust My Blues, accompanied by Elmo Lewis on slide guitar, when Mick Jagger, Keith Richards, and Dick Taylor walked through the door together.

On Keith especially, the effect was instant hero worship, heightened by Keith's tendency to mix up one name with another. 'It's Elmore James,' he kept whispering to the others. 'It is, man – really! It's fuckin' Elmore James!'

They met 'Elmo Lewis', alias Brian Jones, afterwards and, over half pints of beer, talked Blues for the rest of the night. To the Dartford boys, he seemed a raffish figure, only a year older than Mick and Keith but already a 'semi-pro' and – it emerged – the father of a baby. Keith remembers how, at close quarters, Brian's slight body seemed to thicken on his short and powerful legs. 'He was like a little Welsh bull,' Keith says. 'He was broad, and he looked very tough.'

That first conversation produced only an exchange of views. Brian, interested mainly in jazz-influenced Blues, had not yet discovered Chuck Berry. He listened intently to what Keith told him about Berry and Jimmy Reed. He made it clear, though, that his ambitions went somewhat higher than Alexis Korner's part-time student vocalist and a red-nosed, pimply guitarist whose only public appearance to date had been in the garden of a Bexleyheath council house.

The partnership between Elmo Lewis and P. P. Pond lasted only for that one engagement. Paul Pond returned to Oxford to resume his studies and await his destiny with Manfred Mann. Elmo Lewis, on the lookout for partners again, placed an advertisement in *Jazz News*, Soho's club information sheet, grandly inviting prospective sidesmen to audition with him in the back room of a Berwick Street pub, the Bricklayer's Arms.

The first recruit, Ian Stewart, arrived by racing cycle, looking anything but the part of the Blues pianist he claimed to be. Thick-set and muscular, with a long, pugnacious jaw, he entered the rehearsal room in leather shorts, carrying a pork pie he had bought for his lunch. When he sat at the piano, however, all such visual reservations vanished. Pumping with one burly leg, he could make even those nicotine-yellowed keys forget their life of Bye Bye Blackbird and, instead, give out the hectic, tinny airs of ragtime and barrel-house. He then sat back, took out his pork pie and began to eat it nonchalantly.

'Stew' became the nucleus of Brian's group, together with an accompished solo guitarist, Geoff Bradford. Over the next few days, Mick Jagger, Keith Richards and Dick Taylor also drifted in and auditioned to Brian's satisfaction. Stew recognized them from the Ealing Club, but rated none of them as musicians in his or Bradford's class. Tough and short-spoken as he was, there was something about Keith, especially, that put him on his guard. 'I think Keith was very shy in those days. Mick had got very friendly with Brian, and that seemed to make Keith edgy and uncomfortable.'

There were quickly arguments between Geoff Bradford, a pure Blues guitarist in the Muddy Waters style, and Keith, the Chuck Berry acolyte. Bradford refused to have anything to do with 'Rock 'n' Roll rubbish' like Roll Over Beethoven and Sweet Little

Sixteen, and walked out, never to return. By this time, Elmo Lewis, the three Dartford boys and the lantern-jawed Stew had found enough in common to carry on together.

Practice sessions at the Bricklayer's Arms took place three times a week, even though the embryo – and untitled – group still had no prospect of a booking. 'It was a seven o'clock start, and we'd all be there sharp at seven,' Ian Stewart says. 'The one you could never depend on was Brian. He'd suddenly disappear for a few days, then he'd turn up again and want to get another rehearsal going. I never really trusted Brian – mainly because he was always telling you to trust him.'

The solid Stew had a steady daytime job as a shipping clerk with Imperial Chemical Industries in Buckingham Gate. His first impression of Mick and Keith was of semi-vagrants, permanently broke, shabby and ravenous. Mick had no money but his seven pounds per week student grant, plus a few shillings he got for singing with Alex. Keith, at the point of expulsion from Sidcup Art College, was entirely dependent on handouts from his mother. 'They looked like they were going to starve together. But Mick *was* rather better off. Every so often, he'd leave Keith and go off to a slightly better caff. Mick always was very fond of his stomach.'

The first spark of originality in the group was struck by spontaneous interaction between Brian on his Gibson guitar and Keith on his Hofner. They would play, not as 'lead' and subordinate 'rhythm', but as a duet, matching one another solo for solo, merging in a natural two-amp harmony, one zigzagging down the bass notes as the other climbed into treble register. This emergence of a 'two-guitar band' seemed an infinitely more exciting prospect than the skinny LSE student who sat about patiently, awaiting his chance to sing. Even then, in the trio of Mick, Keith and Brian, the joining of two inexorably left the third one out in the cold.

The sound they made could be heard in the main pub and, one night, fell on appreciative ears. Later, in the bar, a middle-aged man came up and introduced himself by visiting card as 'David Norris, Artists' Representative, Cockfosters'. He told them he'd liked what he'd heard, and could get them some engagements in ballrooms and dance halls – perhaps even at military bases on the Continent – provided they got themselves some decent instruments and stage suits. Mr Norris, for his pains, was firmly snubbed. All five had vowed they would never 'sell out' their music to the commercial world, even if it meant they never got a single engagement.

Alexis Korner remained the only real star in the Blues firmament. And in the summer of 1962, it seemed as if Korner's meteoric career was about to leave Mick Jagger behind. Blues Incorporated had been offered their first nationwide broadcast, on the BBC Light Programme's *Jazz Club*. There were, however, two drawbacks. The first was that the BBC appearance, on July 12, clashed with Korner's regular Thursday booking at the Marquee. The second was that the BBC, with typical frugality, would pay for five musicians only. Korner must therefore shed the most dispensable one in his lineup, the vocalist.

Jagger did not mind being dropped. He was, on the contrary, anxious for Korner to seize this chance to bring Blues to a national audience. It was arranged that the Marquee date should be filled by Korner's original Ealing vocalist, Long John Baldry. For an intermission band, the Marquee's manager, Harold Pendleton, agreed to give a chance to the group which had been rehearsing at the Bricklayer's Arms, though with so little hope it did not yet have a name.

The engagement was sufficiently important to merit a paragraph in the July 11 issue of *Jazz News*.

> Mick Jagger, R & B vocalist, is taking a rhythm and blues group into the Marquee tomorrow night while Blues Inc. is doing its Jazz Club gig.
>
> Called 'The Rolling Stones' ('I hope they don't think we're a rock and roll outfit,' says Mick), the line-up is: Jagger (vocals), Keith Richards, Elmo Lewis (guitars), Dick Taylor (bass), 'Stew' (piano) and Mick Avory (drums).

The name was chosen by Brian, in honour of the Muddy Waters song Rolling Stone. Ian Stewart, for one, objected strongly to it. 'The Rolling Stones – I said it was terrible! It sounded like the name of an Irish show band, or something that ought to be playing at the Savoy.' Mick Avory, the drummer they had recruited, felt equally dubious, but accepted – as the others did – that, since Brian had formed the group, he could call it what he liked.

So on July 12, 1962, with a playing order written on a page of Ian Stewart's pocket diary, the six Rolling Stones faced their first audience. Mick wore a sweater, Brian a cord jacket and Keith a skimpy dark suit which left his shirt collar and cuffs exposed like the surplice of the angelic choirboy he formerly had been. Behind them, Dick Taylor, Ian Stewart and Mick Avory glanced at one another ominously. 'You could hear people saying "Rolling Stones . . . Rolling *Stones* . . . "' Dick Taylor remembers. '"Ah . . . Rock 'n' Roll, are they . . . " Before we'd played a note, we could feel the hostility.'

Britain in 1962 was a nation still predominantly interested in recovering from 1939. The only generation that mattered was the one which had survived the war and its scarcely less uncomfortable aftermath, inspired by a common belief that one day, butter would cease to be rationed; that coupons would no longer be needed to buy clothing or chocolate. These miracles had come to pass – and more. In British homes, as in American ones seen on the cinema screen, there were now TV sets, washing machines, garages containing cars with fins. There were transistor radios, cocktail cabinets and 'genuine champagne perry'. Harold Macmillan, Prime Minister since the Suez Crisis, could be believed when he told the country, 'You've never had it so good.' Largely through that powerful superstition, government remained firmly in the hands of an elderly Edwardian whose winged white hair and drooping moustache gave him the appearance of a dilapidated but complacent sea lion.

The decade which still had not defined itself in 1962 was actually starting to form in 1955, with early sightings of that problematical new species, the 'teenager'. It was a species, however, which for the next five years caused little profound effect on British life. For it sprang almost wholly from what was still dismissively called the 'working' class. Rock 'n' Roll music, skiffle, long hair and coffee bars were condemned all in one as a deviation of the lower proletariat. 'Pop', the Rock sound watered down, figured not much higher in the social register. Its most successful British exponent, Cliff Richard, owed his survival to having exchanged the grubby aura of the 'Rocker' for that of a conventional show-business personality.

Change was coming, even now, in a battered van making its way to London from the unregarded northern city of Liverpool. In June 1962, the head of an obscure record label, Parlophone, gave an audition to four young Liverpool musicians who had, up to then, been rejected by all the major companies. Their first record – chosen with difficulty from an eccentric and uncommercial repertoire – was not released until the following October. The record was called Love Me Do; the group was the Beatles.

For the Rolling Stones, in October 1962, the most pressing question was whether they could survive another week. It scarcely mattered that their debut at the Marquee Club had gone better than any of them dared hope. To the club's jazz and pure Blues crowd, merely the sight of Dick Taylor's bass guitar had been reason enough to detest them. But there had also been a contingent of 'Mods', up on the town from Wembley or Shepherd's Bush, who loved Chuck Berry and Bo Diddley as much as Keith did, and – being Mods – had conclusively drowned out the jazz fans' disapproval. That endeared the new group still less to Harold Pendleton, who ran the Marquee on behalf of the National Jazz League, and manifestly disapproved of their music, their clothes, their attitude and – as it seemed to Ian Stewart – their perversely ill-chosen name.

The only further bookings Harold Pendleton would offer them were as dogsbodies, filling in for other bands that had not turned up. Often, after booking them, Pendleton would telephone Brian Jones and say he didn't want them after all. On the nights when they did make it to the Marquee stage, Pendleton would indulge in sarcasm at their expense. Keith Richards was a frequent target, gawky and shy, with his skinny black suit and pimple-chapped face, playing the Chuck Berry guitar riffs that Pendleton so audibly despised.

The slights they continually received from Pendleton and the jazz faction led Brian Jones, in his capacity as leader, to compose a long, erudite letter to *Jazz News*, complaining of 'the pseudo-intellectual snobbery that unfortunately contaminates the Jazz scene . . . It must be apparent,' Brian continued weightily, 'that

Rock 'n' Roll has a far greater affinity for R & B than the latter has for Jazz, insofar that Rock is a direct corruption of Rhythm and Blues whereas Jazz is Negro music on a different plane, intellectually higher but emotionally less intense . . .'

Harold Pendleton had some cause for complaint. The Rolling Stones, though top-heavy with guitarists and their non-playing singer, could persuade no drummer to throw in his lot with them. While anyone could buy a guitar and strum at it, a drummer, with his vast capital investment of £50 or more, conferred instant professionalism and permanence. Mick Avory, on that first Marquee night, had sat in only as a favour. All the drummers they had tried since then were from jazz bands, unable or unwilling to find the R & B back beat. The only exception was Charlie Watts, Blues Incorporated's part-time drummer, who sat in also with a Soho band called Blues By Six. Charlie, despite his jazz background and long, glum face, always gave them just what they wanted. But he seemed altogether too well set up and prosperous to consider joining them for good. 'We were all a bit in awe of Charlie then,' Keith says. 'We thought he was much too expensive for us.'

Brian Jones's double life as a reluctant family man and fancy-free London bachelor took on a new complexity, late that summer, when he, Mick Jagger and Keith Richards took a flat together in Edith Grove, Chelsea. The three shared two rooms halfway up a shabby house racked by the noise of lorries thundering through to Fulham Road. The flat was squalid even by London bedsitter standards, with its damp and peeling wallpaper, grubby furniture, filthy curtains and naked light bulbs that functioned at the behest of a single, ironclad electric coin meter. The lavatory was communal, on the staircase to the flat above. Those who visited it after dark did so with a supply of newspaper, matches and a candle. Keith spoke of buying a revolver, so that he could sit there and shoot at the rats.

The minuscule rent was paid by the pooling of Mick Jagger's LSE grant with Brian's wage as a shop assistant at Whiteley's. Keith – apart from one brief stint as a Christmas relief postman – contrived to remain unencumbered by any activity but playing his guitar. His contribution was a supply of food parcels sent up from Dartford by his mother. Doris Richards would also descend on the flat once a week and take away mounds of dirty underwear and shirts to wash.

To help with the rent, they found a fourth tenant – a young printer whom they knew only as 'Phelge'. 'He was the sort of madman you'd meet around Chelsea then,' Keith says. 'You'd walk in through the front door and there would be Phelge, standing at the top of the stairs with his underpants on his head.'

For Mick, the Edith Grove flat was a chance to break free of the constraints of home and his mother's reproaches for the opportunities he was wasting. He remained, even so, primarily an economics student, tacitly acknowledging that he must one day give up Blues singing to work for his degree. Up all night at the Marquee, and Chelsea's perpetual bottle parties, he would still go off next morning to Aldwych and his LSE tutorials. His father's waning influence could not altogether remove the habit of exercise. The pale, languid Chelsea layabout still turned out at regular intervals to play soccer in the LSE second eleven.

Keith, jobless and almost penniless, spent most of his days at the flat with no other company than the coin meter and his guitar. Brian, at the outset, still had a job at Whiteley's and, it was presumed, an alternative home with Pat Andrews and the baby. The Whiteley's job vanished when Brian was caught pilfering from the cash register. The link with Pat and the baby was similarly broken – although his friend, Dick Hattrell, remained a faithful follower. After that, Brian also had nothing to do, and would sit around the Edith Grove flat all day with Keith, practising their guitar duets, working out on the harmonica he had almost mastered and plotting where their next meal was coming from. He taught Keith the trick, learned in his Oxford wanderings, of creeping into neighbours' flats on the morning after bottle parties, collecting all the empty beer bottles and returning them to a pub or off-licence to collect the twopence deposits.

A tiny trickle of money came from dates arranged by Brian at venues he had already reconnoitred on his travels outside London. The venues were mostly weekend dances, put on in church halls or suburban sports pavilions. The fee – seldom more than a couple of pounds a night – would be received by Brian, then 'shared' among the other five. They did not know, since Brian thought it not worth mentioning, that he had invariably obtained an extra payment for himself as their leader and – he would also say – their manager and booking agent. Brian, in those days, was always ahead by a tiny, surreptitious percentage.

One of their regular dates was at St Mary's Parish Hall, in Hotheley Road, Richmond, playing in alternation with a group from Shepherd's Bush called the High Numbers, later transfigured into the Who. Another was in a dilapidated wooden dance hall on Eel Pie Island in the River Thames at Twickenham, crossed by a footbridge that levied a sixpenny toll. They would go there by public transport, by bus or by tube, accompanied by Dick Hattrell, whom Brian seemed able to persuade to do almost anything. Hattrell acted as their road manager until he left London for a stint of part-time soldiering in the Territorial Army.

At the Marquee, meanwhile, Harold Pendleton's sarcasm continued unabated. Even Cyril Davies, who had liked the Stones at first, now joined the jazzers against them, brusquely sacking them from a bill on which his band was headlining. No one in those days knew Keith Richards well enough to recognize the warning signs. One evening, late that autumn, after carefully considering something Harold Pendleton had said to him, Keith picked up his guitar like a caveman's club and swung it at Pendleton's head.

After that, there could be no more Marquee dates for a while. There was even less hope at Ken Colyer's Studio 51 or Giorgio Gomelsky's Piccadilly Club, where they had had one disastrous flop. The Rolling Stones therefore decided to do what Alexis Korner had when snobbery and prejudice were threatening to extinguish Blues Incorporated. They set out to start a club and a following of their own.

The club was a peripatetic one, convened on Saturday nights or Sunday afternoons in a succession of pubs in Sutton, Richmond, Putney and Twickenham. Each date along the meridian would display the same laconic poster: 'Rhythm and Blues with the Rollin' Stones [sic]. Admission 4s.' Fortunately, Ian Stewart owned a van as well as his racing bike, and could chauffeur them and their equipment to pubs in places even further distant, like Windsor, Guildford and Maidenhead. Stew proved a sterling hand at unloading guitar cases and amps, even though he might not himself always get the chance to play. 'If there was no piano, I'd just settle down in the van and go to sleep. I *did* have to be up the next morning to go to work at ICI.'

The lack of a permanent drummer continued to be vexing. Mick Avory, who sat in with them most often, had little natural feel for R & B. Carlo Little, from Cyril Davies's group, whom they liked much better, had more pressing extra curricular work with Screaming Lord Sutch and the Savages. Unable to approach Charlie Watts, they reluctantly settled for a boy called Tony Chapman, who had played in several semi-pro Rock 'n' Roll groups. But Chapman, a commercial traveller, wasn't always reliable and was frequently out of town on his trips.

Just before Christmas came another setback. Dick Taylor, their bass player, announced he was quitting to begin a course at the Royal College of Art. The others asked Tony Chapman if he knew any bass guitarists looking for work. Chapman said he might know someone, an ex-colleague of his in a conventional pop group called the Cliftons. It was arranged that Tony Chapman's friend should come for an audition with Brian, Keith and Mick at the Chelsea 'local', the Wetherby Arms, one cold, snowy day in December.

Bill Perks had always hated his family name, and wished he could change it to something more in keeping with his nature and ambitions. His grandfather Perks, he knew, had done the same thing 50 years earlier when fighting illegally as a bare-fist pugilist. 'And when he got older and used to breed racing pigeons, he still went on using another name,' the metamorphosed Bill Wyman says. 'He always raced his pigeons under the name of Jackson.'

The son born to William and Kathleen Perks on October 24, 1936, showed little sign of his ultimate destiny for almost the first quarter of his life. As a child, he was thoughtful, steady, quiet, rather pious. His mother remembers how he would spend hours in his bedroom, in Blenheim Road, Penge, just reading the Bible. At Beckenham Grammar School he was proficient in art and mathematics and a useful athlete. With his precise mind and prodigious memory, he would have been natural university material if born just one decade later. Then, amid Britain's post-war and class-ridden chill, the best a bright working-class boy could hope for was respectable clerkship. His father, a bricklayer out of doors in all weathers, was delighted to think Bill might get a 'cushy office job'.

His first employment was with the City Tote, a firm of multiple bookmakers in London's West End. He was then called up for two years' service as a clerk in the Royal Air Force. Some of that time he spent in West Germany, at an RAF station near Bremen. His chief memories of service life are freezing cold, the ritual painting of unlit barrack stoves, and hearing Rock 'n' Roll music for the first time over the American Forces Network. He remembers, too, what a liking he developed for a fellow serviceman called Lee Wyman, not realizing it was the surname that really appealed to him.

He already thought of himself as Bill Wyman when, demobbed from the RAF, he took a job as storekeeper with an engineering firm in Streatham, South London. He organized the stores with fastidious efficiency, cataloguing the stock and recording its level by a neat system of dockets and coloured strings. In 1959, he married a girl named Diane whom he had met at a dance in Beckenham, and moved with her into a flat above a Penge garage.

His first guitar, bought during his RAF service, was a Spanish model, so badly made he could hardly hold down the strings. He played with scratch groups, in and out of the service, for the next year or two. 'I was never much of a guitarist. I was no good at playing chords. That's why I switched to bass as soon as they started coming in.'

In December 1962 he was already semi-professional, playing bass regularly in the Cliftons and, occasionally, in stage shows presented by the great pop impresario Larry Parnes. He had risen as high as backing Parnes's discovery Dickie Pride, a tiny youth then billed as 'Britain's Little Richard'. 'We had to wear stage make-up . . . little suits all the same. Horrible, they were. You always knew they'd been passed on to you from someone else.'

It was, therefore, with no great hope or expectation that Bill Wyman walked into the Wetherby Arms and beheld the group with whom Tony Chapman had arranged for him to audition. His first thought – tinged with working-class resentment – was that they looked off-puttingly 'bohemian' and 'arty'. They, on their side, felt no instant rapport with the hollow-cheeked, unsmiling newcomer, seven years older than Mick and Keith, and whose reserved manner suggested the superiority of a bass player who had once accompanied Dickie Pride.

What made him desirable was the sheer magnificence of his equipment. With his bass guitar, he hauled in *two* enormous black and gold amplifiers. Even the one he airily called his 'spare' was a Vox 850, bigger than Keith Richards had ever seen outside a shop window. Plugging in his bass, he indicated the 850 and said, 'One of you can put your guitar through that.'

'I wasn't sure – I thought I'd just try things out with them for a bit,' Bill says, 'even though I did think they looked too bohemian. Not long afterwards, they decided they wanted to get rid of Tony Chapman as drummer and bring in Charlie Watts. Tony came to me and said, "Well, that's it, Bill. We can form a new group of our own now." I said, "No – I think I'm all right where I am." I think I made a wise decision.'

Initially, it seemed far from wise. Bill Wyman's recruitment to 'the Rollin' Stones' coincided with heavy snowfalls, which, as they grew steadily worse, prevented them from getting to all but a scattered few of their suburban dates. At those they did manage to reach, attendance was disastrously reduced. Even their large Eel Pie Island following seemed reluctant to brave the toll bridge over the fast freezing Thames. Wyman, perched on his amplifier rim, a cigarette dangling from his mouth, regretted his folly in exchanging Larry Parnes's stage shows for arty types like this, who did not even stand up to play, but sat on chairs or stools in a semicircle behind their head-shaking vocalist.

The winter, it turned out, was Britain's worst for more than a hundred years. The entire country became submerged in a featureless white plain, swept by unremittingly savage cold which turned milk to creamy granite and made beer explode spontaneously in its bottles. From December to mid-February, the weather was Britain's sole talking point – apart from a brief scandal, reported from Carlisle just after Christmas, when a group called the Beatles was ejected from a Young Conservatives dance for the impossibly tasteless offence of arriving in black leather jackets.

At Edith Grove, the water pipes were now all frozen solid: Mick, Keith, Brian and Phelge could not wash or pull the lavatory chain. What puny room heaters they had barely took the edge off the biting cold. Bill Wyman, the settled married man, could hardly believe the squalor of the conditions. 'They weren't cooking – just living on pork pies and cups of instant coffee,' Bill says. 'I used to get through pounds, just feeding that electric meter of theirs.'

Their diet was mainly potatoes and eggs, which Brian and Keith would pilfer from Fulham Road grocery shops, and stale bread scavenged from the debris of parties given by other tenants in the house. Bill Wyman, when he dropped by, would bring food and cigarettes as well as shillings for their ravenous coin meter. Once a week, Ian Stewart would hand them a supply of six-shilling luncheon vouchers, bought up at a shilling each from weight-conscious secretaries in his office at ICI.

On many days, Keith remembers, it would not be worthwhile even getting out of bed. 'We hadn't got any gigs. Nothing to do. We'd spend hours at a time just making faces at each other. Brian was always the best at that. There was a particularly horrible one he could do by pulling his eyes down at the corners and sticking his fingers up his nostrils. He called it "doing a Nanker".' Even when every pipe in the flat was frozen, Brian somehow managed to wash his hair every day, and find a shilling somewhere to blow-dry it into its elaborate cresting wave. He seemed, for all his fastidiousness, the most adept of them all at living rough. Even Keith did not have Brian's sublime assurance, as each frozen midday dawned outside their filthy, iced-up windows, that the wherewithal of keeping warm and not starving could always be borrowed, begged or stolen.

An unexpected windfall was the reappearance of Dick Hattrell, fresh from Territorial Army camp, his £80 gratuity in his pocket, and willing as ever to do anything Brian told him. Within a week, Brian had annexed every penny of Hattrell's money for meals, drinks, even a brand-new guitar. On Brian's orders, Hattrell took off his army greatcoat and handed it to the shivering Keith. He would obediently follow them to their local hamburger bar, hand them more money and, at Brian's command, stand patiently in the snow until they came out again. When Dick Hattrell's money ran out, so did his welcome at the flat. One night as he lay in bed, Brian threatened to electrocute him with a guitar lead. Hattrell fled into the snow, terrified, wearing only his underpants. 'He wouldn't come back for an hour, he was so scared of Brian,' Keith says. 'When they finally did bring him in, he'd turned blue.'

The new year 1963 found Britain still snowbound, with villages, towns, even whole counties cut off, most transport paralysed, all sport fixtures cancelled, a whole nation gone to ground and huddled round the fitful blue warmth of its television screens. On

January 12, the Saturday night pop show *Thank Your Lucky Stars* provided its snowed-in bumper audience with the spectacle of that absurd new pop group the Beatles, looking even more outlandish in their mop-top haircuts and crew-necked suits, miming their new record Please Please Me, not with scowls and prissy dance steps like Cliff Richard's Shadows, but jigging about absurdly, grinning at the camera and each other. To viewers over twenty-one, the interlude seemed no more than faintly comic. But on a million British teenagers, pent up by so much more than cold, that zesty 'Whoa yeah' chorus had an altogether different effect. By February 16, Please Please Me was number one on the *Melody Maker*'s Top Twenty chart.

The Beatles were also beginning to make regular radio appearances on the BBC Light Programme's *Saturday Club*, giving 'live' performances from their stage repertoire in a far-off Liverpool cellar club called the Cavern. Much of their material was Rhythm and Blues which they had copied from 'import' discs brought from America to Liverpool by stewards on the transatlantic ships. Brian and Keith, listening to *Saturday Club*, huddled under their blankets at Edith Grove, were astonished to hear Chuck Berry and Bo Diddley songs on the stuffy BBC, albeit filtered through thick Scouse accents and almost audible grins.

Since *Saturday Club* had a reputation for booking groups which had not yet even made a record, Brian sent off one of his prosy letters to the BBC, requesting an audition for the Stones. A fortnight later, they received a summons to report to a BBC rehearsal room. Before they set off, Brian shampooed and blow-dried his hair into a 'Beatle cut' thicker and more eye-enveloping than the Beatles wore. 'It shocked even us a bit,' Keith says. 'He looked like a Saint Bernard with hair all over his eyes. We told him he'd have to be careful or he'd bump into things.'

The audition took place under the eye of the show's producer and of its compere, Brian Matthew, a plummy-voiced ex-announcer. Both men based their musical judgment on the hidebound prejudices of a corporation which, for years, had banned even the phrase 'Hot Jazz' as being sexually suggestive. 'We got a letter back from the producer in the end,' Bill Wyman says. 'He said they liked us as a group but they couldn't book us because "the singer sounds too coloured".'

Wyman still did not quite know why he stayed on in the Stones, especially now that his friend Tony Chapman had left. The country-wide thaw, and consequent improvement in suburban club dates, only emphasized their desperate need of a regular drummer even as semi-reliable as Chapman had been. Brian's idea was to bring in Carlo Little, a bravura – many said 'flash' – performer with Cyril Davis. But to Mick, Keith and Ian Stewart, there was only one possible candidate. 'One night, we all just looked at each other and that did it,' Stew says. 'We went up to Charlie Watts and said, "Right, that's it. You're in."'

The boy with the long, thin, dourly soulful face and the neat mod three-piece suit came from several social worlds away. Charlie Watts was a true Londoner, born at least within a rumour's distance of Bow Bells, and with that air peculiar to many Cockneys of being older than his years. His father worked for British Railways at King's Cross station as a parcel deliveryman. His mother had formerly been a factory worker. The family lived in Islington, North London, in a house which, however modest, was ruled by Charles Sr.'s punctilious tidiness. 'My dad made me cover all my books with brown paper,' Charlie says, ' – even my Buffalo Bill annual.' He cherished that annual, with its colour portrait of William F. Cody, looming ferociously from a Wild West that was – and remains – Charlie Watts's abiding passion.

Charlie, at 21, seemed set on a promising professional career. Since leaving Harrow Art College, he had worked as a lettering and layout man for the Regent Street advertisement agency Charles Hobson and Gray. It was a prestigious and – for that time – well-paid job which Charlie was reluctant to jeopardize, even for his beloved jazz. He had, indeed, recently given up playing with Blues Incorporated for fear that too many late nights would impair the daytime steadiness of his hand.

For the Stones, it was not simply that Charlie Watts owned a handsome set of drums and played them with an unobtrusive skill that held each ramshackle Blues song together like cement. He was also warmly liked by each of them. He seemed to get on best with the group's shyest and most uncertain member, Keith. Dapper as Charlie himself was, something in Keith's incorrigible raggedness stirred him to wistful admiration. He would sit for hours at Edith Grove, listening to Keith play guitar duets with Brian, listening to their accumulated wisdom concerning Chuck Berry B-sides and, every so often, putting another shilling in the electric meter.

The drawback, in Charlie's eyes, was that he loved jazz above everything, and saw no prospect, via these hard-up student types, of realising his ambition to visit New York and see Birdland where Charlie Parker used to play. At the time the Stones pounced on him, he was also considering the offer of a regular place in the far more respectable Blues by Six. 'He came to me, agonizing about it,' Alexis Korner said. 'I told him I thought the Rolling Stones were likely to get more work than the others, in the long run.' So at last, with that resigned shrug – that look of placidly expecting the worst – Charlie Watts was in.

On Sunday evenings in the sedate Thames-side borough of Richmond, crowds of teenage boys in corduroy jackets and peg-top trousers, accompanied by white-faced, bare-kneed, shivering girls, could be seen emerging from the railway station and streaming up a narrow passage-way by the side of a Victorian pub. At the end, under an improvised sign, CRAWDADDY CLUB, a black-bearded young man, somewhat like Captain Kidd in the comic books, stood guard on the door into the pub's mirror-lined 'committee room', chaffing his customers in an accent exotically and indeterminately foreign. 'Any girls who want to come in . . . ' Giorgio Gomelsky would say, 'we're so full, you'll have to sit on your boyfriends' shoulders.'

Giorgio was a 29-year-old Russian emigré, born in Georgia, exiled to Switzerland, educated in Italy and Germany, and now one of the best-known figures on the London jazz scene. He had worked for Chris Barber in the Fifties, helping to set up the National Jazz League and, later, organizing the first of the League's annual Jazz Festivals at Richmond Athletic Ground. He had discovered Blues while working as a courier, escorting American Blues singers on from London to Continental dates booked for them by Barber's organization. 'Sonny Boy Williamson lived in my house for six months. I travelled all over with him. We were in Liverpool when the Cavern was still only a Trad Jazz club.'

In the early Sixties, Giorgio combined the role of assistant film editor and West End jazz club manager, running the old Mississippi Room, with earnest attendance at classes to study

Stanislavsky's Method acting. Among his fellow students in the class was a young Irishman named Ronan O'Rahilly, whose family was rumoured to own the greater part of County Cork, and who was also trying to crash into the London entertainment scene by managing Alexis Korner's Blues Incorporated.

Gomelsky's first Blues Club was the Piccadilly, set up on a Russian shoestring in the old Cy Laurie folk cellar. 'The Rollin' Stones' played there just once, shortly before Harold Pendleton and Cyril Davies squeezed them out of the Marquee. Much as Gomelsky liked them as individuals, he thought their playing 'abominable'. Counting Mick Jagger's younger brother, Chris, only twenty or so people turned up that night to see them.

In early 1963, the Piccadilly Club had closed and Giorgio needed a new venue that could be hired with the single five pound note he had in his pocket. He knew the landlord of the Station Hotel in Kew Road, Richmond, and knew that the pub's substantial back room had not been in use since its regular Trad Jazz sessions had petered out. 'I said, "Let me try Blues here, just for one night . . ."' The club was called the Crawdaddy, after a Bo Diddley song, Do the Crawdaddy. Sessions took place on Sunday nights within the Station Hotel's licensing hours, 7 to 10:30 p.m. Its first resident attraction was the Dave Hunt Group, featuring Ray Davies – who would one day lead the Kinks – and playing in Louis Jordan's 1940s 'jump band' style.

Brian Jones had long been pestering Giorgio to do something to help the Rollin' Stones. 'He had that little speech impediment – kind of a lisp. It used to be part of his charm. "Come and lithen to us, Giorgio," he'd plead with me. "Oh, Giorgio, *pleathe* get us some gigs."'

Since their first disastrous tryout at the Piccadilly Club, Giorgio had seen the Stones again – at the Red Lion in Sutton – and had noticed a vast improvement. 'But what could I do? Dave Hunt's group already had the Richmond gig.

'It was the weather, really, that got them their chance. Dave Hunt's band couldn't make it, because of the snow – and anyway, I didn't go so much for that jump-band stuff Dave was playing. So, Monday, I rang Ian Stewart – it was so funny: to get the Stones you had to go through to ICI. I said, "Tell everyone in the band you guys are on next Sunday."'

That first Sunday night when the Rollin' Stones played the Crawdaddy instead of Dave Hunt's group, attendance was disastrously reduced. 'I even went through to the main pub to try to round some more customers up,' Giorgio says. 'Anyone who'd buy a ticket was allowed to bring in another person for nothing.'

Giorgio himself stood in the half-empty room, watching a group that, in the few weeks since their Red Lion date, had changed almost beyond recognition. The principal change was Brian Jones, with his new, heaped yellow Beatle cut, coaxing and caressing the Blues harp in his cupped hands to produce sounds like silvery minnows darting in and deftly out of Keith's guitar. Another change was the boy in the dapper three-piece suit, seated behind his drums with all the pleasure of a convict trying out an electric chair, yet playing with an impeccable, light-handed touch that pulled every loose thread together – and closed up every crack. Everything had come right behind the lead singer who was so far from right, but compulsively wrong, in the sweater that slipped off one shoulder like a teagown, his smear of a mouth parroting a black man's words as his opaque eyes searched for his reflection in the mirrors all round him. That snowy Sunday night, behind a Thames-side pub, where bottles clashed into basketwork skips and feathered darts thudded against targets, the Stones began to be brilliant.

Within three weeks, they had attracted a huge following, of whom R & B enthusiasts were only a minor part. Richmond, Twickenham and Surbiton on a Sunday night offered little enough excitement of any kind. The larger and larger crowds that converged on the Station Hotel and flooded down its side passageway contained samples of every teenage faction that had ever done battle on Brighton or Margate beach. There were Mods in high-button suits, newly dismounted from Lambretta scooters. There were black-leather Rockers, in studs and cowboy boots. Unified by the bond of the polo-neck, there were art students and shop assistants and well-brought-up 'young people' (as opposed to 'teenagers') from middle-class riverside homes at Putney, Hammersmith and Strand-on-the-Green. 'And do you know – there was never one fight in that place,' Gomelsky says. 'All that glass on the walls, and not even a mirror broken.'

At first, the Crawdaddy crowd behaved like jazz fans, merely standing and watching the Stones in the red-spotlit dusk. Then one night, Giorgio's young assistant, Hamish Grimes, jumped up on a table top and began to leap and flail his arms with the music like a dervish. From Hamish's impromptu outburst there evolved a dance peculiar to the Crawdaddy Club, partly derived from the Twist and the Hully-Gully but unique in that it could be performed by single males or even pairs of males, locked in a strange, crablike embrace, each gripping the other's elastic-sided ankles. The climax of each Stones session was a Bo Diddley song, either Do the Crawdaddy or Pretty Thing, when, at Giorgio's encouragement, the whole 300 would form a solid mass of corduroy, Op-Art stripes and red-spotlit shirt collars, jumping and gyrating together for as long as twenty minutes at a time.

Giorgio Gomelsky became the Rolling Stones' first manager, mainly through his own reluctance to be considered anything so bourgeois. 'It was always a *partnership*. I used to divide the door receipts from each Sunday equally with them. They would help me keep the club going. For instance, we never paid to advertise the Crawdaddy Club. The Stones and I would put illegal fly posters all over. I got them printed for four pounds a thousand, and the Stones mixed up the paste in the bath at Edith Grove.'

From the moment they began pulling in the crowds at Richmond, Giorgio had been urging his contacts in the London music press to come to Richmond and see the Stones perform. He also began shooting 35 mm film of them onstage at the Crawdaddy and arranged for them to make a soundtrack of two Bo Diddley songs at a small studio in Morden. It was typical of the idealistic Russian that, while working to launch the Stones, he never attempted to put them under exclusive contract to himself. His advice, on the contrary, was to let no one have control over them but themselves. 'I kept telling them, "Wait. Get strong, so that you can handle all of it yourselves and don't have to ask anyone for anything. Don't run the risk of someone walking in here and taking you over."'

Giorgio, in fairness, had a somewhat larger project on his mind. Two years previously while living in West Germany, he had visited Hamburg's sleazy St Pauli district and had seen the Beatles in their earliest incarnation as black-leather Rockers, pouring out bowdlerised R & B and their own primitive compositions to an audience of whores, transvestites and merchant seamen. Watching them now, in their crew-necked suits, bobbing and frolicking on the torrents of ever wilder hysteria, Giorgio Gomelsky realized they wer something more than merely the biggest pop attraction since Cliff Richard and the Shadows.

The tiny world of London impresarios soon brought Giorgio Gomelsky into contact with the Beatles' 27-year-old manager, Brian Epstein. 'I would be there when dance hall promoters rang up Epstein, offering him £50 for one appearance by the Beatles. He'd say, "I don't know . . ." and start looking in his diary. So then the promoter would offer him £60. "I don't know . . ." he'd still say. The promoter would offer £70, thinking Epstein was stalling for more money. He wasn't. He just couldn't find the right date in his diary.'

Giorgio approached Brian Epstein in his role as avant-garde movie director, proposing a film that would bring out the still unperceived wit and knockabout charm of the Beatles' offstage characters. He was now working on a rough script, helped by Ronan O'Rahilly, his fellow Method-acting student, and the jazz writer Peter Clayton. With the Beatles themselves he was on good enough terms to invite them to the Crawdaddy one Sunday after their appearance on *Thank Your Lucky Stars* at the ABC-TV studios in nearby Twickenham.

As the Stones played that night, they were astonished to see all four Beatles, in expensive leather overcoats, being escorted by Giorgio to a special vantage point beside the stage. Still more astonished were they, later, to be approached by people they looked on as big-time celebrities, and to be told in thick, pally Liverpool accents that their music was 'fab' and 'gear'. John Lennon, in particular, looked at Brian Jones with something like hero-worship. 'You really play that harmonica, don't you,' he said. 'I can't really play – I just blow and suck.'

A lengthy and amicable conversation ensued. For the Beatles, it had been a poignant experience to see a group so much like their former selves, before Brian Epstein cleaned up their music and appearance. The Stones, on their side, recognised blood brothers in the R & B cause who had only reluctantly dropped Chuck Berry in favour of original compositions the pop public increasingly demanded. It fascinated Mick Jagger, especially, to learn that John Lennon and Paul McCartney had already written more than a hundred songs together and that, after just one Top Ten hit, they had a share in their own music-publishing company. For a brief while, Mick cast aside his reserve and quizzed the Beatles closely about how much per song one could earn in royalties.

A week later, the Beatles appeared in their first major London concert, a 'Pop Prom' run by the BBC at the Royal Albert Hall. The Rollin' Stones received front-row tickets and access to the Liverpudlians' embattled dressing room. Later, Giorgio and Brian Jones helped the Beatles' two road managers, Mal and Neil, to load their stage equipment into their van. Some girls, spotting Brian's blond dome of hair, mistook him for a Beatle, crowded round him, despite his protests, and clamoured for autographs.

The incident, Giorgio remembers, had a transfixing effect on Brian. 'As we walked away from the Albert Hall, down the big steps at the back, he was almost in a daze. "That's what I want, Giorgio," he kept saying. "*That's* what I want."'

Knowing the Beatles was all very nice – but it did not help Giorgio in his efforts to interest powerful London people in a group whose venue, ten miles from the West End, might as well have been another hemisphere. For record company 'Artist and Repertoire' men, the only worthwhile journey, if not to Soho, was 200 miles north to Liverpool, in their frenzied search for new groups in the Beatles' image. It was a quest pursued with especial fervour by Decca, whose head of A & R, Dick Rowe, was celebrated as The Man Who Turned The Beatles Down. A letter from Giorgio Gomelsky about a new Blues group in Surrey did not even reach Dick Rowe's in-tray.

The Stones themselves knew only one person connected with the record industry. This was a school friend of Ian Stewart's named Glyn Johns, who worked at IBC Studios in Portland Place. Part-owned by the orchestra leader Eric Robinson, IBC had very little to do with pop music. But Glyn, a talented engineer, was allowed to record any artists he thought promising. At his invitation, the Rollin' Stones came to IBC and, in a single evening, recorded four songs from their stage act, including Chuck Berry's Come On.

The excitement of being in a real studio, supervised by a young engineer who was also a Crawdaddy fan, rather tailed off, since IBC carried little weight with the major record companies. A colleague of Glyn's knew someone at Decca – but on the clasical music side. It seemed just more effort wasted on a world whose ears were deaf to all but the Beatles' second Number One single, From Me to You.

On April 13, when the Stones' spirits were at their lowest ebb, Giorgio Gomelsky's hustling of newspapers, small as well as large, finally began to pay off. The weekly *Richmond and Twickenham Times* devoted a full page to the Blues club behind the Station Hotel and its effect in taking custom from Trad Jazz clubs in the area. 'The Rolling Stones' – the 'g' once more reinstated – received a somewhat incidental mention: 'Save for the spotlit forms of the group on the stage, the room is dark . . . A patch of light catches the sweating dancers and those who are slumped on the floor, where no chairs are provided . . . '

A few days later, Peter Jones of the *Record Mirror* succumbed to Giorgio's entreaties and agreed to give up his Sunday lunchtime to watch Giorgio's group being filmed onstage at their Richmond pub club. Jones was a prescient as well as a prolific journalist, the first to interview the Beatles in any national music paper. He watched the Stones perform on camera, and afterwards met them in the Station Hotel's saloon bar. 'They were hungry, and they were very bitter,' Peter Jones says. 'They told me no one had even been bothered before to drive ten miles out from London to see them. I promised to do my best to get a story about them into the *Record Mirror*.'

Jones was as good as his word. He persuaded the *Record Mirror*'s star reporter, Norman Jopling, to go out to Richmond with a photographer the following Sunday. Jopling – a Blues and Soul fanatic – was even more impressed than Peter Jones had been. 'The Stones had got the *real* R & B sound, not just a copy of it,' Jobling remembers. 'When they played a Bo Diddley number, it *sounded* like Bo Diddley. And the whole scene around them in that room was unbelievable.'

Norman Jopling's feature article in *Record Mirror*, the following Thursday, surpassed Giorgio's wildest hopes:

> As the Trad scene gradually subsides, promoters of all kinds of teen-beat entertainments heave a sigh of relief that they've found something to take its place. It's Rhythm and Blues, of course. And the number of R & B clubs that have suddenly sprung up is nothing short of fantastic.

> At the Station Hotel, Kew Road, the hip kids throw
> themselves about to the new 'jungle music' like they never did in
> the more restrained days of Trad.
>
> And the combo they writhe and twist to is called the Rolling
> Stones. Maybe you haven't heard of them – if you live far from
> London, the odds are you haven't.
>
> But by gad you will! The Stones are destined to be the biggest
> group in the R & B scene, if that scene continues to flourish . . .

It was, indeed, an astounding 'plug' for unknown musicians in a
paper read throughout the tight community of agents and A & R
men. As Norman Jopling recalls, the feedback was instantaneous.
'*Record Mirror* hit the streets at about 1 p.m. in the West End. By
four o'clock that afternoon, three different record companies had
phoned me, saying "Where can we get hold of these guys?" ' Jopling
supplied particulars, although fully aware – as Peter Jones was –
that the guys had by now been well and truly got hold of.

## 3

# 'I belong to you and you belong to me, so come on'

At the age of eleven, Andrew Loog Oldham was already incorrigibly addicted to glamour. While other boys read the *Eagle* comic or swapped matchbox labels, Andrew Loog Oldham walked the Soho streets, breathing in with delight the mingling scents of coffee beans, salami, striptease and primitive Rock 'n' Roll. Glamorous as these surroundings were, they paled next to the glamour he already perceived in himself. From an even earlier age, he had visualised his own life as an epic film of which he was both the star and the rapt audience. 'It was the only way I could get to school in the morning. As I walked in through the gates, I'd see the opening credits start to roll . . .'

The name which in later years seemed so typical a product of its owner's imagination was, in fact, genuine. Andrew Loog Oldham was the son of a Dutch-American air force officer, killed on a bombing mission over Germany in 1944. Born out of wedlock, the baby received both parents' names. His Dutch origins were always faintly manifest in a pink complexion, butter-coloured hair and eyes whose myopic pallor gave Oldham, even at his most uppity and outrageous, the look of a rather studious small boy.

A private boarding school to which his widowed mother sent him provided an early object lesson in the relation of fantasy to profit. The school – in Witney, Oxfordshire – was run by an ex-army officer, a dashing figure whose frequent absences were rumoured to be connected with vital work for the War Office. The head was, in fact, a prisoner on parole who moved around the country, setting up small schools, collecting fees, running up bills, then vanishing without trace. That headmaster was Andrew Loog Oldham's first lesson in the principle that, provided you had nerve and style enough, you could get away with almost anything.

In 1955, the pink-faced Hampstead schoolboy was a familiar

figure among the teenage crowd at Soho's famous 2 I's coffee bar. Norah, the doorkeeper, knew him well and would let him downstairs into the skiffle cellar without paying the usual one-shilling cover charge. His taste in pop heroes was eccentric even then – Wee Willie Harris, green-haired and wizened; Vince Taylor, an early American rocker, afterwards famous in France. 'It was always the sex in Rock 'n' Roll that attracted me . . . the sex that most people didn't realize was there. Like the Everly Brothers. Two guys with the same kind of face, the same kind of hair. They were meant to be singing together to some girl, but really they were singing to each other.'

From the age of thirteen or so, Andrew Loog Oldham saw himself as an amalgam of two movie roles, both portrayed by his screen idol, the suave if faintly reptilian Laurence Harvey. He wanted to be Harvey's version of Joe Lampton, ruthless working-class hero of *Room at the Top*. He wanted just as much to be the jive-talking young Jewish hustler whom Harvey played in *Expresso Bongo*, sashaying round Soho in Italian box jacket and rakish trilby hat, scouring the pasteboard streets for any quick way to a dividend.

He left Wellingborough College at sixteen with three GCE 'O' Levels – in English, Divinity, and, he claims, rifle shooting – and at once set about making his way in the world as Laurence Harvey had shown him. His first coup was to go to Chelsea, walk into Mary Quant's clothes boutique and ask for a job in any capacity whatever. Mary Quant and her husband, Alexander Plunkett-Green, were amused by the blond-haired youth and his barefaced effrontery. They agreed to take him on as an odd-job boy, teamaker and messenger.

He worked for Mary Quant throughout the period when her plungingly simple black and white dresses, short skirts, sailor necks and oversized bows altered the look of haute couture, and of London, forever. In February 1962, the first issue of a 'colour supplement' by the hitherto stuffy *Sunday Times* featured a Quant dress worn by a new young model, Jean Shrimpton, and photographed, not by the customary middle-aged Society acolyte but by a young man, David Bailey, who came from London's East End and – still more outrageously – made no attempt to conceal it. This first 'in crowd', as defined by the *Sunday Times*, did not, of course, include anyone named Andrew Loog Oldham; still, he was happy. 'I was where I wanted to be – around stars.'

At this stage, the only way of achieving stardom himself, as his mental scenario had dictated, was to become a pop singer. The fact that he could neither sing nor play an instrument seemed hardly relevant. Over a period of months, London agents and managers would be intermittently persecuted by the same blond, bespectacled, unmusical youth, posing under such aliases as 'Chancery Laine' and 'Sandy Beach'.

By working for Mary Quant all day, and by night as a waiter at Soho's Flamingo Club, he saved enough to migrate to the French Riviera. There, for several months, he worked in sea-front bars and as an itinerant window-dresser. There, too, in company with two freelance journalists, he concocted his first great money-making scheme. The plan was to kidnap a wealthy heiress. Andrew would keep her, drugged, in a flat in Monte Carlo while the journalists sold the story to the London *Daily Express*. It would give the story a piquant twist, they said, if Andrew were subsequently to marry the heiress. This he was quite willing to do. Unfortunately, the scheme foundered after the, not unwilling, girl had been taken to the Monte Carlo flat. Her father had friends in the British government, and got an official D-notice issued, prohibiting any newspaper from running the story. Andrew Loog Oldham thus failed to become nationally famous either as a kidnapper or as a cad.

Back in London, a job with the Leslie Frewin publishing house provided an entrée into the decidedly glamorous world of public relations. He left Frewin to join a PR company whose clients included the pop singer Mark Wynter. Handsome, blow-waved and insipid in the prevailing American style, Wynter was following what seemed an inexorable course from Top Twenty hit to low-budget 'exploitation' feature film. One of Oldham's jobs was to accompany him on location to Twickenham studios and share a bedroom with him at a nearby small hotel. 'Every morning, Mark used to get up very early and creep off to the bathroom to wash and shave and fix his hair. Then he'd come and get back into bed. A bit later, he'd sit up and say "Well, Andrew – time to set off for the studios." He was convinced I thought he always woke up looking like that. I thought that was great – that really *was* looking after your image.'

Two major pop impresarios, Larry Parnes and Don Arden, between them controlled all the singers and groups for whom Oldham hoped to work as publicist. Parnes ran a 'stable' of singers from offices in Cromwell Road, opposite Boy Scout headquarters. Don Arden, an authentically frightening figure, rivalled Larry Parnes in promoting pop package tours, cobbled from the hit-makers of the moment. Andrew Loog Oldham joined Arden for a while but was fired after inviting journalists to view cinema seats which, during a particularly well-appreciated package show, had been slashed with razors and drenched with female urine.

He was by this time a well-known figure around ABC-TV's studios in Aston Road, Birmingham, where *Thank Your Lucky Stars* was recorded. In February 1963, he stood and watched the Beatles give their first nationwide performance of Please Please Me. He later approached Brian Epstein, and offered himself as publicist for Epstein's company, NEMS Enterprises. Brian Epstein, it happened, was preparing to launch two other Liverpool acts, Gerry and the Pacemakers and Billy J. Kramer and the Dakotas. He agreed to hire Andrew Loog Oldham to promote the two groups on a monthly retainer of £25.

The arrangement was somewhat hampered by Tony Barrow, a London-based Liverpudlian already writing press releases about the Beatles and sleeve notes for their first LP record. Brian Epstein ordained that Barrow should concentrate on written handouts while Oldham – by now running his own PR company – dreamed up stunts to get paragraphs into the papers. The Beatles themselves, watched over with obsessive jealousy by Epstein, remained always tantalizingly out of reach. His NEMS work was for the advancement of Gerry Marsden and Billy J. Kramer, each awaiting Top Twenty success in cardboard shoes and cheap little 'shortie' overcoats.

His journeys north, though chilly and unglamorous, brought one further big advance. In Manchester, he met Tony Calder, a young agent handling local groups like the Hollies and Wayne Fontana and the Mindbenders. Manchester groups were by now starting to benefit from London's obsession with the Mersey Sound. Tony Calder also took on Oldham as publicist for his firm, Kennedy Street Enterprises. 'It felt just like tiddlywinks. I'd already got Liverpool sewn up, with Epstein and NEMS. Now I'd got Manchester as well.'

A chance PR assignment for the American record producer Phil Spector, early in 1962, altered Andrew Loog Oldham's conception of how he might seize his still unspecified destiny. Up to then, in pop music, celebrity had come only to performers – the singers first, then the star guitarists and, latterly, the groups. No fame, or even credit, was given to the A & R men who arranged and supervised even the biggest hit recordings. Phil Spector was the first A & R man to be as well known as the artists he recorded – to 'produce' each three-minute disc in his individual and unmistakable style of complex multitrack effects and cavernous echo: the Spector Wall of Sound.

Phil Spector became the epitome of all Andrew Loog Oldham wished to be. His persona was that of a semi-gangster, riding round in dark-windowed limousines protected by ugly bodyguards with bulges under their arms. While Spector was in London, Andrew Loog Oldham rode round with him, devoutly questioning him about the secret of his success. Instead of the hoped-for technical hints, Phil Spector imparted a piece of advice which Oldham at the time found rather disappointing. If Oldham ever found a group to record, Spector said, he should on no account let them use the record company's studio but should instead pay for an independent studio session and afterwards sell or lease back the tapes to the record company. That way, you had control and you had much more money.

In April 1963, the Beatles were Number One in every chart with From Me to You. Gerry and the Pacemakers were Number Two with How Do You Do It? Andrew Loog Oldham lost his retainer from NEMS Enterprises, and began looking around for something else to make up that monthly £25. Calling in at the *Record Mirror* office – a habitual haunt of his for picking up tips – he found Peter Jones enthusing over an unknown Blues group whose fortunes Norman Jopling was about to change with a eulogistic article. As Andrew Loog Oldham listened, the pop singer and the publicist faded; a brand-new incarnation of himself took shape on his mental Cinerama screen.

He drove to Richmond the very next Sunday. In the narrow passageway beside the Station Hotel, he met a boy and girl coming out into the warm spring dusk. Neither Mick Jagger nor his girlfriend Chrissie Shrimpton noticed Andrew Loog Oldham, for the simple reason that they were having a furious argument.

The Crawdaddy that night was anything but the wild spectacle

95

Norman Jopling had described. Giorgio Gomelsky had been called away to Switzerland by the death of his father. Without Giorgio to enliven it, the club was in a torpid mood. The Stones had even resumed their old purist habit of playing seated on a ring of bar stools. 'There was no production,' Oldham says. 'It was just a Blues roots thing . . . "Here I am and this is what I'm playing." Even so, I knew what I was looking at. It was Sex. And I was just ahead of the pack.'

His initial approach to them was to the group's apparent leader, Brian Jones. He remembers with what determination Brian's slight figure blocked him from making any similar overtures to either Mick or Keith. 'Brian really was a weird shape with that big head, broad body and little short legs. But he had incredible power. He could make you focus just on his head and neck.'

A short conversation elicited the fact that the Stones, for all their big cult following, still had only three regular bookings – at the Crawdaddy, Eel Pie Island and Ken Colyer's Studio 51 club. The plans Giorgio Gomelsky had made – the feature film and so forth – sounded much less substantial without Giorgio there in person to explain them. Hearing about Giorgio gave Andrew Loog Oldham another reason to act like lightning.

There and then, he offered himself to the Rolling Stones as manager. It was by all accounts the most brilliant selling job of his nineteen years, expertly mixing brazenness with intuition. He approached them as a London big shot but at the same time as an equal, contemptuous, like themselves, of the respectable world, the 'wankers' and 'erdies' and other synonyms for stuffy middle age. Even the cautious Bill Wyman could not help but be impressed. 'Andrew talked the same way we did, and wore the same clothes. He seemed to care about what we cared about – just the Blues and getting it better known in Britain.'

Oldham, for all his big talk, knew he was in no position, on his own, to manage any pop group. As a PR man, he could exist on the wing, using other people's desks and telephones. As a manager, he could not function unless connected to the right network of tour promoters, song pluggers and record A & R men. He decided there was no alternative. His secret would have to be shared.

His first choice was his late PR client, Brian Epstein. Oldham offered Epstein 50 per cent of the Rolling Stones in exchange for the office space and facilities needed to launch them. But Brian Epstein, busy with the Beatles and his other Mersey groups, declined the opportunity.

Oldham's next approach was to Eric Easton, an old-established London agent, handling such middle-of-the-road artists as Bert Weedon, Julie Grant and the pub pianist 'Mrs Mills'. A former electronic organist, bald-headed and quiet, he seemed the least likely patron for a shaggy R & B band. Nonetheless, he agreed to accompany Andrew Loog Oldham to Richmond the next weekend, even though it meant missing his favourite television programme, *Sunday Night at the London Palladium*.

Eric Easton saw the Stones, winced once or twice, but was astute enough to realize what a find Oldham had made. His one qualification was that Mick Jagger ought to be dropped in favour of a vocalist who could *really* sing. When Brian Jones was brought into the discussion, he seemed quite amenable to getting rid of Jagger. But Oldham – for reasons he himself did not quite understand – insisted that Jagger should stay.

When Giorgio Gomelsky returned from Switzerland early in May, he found that the Stones had signed an exclusive management agreement with Andrew Loog Oldham and Eric Easton. Brian Jones broke the news to Giorgio, mysteriously claiming that Oldham was a school-friend of his. Brian, in fact, had signed the agreement on behalf of all the Stones and had, additionally, done a private deal with Easton to receive £5 a week over and above what the others were paid in salary.

In 1962, the most unenvied figure in British pop music was Dick Rowe of Decca Records, The Man Who Turned the Beatles Down. It made no difference to remind himself – as Rowe constantly did – that his decision at the time had seemed entirely logical. Two auditions, in Liverpool, then London, had failed to detect any noticeable merit in a quartet of juvenile eccentrics singing Besame Mucho, Your Feet's Too Big and other items perversely unsuited to current teenage fashion. So, in January 1962, Dick Rowe passed on the Beatles, instead signing up a group with the altogether more desirable and commercial name of Brian Poole and the Tremeloes.

Ten months later, the calamity of Dick Rowe's decision confronted him each day of his working life. The Beatles had become the biggest thing in teenage entertainment since Elvis Presley. Dick Rowe had let them slip through his fingers and into the waiting clutches of Decca's deadly rival, EMI.

For twenty years, these two giant companies had controlled British popular music, producing 95 per cent of all discs on their agglomerated labels as well as manufacturing the wireless sets, record players – and even needles – required to bring their product to life. Of the two, Decca seemed more wholeheartedly devoted to entertainment. The blue Decca label, the white Decca factory at Wimbledon, were synonymous with the age of the wind-up gramophone. Decca introduced the first long-playing record into Britain when EMI was still mainly an electrical company, manufacturing TV sets, radiograms and weapons systems for the then War Office.

Decca was the creation – and, substantially, the property – of Sir Edward Lewis, a white-haired, gangling man who, even on days that paid high dividends, was seldom observed to smile. For Sir Edward, recorded music was a commodity little different from soap or safety pins, and only really in tune if it harmonised with a good showing on the Stock Exchange, Sir Edward Lewis's favourite place in the world. 'I only ever knew of one person who could make him laugh,' Dick Rowe says. 'That was Tommy Cooper. If Sir Edward ever left the office early, you could be sure Tommy Cooper was on television that night.'

Decca's pre-eminence as a record company ended in 1954 with the arrival of Sir Joseph Lockwood, a successful flour miller, to the EMI chairmanship. Lockwood instantly halted EMI's decline, ending the manufacture of radiograms and investing in new record-pressing plant just in time for the first pop music boom. Sir Edward, for his part, took Lockwood's success as a personal insult, and would speak of him only in the most feline terms. He took some comfort from the fact that Lockwood, unlike himself, owned no substantial part of his company's stock and was, therefore, 'just an employee'.

Now, thanks to Dick Rowe, Lockwood had carried off the greatest prize of all. Not only the Beatles but all other northern groups and their new money-spinning sound seemed to have been engorged by EMI. No one wanted Decca after the preposterous mistake of its hapless A & R chief. 'Things got so bad,' a former

Decca employee says, 'that if a boy with a guitar had just walked along Albert Embankment past our office, the whole A & R staff would have rushed out to sign him up.'

Rowe's only consolation was that no group, however big, could possibly appeal to British teenagers for longer than six months. He might have lost the Beatles, but he had a sporting chance of finding the *next* Beatles. It was to this objective that Rowe's entire A & R department was now frenziedly devoted. Like every other record company, Decca had sent teams of talent scouts up to Liverpool to scour the Merseyside clubs and ballrooms. The fact that the Beatles' home town was a seaport acted powerfully on the A & R men's overheated minds. The search for new Beatles was widened to other seaports, Cardiff, Bristol and Southampton.

Dick Rowe himself was still drawn back, with remorseful fascination, to Liverpool. He was there again in the first week of May 1963, hoping to find the next Beatles in a talent contest he had been asked to help judge at the city's Philharmonic Hall. To add to his discomfort, an original Beatle, George Harrison, sat with him on the judging panel. Rowe remarked to George with a brave show of lightheartedness that he was still kicking himself. Though John Lennon had been heard to say he hoped the Decca man kicked himself to death, George seemed to cherish no animosity. 'In fact,' Dick Rowe says, 'he told me I'd been right to turn the Beatles down because they'd done such a terrible audition.'

Halfway through the talent contest, the next Beatles still had not materialized. George Harrison remarked to Dick Rowe that there was a group down in London he should consider signing; a group called the Rolling Stones who played each Sunday night at the Station Hotel, Richmond . . . When George turned round, he found he was talking to himself. Dick Rowe's chair was empty.

He remembers that, as he drove through Richmond after his headlong journey down from Liverpool, the sun was low in the sky, red and warm like a portent of redemption. 'The sun was so bright that when I got into the club, I could hardly see anything at all. Just crowds of boys – I couldn't see any girls. Crowds of boys, rising and falling on the balls of their feet.' Unannounced – unnoticed in the Crawdaddy's Sunday-night crush – Dick Rowe stood and watched the five figures who were about to rescue his reputation.

Elated as he was, he forced himself to follow A & R protocol. 'I'd *never* speak directly to a group that interested me. It was *always* to their agent or manager. I couldn't find anything out in the club about who managed the Stones. Next morning, I was in my office at eight o'clock, ringing round all the main agencies. No one I spoke to seemed to have heard of the Rolling Stones. Eventually someone said, "Try Eric Easton." I knew Eric, of course. Once I'd spoken to him, the whole deal went through in a matter of days.'

Before the Stones could sign with Decca, one small difficulty had to be overcome. The tape of five songs they had recorded with Glyn Johns at IBC studios was still held by IBC, and could thus be termed a prior recording commitment. Eric Easton's advice was that the Stones themselves should approach IBC, saying they had now split up and wanted to buy the tape back as a souvenir. An unsuspecting IBC agreed to return the tape for what it had cost in studio-time: £109.

Within less than a week, Easton and Dick Rowe were concluding what Decca's A & R chief presumed would be a straightforward two-year recording contract. If anything, Rowe considered, it showed largesse on Decca's part. When Brian Epstein signed the Beatles with EMI, he had been forced, after many previous rejections, to accept a miserly rate of one old penny royalty per double-sided record, rising in yearly increments of one farthing. Rowe, therefore, felt it almost a point of honour to offer the Rolling Stones, however unknown and untried, the standard record royalty rate, five per cent of the retail price of each copy sold.

Thus far, Dick Rowe's dealings had been with his pleasant and obliging contemporary, Eric Easton. The familiar process, of doing deals quietly over the heads of inexperienced boys, was now rudely shattered by Easton's nineteen-year-old associate. Andrew Loog Oldham, even before he walked into Decca, had imagined the film cameras starting to roll on yet another version of himself. 'I'd decided I was going to be a nasty little upstart tycoon shit.' At his first meeting with Decca's managing director, Bill Townsley, Oldham sat down, uninvited, and coolly put his feet up on Townsley's desk.

Dick Rowe gazed just as expressively at the fair-haired youth who had peremptorily cut across his genial suggestions to Eric Easton about possible dates for the Stones to cut their first record at

Decca's West Hampstead studios, and which of Decca's staff producers might supervise them. Oldham replied that the Stones would not be using Decca studios and, while Rowe was still goggling, added that they did not need a producer. They already had one, named Andrew Loog Oldham.

Oldham had never forgotten the advice imparted to him in the mysterious depths of Phil Spector's limousine. That advice was, simply, that all material taped in the studios of a record company remained the company's copyright. By recording the Stones independently, then leasing the record 'masters' back to Decca for manufacture and distribution, Oldham would retain the copyright and, simultaneously, rob Decca of control over what was recorded. Such a deal had not been proposed in the whole history of British recorded music. It was a measure of Decca's desperation to launch the 'new Beatles' that Oldham's conditions were accepted.

The sunglasses through which Andrew Loog Oldham blandly surveyed his disgruntled new associates were a further ploy borrowed from Phil Spector. Through his mind's movie camera, he saw himself already as an English Spector – an entrepreneur as famous and glamorous as any performer in his care. So Andrew Loog Oldham, despite never before having set foot in a record studio, announced to Dick Rowe and Decca that the Rolling Stones' first single would be under his exclusive direction.

It was a simple matter, anyway, to hire a studio at Olympic Sound, just off Baker Street, at a fee of five pounds per hour. There, on May 10, 1963, Andrew Loog Oldham met the six Stones under the slightly bemused eye of the single engineer, Roger Savage, whose services were included in the price.

Oldham had instructed the Stones to choose what they considered the five best numbers in their repertoire. He himself would then decide which would be the A-side and which the B-side of the single. That decision proved more troublesome than he had expected. The Stones' best stage numbers were Roll Over Beethoven, Dust My Blues, Roadrunner – Rhythm and Blues standards, now so widely in use among other groups they could have little impact on the commercial record charts.

The final choice for the A-side was Come On, the Chuck Berry song they had already taped at IBC studios. As a number, its chief virtue was its obscurity. Few of Berry's British fans had heard the original version with its uncharacteristically ill-humoured lyric, its odd rumba beat and prissy boy-girl duet. The B-side – which did not have to be so commercial – was another song already taped at IBC, Willie Dixon's I Want To Be Loved.

For three hours or so, the Stones worked to polish a version of Come On, which, even at its best, would still betray for all time their sense of uneasy self-compromise. Chuck Berry's perverse rumba was stripped down to bare guitars and bass, played at the tempo of rapid feet pattering in and out of a wah-wah harmonica riff. Mick Jagger's vocal similarly purged the lyric of its exasperation at ramshackle cars and crossed telephone lines. Where Chuck Berry sang of 'some stupid jerk', Jagger felt it more judicious to say 'some stupid guy'. Even with a key change, allowing much of the song to be repeated, the finished track lasted barely a minute and three-quarters.

As 'producer', Andrew Loog Oldham confined himself to watching the studio clock, fretting that another hour had passed and another five pounds had been spent. The final take was finished at just before 6 p.m. Unwilling to spend five pounds more, Oldham said that one would do and began to walk out of the studio. 'What about mixing?' the engineer asked in bewilderment. Britain's putative Phil Spector had not realized that, after a song was taped, its separate vocal and instrumental tracks were then 'mixed' for internal balance. 'You mix it,' Oldham said airily. 'I'll drop in and pick it up in the morning.'

The result, even after mixing, was clearly far below even the very moderate standard of a 1963 pop single. Dick Rowe said so, and the Stones agreed. They were now as keen as Rowe that the single be recorded under experienced supervision in Decca's own studios. There, at last, both Come On and I Want To Be Loved reached a standard satisfactory to musicians and A & R man. The release date was fixed as June 7.

The Stones were now 'Decca recording artists', part of a galaxy of talent that included Little Richard, Tommy Steele, Duane Eddy and the works of Buddy Holly. For all that, while Eric Easton worked on their future career, present circumstances remained much as before. They continued playing the same few club dates for the same few pounds each – Giorgio's Crawdaddy, the Marquee, Ken Colyer's Studio 51. Even that former nest of folk purists was now so packed out each Sunday afternoon that girls could reach the lavatory only by letting themselves be lifted up and passed along over people's heads.

One Sunday at Studio 51, the crush was so fierce that a girl named Shirley Arnold fainted. She came to in the band's changing room, under the solicitous gaze of the Stones and their young manager. Shirley was a passionate Blues fan, then going out with a member of another R & B group, the Downliner Sect. She got talking to Oldham who, after very few minutes, offered her the job of organizing the Stones' embryonic fan club. 'I said I'd give it a go. There and then, Andrew handed me about 300 postal orders that girls had sent in as subscriptions and said, "Okay, get on with it."'

Decca, meanwhile, prepared to launch their new acquisition with all the fire and verve of a government office on a Friday afternoon. Decca's promotional strategy – in common with everything else – came directly from the chairman's office. Sir Edward Lewis did not 'believe' in publicity. In his experience, greater profits accrued from artists whose private lives remained obscure. So it had proved in the case of Ted Heath the bandleader, whose very death had gone largely unnoticed by his sizeable American public, thus allowing Decca to go on recording the Heath band as if he were still conducting them.

As Andrew Loog Oldham knew from his months as a publicist, there was only one sure way of pushing a debut single by an unknown group into the national Top Twenty charts. The group must appear on ABC-TV's hugely popular Saturday night pop show, *Thank Your Lucky Stars*.

It seemed a great stroke of luck that Brian Matthew, compere of *Thank Your Lucky Stars* – and of BBC Radio's equally influential *Saturday Club* programme – was also one of Eric Easton's clients. Unfortunately, Matthew had so far reacted adversely to the Stones, criticising Mick Jagger's vocal style and their general scruffiness. To get a booking on *Thank Your Lucky Stars*, the Stones must conform to the pattern for all pop groups that the Beatles had ordained. They must wear matching stage suits, and look neat and clean and amiable.

Whatever outrage the Stones felt at this proposal was subdued by their eagerness to get in front of the TV cameras. They allowed themselves to be presented to Brian Matthew and his producer,

103

Philip Jones, in uniform outfits whose Carnaby cuteness might better have suited a team of chorus boys. The jackets were 'bumfreezers' of houndstooth check, high-buttoning, with velvet half-collars. With the jackets went round-collar shirts, slim ties and Cuban-heeled Beatle boots. The ensemble had been financed – and chosen – by Eric Easton, and earned nods of approval from all but those compelled to button and tab themselves into it. The humiliation, though, was more than worthwhile. The Stones were booked to mime their single on *Thank Your Lucky Stars* on the day of its release, June 7.

The alterations did not stop there. Keith Richards, to his eternal mystification, was told to drop the 's' from his surname to give it a 'more pop sound', like Cliff Richard. And Ian Stewart, the Stones' piano-player, chauffeur and provider of luncheon vouchers, was dropped from the stage line-up. Six in one group was too many, Andrew Loog Oldham had decided. And Stew, with his short hair, beefy arms and pugnaciously sensible face, looked 'too normal' for what Oldham's mental movie camera was already starting to run.

'It wasn't done very nicely,' Stewart says. 'I just turned up one day to find the others had stage suits and there was no stage suit for me. None of them even mentioned it to me – apart from Brian. "You're still a full member of the group, Stew," he kept telling me. "You'll still get a sixth share, I promise you."'

The Stones, however, did not ditch Stew with the amnesiac finality with which the Beatles had ditched their first drummer, Pete Best. Oldham's request was that he stay on as their 'roadie', driver and packhorse and occasional backup pianist. Stew agreed, though his pride was badly hurt. 'I thought, "I can't go back to ICI after this. I might as well stay with them and see the world."'

*Thank Your Lucky Stars* on June 7, 1963, offered Britain's teenagers the customary spectacle of records mimed by their artists, not always accurately, dwarfed by elaborate stage sets and half-drowned by pre-recorded female screams. Top of the bill was Helen Shapiro, a sixteen-year-old got up to look 40, in bouffant hair and flouncy petticoats. The Viscounts, and English close-harmony trio, sang their cover version of the American novelty hit Who Put the Bomp? Two disc jockeys, Pete Murray and Jimmy Henney, delivered judgment on new singles with all the fatuous disinterest of men in their late 30s, aided by a local girl named Janice Nicholls, whose invariable adjudication, 'I'll give it five' – or, in Birmingham dialect, 'Oi'll give eet foive' – had become a national catch-phrase. Brian Matthew introduced each act wearing a V-necked sweater and speaking in what determined efforts to talk down to 'the kids' could not disguise as anything but the voice of a BBC newsreader.

The Stones were bottom of the bill and, as such, merited only a simple, two-sided set, decorated with cut-out playing-card shapes. Mick stood on a low plinth, just to the rear of Brian and Bill. Keith, seated on a stool, and Charlie at his drums were seen in profile. Their 'spot' in all lasted barely a minute and a half. As the cameras moved up and back, and pre-recorded screams raged around them, the hounds-tooth-checked, velvet-collared Rolling Stones tried as hard as they could, or ever would again, to be a conventional pop group.

A minute and a half proved enough for many viewers, when the recorded show was broadcast the following weekend. Afterwards, ABC-TV's Birmingham switchboard was jammed with calls protesting that such a 'scruffy' group had appeared on *Lucky Stars*, and hoping they would not be invited back.

First reviews of Come On in the trade press new release columns were no more than lukewarm. *Record Mirror*, the most enthusiastic, commended 'a bluesy, commercial group which could make the charts in a small way'. For the pop-oriented *Disc* and *New Musical Express*, Come On fell between two stools, being neither 'Mersey Sound' nor imported American ballad. What little radio play the single received made it sound thin and anaemic. A month after its release, the *New Musical Express* chart showed it at Number 26, only one place higher than the Beatles' From Me to You, issued almost three months earlier.

The only significant piece of publicity, apart from *Thank Your Lucky Stars*, came about thanks to Giorgio Gomelsky's good nature. Giorgio bore the Stones no ill will for his peremptory squeezing out, and had gone on plugging them enthusiastically to his friends in Fleet Street. Patrick Doncaster, the *Daily Mirror*'s rather elderly pop columnist, was at length persuaded to come to Richmond and write about the Crawdaddy Club, the Stones and a new young group, the Yardbirds, whom Giorgio now promoted.

Doncaster's full-page *Mirror* piece on June 13 set the scene only too well. The Ind Coope brewery – which had not previously been aware of the frolics conducted on its property – summarily evicted Giorgio Gomelsky from the Station Hotel's back room. Thereafter, the Crawdaddy Club convened in the open air at Richmond Athletic Ground. The Stones, the Yardbirds, Cyril Davies and Long John Baldry played on a rugby pitch in front of the main grandstand, to promenading audiences of up to a thousand.

Eric Easton, meanwhile, laboured to set the Stones on the path ordained for an aspiring 'beat' group – the dreary round-Britain path of the pop package show. It was no mean achievement, after the poor chart performance of Come On, for Easton to book them into a nationwide tour beginning on September 29, headed by America's famous Everly Brothers and featuring the Stones' own R & B hero, Bo Diddley.

The prospect was one alluring enough to make up Mick Jagger's mind, at last, about the direction he wanted his life to take. Even after the Stones had signed with Decca, he had continued to hover between music and the London School of Economics, keeping all options open to a point where the other Stones became irritated hardly less than Joe and Eva Jagger, and even threatened to drop him as vocalist if he were not available to go on tour. So Mick Jagger went to the LSE registrar and announced he would not be completing his economics course. To his surprise, and relief, no obstacle was put in his way. 'The registrar said I could go back later if I wanted. It was all surprisingly easy.'

On August 12, the Stones made their last appearance on their Richmond home turf, playing at the *Evening News*-sponsored National Jazz and Blues Festival with Acker Bilk, Cyril Davies and Long John Baldry. It was to be almost their only London booking prior to leaving on tour with the Everly Brothers. The next step in Eric Easton's strategy was to launch them into a practically non-stop schedule of 'one-nighters' at ballrooms in remote East Anglian towns like Wisbech, Soham, Whittlesey and King's Lynn.

For most of Britain throughout that unseasonably wet summer, interest had centred on the developing scandal of John Profumo, a Conservative cabinet minister, Christine Keeler, his twenty-two-year-old mistress, and the subsequent lurid press exposures which had revealed Britain's High Tory establishment to be sexually

106

linked with an underworld of call girls, Mayfair pimps, property racketeers and even – it was suggested – Russian spies. For once, Britain suspended disapproval of its renegade young to contemplate the possibility that senior government ministers indulged in public fellatio; that 'up to eight' High Court judges had been involved in a single sex orgy; that at a fashionable London dinner party, another eminent politician had waited at table naked and masked and wearing a placard which read 'If my services don't please you, whip me.'

By contrast with Profumo, Christine Keeler, Stephen Ward and Mandy Rice-Davies, the preoccupations of teenagers seemed positively wholesome. The exact nature of that preoccupation was earnestly sought by London's commercial TV Company, Associated-Rediffusion, in planning a new weekend pop-music show to pre-empt *Thank Your Lucky Stars*. The A-R show was to be called *Ready, Steady, Go* and be introduced – unprecedentedly – by people the same age as its audience. The producer, Elkan Allan, auditioned each applicant for the job by asking one question: 'What do you think young people in this country care about most?' A girl named Cathy McGowan was hired for answering, simply, 'Clothes.'

It was the clothes of its audience – not confined to seats as before in such shows, but thronging a large, high-ceilinged, multi-level studio – which established *Ready, Steady, Go* as the epitome of a new pop style, a fashion changing almost as quickly as did the Top Ten sounds. Hipster trousers, flared jeans, leather jackets, Op-Art dresses, the girls' Quant crops, the boys' Beatle cuts, seethed all around Cathy McGowan and the deliberately exposed TV hardware. The atmosphere was that of a King's Road party where the performers themselves had just chanced to drop by. It was an atmosphere powerfully established by the show's Friday-night slogan 'The weekend starts here'; a feeling projected to millions that all belonged to the same quintessentially fashionable club whose only qualification was that you must be under 21.

The Stones, to their great chagrin, spent those same Friday nights packed into Ian Stewart's van, heading out through the East End to Hertfordshire, Bedfordshire or the Cambridgeshire Fens. It irked them particularly to think that the Beatles, mere northerners, were kings of the new London while they themselves

107

suffered this provincial banishment. In Stew's van, Bill Wyman always insisted on the front passenger seat as safeguard against the travel sickness from which he claimed to have suffered since childhood. Not for years did the others realise that was Bill's way of securing the van's most comfortable seat.

The town halls and ballrooms of Whittlesey, Soham and Wisbech were about as far as one could travel from *Ready, Steady, Go:* big, draughty vaults of municipal brickwork, filled with boys in Fifties cowlicks and girls in 'twinsets' and ballooned petticoats. The Stones' R & B repertoire was greeted with puzzlement, if not downright hostility. Better things happened when they tried American songs in the pop-soul idiom – Lieber and Stoller's Poison Ivy; Arthur Alexander's You Better Move On. Even after Come On became a minor hit, the Stones were so ashamed of their performance on record, they refused to do the song on stage.

Somewhere between Whittlesey, Cambridgeshire, and the Everly Brothers tour, Eric Easton's houndstooth-check jackets were cast off for good. It was a discreet rebellion, led – surprisingly – by Charlie Watts, the first to leave his stage suit 'accidentally' in some Fenland dressing room. Keith Richard made his unwearable by multilayered whisky and chocolate stains. The group photograph taken for the tour poster shows them restored to their corduroys and polo-necks, standing on a jetty beside the Thames, not far from Edith Grove. A short pretour feature in *New Musical Express* began: 'They are the group who prefer casual wear to stage suits and who sometimes don't bother to change before going onstage . . .'

The tour that opened at the London New Victoria Cinema on September 29 was an odd mélange assembled by its promoter – the frightening Don Arden – to attract all possible levels of the pop listening public. The Everly Brothers were fading legends of the Rock 'n' Roll Fifties. Bo Diddley was a cult R & B star. The Flintstones were a heavy saxophone 'combo'. Julie Grant – another Eric Easton client – was a middle-of-the-road ballad singer. When, after barely a week, the mixture proved insufficiently powerful at the box office, Don Arden hastily flew in a second Rock 'n' Roll legend, Little Richard, to co-star with the Everlys.

For the Stones – given small-type billing equal to Julie Grant –

what mattered most was the honour of appearing on the same programme as their idol, Bo Diddley. To show their respect, they dropped all Bo Diddley material from their tour act. Diddley was flattered by the homage of his five shaggy acolytes and was sufficiently impressed by Bill's and Charlie's playing to ask both to appear with him as session men on BBC Radio's *Saturday Club*.

From its opening London date, the tour headed out into the dim, dark hemisphere beyond Watford which, in pre-motorway Britain, was referred to with vague forboding as 'the North'. 'A few miles out, and it was all new to me', Keith says. 'Up to then, I'd never been further north than North London.'

Derby, Nottingham, Sheffield, Birmingham, Manchester, Bradford, Newcastle and twenty other cities – ancient and important and even beautiful cities, as yet undespoiled by planners – all clotted indistinguishably into the Stones' first experience of 'the road'. Shows, twice nightly, in some huge old Art Deco circuit cinema, a Gaumont, a Regal or Odeon. Dark alleys, scratched stage doors and freezing backstairs passages. Dressing-rooms littered with beer bottles and old fish and chip wrappings. Hooks for coats, squalid lavatories, naked light bulbs. A peep through dusty plush curtains into the buzzing, twilit auditorium. Managers and under-managers, short-haired and nylon-shirted, hovering in anxious hostility. Sound systems as a rule no more elaborate than the same two extending mikes used in last Christmas's pantomine. The curtains parting, on shrieks as from damned souls, and dark plush darkness bejewelled with green Exit signs, smudged here and there by the white crossbelts of the St John Ambulance Brigade.

Cinema managers, fearful of riots and torn seats, had looked sufficiently askance at pop groups who invaded their backstage region in mock sharkskin suits and ruffle-fronted evening shirts. 'When we used to walk in,' Bill Wyman says, 'some manager guy would look at us and say, "Go on, get down to your dressing room. You've only got ten minutes to get changed for the show." We'd say, "We're ready to go onstage *now*. We're ten minutes *early*."'

The initiation was also into cities still walled in Victorian darkness, where the only restaurants open late were Indian or Chinese; where hotels smelled of cabbage and beer slops, heat in the rooms was available only by coin meter, and bedclothes passed on a rich legacy of fleas, ticks and scabies. For most of the tour – thanks to another private deal he had done as 'leader' of the Stones – Brian managed to stay in slightly more expensive hotels than the others.

On Sunday, October 13, at the Odeon Cinema, Liverpool, Little Richard, the Everly Brothers, Bo Diddley, Julie Grant and the Rolling Stones performed to a barely half-filled house. The same night, the Beatles topped the bill of ATV's variety show *Sunday Night at the London Palladium* after a day in which their fans had kept the Palladium virtually under siege. An audience of fifteen million watched the four little figures in halter-neck suits, with wide grins and bouncing-clean hair, who in that moment ceased to be a teenage fad and became a national treasure.

It was with some nervousness, later on, that the Stones played the Cavern Club in Mathew Street, the Beatles' now celebrated Liverpool home. They need not have worried. The Cavern crowd, urged on by Bob Wooler, the resident disc jockey, gave the visitors a tumultuous welcome. Later, they sampled the pleasures of an all-night city, first at Allan Williams's Blue Angel club, then with some local girls who concluded the entertainment by inviting them home to breakfast.

On October 16, it was announced that the Beatles would take part in the 1963 Royal Command Variety Show in the presence of the Queen Mother, Princess Margaret and Lord Snowdon. Fleet Street had found the ideal antidote to Profumo, Keeler, that whole summer of upper-class sordidness. With the encouragement of the press, Britain gulped down the Beatles like a reviving tonic. Even those who found their music loud and their hair ludicrous could not help but be charmed by their freshness and cheekiness, the sharp-witted yet amiable back-answers – uttered mainly by John Lennon – which seemed to reassert the essential honesty and integrity of the working man.

The Rolling Stones, like everyone else on the Everly Brothers package tour, grew even more conscious that the centre of the world was far from the Gaumont Cinema, Bradford. Nor did a visit from their nineteen-year-old co-manager greatly bolster up their self-esteem. Andrew Loog Oldham, having breezed in, made perfunctory inquiries and looked aghast at the encircling grimness, wished them good luck and disappeared again.

Oldham went straight to Liverpool, and the more promising company of John Lennon and Paul McCartney, both simultaneously visiting what was still their home base. The three afterwards drove back down to London. 'It was a very weird journey,' Oldham remembers. 'I don't know if we were drunk or stoned, or both. John and Paul started talking about getting themselves disfigured so that the fans could never recognize them and chase them anymore. They were talking about all the different ways their faces might be mutilated. "We could get caught in a fire," Paul said. "We could have special rubber masks made, like skin . . ."'

Oldham's main worry on the Stones' behalf was finding them something to record as a follow-up to Come On. He had ransacked the entire catalogue of the American Chess and Checker R & B labels for something which was neither too well known in its original version or covered already by the proliferation of new British Blues groups. It was an unsuccessful search which made Andrew Loog Oldham wish even more fervently, as he sat in John and Paul's black-windowed limousine, that the Rolling Stones could knock off their own hit songs with the same nonchalant ease as the Beatles.

The final choice, agreed with Decca's Dick Rowe, was a cover version of the Coasters' semi-comical Poison Ivy and, for the B-side, Benny Spellman's Fortune Teller. At Rowe's suggestion, the session was entrusted to one of Decca's younger staff producers, Michael Barclay. 'It was a disaster,' Dick Rowe says. 'The Stones thought Mike was a fuddy-duddy; he thought they were mad.' The result was a version of Poison Ivy which Decca and the Stones hated in almost equal measure. The single appeared on Decca's schedule of new releases but was then cancelled.

A further long discussion-cum-rehearsal at the Studio 51 club in Great Newport Street produced nothing else that Andrew Loog Oldham considered remotely promising. Exasperated, he left the Stones to their tinkering and arguing and started mooching round the Soho streets like Laurence Harvey in *Expresso Bongo*, hoping – as that inspirational film idol had hoped – that something or other might turn up.

111

Miraculously enough, something did. A London taxi stopped next to Oldham, and out jumped John Lennon and Paul McCartney. The Beatles, that day, had been at the Dorchester Hotel, receiving awards from the Variety Club of Great Britain. John and Paul were now on the loose together, looking for more excitement.

'The dialogue,' Oldham says, 'really did go like this. "'Ello, Andy. You're looking unhappy. What's the matter?" "Oh, I'm fed up. The Stones can't find a song to record." "Oh – *we've* got a song we've almost written. The Stones can record that if yer like."'

The song was I Wanna Be Your Man, one of a clutch of new Lennon-McCartney numbers written for the Beatles' forthcoming second LP. Susceptible to fashion as ever, and natural mimics, they had produced their own two-minute blast of Rhythm and Blues. As it was still not quite finished, John and Paul went back with Oldham to Studio 51 and put the final touches to it while the Stones waited.

This casual gift from pop music's hottest songwriting team provided the lethargic Stones with a rush of adrenaline. It required only an hour or two at Kingsway Sound Studios, Holborn, to produce their own Chicago Blues interpretation of I Wanna Be Your Man, replacing winsome Beatles' harmonics with the belligerent simplicity of Mick Jagger's voice and Brian Jones's slide guitar. For a B-side, it was enough to tape a twelve-bar blues instrumental, hastily ad-libbed, as was its title: Stoned. Plagiarism as it was (of Booker T's Green Onions), this counted as an 'original' composition. Andrew Loog Oldham set up a publishing company to handle such collective efforts, its proceeds to be divided between the five Stones and himself. The company was called Nanker Phelge Music, combining Brian Jones's word for a grotesque facial contortion with the name of their Edith Grove flatmate, Jimmy Phelge, the youth who at unexpected moments used to wear his underpants on his head.

I Wanna Be Your Man was released on November 1. The Stones were still on tour with the Everly Brothers and Little Richard, playing two shows at the Odeon Cinema, Rochester. Two nights later, the tour wound itself up at length at the Odeon, Hammersmith. Here at last the Stones were on home territory.

The show's compere, Bob Bain, had to plead with the audience to stop shouting, 'We want the Stones' and instead shout, 'We want the Everlys.'

To the rest of Britain, however, even big-name groups like the Searchers and the Shadows hardly impinged on an obsession born in the trickery of Fleet Street but now rampant beyond any newspaper's manipulation. On November 4, the Beatles captivated the Royal Command Variety Show by suggesting that a blue-blooded audience containing both the Queen Mother and Princess Margaret should either clap or 'rattle yer jewellery'. On November 22, their second LP, *With the Beatles*, launched them, looking like soulful art students, into the upper as well as lower social sphere, selling enough copies on advance orders to push the whole album into the Top Twenty *singles* chart. In early December, the *New Musical Express* chart showed yet another Lennon-McCartney song, I Wanna Be Your Man by the Rolling Stones, at number thirteen. For influential critics like Brian Matthew, more interest lay in the song's composers than in the group which had been lucky enough to record it. 'Do you realize,' Brian Matthew repeatedly asked his BBC radio audience, 'how many songs in the current Top Ten are written by, if not sung by, the Beatles?'

# 4

# 'Beatle your Rolling Stone hair'

We owe this intimate backstage visit to one of Britain's last surviving newsreels, in happier days devoted exclusively to sport and Royalty but now, in 1964, bravely attempting to fathom an uproar more raucous, to its elderly editors, than the cry of their own screen emblem, the Pathé cockerel.

We follow as the camera tracks uncertainly down a dark passageway, round a corner and through a suddenly opened door into the Stones' dressing room. It is, however clumsy, an attempt at *cinéma vérité* – a pop group on tour, caught between performances. The camera settles first on Keith Richard, leaning forward, a cigarette clamped between his lips, to fasten a shirt collar as high as a Regency beau's hunting stock. Beyond Keith, Brian Jones, in black coat and snow-white jeans, holds up his lozenge-shaped guitar, the better to show the complex chord he is shaping. His hair is now peroxide blond, an aureole of metallic gold covering his eyes, almost encircling his face. The camera moves to Mick Jagger, in a matelot-striped jersey, then it moves on somewhat hastily. His face wears an expression not wholly welcoming; besides, he isn't holding a guitar.

The stage sequence filmed by Pathé shows how undeveloped Mick Jagger still was as a performer or personality. The song is the Stones' old club standby, Chuck Berry's Round and Around. Jagger sings it, hunched around the old-fashioned stand-mike, his face turned diffidently into one matelot-striped shoulder. His lips open just enough to moisten themselves. His eyes seem cloudily preoccupied. At intervals, he claps his hands automatically above his head. Beside him, Keith Richard jigs around, wearing a happy, rather dizzy grin. Far on the other side, with heaped gold hair shutting out his eyes, Brian Jones stands, motionlessly provocative. The camera cuts away to girls with Beatle fringes, alternately screaming and stuffing handkerchiefs into their mouths. Now we see the full stage, empty but for the Stones, their vestigial equipment and a red-curtained backdrop. Jagger leaves the microphone and – the only word is – waddles like a duck shaking water from its tail.

On January 6, they were out on tour again, in the George Cooper Organization's 'Group Scene 1964' show. By now they were big enough to merit equal top billing with the Ronettes, an American girl group, highly successful on Phil Spector's Philles record label. Spector had already sent his acolyte Andrew Loog Oldham a telegram, sternly warning 'Leave my girls alone.' As both individual Stones and Ronettes have since corroborated, that warning was to no avail.

The combination of svelte, sinuous black girls and snarling, scruffy white boys attracted much interest in a music press jaded equally by Christmas indulgence and Beatle overkill. In *New Musical Express*, under a heading 'Girls Scream At Stones, Boys At Ronettes,' Andy Gray praised the show's 'vocal volume and body action'. Gray's review – which set the seal of box-office success on the tour – is revealing as a sample both of 1964 Rock prose and also the pitifully short performances given by even top-of-the-bill attractions:

> Two packed houses greeted with cheers, screams and scarf-waving the local lads who have made good – the Rolling Stones. Fever-pitch excitement met compere Al Paige's announcement of them, and they tore into their act with Girls, followed by Come On. This group certainly is different – members wear what they like, from shirts to leather jackets, but they have long hair in common.
>
> Lead singer Mick Jagger whips out a harmonica occasionally and brews up more excitement while the three guitars and drums throb away in back. Hey Mona was another R & B compeller before a quiet number, very appealingly sung by Brian Jones [sic], You Better Move on. Back to the torrid stuff for the last two numbers, Roll Over, Beethoven and I Wanna Be Your Man, taking the act to encore applause . . .

Decca's release of an EP – extended play – record on January 17 redoubled the nightly pandemonium. The EP, with its handful

115

of tracks and cheap picture cover, was a well-tried device for getting additional mileage from a pop act whose success did not yet warrant a full twelve- or thirteen-track LP. The Stones' first EP was in this catchpenny tradition, offering their cancelled A-side Poison Ivy, together with slipshod versions of Chuck Berry's Bye Bye Johnny and Berry Gordy's much imitated Money. The exception was an Arthur Alexander song, You Better Move On, sung by Mick Jagger with care and almost without affectation. You Better Move On proved popular enough to take the entire EP into the Top Ten singles chart barely a week after its release.

The Stones' third single, it was already decided, would be a cover version of the Buddy Holly song Not Fade Away – which Mick Jagger had first heard with Dick Taylor at Woolwich Granada back in 1957 – but drastically rearranged by crossbreeding with an equally important stylistic source. On to the mild, reflective Holly song, Keith Richard had grafted guitar chords played in the shuffling, stop-start 'Bo Diddley' beat. 'To me,' Andrew Loog Oldham says, 'when Keith sat in the corner and came up with those chords, *that* was really the first song the Stones ever wrote.' The result was played at twice the speed of the Holly original, flashed across, each second verse, by a whinny from Brian Jones's harmonica.

The taping of Not Fade Away, at Regent Sound, towards the end of January 1964, was an occasion that would have horrified conventional A & R men like Dick Rowe. Oldham and the Stones had hit on the ideal way of escaping interference from Rowe or anyone else from Decca. They recorded by night, not even starting until long after all A & R men were safely back in their suburban mock-Georgian villas, tucked up between their fitted nylon sheets.

Not Fade Away could thus be taped as the culmination of a drunken studio party at which the Stones and Oldham were joined by Phil Spector and two members of the Hollies, Alan Clarke and Graham Nash. Later on, the American singer Gene Pitney also dropped in, bringing with him an outsize bottle of brandy. The final Not Fade Away take featured the two Hollies, appropriately, on back-up vocals and Phil Spector shaking the maracas of which the rhythm track is mainly composed. Spector also cobbled up a B-side song called Little By Little, a pastiche of

Jimmy Reed's Shame, Shame, Shame, dashing it off in minutes, with Mick Jagger's help, in the corridor. Little By Little was recorded as a simple jam session of guitar, harmonica, piano – played by Gene Pitney – and a Jagger vocal, like the maracas, audibly plastered. At frequent intervals, the session disintegrated into tomfoolery, with Jagger rudely mimicking Sir Edward Lewis, the Decca chairman, and Phil Spector ad-libbing an obscene recitative under the title Andrew's Blues.

On February 4, at New York's Kennedy Airport, the Beatles emerged from their BOAC aircraft to behold a 5,000-strong crowd, keening and howling in the grip of that European virus which the *New York Post* had predicted would definitely *not* spread to America. Their appearance, four nights later, on NBC-TV's *Ed Sullivan Show* – for a knockdown fee of $3,500 – was watched by an estimated 70 million, or 60 per cent of the American TV audience. It was a moment destined to remain stamped on a whole nation's memory, when Ed Sullivan waved a patronising arm and the four little figures appeard, in their neat, skimpy suits and polished fringes, and all America's xenophobic wariness dissolved into charmed fascination.

The Beatles' conquest of America took them out of the orbit of mere pop. In one two-week visit, all unconsciously, they changed the entire basis of Anglo-American relations. No longer was Britain, to American eyes, a picturesque backwater, producing Scotch whisky, Shakespeare and entertainers laughably inferior. Britain, through the Beatles, became the apotheosis of New York fashion. In Britain, those who had once damned and denounced them now commended them as an invaluable addition to the export drive. Their name took on almost a talismanic quality, securing newspaper headlines impartially for anyone who invoked it. Members of Parliament, peers of the realm, archbishops, even Royalty itself, now talked and talked about the Beatles.

To their teenage audience this was, of course, the most gratifying turnabout from last year's parental ridicule. Just the same, to find one's idols shared by one's mother, and even one's grandmother, made pop seem suddenly rather tame.

No one's mother or grandmother liked the single, released on February 27 and now climbing up the Top Twenty, spurred on by alternate kicks of delight and hostility. The Stones' late-night carousings with the Hollies and Phil Spector had produced a noise which sold itself, both as instant hit material and instant anti-heroism, from its first chaotic, maraca-shaking chord. Phil Spector's presence is widely supposed to have brought about the Stones' vastly improved cohesion in Not Fade Away – guitars sharper, harmonica more savage, the general onslaught resembling a miniature wall of sound.

The national press, its nicotine-yellow finger now firmly attached to the British teenage pulse, was quick to spot the new fad – or, in other words, to take up Andrew Loog Oldham's suggested story angle. 'They look,' said the *Daily Express*, 'like boys whom any self-respecting mum would lock in the bathroom. But the Rolling Stones – five tough young London-based music-makers with doorstep mouths, pallid cheeks and unkempt hair – are not worried what mums think . . . For now that the Beatles have registered with all age groups, the Rolling Stones have taken over as the voice of the teens.'

Last year's Beatle crowds, it was becoming clear, had behaved moderately in comparison with those who followed the new 'voice of the teens'. The Stones' third tour, early in February, played each night to an uproar, not merely of screaming girls corralled in cinema seats, but also of spontaneous battles between Mods and their sartorial foes, the Rockers. Other groups to whom this happened would hug their precious guitars to them and hurry from the stage. But the Rolling Stones played on. Brian Jones in particular loved to see 'bother' starting and to encourage it subtly by brief, goading shakes of his hair and tambourine. It was largely from this trick of Brian's that Mick Jagger learned how small, tantalizing body movements could tease up conventional screams to a banshee-like howl. He, too, began to experiment, slipping off his Cecil Gee Italian jacket and dangling it on his forefinger like a stripper's G-string.

Their television appearances, on *Lucky Stars* and *Ready, Steady, Go*, had precipitated a blizzard of hate mail. 'The whole lot of you,' wrote a typical correspondent, 'should be given a good bath, then all that hair should be cut off. I'm not against pop music when it's sung by a nice clean boy like Cliff Richard, but you are a disgrace. Your filthy appearance is likely to corrupt teenagers all over the country . . . '

118

One feature of those TV appearances, above all, had caused adult Britain to recoil with almost speechless revulsion. The Beatles, for all their mop-top fringes, had always been assiduously barbered and groomed. The Stones' hair, its length, its volume, its wild lack of shape, made the Beatles' look decorously short by comparison. Not since the early Victorian age had young British men been seen with hair that hung down their necks and curled over their shirt collars, half obliterating their eyes and ears. To a nation whose collective memory of army life was still strong, the Stones' hair signified almost rabid uncleanliness. And, indeed, the voice of adult Britain rang out like so many sergeant majors. The president of the National Federation of Hairdressers, offering to give the next number one pop group a free haircut – and, by implication, a disinfecting and de-lousing – added: 'The Rolling Stones are the worst. One of them looks as though he has got a yellow feather duster on his head.' Brian Jones was deeply offended, especially since he nowadays washed his newly golden hair on average *twice* each day and was known within the Stones, not affectionately, as Mister Shampoo.

All who attacked the Stones fondly imagined themselves to be part of a process that must ultimately consign the ugly little upstarts to ear-burning oblivion. A great many worthy citizens might have held their peace if they had realized what Andrew Loog Oldham did by early 1964: that the more ferociously grown-ups attacked and derided the Stones, the more their teenage fans would love and support them.

Coverage of the Stones from spring 1964 onwards testifies to Andrew Loog Oldham's artful success in making their name synonymous with surliness, squalor, rebellion and menace. Newspaper reporters then were usually middle-aged, baffled by pop music, and only too glad of the phrases which Oldham provided. Almost every story began in the same way: 'They are called the Ugliest Group in Britain . . . ' Other stories described the Stones' habit, when exasperated by pressmen's questions, of sticking their fingers up their noses and dragging down their eyes in a collective version of Brian Jones's 'nanker' grimace. Perhaps Oldham's greatest thematic coup was a headline in *Melody Maker:* WOULD YOU LET YOUR DAUGHTER GO WITH A ROLLING STONE? The words mutated into what became

119

almost a national catch-phrase whenever the Stones appeared on television. 'Would you let *your* daughter marry one?' people said to each other, or, 'Mothers turn pale . . .'

To the fans, they were presented in the mode of Elvis Presley a decade previously – as rebels who were nice boys when you got to know them. No less an authority than Jimmy Savile confided to his pop column audience in *The People* newspaper that 'they're a great team for having a laugh, and dress very clean and smart when they relax.' Oldham ensured that they did everything that pop fans expected, posing as lurid colour pin-ups for teen magazines like *Rave* and *Fabulous 208,* grouped in uniform leather waistcoats or jumping up together in zany Beatle style. Their clothes – Brian Jones's especially – were discussed at inordinate length. Like every other group, they filled in their 'Life Lines' for *New Musical Express,* tempering sarcasm with what was usual, including the ritual white lie about their ages. Mick Jagger ('born 1944') gave his Favourite Colour as 'red, blue, yellow, green, pink, black, white', and his Favourite Clothes as 'my father's'. Keith Richard gave his Year of Birth as '1944', his Parents' Names as 'Boris and Dirt', his Favourite Actor as 'Harold Wilson', his Miscellaneous Dislikes as 'headaches, corns, pimples, gangrene'. Brian Jones ('born 1944') gave his Sister's Name as 'Hashish' and his Biggest Career Break as 'break from parents'. Though Bill Wyman subtracted the largest amount from his age – five years – he admitted the existence of his wife, Diane, and his four-year-old son, Steven. Only Charlie Watts did not lie about his age or his Hobbies: 'collecting antique firearms and modelling in plaster'.

The 'voice of the teens' no longer needed their manager to whip up notoriety for them. On March 27, under a headline BEATLE YOUR ROLLING STONE HAIR, the *Daily Mirror* reported that eleven pupils at a boys' school in Coventry had been suspended for imitating the Stones' hair-style. The headmaster had refused to reinstate them until they returned to school with hair 'cut neatly, like the Beatles'.' By April 1964, they had spent so many consecutive weeks on tour that when Bill Wyman finally went home, his dog mistook him for a burglar and tried to bite him.

Bill had moved with his wife and son from their flat in Penge to a modest house in Farnborough. He was still conspicuously the older man of the group, weighing the pleasures of stardom against the need to support a family and pay off a mortgage. That was only just possible on the wage each of the Stones drew from Eric Easton, pending Decca's first payout of royalties – which, their contract now revealed, might not be for up to a year after the actual record sales. When Bill drove home to Farnborough, he did so in the mood of an overworked commercial traveller, minus commission.

Mick, Keith and Brian had left the Edith Grove flat and gone separate ways which, at the time, seemed dictated by Brian's eternally complicated love life. He now wanted nothing to do with Pat Andrews and baby Julian, being deeply involved with a pretty young model named Linda Lawrence. Within a matter of only months, the inevitable happened. Linda, too, discovered that she was pregnant.

Mick and Keith were now sharing a flat with Andrew Loog Oldham in Willesden, North London. 'We had two rooms between us,' Oldham says. 'And we had to share a bathroom. It was rather a quiet place, really. Half a bottle of wine in that flat was a big deal. And anyway, all three of us were going steady.'

Mick Jagger was 'going steady', in almost every sense of that winsome Fifties phrase, with Chrissie Shrimpton, seventeen-year-old younger sister of Jean Shrimpton, the famous new face of *Vogue* and Sunday colour supplements. A year earlier, watching the Stones play at a basement club in Maidenhead, a friend of Chrissie's dared her to go up to Jagger and ask him to kiss her. The encounter was symbolic of the new kind of Sixties girl. Chrissie Shrimpton was, no less than the kind of Sixties man Mick Jagger would shortly become. He did kiss her and afterwards, in a resurgence of tradition, asked her out to a cinema in Windsor.

Chrissie's father was a prosperous builder in the Buckinghamshire town of High Wycombe, with a substantial house and farm a few miles into the country. Mr Shrimpton did not at first care at all for the thin, spotty boy his younger daughter had been bringing home after excursions to music clubs in the neighbourhood. The fact that he was an LSE student, a cut above the usual pop-group type, somewhat mollified Chrissie's parents. And Mr Shrimpton, self-made man that he was, perceived that, under the hair and spots and sullen lips, there was an acute and calculating intelligence.

Though Chrissie did not share her sister Jean's cool, unfussed beauty, she was in every way an improvement on Mick's Dartford girl-friends. She was also, despite her elfin appearance, strong-minded and forthright, with a temper that Mick soon provoked by his cool and careless attitude to the obligations of a steady boyfriend. Their romance from the beginning was punctuated by fights like the one Andrew Loog Oldham had witnessed in the Crawdaddy Club passage.

They were, even so, genuinely and often happily in love, and had made plans to marry as soon as Mick earned enough money to support a wife. This was in the days when he still planned to finish his LSE course and choose some respectable career in business, economics or – he once told Chrissie's father – perhaps even politics.

The Shrimptons, with their farm and country house, gave Mick Jagger his first social step up from suburban Dartford. Still more attractive was the connection through Chrissie's famous sister with the world of fashionable young London – David Bailey, Mary Quant, the *Sunday Times*, Whipp's and the Ad Lib. Though Chrissie herself was at secretarial college, her name sometimes appeared in magazine stories about Jean. Mick, though hardly even semi-famous, liked to imagine their romance to be the stuff of newspaper gossip columns. So he would refer to it, in tour interviews with provincial journalists, sitting on the cold back stairs of some northern Gaumont or ABC, sniffing with the faint flu that plagued all the Stones and tilting a Pepsi bottle against his lips. '. . . there's all those lies being written about me and Chrissie Shrimpton . . .'

He was now palpably a being apart from the other Stones, in his cable-stitched fisherman's sweater, his languid eyes appraising his interviewer's cheap suit as he dismissed this or that question as 'too much of a drag to talk about'. Offstage, he seemed the most antisocial and isolated: a rebel against his home and background, more vehement even than Brian Jones. For weeks on end, Joe and Eva Jagger down in Dartford would hear nothing from him. Keith, by contrast, kept in touch with Doris Richards and showered her with gifts to delight her eccentric heart. Charlie Watts was a model of filial affection who presented his mother with a coffee gateau religiously every Friday night. When buying a gateau for his girl-friend also, Charlie would take the walnut from the centre of the girl-friend's cake and put it on his mother's, so that she'd have two walnuts.

In those days, there were people who could talk to Mick about his apparent rejection of two very pleasant, if deeply ordinary, parents. Paul McCartney had a long talk with him about it one night when the Beatles and Stones were out together. McCartney got on well with his widower father, and all old people, and was depressed by Mick's dogged insistence, against much evidence to the contrary, that parents were 'a drag'. Everything was 'a drag', it seemed, which did not supply lustre to his still undecided image.

To so natural a mimic, those early road shows as supporting attraction to big American stars were like a series of lessons in pop idol behaviour and deportment. He had watched the Everly Brothers, singing to one another like blow-waved, cooing narcissists. He had seen Little Richard, a Rock 'n' Roll master whose music had always been strangely ambiguous of gender, and who now took the stage in full make-up, complete with nail varnish. It was on the Little Richard tour that Jagger asked a Liverpool musician, Lee Curtis, how he could find out about theatrical make-up. Curtis's brother, Joe Flannery, sat him down backstage and showed him how to apply actors' pancake and rouge.

Chrissie Shrimpton had watched Jagger's growing awareness of himself as something more than merely a constituent of the Stones' democracy. To Chrissie, he still pretended it was all for a laugh; that the normal, sensible part of him stood back and laughed when little girls screamed for him. But then, if they were out together and girls waylaid them, to Chrissie's great irritation, Mick would pretend not to be with her – even ask her to make herself scarce. The Beatles might have lost followers after the revelation that John Lennon had a wife. It was better for Mick's image – so Andrew said – if he seemed to have no steady girl-friend.

Chrissie felt slighted by Mick's apparent willingness to let Andrew Loog Oldham rule and dominate him – accepting, for instance, Oldham's firm rule that girl-friends were barred when the Stones travelled on tour. Mick's closeness with Oldham was starting to cause comment among Chrissie's friends who saw them together in pubs, deep in purported musical strategy. Chrissie Shrimpton, in no doubt about Mick's virility, was nettled when a female acquaintance asked, 'At that flat, do Mick and Andrew sleep in the same bed?'

Brian Jones was now living in considerably greater comfort than his former flat-mates, having managed to billet himself with the parents of his girl-friend, Linda Lawrence, at their house in Windsor. The arrangement was, of course, based on the idea that Brian's intentions towards Linda were honourable. Before the opposite proved to be the case, the Lawrences showed him every consideration. He was allowed to use Mr Lawrence's car whenever he wished. The name of the house was even changed, in Brian's honour, to 'Rolling Stone'. And he did seem infatuated with Linda. On tour, he would shower her with postcards – to 'darlin' Linda' – and on his return buy her expensive presents. These included a French poodle and a goat which Brian liked to take for walks through Windsor on a lead.

His passion for Linda seemed to fade in proportion to the progress of her pregnancy. He was soon on the move again, forsaking the Lawrences' hospitality for a small flat in Chester Street, Belgravia. The birth of a son to Linda completed the alienation process. Brian was seldom other than indifferent to the baby, to whom, in a mood of mischievous malice, he gave the same name as his child by Pat Andrews – Julian Mark. 'He was so rude about that poor little kid,' Shirley Arnold, the Stones' fan club secretary, remembers. 'He used to call it Broad Bean Head.'

As Brian tired of Linda, his indifference curdled into physical cruelty. On her visits to him in Chester Street, he would sometimes knock her about so violently that his downstairs neighbours – another group, the Pretty Things – could hear bumps and crashes through the ceiling.

To Brian all that mattered was the living of his longed-for role as a pop star. He loved being famous, being recognized, pursued and mobbed by girls – for himself now, not as a counterfeit Beatle. He loved having money, having girls, having wine, having clothes. He loved the pop-star night life at 'in' clubs like the Ad Lib, The Establishment, Whipp's and Scotch of St James's. He loved the shopping raids on boutiques in corduroy, button-down blocks on either side of Carnaby Street. Brian was the Stone nominated as *Rave* magazine's Best-Dressed Pop Star of the Week. He thought nothing of spending thirty guineas on one French jacket from Cecil Gee's, a 'tenner' on a single silk shirt from Just Men. What he did not buy he would cheerfully steal. The striped jersey, copied by boys all over Britain after Brian wore it on *Ready, Steady, Go*, had in fact been stolen from the wardrobe of one of his Pretty Thing neighbours.

The Pathé newsreel film, shot backstage at Hull ABC cinema, shows what a masterly performer Brian was offstage as well as on. In that film, he appears choirboy innocent, concerned only with tuning his guitar. He would sit down with pimply teenage provincial journalists, the soul of amiability, speaking in that voice so soft, it was almost effeminate, his gold-fringed eyes open wide with incredulity at the attitude of the latest hotel to refuse the Stones accommodation, though – as likely as not – it would have been Brian's own behaviour that precipitated the ban. 'The Scotch Corner Hotel . . . near Darlington . . . ooh, that's a *terrible* place. So *aggressive*.'

Within the Stones, in their claustrophobic tour life, Brian was invariably the source of any disagreement or disruption. They were all waiting in the wings one night when Keith went for him with both fists, shouting, 'Where's my chicken, you bastard?' Brian, before the show, had filched and eaten Keith's portion of the only food they would be likely to get that night.

Brian continued to regard himself as leader of the Rolling Stones, and as such entitled to a higher pay-out and superior hotel rooms, all the time in blissful unawareness that his secret negotiations and subterfuges were well known to the other four.

In those heady 1964 days, the others were content to take out their resentment of 'Mr Shampoo' in comparatively harmless ways. Mick and Keith both developed impersonations of Brian based on his physical defects – the too short legs he attempted to hide on stacked-up Cuban heels; the foreshortened neck which made his chin rest, never quite comfortably, on the roll-top of his sweater. The subtle ragging of Brian increased on a trip with Oldham to Northern Ireland to make a documentary film, directed by Peter Whitehead and entitled – in honour of its least willing participant – *Charlie Is My Darling*. 'Brian really went over the top whenever Peter Whitehead's camera was on him,'

125

Oldham says. 'He'd do these long soliloquies to camera. "Why am I a musician . . . and who am I?" He didn't realise the others were sending him up rotten.'

What no one could deny was the strength and drive Brian gave to the Stones by sheer musicianship. His preposterous egotism, his amoral willingness to do anyone down and filch anything, were forgotten as soon as he picked up his slide guitar or played harmonica, his cheeks filling and hollowing with the quick, light, dancing breath that kept the whole sound together.

'Brian was a power in the Stones as long as he could pick up any instrument in the studio and get a tune out ot it,' Andrew Loog Oldham says. 'As soon as he stopped trying, and just played rhythm guitar, he was finished.'

The process had already begun which was to define the power structure within the Stones, binding Mick and Keith together in their unstoppable alliance and leaving Brian irretrievably out in the cold. It began on the night that Andrew Loog Oldham locked his two flatmates in the kitchen of their Willesden basement and threatened not to let them out until they had written a song.

For Oldham, it was a matter of sheer convenience. He was tired of rummaging through Chappell's R & B song catalogue in the perpetual search for material acceptable to the Stones' purist conscience and to Decca's A & R department. Their two Top Twenty singles seemed to confirm what Andrew Loog Oldham told them with ever increasing frequency: 'You can't be a hit group just on Rhythm and Blues.' Nor – it was implicitly added . . . could Oldham become the teenage Svengali of British pop just by sorting through sheet music and listening to song pluggers' demo tapes.

The necessity of putting together a twelve-track LP, to capitalize on their singles' success, intensified Oldham's fear that the Stones were in imminent danger of running out of material. Yet again, he looked enviously towards the Beatles, whose own original songs had comprised a good 50 per cent of their second, million-selling album, *With The Beatles*. Mick and Keith, too, though far from convinced they could concoct a song together, had been deeply impressed by the exercise in instant Lennon-McCartney composition that had produced I Wanna Be Your

Man. So, when Andrew locked the kitchen door on them in Willesden, they agreed, for the moment, not to kick it down.

Their first attempts at songs were ballads of a glutinous sentimentality, quite unsuitable for the Stones' repertoire, or for anyone else's, despite all Oldham's bullish attempts at syndication. The first ever Jagger-Richard composition, It Should Be You, was eventually recorded by an obscure white soul artist named George Bean. Slightly more success befell another early ballad, That Girl Belongs to Yesterday, when recorded by Gene Pitney, their erstwhile pianist and booze peddler. Pitney had a minor hit with the song only after drastic rearrangement to suit a piercing voice which, it was said, hit notes that only record engineers and dogs could hear.

Only one Jagger-Richard song, Tell Me, was considered good enough for the album released by Decca in April 1964 (although two more tracks bore the Stones' collective songwriting name, Phelge). Tell Me has curio value as a heavy-handed attempt by Mick and Keith to imitate the Mersey Beat sound of the numerous post-Beatle groups from Liverpool. Strange it is to hear the Stones trying to sound Beatle-ish, with tolling bass drum, minor chords and choked-up close harmony. Mick Jagger's 'Whoa yeah' rings out in patent embarrassment. Keith Richard descants him, a McCartney made of cigarette ash and scouring pads.

The other eleven tracks are a belligerently alive memento of the Stones as an R & B band, the way they used to sound at Ken Colyer's or the Crawdaddy. Given the limitations of a tiny, primitive studio, and severely rationed time there, they could do little else but blast out the best of their club repertoire, imagining an audience in place of Regent Sound's egg-box walls and Andrew Loog Oldham's agitated eye on the clock. 'Andrew told us we couldn't afford retakes,' Bill Wyman says. 'The only time we broke was for food, or to let Mick run out and get sheet music for the words of Can I Get A Witness?'

The tracks are a squirming medley from the Soul and Blues bag: Chuck Berry's Carol, Bo Diddley's Mona, Jimmy Reed's Honest I Do, Willie Dixon's I Just Wanna Make Love To You. Even then, they could not find quite enough songs, and were forced to throw in a lengthy instrumental sequence vamped around the chords of Can I Get A Witness? featuring Ian Stewart on electric organ, with instrumental breaks by Keith and Brian. There is even a comedy number, Walkin' the Dog, with Mick Jagger skilfully mimicking Rufus Thomas's pop-eyed jokiness. The Jagger of this first album is simply a singer with the band, stepping back to allow others their turn. But in every syllable he sings, there are signs of the Jagger to come. There are signs, most powerfully, in Slim Harpo's I'm A King Bee, a slow blues, torrid with sexual warning – 'I'm a king bee, baby, buzzin' round your hive' – intoned by Jagger in a somnolent drawl, his tongue and lips playing an audible, almost visible part.

The album sleeve was a Loog Oldham tour de force. Borrowed unashamedly from the famous black and white portrait on the cover of *With The Beatles,* it had one big difference – the subject of prolonged battle between Oldham and Decca's design department. Even the epoch-making Beatles sleeve bore a title and the artists' name. Andrew Loog Oldham, however, insisted that the Stones' sleeve should make no statement other than its pictorial one. The five Stones stood sidelong, glowering from shadows so intense, one could barely see the buttons on their Carnaby Street clothes. It was left to the buyer to know who they were and to peer closer at their faces for evidence of animal sullenness or poetic sensitivity. Twenty years on, the look is still modern, the nerve still coolly audacious. On the back, convention returned with song titles, photographs and a sleeve note by Oldham that began: 'The Rolling Stones are more than a group. They are a way of life . . .'

By the day of its release, the album had sold 100,000 copies in advance orders. The Beatles – as Oldham jubilantly pointed out – had sold only 6,000 advance copies of their debut album, *Please Please Me.* He had further cause for glee when the Rolling Stones, climbing up the trade press album charts, displaced *With The Beatles* on its way down. Oldham, naturally, dismissed the fact that the Beatles album had been in the charts since the previous November. Everywhere he went, to everyone he met, he uttered the same cry of triumph: 'The Stones have knocked the Beatles off.'

London (AP) Americans – brace yourselves.

In the tracks of the Beatles, a second wave of sheepdoglooking, angry-acting, guitar-playing Britons is on the way.

They call themselves the Rolling Stones and they're due in New York Tuesday.

Of the Rolling Stones, one detractor has said:

'They are dirtier and are streakier and more dishevelled than the Beatles and in some places, they're more popular than the Beatles.'

Says Mick Jagger:

'I hate to get up in the morning. I'm not overfond of being hungry either.'

From Keith Richard:

'People think we're wild and unruly. But it isn't true. I would say that the most important thing about us is that we're our own best friends.'

More than the others perhaps, Brian Jones likes clothes. He puts his philosophy this way:

'It depends on what I feel like really. Sometimes I'll wear very flamboyant clothes like this frilly shirt. Other times I'll wear very casual stuff. I spend a lot of my free time buying stuff.'

Then he adds:

'There's really not much else to do.'

Misgivings about this first trip to America were by no means all on America's side. The Stones took off from Heathrow Airport on June 6 almost as unhappy about the whole idea. They knew only too well that when the Beatles had reached America four months earlier, it was on the strength of a single lodged firmly at the top of *Billboard* magazine's Hot Hundred. Their own first US single, Not Fade Away, coupled with I Wanna Be Your Man, had, since its mid-May release, barely scraped into the *Billboard* list. Only Andrew Loog Oldham remained unperturbed. The Beatles, he reminded them, had taken two years and three flop singles to 'break' in America. Oldham believed he had the contacts and the nerve to make things happen a lot faster than that.

The Rolling Stones were to be launched in America, not as R & B iconoclasts but – in the subtitle of their US debut album . . . as 'England's Newest Hitmakers', overtly exploiting the craze for British pop which the Beatles had started and which was now too great for even the Beatles to satisfy alone. In this 'British Invasion', the Stones were following some of the groups they most despised – Herman's Hermits, Billy J. Kramer, the Searchers. 'Everyone we really hated seemed to be doing far better in the States than we were,' Bill Wyman remembers. 'They'd had a number one record, done a good tour, good TV. We'd got nothing like that to look forward to. No wonder we were depressed on the way over.'

What few newspaper reports of their coming had appeared in America all picked up from the line from Associated Press – that the Stones' chief characteristic as a group was barely believable 'dirtiness'. The one exception was *Vogue,* a magazine then under the inspired editorship of Diana Vreeland. *Vogue* devoted a full page to David Bailey's portrait of Mick Jagger, looking upward from his penny-round collar with big-eyed, schoolboyish winsomeness. 'To the inner group in London, the new spectacular is a solemn young man, Mick Jagger,' *Vogue* reported. 'For the British, the Stones have a perverse, unsettling sex appeal, with Jagger out in front of his team-mates . . . To women, he's fascinating, to men a scare . . . quite different from the Beatles, and more terrifying.'

The scene at Kennedy Airport, when the Stones landed on June 2, was all too obviously an attempt to re-create the Beatles' famous touch-down four months earlier. A crowd, numbering hundreds rather than thousands, screamed somewhat wanly as a bevy of girls came forward to greet the arrivals, accompanied by four symbolic English sheepdogs. The screams were over well before the Stones entered the terminal, watched by US Customs and Immigration officials whose thunderstruck revulsion suggested them to be irregular readers of *Vogue*. That first walk down the synthetic red carpet unloosed, on every side, a cry which would be repeated in scales of horror and derision throughout all fifty states: 'Why dontcha get ya goddamned hair cut?'

With no hit single to their credit, the Stones merited scant promotional help from their US record label, London. It was left to Andrew Loog Oldham to whip up a rather pallid semblance of the Beatles' celebrated imprisonment inside the Plaza Hotel. The London *Daily Mirror,* next day, was persuaded to run a story that the Rolling Stones were barricaded inside their – much less grand – Manhattan hotel for fear of girls with nail scissors, threatening to cut off lumps of their hair. The tale was rather spoiled by an agency picture of Brian Jones strolling down Broadway in a loose silk shirt and sleeveless bolero but producing no more public reaction than any other freak encountered at noon in midtown Manhattan.

For the Stones' American TV debut, Oldham could arrange nothing grander than the Les Crane programme, an obscure talk show transmitted in competition with the Late Late Movies, whose semi-somnambulistic host contrived such penetrating questions as 'You guys all dress different – how come?' 'Because we are all different persons,' Mick Jagger answered in the lisping public school accent he had adopted for transatlantic use.

Worse was to come in Los Angeles two nights later, when the Stones appeared on Dean Martin's *Hollywood Palace* TV show, sharing the bill with circus elephants, acrobats and rhinestone-studded cowboys. As the show was pre-recorded in separate segments, the Stones could not know that Dean Martin's script was full of ponderous attempts to be funny at their expense. 'Their hair isn't long,' quipped the crooner in his well-loved slur. 'It's just smaller foreheads and higher eyebrows . . .' 'Now don't go away, everyone,' he pleaded humorously as the show broke for commercials. 'You wouldn't want to leave me with these Rolling Stones, would you?' Later, introducing a trampolinist, Dean Martin quipped, 'That's the father of the Rolling Stones. He's been trying to kill himself ever since.'

The West Coast pop fraternity, by contrast, provided good friends and still better object lessons. As protégés of Phil Spector, the Stones were received as VIPs in what was, after New York, the world's recording capital. Spector's advice to Andrew Loog Oldham at the Not Fade Away session had been to get the Stones with all speed into an American recording studio. In addition to touring, they were booked for a session at RCA's Hollywood studio and, later in Chicago, at Chess Records, the self-same studios used by Chuck Berry, Muddy Waters and virtually every other Blues master they had ever idolized. Even Mick Jagger could barely contain his excitement at being so close to the place that had fed his teenage dreams with its checkered logo and its mail-order catalogue.

A good friend on the West Coast was Sonny Bono, soon to find fame with his half-Indian wife as Sonny and Cher, but at this time an energetic music PR and promotion man. 'Sonny met us at the airport in these way-out clothes – striped trousers and scarves and bangles,' Andrew Oldham says. 'The Stones had never seen clothes like that before. When Sonny opened the boot of his car, there were *stacks* of records in there – about a thousand. That blew our minds as well. In England, you never *saw* the records like that, actually on their way to the punters.'

From the West Coast, they embarked on what was not so much a tour as a series of random one-nighters, booked by Eric Easton in London, often with no knowledge of the event, the promoter or the venue. Their first American performance, at San Bernardino on July 5, was in an old-fashioned pop jamboree, sharing the bill with Bobby Goldsboro, Bobby Vee and the Chiffons. Here, the omens seemed promising. The Stones easily outplayed their competition and finished their show fronted by kneeling, crash-helmeted police to fend off hundreds of entreating arms. 'It was a straight gas that night,' Keith remembers. 'The kids knew all the songs and sang along with them. Especially when we got to Route 66 – they roared out "San Bernardino" like a football crowd.'

That euphoria was to be short-lived. At the Stones' next date – a 'teen fair' in San Antonio, Texas – they were required to play standing on the edge of a water tank full of trained seals. In a 20,000 capacity arena, only a few hundred seats were filled. The London *Daily Mirror* reported that the Stones had been booed – although a tumbling act and a performing monkey on the same bill were both called back for encores. The *Mirror* quoted a local seventeen-year-old's scornful remark about the 'New Beatles': 'All they've got that our school groups haven't got is hair.'

In Omaha, Nebraska, the arrival of the New Beatles was taken ludicrously in earnest. The Stones were met at the airport by a squad of twelve motorcycle cops and delivered, with wailing sirens, to a 15,000 seat auditorium where approximately 600 people awaited them. 'We couldn't see it at the time, but all that was really doing us some good,' Keith says. 'In England, we'd been used to coming onstage, blasting off four numbers and going. America, that first tour, really made us work. We had to fill up the spaces somehow.'

In New York and Los Angeles, the Stones had seemed wild enough. In the American Midwest in 1964, their effect was literally traumatizing. Incredulous revulsion, on the faces of policemen, town sheriffs, hotel clerks and coffee-shop waitresses, greeted them wherever they went. 'I've never been hated by so many people I've never met as in Nebraska in the mid-Sixties,' Keith says. 'Everyone looked at you with a look that could kill. You could tell they just wanted to beat the shit out of you.'

The bright spot of their journey was to be their recording session at Chess studios in Chicago. Andrew Loog Oldham had been determined not to waste this precious opportunity on run-of-the-mill R & B material, and had succeeded in finding the Stones a first-class Soul song to record at Chess as their next single. The song, It's All Over Now, had already been a minor hit for its composer Bobby Womack and his group the Valentinos. The publishing rights, Oldham learned, were controlled for Womack by his business manager, a New York accountant named Allen Klein.

Chicago was all but poisoned for the Stones by the spectacle of themselves on the *Hollywood Palace* TV show, recorded a week previously. Even after doing the show, they had not realized the extent to which they had been just fodder for Dean Martin's boozy jokes. Jagger was particularly outraged that they should have been set up as stooges, and at once telephoned Eric Easton in London to scream at Easton for having booked the spot. In fact, as Oldham said, the Stones probably gained fans as a result of Dean Martin's disapprobation.

Next day, they arrived at Chess studios, on South Michigan Boulevard. As they walked in, so did a black man with a chubby, kindly face and a small Oriental moustache. 'It was Muddy Waters,' says Bill Wyman. 'He helped us carry our gear inside.'

Two formative days passed at Chess, under the supervision of Ron Malo, a house engineer responsible for some of the greatest work ever recorded by Chuck Berry and Bo Diddley. What Malo had done in the Fifties for Berry and Diddley, he now did for the Rolling Stones, cutting back their native looseness and disorder, focusing tight on the essentials which they themselves still could not see. Under Ron Malo, for the first time, they played, not as a scrabbly rhythm section but in the 'broken up' style developed by Blues masters who had sung and played lead guitar simultaneously.

133

The first few seconds of It's All Over Now, with Keith Richard's bass tremolo growling like the bark of a large dog against Brian Jones's country pizzicato, represents the start of the Stones, as, above all, an irresistible compulsion to dance.

No less formative was the mood of the song itself: a lyric about losing love, sung by Mick Jagger with a triumphant and delighted sneer, released at last from the tedious affair and its tiresome 'half-assed games'. Perfectly in counterpoint with the fang-sharp sound, that callow voice grimaced its poison-pen phrases, uncertain – as it would ever be – whether it spoke as victor or victim. The mimic had become his own man at last.

Muddy Waters dropped in frequently to talk to the Stones during their session. So did two more of their great Chicago Blues idols, Willie Dixon and Buddy Guy. The Bluesmen were naturally full of benevolence towards the young Britishers who had given their songs a new lease of life. Later on, even the great Chuck Berry came in to inspect them. Rock 'n' Roll's poet laureate, though not best known for charity towards young musicians, thawed considerably in the light of the composer's royalties the Stones were earning him. He praised their version of Reelin' and Rockin', stayed to watch them work on an EP track, Down the Road Apiece, and invited them to visit his stately home and pay-as-you-enter fun fair, Berry Park.

The session concluded, the Stones euphorically called a press conference outside the Chess building on South Michigan Avenue. Several dozen screaming girls turned the occasion into a riot which ended only after a senior Chicago police officer strode up to the Stones and snarled, 'Get outta here or I'll lock up the whole goddamned bunch.'

They had been back on tour only a day or two when Phil Spector, in New York, picked up his office telephone to hear Mick Jagger's voice, speaking from a hotel room in Hershey, Pennsylvania. 'Everything here,' Jagger moaned, 'is fuckin' *brown*!' The Stones that night were performing in a town named, and largely decorated, in honour of its principal product, the Hershey chocolate bar. 'The phones are brown,' Jagger wailed, 'the rooms are brown, even the fuckin' *streets* are brown . . .'

The tour's last weary leg through Pennsylvania and New York State was interrupted by some cheering news from home. In

*Record Mirror*'s annual popularity poll, the Stones had pipped the Beatles as Top British Group. Mick Jagger had been named Top British Group Member. The Beatles held their lead only in the Year's Best Single category, She Loves You winning narrowly from the Stones' Not Fade Away.

With the release of another US single, Tell Me, and strategic plugging of their 'England's Newest Hitmakers' album, the Stones, at long last, seemed to be penetrating the consciousness of teenage America. The tour ended in New York on a definite high note with two concerts at Carnegie Hall, scene of the Beatles' triumph six months earlier. Both concerts were promoted by Murray 'the K' Kaufman, the influential New York disc jockey whom John Lennon had first introduced to the Stones (largely to get the egregious deejay off the Beatles' long-suffering backs). Thanks to Murray the K's promotion, the Carnegie Hall concerts were each an immediate sell-out. At the first, Stones fans started running wild before a note had been played. The police forbade the Stones to close the show as planned: instead they were forced to appear halfway and escape during the first interval.

Their return to London, just as America was waking up to them, struck converts like Murray the K as perversely ill-advised. The truth was that Andrew Loog Oldham could not afford to keep them, or himself, in New York a minute longer. Oldham had already calculated that, for the whole tour, he and the Stones would receive earnings of approximately ten shillings each. The story for the British press was that the Stones were returning – £1,500 out of pocket in air fares – to honour a booking, made months earlier when they weren't famous, to play at the annual Commemoration ball of Magdalen College, Oxford.

At Heathrow, they were met by a hundred girls and a bevy of newspapermen whose interest was now something more than perfunctory. To one reporter, Keith ingenuously showed the hand gun he had bought in America, he said 'as easily as candy floss.' Mick Jagger was met by his girl-friend Chrissie Shrimpton and inquiries about how he felt at having been placed sixth in *Record Mirror*'s Best Dressed Pop Star list. 'It's a joke,' Jagger replied, speaking in a Cockney accent once again.

It's All Over Now was released in Britain on June 26. Advance orders of 150,000 copies put it instantly into every trade paper's

Top Ten. Within a week it had risen, through the Merseybeat barrier, to challenge and then displace that summer's big surprise hit single, the Animals' House of the Rising Sun.

The organizers of the Magdalen College 'Commem' were thus not a little astonished when, halfway through the night's open-air junketings, it was reported that the Stones had turned up as arranged and were bringing in their equipment. Even the Beatles, generally honourable about bookings, had, the previous year, accepted £500 to play at the Christ's College May Ball and had then failed to appear. The Stones' fee had likewise been settled months earlier when they were still only semi-famous. Nonetheless – for reasons never fully apparent – they insisted they must keep their word. It doubtless weighed with them that a major Blues artist, Howlin' Wolf, was also due to appear at the Magdalen Commem, and that they ought not to give ground to its other main pop attraction, Freddie and the Dreamers.

The writer John Heilpern was one of Oxford University's few dedicated Stones fans who purposely crossed the floodlit college lawns, uproarious with patrician cries and steel-band music, to the marquee where the Stones were setting up their equipment in a mood of evident disenchantment. 'They were all deeply pissed off about having to play,' Heilpern remembers. 'They'd been booked to do an hour, so they managed to spend at least the first forty minutes tuning up. Brian Jones already looked zonked out of his mind. There was a sense of vague leadership from Mick Jagger. When he started, everyone did. At first, they didn't try; they were hissed and booed, which obviously delighted them. Then, all of a sudden, they all snapped into it.'

It was a moment, for John Heilpern and many others, signifying the start of what would one day be termed 'the counterculture' but what, that night at Oxford, seemed more a question of class turned upside down. The surly, middle-class boys, playing American R & B, were patently a new aristocracy, just as the dinner-jacketed throng, jigging up and down before them, would become part of a willing new proletariat. The noise spread, through the canvas walls, across grass strewn with debs and duckboards, drowning the steel band. More and more young men in tails, clutching girl-friends and open-mouthed champagne bottles, came in to hear the Stones, and dance.

# PART TWO

# 5

# 'My client has no fleas'

The town of Reading, Berkshire, is distinguished by very little. Huntley and Palmer's biscuit factory and the prison where Oscar Wilde was incarcerated loom with equal glumness over terraced streets whose uniform orangey brick and mean proportions betray the handiwork of the Victorian speculative builder. Reading is the very last place in England one would expect to find glamour or eccentricity. Nevertheless, in the late Fifties, the town's population included one notably exotic personage: Eva Sacher-Masoch, the Baroness Erisso, who lived in Millman Road with her small daughter, Marianne.

The Sacher-Masochs are an ancient and illustrious Austrian family dating back to the reign of Charlemagne. Europe's *Who's Who*, the *Almanach de Gotha*, testifies to almost nine centuries of Sacher-Masoch involvement in warfare and the arts, culminating in the nineteenth-century novelist who first described the giving of pain for sexual pleasure, and used his own name to define it: Masochism.

Eva's childhood was dominated by her father, an Austrian count of the old school, who went off to the Great War much as his forebears had accompanied Charlemagne, with a silver helmet, a cloak and a string of seven Arab chargers. The Count survived, with his grandeur almost all intact. Eva spent her girlhood in surroundings of nineteenth-century splendour, albeit tinged with the growing menace of Nazism. A gifted dancer, and very beautiful, she won a place with the famous Max Reinhardt company in Vienna. But for the war in 1939, she would have joined Max Reinhardt in Hollywood and would, undoubtedly, have become a major film star.

It was to be her destiny, instead, to live out the Nazi terror, and so meet and fall in love with an Englishman, Glyn Faithfull, whose peacetime study was research into ancient words and languages. As a philologist, Glyn had been drafted into British wartime intelligence and was in Yugoslavia as a liaison officer with a unit of Tito's partisans that included Eva's brother, Alexander. The story in the family goes that Glyn Faithfull saved Alexander's life. He, in gratitude, recommended the Englishman to the affections of his beautiful sister, herself active in the Viennese Resistance attempting to save Austrian Jews from extermination.

The war over, Glyn Faithfull married his Austrian baroness, brought her home to England and resumed his academic career with a teaching post at Liverpool University. Their only child, Marianne, was born in 1947 and first came to consciousness in the deeply unlikely surroundings of Ormskirk, Lancashire.

Marianne's first real memories begin after the age of six, when her parents separated and Eva took her to live in Reading, in a tiny house which, even so, contained rich reminders of her high-born Austrian heritage. There were the ceremonial dinner plates, from banquets long unaffordable, and leather books from private libraries long dispersed. There was the discovery that Eva spoke in a voice quite different from other girls' mothers; that her speech, her gestures, her very posture belonged to somewhere far from Millman Road. 'Eva had to adapt her whole body to that house,' Marianne says. 'She'd grown up in rooms so big you could just *sweep* across them. At Millman Road there was no room big enough to sweep across. She'd trained herself to be very careful and contained, to suit the size of the rooms we had.'

Marianne remembers with what grande dame style Eva used to invest even the most mundane parts of their life in Reading. 'She'd go round the shops, talking to everyone as if she was touring her estate. One must always be gracious, she said. She told me I had to smile at everyone. And the poorer they were, the nicer I had to be to them.'

The dour Reading shopkeepers were, if anything, more captivated by the little girl who would, in time, do her mother's shopping, carefully repeating Eva's ceremonious: 'One pound of tomatoes – not too big. One ni-ize lettuce . . .' 'Millman Road wasn't in the worst part of Reading, but it was near the worst part. There was one very frightening street I had to go down to the shop where I used to buy my mother's Woodbines.

140

"Darleeng . . ." she'd say, "you go out and get me some Voodbines . . ."'

The baroness was a cultivated as well as formidable woman. From her mother, at the earliest age, Marianne learned to read voraciously and appreciate paintings and music. Though money was short, Eva took her back to Vienna to show her where she had come from and visit the city's great museums and galleries. 'My mother taught me something else as well at an early age. She taught me that to be beautiful – as I knew I was – shouldn't be a passive thing. It was something to be put to use, the way that, in the past, she'd put her own beauty to use. I was trained by a highly trained professional.'

A local Catholic convent, St Joseph's, agreed to accept the baroness's daughter as a weekly boarder on semi-charitable terms. 'When I first brought a friend home to Millman Road, I got this terrible shock,' Marianne says. 'I realized that my home wasn't the same as other girls'. I realized my mother was quite different from everyone else's.'

St Joseph's was run by an order of nuns, on principles medievally strict. When bathing, the girls had to wear shifts, to avoid the sin of looking at their own nude bodies. It was a system which Marianne, a non-Catholic, found especially repressive and fought against with the inquiring mind her mother had fostered in her. At home, none of the bookcases was ever locked. Marianne and a schoolfriend set about methodically reading through the entire Index of books forbidden to Catholics.

At sixteen, both beautiful and intelligent, her future seemed overburdened with promise. Her academic prowess – especially in languages – would have gained her admittance to any of Britain's top universities. Her talent for drama, allied to her looks and pure mezzo-soprano singing voice, would likewise have taken her to the best academies of either drama or music. 'There was no doubt, in my mind or my mother's, that I'd go on the stage. The only question was, how?'

Meanwhile, to use her own wistful phrase, Marianne Faithfull 'lived in a Renoir painting – long blonde hair, sunny days, straw hat with ribbons . . .' She had begun to sing semi-professionally – folk songs, with guitar accompaniment, in a Reading coffee bar to an adoring circle of local college boys. 'I'd learned my lesson from Eva – that beauty was something I had to put to use. I knew things *must* happen to me – that my looks and my voice together were a devastating combination.'

At sixteen, she began going steady with John Dunbar, a Cambridge undergraduate studying fine art at Churchill College. She remembers standing for hours outside the telephone box near her house, waiting to talk to John until her money ran out. He was the first boy to make love to her – in her innocence, she thought he would be the only one. Her life moved away from Reading to Cambridge, where she would visit Dunbar at his brand-new college, or to London, where his family lived and where he had many friends among the new pop 'in' crowd.

In the early summer of 1964, Marianne went with John Dunbar to a party in London, given to launch a new girl singer named Adrienne Posta. Many of the 'in' crowd were there – among them an old friend of John Dunbar's, whose sunglasses and puff-sleeved silk shirt made it hard for Marianne to believe John had first met him through a shared interest in Hampstead left-wing politics. So she was first introduced to Andrew Loog Oldham while at the same time, across the noisy room, receiving her first sight of her future lover, supporter and destroyer, Mick Jagger.

Just then, Jagger's glance was only one in the swarm that settled on honey-blonde hair and the face it framed, in which virginal innocence co-existed with a kind of helpless sensuality, brimming of its own accord in her wide blue eyes and a mouth as tender, as bruisable, as soft, red fruit. Marianne was well aware she had captured the attention of every man in the room. 'I knew I was at that party just as a beautiful woman, to go to the highest bidder,' she says. 'I knew I had to use my looks, the way Eva had said, to create a situation; to make things happen that I wanted to happen.'

What happened was that Andrew Loog Oldham came swaggering up and, on being introduced to Marianne Faithfull, said: 'With a name like that, you ought to be making records.' The name added to the lovely, misty face had set wheels awhirl in Oldham's mind, even before Marianne told him she was already singing semi-professionally. Within literally minutes, Oldham

142

informed her she could become a big star, provided she placed herself under his exclusive management.

She met Mick Jagger, with Keith, a few minutes afterwards, but was not impressed. She disliked Mick's pallor, his spotty face and the studied crudeness of his voice and manner. Jagger's invariable approach to girls he considered 'high class' was ' 'Ello, darlin'. 'Ow yer doin'?' Their first brief conversation ended with Jagger deliberately slopping wine down the front of Marianne's dress.

Oldham, it transpired, had been absolutely serious. Within a few days of the party, Marianne found herself offered a formal management contract and a recording test with the Stones' label, Decca. Since she herself was only seventeen, all contracts had to be endorsed by her mother, the baroness. 'Eva signed everything, even though she didn't really know what it was about,' Marianne says. 'Her one stipulation was that when I went out on tour, I must always have a chaperon.'

Oldham's real plan, as always, was for the greater expansion of Andrew Loog Oldham. The manager of the pop group which had outraged Britain now saw his chance to perpetrate an even greater surprise. What more surprising contrast could there be to the shaggy, surly Rolling Stones than a sweet-faced ex-convent girl whose voice was softly elegant and whose mother was an Austrian noblewoman? With a chaperon thrown in as well, Oldham's promotional script was practically writing itself.

To launch Marianne Faithfull on record, Oldham planned to use a song by Lionel Bart, a composer of stage musicals then at his apotheosis. The B-side was to be Greensleeves, with slight modifications that would allow Andrew Loog Oldham, not King Henry VIII, to claim the composer's credit.

The Lionel Bart song, unfortunately, did not suit Marianne's voice. Oldham therefore had no alternative but to order a song from a composing team whose efforts thus far had been confined to sentimental ballads – Mick Jagger and Keith Richard. 'I told them, Marianne's a convent girl. I want a song with brick walls all round it, and high windows and *no* sex.'

These tight restrictions, paradoxically, set free the creative chemistry between Mick and Keith that they had almost despaired of discovering. As Time Goes By – subsequently retitled

As Tears Go By – was their first *real* song in the sense that it sprang wholly from within themselves, stamped unmistakably with a shared character. Simple, even elegant, imbued with overtones of Tennyson's Lady of Shalott, its qualities startled no one more than its two composers. For weeks afterwards, Mick remembers, they would rack their brains in fruitless attempts to write something else as good.

Marianne went into the Decca studios under much the same strictures, performing the song in the most muted possible version of her rich mezzo voice. The result was what Oldham had wanted: a convent girl singing sweetly and shyly, with high walls and no sex. In August 1964, As Tears Go By was number nine in the charts. Marianne Faithfull was Britain's leading female singing star. 'Greensleeves goes Pop,' the *Daily Mirror* said.

Caliban's island was not more full than Great Britain, in August 1964, of the sound of voices and 'twangling instruments', beamed from insecure moorings three miles distant, their harbinger a watery ship's bell.

Giorgio Gomelsky's fellow Method actor Ronan O'Rahilly was the first – by a cat's whisker – to get the idea. For years, British entrepreneurs had dreamed of starting pop radio stations in the American style, but had always been thwarted by the BBC's legally enforced monopoly. O'Rahilly's wheeze was to fit out a ship as a radio station and begin transmitting off the Essex coast, outside Britain's three-mile territorial limit. 'Radio Caroline' announced itself over the 1964 Easter Bank Holiday, with a record clearly chosen to echo its own piratical effrontery: Not Fade Away by the Rolling Stones. Almost simultaneously, a rival ship, Radio Atlanta – fitted out in the same Irish port, despite heavy sabotage from O'Rahilly's supporters – began pouring the same heady mixture of continuous pop, American-style commercials and station identification jingles into Britain's radio sets.

Within a few weeks, the two pirate stations, as they were instantly dubbed, together had an audience numbering hundreds of thousands. Official attempts to ban them under the Wireless Telegraphy Acts revealed that they were indeed beyond parliamentary jurisdiction. It became evident also that Radio Caroline and Radio Atlanta were providing something the public wanted, despite years of BBC insistence to the contrary. The pirates therefore could continue, and multiply. Soon there was Radio London; Radio Scotland; Radio Clyde; Radio Sutch; Radio Invicta; Radio City. Transmitter ships littered the North Sea, locked in a wavelength war that occasionally spilled into actual violence. A man was even killed in a night attack on the disused Thames Estuary fort which housed Radio City.

The muffled creaks of pirate ship timbers, and groans of their intermittently seasick young disc jockeys, are an essential element in recalling the 1964 'Beat Boom'. The sounds were the more exciting for rising and falling somewhat, as the vessel did; being smuggled into the radio dial, between tedious Light Programme and smug Home Service, like so much contraband.

With those thousand twangling instruments – bought usually on the instalment plan – came voices, multifariously accented. Following Liverpool's glorification, other far-flung provincial capitals could also now pique themselves on emitting a competitively fashionable 'sound'. As well as Mersey groups (Pacemakers, Searchers, Mojos, All Stars, Chants, Undertakers, Flamingoes) and Manchester groups (Hollies, Dakotas, Mindbenders, Hermits, Dreamers), there were Birmingham groups (Applejacks, Fortunes, Ivy League); there were Tyneside groups (Animals, Bluechips); Scottish groups (Luvvers, Poets) and Irish groups (Bachelors, Them). London restored its dented cultural superiority with groups mingling club R & B with aggressive Mod culture (The Who, Small Faces, Kinks). There were all-instrument groups (Jaywalkers, Blue Inc) and all-vocal groups (Four Pennies, Walker Brothers). There were earnest groups (Manfred Mann, Yardbirds) and comical groups (Fourmost, Rockin' Berries, Barron Knights). There were, in short, dozens, if not hundreds, of groups. And, presumably, that Decca executive who had pronounced guitar groups to be 'on the way out' was still in his Albert Embankment office, trying to kick himself to death.

Whatever the passing allegiance for this or that newly fashionable group, being a pop fan in 1964 Britain depended on one fundamental question: 'Are you Beatles or are you Stones?' asked with the searching ferocity of rival factions in a football crowd. Even football factions, though, had scarcely been as rife with implications of reflected character.

145

To answer 'Beatles' implied that one was oneself similarly amiable, good-natured, a believer in the power of success to effect conformity. To answer 'Stones' meant, more succinctly, that one wished to smash up the entire British Isles. On June 24, a Stones concert in the Winter Gardens, Blackpool, provoked a riot that seventy policemen could not contain. The Stones themselves came under heavy attack, from hails of spittle and grabbing hands that eventually succeeded in pulling a Steinway grand piano off the stage. The journalist Roy Carr – then a musician in a backup band – remembers with what deep gratification he saw Keith Richard persuade an over-eager fan to retreat from the stage rim by sinking one pointed boot toe in his face. Afterwards, Ian Stewart, the imperturbable, came round to their dressing room to distribute various chips of splintered wood, saying, 'Here's your guitar . . . and here's your amp . . .'

On July 3, a Stones concert in Belfast was cancelled for fear of some similar outbreak. What Belfast avoided, Holland received in double measure eight days later, when the Stones caused the virtual annihilation of a cinema in The Hague. Next day, when they arrived back in Manchester for a *Ready, Steady, Go* appearance, a door was wrenched bodily from their hired limousine. So it continued, in Liverpool, Manchester, Carlisle and Edinburgh, the splinter of chairs and woodwork threatening to drown even the chart success of their new EP, Five by Five. Their progress, viewed on old newsreels and TV film, shows what a change was coming over pop concerts. More police, more 'stewards', of more and more doubtful probity, massed along the stage front. More foolhardy lunges at Mick Jagger by desperate girls. More nonchalant violence in the seizing of such girls by their arms, legs, even their hair, to toss them back into the crowd.

The virus was spreading into parts of Europe where even Beatle-mania had not taken root. On October 18 – despite an attempt to ban them by Belgium's Minister of the Interior – the Stones played to a howling sea of heads at the Brussels World's Fair ground. Two nights later, in Paris, the pop concert in its old, innocent, sedentary form was finally laid to rest. The Stones' show at the Olympia theatre ended in running fights between gendarmes and youths who ran amok through the boulevards, breaking shop windows, slashing at newspaper kiosks, overturning café tables and hurling customers on to the pavement. The *Daily Mirror* reported that 150 arrests had been made.

On October 23, the bacillus was once more reported en route to the American continent. America's worst fears were confirmed by a publicity photograph, showing the Stones apparently in an advanced state of destitution, Mick Jagger engaged in scratching himself like a baboon while Keith peered with absorption inside the waist band of his jeans. 'The Rolling Stones, who haven't washed for a week . . . ' the caption began.

At Kennedy Airport, girls who broke from the crowd barriers were felled by policemen with flying football tackles. One of them, pulled forth for a random TV interview, proved surprisingly lucid in answer to the stock question, 'Why do you like the Stones?'

'Because . . . Keith is beautiful, and because . . . they're so ugly, they're attractive.'

Their appearance on the Ed Sullivan TV show on October 26 presented Sullivan's coast-to-coast audience with the interesting spectacle of a studio apparently being torn to shreds by its audience. Sullivan issued a statement, disclaiming responsibility for the Stones' engagement and vowing they would never pollute his air time again. 'I promise you, they'll never be back on our show . . . Frankly, I didn't see the Rolling Stones until the day before the broadcast. They were recommended by my scouts in England. I was shocked myself when I saw them.

'Now the Dave Clark Five *are* nice fellows. They're gentlemen and they perform well. It took me seventeen years to build this show. I'm not going to have it destroyed in a matter of weeks.'

Another TV clip shows Mick Jagger being interviewed, next to a deeply anxious-looking Charlie Watts. The usual interviewer, bald and bow-tied, speaks devoutly into his microphone, then thrusts it outward as if only half convinced Jagger is capable of speech. 'Er, Mick . . . er, how are you all enjoying your first trip to the States? I'm sorry: your *second* trip.'

'Yes, our second trip,' Jagger replies. 'Yes, it's been very enjoyable. Highly enjoyable, yes.' His voice is deliberately polite and hushed to semi-audibility.

'But that's not the way it was the first time you came over.'

'Oh, *no*,' Jagger says, contriving in the same moment to be both emphatic and utterly uninterested. 'When we first came over here, it was just to get ourselves known about so to speak.' His voice softens to a sing-song, little-boyish lisp, like Brian's. 'And then we went back. And things started happenin' for uth.'

'And, uh . . . why was that?'

'Dunno.' Jagger smiles his shy smile and shrugs. 'Some . . . chemical reaction.'

On the West Coast, between studio sessions at RCA, Hollywood, the Stones appeared on a TAMI (Teenage Music International) pop package show, filmed at Santa Monica Civic Auditorium and shown later in cinemas throughout America. Technically, they topped the bill, headlining above Gerry and the Pacemakers, Jan and Dean, Chuck Berry, the Beach Boys, Marvin Gaye and Smokey Robinson and the Miracles. Even James Brown, grand master and autocrat of all black Soul singers, had his name in smaller type than the Stones. 'We were all terrified about appearing on the same bill as James Brown,' Bill Wyman says. 'He'd told everybody that when he went onstage, he was going to make the Rolling Stones wish they'd never set foot in America.

'We were all in the dressing-room beforehand, really scared. And Marvin Gaye and Chuck Berry came in to see us. Marvin Gaye said, "Are you guys nervous?" We said, "Petrified." He was really nice. He said, "Hey, go out there and just do your best. Nobody wants to know if you're better than anybody. They only want to know that you're on."'

They stood in the wings, a little comforted, watching 'Mr Dynamite' steal the show as expected with his frantic energy and whooping lust, with shrieking and pleading and impossible preening, a sweat-shiny dynamo trapped on the moving staircase of his own feet. They watched the bizarre multi-encore finale in which Brown, on his knees, was forcibly wrapped in a cloak by bodyguards and strongarmed towards the wings, before turning and throwing off the cloak – exact to a drum roll – and starting to sing and dance and sweat anew.

The Stones did not expect to surpass that. But they still gave a performance impressive enough for Brown to grant them an audience in the dressing-room where he sat, surrounded by black retainers and stage shoes and tubs of champagne on ice. It was the first time that Mick Jagger had realized that a musician could be a monarch and despot also. Jagger, indeed, returned to London having learned the most crucial object lesson of his life. To Chuck Berry's voice and Rufus Thomas's grimaces were now added James Brown's dance steps – the very way Brown boogied up to unclip his microphone.

'That was when the Mick Jagger we know began,' Giorgio Gomelsky says. 'After that second trip to America. When Mick got off the plane back in London, he was doing the James Brown slide.'

The presentation of the Rolling Stones' new single, Little Red Rooster, on *Ready, Steady, Go*, had an avant-garde audacity which would have done credit to Samuel Beckett. At first, all the viewer saw was a mouth, unmistakable for its sullen and insolent, overstuffed lips. 'I am the little red rooster,' sang this oracle wetly, 'too lazy to crow for days . . .' The mouth on its own sang a full chorus before the camera pulled back to show Jagger's face and, at length, the other Stones behind him, misty and subservient in the sleepwalking beat whose only ornamentation was the tremulous swoops and shocks of a lone bar slide guitar.

It had seemed like a gamble for the Stones to follow up a pop hit like It's All Over Now with an unreformed Blues classic, written by Willie Dixon and first recorded by Howlin' Wolf. In the event, Little Red Rooster proved the ideal vehicle, both for the Stones as Blues purists and for Mick Jagger as an increasingly audacious purveyor of sexual innuendo. It was a production as compulsive instrumentally as vocally, with Brian Jones's slide guitar seesawing from a low throb, like blood through an artery, up to its palpitant, quivering high.

Jagger, performing the song on *Ready, Steady, Go,* seemed less like a pop vocalist than a young lord posing for some Mayfair portraitist with barely good grace. It confirmed what the 'RSG' audience was beginning to suspect – that he and the Stones inhabited a world more private and privileged than even Associated-Rediffusion's Kingsway studios. The fact was corroborated by the London *Daily Express*'s 'William Hickey' column, hitherto the exclusive preserve of Society's hostesses, playboys and debutantes. 'There's no harm these days in knowing a Rolling Stone,' the Hickey columnist wrote. '. . . some of their best friends, in fact, are fledglings from the upper classes . . .'

Robert Fraser, the London art dealer, was such a friend, though scarcely a fledgling. The son of a Scots merchant banker, he had been educated at Eton and then taken a commission in the army, serving with distinction in the Kenya Mau-Mau emergency. In 1964, he already enjoyed high standing in the London art world for his prescient championing of American pop artists like Andy Warhol and Jim Dine. Slight and dark and nervous-looking, he combined formidable taste with a passion for novelty, adventure and low life. With these the Rolling Stones would furnish Robert Fraser in all too great abundance.

He had met them first in Paris after their Olympia concert, while police were still scooping up rioters from the debris of wrecked pavement cafes. 'I'd bumped into Teddy, the disc jockey from the Ad Lib, who'd come over specially to see the Stones. They knew Teddy well, of course, because he was so into their black music. Through Teddy I got talking to Brian Jones – who even then seemed very paranoid. Later on, I took them all to a party at Donald Cammell's studio.'

Cammell, an American painter and would-be filmmaker, would also figure prominently in the Stones' social conversion. That night in 1964, he was simply host at a party where five British pop musicians were the very least glamorous and fashionable guests. 'They all looked very ugly, very scruffy,' Robert Fraser says. 'Mick was just a rude slob. You could tell it was the first time any of them had been to a place like Donald's or to a party like that – big studio . . . low lights, wonderful-looking women . . . drugs . . .'

Fraser subsequently introduced them to his Old Etonian friend Christopher Gibbs, a young antique dealer whose Chelsea shop was credited as source of the current mania for Moroccan decor in fashionable Mayfair and Belgravia homes. Gibbs was nephew of the Governor of Rhodesia, a friend of Cecil Beaton, whose diary describes him as 'a most cultivated young man'. He was also a unique mixture of modern wit and old-fashioned courtliness. With Fraser and Cammell, he was the Stones' initiator into an older metropolitan clique whose raffish doings had titillated Society columns during the middle and late Fifties. Brian, Mick and Keith, as modern counterparts – with the added attraction of money to burn – were welcomed with open arms into the 'Chelsea Set'.

John Lennon, with his infallible gift for an apt phrase, said that fashionable young London in 1964 was 'like a gentleman's smoking club'. The 'in' crowd, yearningly celebrated by pop song and newspaper report, in fact consisted of no more than a dozen faces, moving in a pack around the same tiny circuit of late-night West End clubs. And no club was truly 'in' until its high-priced darkness could disclose the chalk-pale face of a Beatle or a Rolling Stone or – in the innermost in-ness – a Beatle and a Stone conversing together.

The deadly rivals of the Top Twenty and music press popularity polls were, in private life, very good friends. The Stones readily admitted that without George Harrison they might never have got their Decca contract, just as without Lennon and McCartney, they would never have had a hit single. The Beatles, on their side, felt sneaking envy of the Stones' refusal to compromise themselves with stage suits and insincere smiles, the way even John Lennon had been forced to do.

The Stones' challenge to the Beatles as a pop attraction had, if anything, increased the bond between them. Being so famous that one constantly risked being torn limb from limb, was a predicament that no one else understood quite so well. Likewise, the predicament of being showered with pocket money while, at the same time, vaguely realizing one was not half so rich as one might think. In the dark of 'Scotch' or the Ad Lib, Beatles and Stones first compared notes about their record contracts and royalty rates. The surprise was that the Beatles, for all their international money-spinning, actually earned less per copy of each single and album than did the Stones.

Robert Fraser was a friend of both Beatles and Stones – one of many they had in common. Andrew Loog Oldham's crony Peter Asher was the brother of Paul McCartney's actress girlfriend, Jane Asher. Paul had for some months lodged at the Ashers' Wimpole Street house, in an attic room occupied by a bed, a wardrobe, two Cocteau drawings and a cache of Gold Discs. Paul was friendly with John Dunbar, boyfriend of Oldham's protégée, Marianne Faithfull – herself the strongest infusion of gentility into

151

the Stones' background. When Marianne broadcast a charity appeal on Radio Caroline in the winter of 1964, it was with all the quiet, self-effacing dignity of minor Royalty.

The Beatles were now making their second feature film, *Help!*, in a state of helpless hilarity which even their director, Richard Lester, did not recognize as their first 'high' from smoking marijuana. Bob Dylan, a rising American folk singer, had introduced them, in New York, to this traditional resort of American Jazz and Blues musicians. Illegal in Britain, it was supposed – by the police as much as anyone – to have died out with the novels of Sax Rohmer. The small, draggled cigarette thus carried minimal risk, passing from the Beatles to their friends the Rolling Stones, the next novelty after hipster trousers or tinted sunglasses or Mateus rosé or Scotch and Coke.

Those little transparent packets of 'grass' added the merest wavelet to a narcotic ocean which, long before 1964, had made London the drug capital of the Western world. It had begun in Victorian times, when Britain's imperial possessions encompassed the Chinese opium trade, and every local tobacconist sold 'opium lozenges' as a cough remedy available to all. Narcotic substances, long outlawed in other countries, continued to be present in mundane British products like nose inhalers, stomach mixture, even 'laughing powder' from joke shops. Britain was the only country where pure heroin was available by prescription from any doctor, and could be bought on the street with considerably less risk than attended the passing of a bet for horse racing. 'I remember when you could buy heroin jacks [tablets] for a pound each,' Robert Fraser says. 'A phial of pure cocaine for £50. There were smart doctors all over Mayfair who'd prescribe it for you.'

'Hard' drugs, in other words, had been an upper-class pursuit long before pop musicians started giggling over marijuana. Fraser himself had smoked grass years before, in New York's avant-garde art circles. Like others before, and since, he was not so much hooked by heroin as seduced by it. Long cured from addiction, he shudders to remember that first 'rush', so very different from soft-drug fuzziness. 'That's the thing about heroin. It doesn't disorient you. It seems to *stabilise* you. It's a feeling like you've been wandering around in the Antarctic for days, and you suddenly walk into a nice warm room with a bar.'

\* \* \*

As Andrew Loog Oldham stood in the howling throng, his bodyguard, Reg – alternatively known as Reg the Butcher – would struggle up to join him, looking cautiously over one shoulder and speaking, as far as possible, in an urgent undertone. 'Don't move a muscle, Andrew,' Reg the Butcher would caution. 'There are eight blokes standing right behind you . . .'

It was the newest of Oldham's fantasies that he needed a muscle-bound protector, like those Phil Spector employed, to shield him from the righteous fury, or murderous envy, of the world on which he had unleashed the Rolling Stones. So Reg the Butcher rode round with him in his powder-blue American Chevrolet. Reg the Butcher sat in on meetings, imparting a piquant possibility to all business negotiations. The idea was that Oldham, if thwarted, would say 'Go and thump that guy, Reg,' and Reg would go and thump the guy.

'Actually,' Oldham says, 'he got me into more fights than he got me out of. Like when he'd come up and say "Don't move. There are eight people behind you . . ." "Reg," I'd say. "We're at a concert. This is a crowd. There are *bound* to be eight people standing behind me . . ."'

The Stones' second album, released on January 30, 1965, launched Andrew Loog Oldham into a new phase of egotistical fantasy. Once again, Decca's art department had been compelled to accept a front cover devoid of title or artists' name, and adorned by a David Bailey photograph calculated to make every British parent reach for the DDT. Five faces in close-up glowered from deep shadow that still did not hide the many scars and pimples and craters left by former pimples on Keith Richard's face. Mick Jagger stood right at the back, craning his neck to see over the others' heads. 'I put Mick there deliberately,' Bailey says. 'I didn't want the others to think he was getting special treatment because he was a friend of mine.'

On the back of the album was Andrew Loog Oldham's artistic debut: a sleeve note written in the prose style of his current literary obsession, Anthony Burgess's *A Clockwork Orange*.

It is the summer of the night London's eyes be shut tight all but twelve peepers and six hip malchicks who prance the street. Newspaper strewn and gray which waits another day to hide its dingy countenance the six have been sound ball journey made to another sphere which pays royalties in eight months or a year.

. . . This is The Stones' new disc within. Cast deep in your pockets for loot to buy this disc of groovies and fancy words. If you don't have the bread, see that blind man, knock him on the head, steal his wallet and lo and behold, you have the loot. If you put in the boot, good. Another one sold.

The album itself was rather routine – predominantly R & B in content, yet somehow lacking the manic live quality of its predecessor. The tracks had been made at three different studios, so varied in texture from the thrilled discipline of Chess, Chicago – evident on a version of Chuck Berry's Down the Road Apiece which Chuck Berry himself had heard and commended – through rather muted Soul gushers, recorded at RCA, Hollywood, with Phil Spector's arranger Jack Nitzsche on piano, to Regent Sound's egg-box echo, featured on a limp Jagger-Richard effort, Grown Up Wrong. Mick and Keith were wholly successful, however, with Left Off the Hook, a bedsitting-room vignette suffused with Jagger's sneering imperviousness to feminine wiles. Conversely, Time Is On My Side – copied from the Irma Thomas version – reminded him of close moments with Chrissie, and became a tender soliloquy more personal than anything he would ever write for himself.

Oldham cannot now remember whether it was a conscious or merely subconscious instinct to galvanize their rather anticlimactic production with a sleeve note exhorting people to knock down blind men and steal their wallets. Certainly the ensuing furore had a stage-managed element, not breaking out until a full month after Rolling Stones No. 2 had hit the shops. Then all at once a Mrs Gwen Mathews, secretary of the Bournemouth Blind Aid Association, was quoted as saying 'They're horrible. It's putting ideas into people's heads. I'm writing to Decca to ask them to change the cover . . .'

Within a week, Oldham had a scandal which, for the first time, caused his name to appear in print as many times as the Stones'. The Daily Telegraph quoted him as saying he had written the offending passage 'for fun, in the bath'. Decca, bowing to pressure

154

from Mrs Gwen Mathews and others, called back as many copies of the LP as possible, and reissued them in a new sleeve with the offending paragraph deleted. But the scandal would not subside. In the House of Lords, a former Conservative minister asked for the Director of Public Prosecutions to investigate what appeared to be 'a deliberate incitement to criminal action'. A Home Office spokesman replied that there were insufficient grounds, adding: 'If it is any consolation to the noble lord, research I made at the weekend supports the view that, even when they are intelligible, the words of a pop song are not considered important, and teenagers have even less regard to the blurb on the envelope.'

On their first Australian and Far East tour earlier in January, Oldham had definitely cast himself as the sixth Stone – if not the first. 'The boys and I,' he told pressmen, with mock-regal sarcasm, at Sydney Airport, 'were moved as we stood on the steps of the airliner which had brought us to this distant land, receiving a tremendous welcome from these warm-hearted and wonderful colonials.' The warm-hearted colonials, 3,000 of them, were even now tearing down a chain-wire perimeter fence and wrenching up rails from their steel floor bolts.

The thirty-day tour of Australia and New Zealand established the Stones as a menace to antipodean stability, with newspaper headlines like SHOCKERS! UGLY LOOKS! UGLY SPEECH! UGLY MANNERS! on the one hand and on the other, hysteria-sodden concerts in Sydney, Melbourne, Brisbane, Perth, Adelaide and Wellington. By the end of the tour, the Stones had four records in the Australian Top Ten, including their unlikely and unsteady cover version of the Drifters' Under the Boardwalk. A disbelieving Britain had meanwhile seen wire service photographs of them immersing themselves in Auckland's hot springs and all five – even Keith Richard – apparently enjoying the sunshine and open air.

On February 26, Decca released a new Stones single that was to prove to Andrew Loog Oldham beyond all doubt that he could make hits happen by the mesmeric power of his will. With The Last Time, Mick Jagger and Keith Richard, under duress from their manager, had at last written something good enough for an A-side. The song itself was basic and Bo Diddley-esque. What lifted it out of the ordinary was a four-note guitar phrase by Keith

155

Richard that slithered through the lyric with a malign, unignor-able persistence, like migraine rendered into sound.

The Last Time went to number one in Britain eight days after its release. With the top-selling British single as well as top LP *and* EP (Five By Five), the Stones might reasonably have expected a rest. Instead, Oldham and Easton launched them afresh on a British tour, itself to be turned into a further EP, Got Live If You Want It, engineered by their IBC friend, Glyn Johns, and containing scream-rent versions of Pain In My Heart and Everybody Needs Somebody to Love. One track consisted solely of the audience chanting 'We want the Stones.' 'It was *technically* a song,' Oldham says. 'So we thought Nanker Phelge might as well cop the proceeds from the publishing.'

Oldham's ambitions had by now outgrown any simple group of five. From January 1964, he began recording for Decca in his own right as director of 'the Andrew Loog Oldham Orchestra'. Studio session men in huge numbers – sometimes including individual Stones – would be assembled periodically to perform such Oldham orchestral compositions as Funky and Fleopatra; 365 Rolling Stones; and the tortuously punning Theme for a Mod Summer Night's Ball.

Only one obstacle remained between Oldham and total fulfilment. This was, alas, not something which Reg the Butcher could arrange by going over and thumping somebody. It could only come in a letter such as Paul McCartney in his Wimpole Street bedsitter had just received from his Mayfair accountants. Andrew Loog Oldham, despite his hold over Britain's number one hit-making pop group, still, somehow or other, had not managed to become a millionaire.

The Stones, despite selling something like a million singles and albums for Decca, remained victims of an accountancy system which did not pay artists their royalty earnings for anything up to a year. Decca saw no reason to modify this practice, even though the Stones' initial two-year recording contract was due to expire in May 1965, and several other major labels – notably American CBS – had already expressed passionate eagerness to sign them.

The present British tour, though sold out at all its 70 shows, was still resolutely failing to make anyone's fortune. Oldham and Eric Easton were in legal dispute with their co-promoter, the

Australian Robert Stigwood, for allegedly not paying their agreed percentage of the box-office receipts. Keith, in particular, felt so strongly about the £10,000 involved that he confronted Robert Stigwood at a London club and – in the words of journalist Keith Altham – 'started to beat the shit out of him. Every time Stigwood tried to get up, Keith would belt him again. "Keith," I said, "why do you keep *on* hitting him?" "Because he keeps getting up," Keith said.'

The Swinging Summer of 1965 found Andrew Loog Oldham still eager and eagle-eyed for every possible farthing. It was his reason, that August, for going to London's Hilton Hotel to have breakfast with Allen Klein, the famous New York accountant. Klein was Sam Cooke's manager, and also proprietor of the song-publishing company which held copyright on the Rolling Stones' recent big hit, It's All Over Now. Oldham, as usual, hoped to obtain a share of the song's publishing royalties.

At the Hilton – after brief general pleasantries – Allen Klein asked Andrew Loog Oldham a simple but devastating question, 'Andrew,' he said. 'How'd you like to be a millionaire?'

Oldham replied that he would, very much.

'Okay,' Klein said. 'Whaddaya want for now?'

'I want a Rolls-Royce,' Andrew Loog Oldham replied.

'You got it,' said Allen Klein.

It was the summer when British life broke up and rearranged itself in a kaleidoscopic array of seeming brand-newness. Everywhere, there seemed to be new clothes, new trends, new sounds, new looks, new promises for the future. Matters far more important than mere pop music had come to be computed in terms of image. National euphoria reached its highest point in 1965 when almost everyone seemed to have got their image just right.

Harold Wilson had brought the Labour Party back to power after thirteen years in exile, with a slogan borrowed from teenage music (Let's Go With Labour) and promises of national revival, after decadent Toryism, administered by clean, bright, classless young ministers, 'forged in the white heat of the technological revolution'. So stupendously successful had been Harold Wilson's verbal gimmickry that the Conservatives, too, now looked to their image, dismissing the skeletal Scottish laird who had been their last Prime Minister and choosing as leader a middle-class, ex-grammar-school boy whose recreations were not grouse-shooting and port drinking but yachting and playing the church organ. Amazing as it must seem to posterity, Edward Heath was intended to fire the imagination of the young.

The Tories, colouring Heath's shirt a shade darker blue on campaign posters, did not yet realise they were competing with a master. In May 1965, the Queen's Birthday Honours list – drawn up by her Prime Minister – created each of the four Beatles Members of the Most Excellent Order of the British Empire. By that brilliant stroke, Harold Wilson's Socialist government and the bigger and bigger booming youth market became synonymous. Those who had feared Labour's restoration would mean a return to postwar austerity saw with amazement that it meant Op-Art dresses, Carnaby Street boutiques and pop stars skipping into Buckingham Palace like an extra scene from *A Hard Day's Night*.

Throughout that whole deluded summer, Britain could be said to contain only one genuinely and unapologetically wicked element. One stubborn obstacle to Harold Wilson's yeah yeah Utopia reaffirmed its disruptive presence on July 22 at West Ham magistrates' court in a case which was to arouse comment and disgust across the nation.

Mr Charles Keeley, manager of the Francis service station in Romford Road, Stratford, testified that late on the night of March 18, a chauffeur-driven Daimler had pulled on to his garage forecourt and a 'shaggy-haired monster' – identified in court as Bill Wyman – had got out and asked 'in disgusting language' whether he could use the toilet. Mr Keeley – whose whole testimony suggested that before he took up garage work he had been resident in a monastery – replied that the public lavatory was out of order, and refused to allow use of a staff one inside. At this, he said, 'eight or nine youths and girls', including Mick Jagger and Brian Jones, got out of the car and Jagger pushed him aside, saying, 'We piss anywhere, man.' The phrase was taken up by the others in what was described as a 'gentle chant', with one of the party even dancing in time to it. Jagger, Jones and Wyman, it was alleged, then walked across and urinated in a line against the forecourt wall.

Convicted for 'insulting behaviour', they were fined three

pounds each, with fifteen guineas court costs. 'Because you have reached exalted heights in your profession, it does not mean you can behave in this manner,' the chairman of the magistrates said, speaking against female uproar from the public gallery which suggested precisely the opposite.

The story of Charles Keeley's midnight ordeal was splashed in every national newspaper, accompanied by pictures of the five Stones (Keith and Charlie had appeared as character witnesses) emerging from the court in handy juxtaposition to headlines like the *Sunday Express*'s LONG-HAIRED MONSTERS. Buried deep in each spun-out narrative was the significant fact that the prosecution had not been a police matter, but had been brought privately by Mr Keeley and a garage customer, Mr Eric Lavender, 'former chief warden at the Dunning Hall Youth Club'. Both asked to give their addresses to the court in writing for fear of reprisals from Stones fans.

The gift bestowed on Charles Keeley's service station represents, all in all, a rather moderate retaliation to what the Stones themselves had suffered, from garage attendants and many others intent on striking some similar ad hoc blow for common decency. Wherever they stopped, however well-mannered their behaviour, they still faced persecution, in open insults and arbitrary bans from roadside hotels, restaurants and cafes. A scattered few places like the Ram Jam Inn or the Blue Boar Cafe – as their food-spattered walls bore witness – catered specifically for travelling pop groups. Otherwise, the Stones had no choice but to use lorry-drivers' pull-ups and motorway service areas, which brought them into direct contact with a public literally thirsting for their blood.

Loudly insulted from almost every surrounding table in one particular motorway restaurant, they managed to consume a greasy, over-priced breakfast, evincing no reaction whatever. 'When we got up to leave,' Bill Wyman says, 'we went and ordered one fried egg to be served to everyone in the place. All the people who'd been abusing us suddenly got a single fried egg each put in front of them and were told that it was from us. This really British thing took over – everyone started nodding at us and smiling and saying "Oh – thanks very much . . ."'

Police patrol cars were simultaneously waking up to the fact

159

that enormous black limousines with dark-shaded windows did not transport only cabinet ministers and foreign diplomats. From mid-1964, the Stones had to contend with ritual police checks and exuberant prosecution for minor traffic offences, pumped up by gutter-press headlines into yet further evidence of Britain's moral disintegration. When, in late 1964, Mick Jagger was summonsed on three such minuscule charges at Tettenhall, Staffs., his solicitor felt obliged to deliver a long and eloquent plea that the length of Jagger's hair should not count as an additional offence. 'The Duke of Marlborough had hair longer than my client, and he won several famous battles. *His* hair was powdered, I think because of fleas. My client has no fleas . . .'

The Stones' tour of America and Canada, in April and May 1965, brought them up against police methods hurriedly evolved under the joint stimulus of pop and the civil rights movement. At their Ottawa concert, a fifty-strong police cordon stood on the stage with them, literally blotting them from sight. In London, Ontario, the police stopped the show after fifteen minutes by turning on the house lights and cutting off the power to the Stones' amplifiers. 'We felt sorry for the fans, not getting a proper show,' Mick Jagger says, 'so we *did* sort of gang up on the police.' CRUDE AND RUDE ROLLING STONES HURL INSULTS AT POLICE was the next day's banner headline. Hundreds of calls to local radio stations, however, made it clear who the audience blamed for the shambles.

Sometimes, backstage, Keith or Brian would be approached by a mountainous cop with a Rolling Stones album in his hand, and words to the general effect: 'Sign this, ya long-haired sissy pervert, or I'll bust ya goddamned head open.' Other officers made it clear that, though they might regard the Stones as semi-human, they were still prepared to be insulted by a sufficiently large bribe. 'That happened when we first went on the *Ed Sullivan Show*,' Bill Wyman says. 'Hundreds of girls were screaming and yelling outside the theatre. The police came and told us that if we wanted protection, we'd have to pay them off. Every hour, they came back and told us we'd have to give them more money or they'd go away.'

With The Last Time at number eight in the *Billboard* Hot Hundred, there was naturally no more talk of their being banned from the Sullivan show. They made a return appearance on May 2, looking slightly smarter, at their host's earnest insistence, and even agreeing to be cooped up in the studio for eight hours before transmission. This time they appeared twice, playing The Last Time, then coming back for an unprecedented four-song encore. Sullivan afterwards sent them a telegram. 'Received hundreds of calls from parents complaining about you but thousands from teenagers praising you. Best of luck on your tour . . .'

Their other main TV spot was on *Shindig*, a nationally popular music show directed by the British emigré Jack Good. 'Howlin' Wolf had come up from Southern California or somewhere to be with us on *Shindig*,' Keith says. 'I'll always remember Jack Good's voice on the set, very English, calling out, "Er – Howlin', could you do that again?" and "Er, Mr Wolf . . ."'

It also became the target for scandalized attack from the adult Clearwater, Florida – that Keith played over to Mick Jagger a guitar riff which, he thought, might be the basis of a makeweight track for the Stones' next LP. 'I'd woken up in the middle of the night, thought of the riff and put it straight down on a tape. In the morning, I still thought it sounded pretty good. I played it to Mick and said, "The words that go with this are *I can't get no satisfaction*." That was just a working title. It could just as well have been Auntie Millie's Caught Her Left Tit in the Mangle. I thought of it as just a little riff, an album filler. I never thought it was anything like commercial enough to be a single.'

Even after Jagger had gone away and written words developing this basic 'hook', Keith could not be persuaded that he'd hit on an inspirational new Stones A-side. 'I think Keith felt it was too basic . . . just a silly kind of a riff,' Jagger says. 'And he was afraid it would sound like folk rock. Doing Satisfaction was the only real time we ever had a disagreement.'

The song was tried out on tape, first at Chess studios, Chicago, then at RCA, Hollywood, under Dave Hassinger's supervision and in the stimulating atmosphere of having recently escaped being crushed to death together in a limousine. After the Long Beach concert, 10,000 fans surged forward, through security barriers and around the Stones' black Chrysler motorcade. For some minutes they were entombed by bodies and wrenching fingers and faces upside down, silently screaming, until police managed to clear a path ahead.

At RCA, Keith worked on his silly little riff some more, feeding it now through a Gibson fuzzbox that lacquered each note into the malign darkness of ink or ebony. The result, as mixed by Dave Hassinger, struck everyone – save Keith – as the best thing the Stones had ever done in a studio. Keith still argued with Mick that (I Can't Get No) Satisfaction was too weak for an A-side, and that people would recognise his intro as a copy from Martha and the Vandellas' Dancing in the Street.

Proof of this internal dissent was the single's appearance in America in May, three full months before its British release. Within two weeks, it had jumped sixty places in the *Billboard* chart, from 64 to 4. On June 15, (I Can't Get No) Satisfaction became the Stones' first American number one.

It also became the target of scandalised attack from the adult world, unparalleled even in the early days of the anti-Rock 'n' Roll crusade. Up to then, moral outrage against pop music had centred on its alleged suggestiveness – the intimations and innuendoes beyond which no song lyricist dared go and few teenage listeners dared imagine. Here, for the first time, a pop song turned from the vocabulary of calf love to the vocabulary of sex. Since duellists ceased to meet each other on parade grounds at dawn, there had been but one, universally recognized, source of 'satisfaction.'

No song in history, probably, has gained so much notoriety from its title. Few enough people realized then – and few realize now – that (I Can't Get No) Satisfaction was not about sex (or, as many believed, about male masturbation). It was Mick Jagger's reaction against the Stones' American tour life, penned in motel rooms or streaming along endless interstate highways. The non-providers of satisfaction are not promiscuity or playing with oneself, or being unable to piss against garage walls. They are men on TV, advertizing detergent, and voices on car radios, giving out 'useless information', and the general, head-whirling emptiness of 'drivin' round the world – doin' this and signin' that – and tryin' to make some girl' (the song's one overt sexual reference). Satisfaction was a Blues song transferred to the pop idiom: a hymn of hate against a world, not oppressing but pampering; a lament on the empty feeling of having too much, whose cosseted fury

162

every over-indulged Western teenager could instantly recognize.

Not that such a definition occurred to anyone in 1965. What took Satisfaction to the top of the British and American charts was the guitar phrase whose guttural malevolence makes it still the best-known intro in pop, and the voice, rising from artificial coo to infuriated snarl, in which all the perversions the lyric doesn't possess seem to flaunt and fondle themselves.

Bound up with that venomous noise, and the editorial uproar it provoked, there is the black and white image of the Stones performing Satisfaction on the *Ed Sullivan Show,* when Sullivan's censors ordered a bleep to cover the reference to 'tryin' to make some girl'; as if that absurd squibble of sound could purge the sight of Mick Jagger, in his cuddly sweater and Rupert Bear checked trousers, wide-eyed and whispering mayhem.

# 6

# 'Everybody's got something to hide'

In 1964, shortly after the Beatles' conquest of America, Brian Epstein received a visit which caused that elegant, doomed young man considerable amusement. Allen Klein, the New York accountant, took advantage of a trip to London to call on Epstein and offer his client, Sam Cooke, as a possible supporting act on the Beatles' next American tour. It soon became obvious, however, that larger matters were on Mr Klein's mind. Halfway through the meeting, in his hoarse and homely New Jersey accent, he made an outrageous suggestion, which was basically that he, Allen Klein, should manage the Beatles' finances instead of Epstein. Touching his foulard scarf with a too well-manicured hand, Brian Epstein smiled at the preposterous notion.

People about to do business with Allen Klein would often smile in just that tolerantly patronising way. One could easily laugh at the short, squat figure, in shape so much like a tenpin bowling pin, which would stump into executive boardrooms wearing only jeans and sneakers and none-too-clean turtleneck sweater. One could smile at the podgy face, topped by a cowlick of greased hair, jammed down ferociously on a chin that had already published a second edition and seemed to be contemplating a third. One could smile – one was positively encouraged to do so – with the sidelong quirky mouth and the dark brown, button-bright eyes, which, despite their fixed stare, moved from side to side continually as if studying the columns of invisible balance sheets.

Allen Klein's appearance, in short, was as completely at odds with his reputation as is the outward aspect of the bright-eyed, cheerfully striped piranha fish. And indeed, as anyone would testify who has conducted negotiations with Klein or survived one of the plethoric lawsuits with which, routinely, he pursues his heart's desire, a piranha might conceivably have the edge in politeness.

Much about Allen Klein may be explained by an early life of

almost Dickensian hardship and lovelessness. He was born in 1932 in Newark, New Jersey, the son of a neighbourhood kosher butcher. His mother died when he was small and his father, unable to cope with both shop and family, put him and his two sisters into the care of the Hebrew Shelter Orphanage. Allen remained there for ten years, growing up in conditions of austere orthodoxy. Even today, he can recite all the Hebrew prayers by heart and, when described in print as a 'Jewish businessman', will telephone the journalist concerned and inquire with dignity: 'Why do you have to mention what religion I am?'

The many contenders for the title of Allen Klein's worst enemy would not gainsay the solitary virtue he claims for himself – his astonishing capacity for work. It was a virtue instilled in him in early childhood. As an accountancy student at the Lutheran Uppsala College, he completed a four-year course in three years, paying for his own tuition with two simultaneous part-time jobs. In class, he would frequently collapse forward on to his desk with exhaustion. Half-asleep as he was, he could still do a mental arithmetic sum quicker than any other student, rattling off the answer without lifting his head from his arms.

On graduating from Uppsala College, Allen Klein took his first ever holiday, in Miami. There he met a girl named Betty, a student of political science, and there and then decided he must marry her. The proposal was made with typical Klein abruptness. 'When I took her home that first time, I told her I'd never hurt her,' he remembers. 'She started to cry. "Don't tell me you love me . . ." she's saying. "Don't tell me you want to marry me . . ."'

They were married in 1958. Klein's income as a junior in a firm of New York accountants was $182.50 per month. Banished from his father's home by an unsympathetic stepmother, he had lately been reduced to sleeping at seamen's hostels, in genuine danger from a nightly cast of drunks, homosexuals and psychopaths.

His income sank further when, shortly after marrying Betty, he took a one-room office and set up as the newest and hungriest in the swarm of Manhattan's accountants. Despite their poverty, Betty remembered, he would always take cabs to meetings across town. 'To be successful, you gotta *look* successful,' was another of his axioms. 'Who's going to put any trust in a guy who arrives on the subway?'

165

His big break came when he accepted a small retainer to handle the affairs of Buddy Knox, a teenage pop singer who had enjoyed huge success in 1957 with a song named Party Doll. Klein discovered that Buddy Knox's record company, from a mixture of inefficiency and contempt for one so young, had failed to pay over a substantial part of what they owed him in royalties. A more interesting discovery was the worried confusion on the faces of record-company men whom Klein confronted with these discrepancies. The upshot was that Buddy Knox got what he was owed. Klein received $3,000 commission – enough to buy him and Betty their first new car.

To each of his subsequent clients from pop music and show business, Klein's offer was bluntly simple: 'I can find you money you never even knew you had.' He would find it, as for Buddy Knox, trapped and forgotten in ponderously slow accounting systems, or in unpaid performance fees or miscalculated box-office percentages. He would then confront the miscreant company in the role of avenging angel, armed with writs and warrants and, occasionally, real live federal marshals. In a business traditionally fuelled by fuzzy bonhomie, the Klein experience was traumatic. Even record companies which treated their artists well and paid them properly could never feel completely sure that Klein's intervention would not cause pain and embarrassment. 'If a corporation is big, it *has* to make mistakes,' was his dogged maxim. 'There's no corporation in the world that doesn't have something to hide.'

The technique worked with spectacular success in the early Sixties on behalf of Steve Lawrence, Eydie Gorme, Bobby Darin and, most notably, Bobby Vinton, an adolescent crooner whom Klein approached at a mutual friend's wedding with the unnerving inquiry: 'How would you like to make $100,000?'

'What do I have to do?' the startled crooner asked.

'Nuthin',' Klein answered. 'It's what *I* have to do.' Shortly afterwards, a cheque for $100,000 in ferreted-out fees and back royalties was delivered to Bobby Vinton's home.

It was a devastatingly simple way, not only of attracting big clients but also of achieving power over them immeasurably greater than any conventional theatrical agent. 'It's natural . . .' Klein's nephew and ex-employee, Ronnie Schneider, says. 'You hand someone a cheque for $100,000 and you're a hero . . . you work miracles. After that, the guy is going to do anything you tell him.'

Klein's other reputation in the music business was as a contract-buster, peerlessly adept in the extrication of his clients from seemingly ironclad recording agreements in order to sign them to rival companies for large advances. Klein in negotiation could draw on an immense store of disconcerting devices, from cab-driver obscenity to lofty hauteur; from little-boy false naiveté to conspiratorial winks and nudges; from predatory exultation to pained surprise that the world could be so indelicate. Two things sustained him through these marathons of boardroom bluff, bile and bad-mouthing. One was the unshakable belief that he, Allen Klein, was the very fount of all honour and square-dealing rectitude. The other was a readiness to engage in lawsuits that practically amounted to collector's mania. At the peak of Klein's career, his company was involved in some 50 lawsuits, their plaintiffs ranging from the US Internal Revenue Service to Diner's Club.

Klein's ambitions to expand into film production date back to a company with the odd name of Hunger Incorporated and a film entitled *Without Each Other*, whose appearance in the 1962 Cannes Film Festival resulted from a remarkable piece of hype. The film somehow got itself tipped in the American Trade Press as a winner of five awards, despite not having been seen by the voting jury or, for that matter, entered officially in the festival. 'What I did at Cannes,' Klein will frequently chuckle nostalgically. 'That really was *fantastic* . . .'

Unable to make headway as a film mogul, despite a growing hoard of movie corporation stock, Klein devoted himself to a pop music market that had expanded beyond even his expectations. In 1964, he took over the affairs of Sam Cooke, a talented black Soul singer then riding high on the twist craze. Klein negotiated an unheard-of million-dollar advance for Cooke from the RCA label against royalties which, unhappily, would never be earned. In December 1964, Sam Cooke was shot to death in a lonely motel while with a lady other than his wife. It has since been suggested that Cooke was murdered by the crime syndicate which had pre-viously owned him and was unwilling to relinquish him to Klein.

Klein's failure to annexe the Beatles in 1964 he accounted but a momentary setback. He continued to boast that he would have Brian Epstein's treasure, even setting the deadline as Christmas 1965. Meanwhile he applied himself to wooing the Beatles' temporary chart rivals, a group of white-trousered Londoners called the Dave Clark Five. His next conquest was the young South African impresario Mickie Most, who had built up a roster of British pop management. Donovan, a gipsyish, slightly groggy Most's groups, the Animals and Herman's Hermits, the 'British Invasion' was practically in Allen Klein's pocket.

His acquisition of the folk singer Donovan served as a foretaste of Klein's awesome effect on the amateurish and ingenuous world of British pop management. Donovan, a gipsyish, slightly groggy seventeen-year-old, had been discovered playing his guitar on the beach at Westcliff-on-Sea, and successfully launched by two young agents as Britain's 'answer' to Bob Dylan. In 1965, Allen Klein decided he wanted Donovan, and flew to Britain in person. Within days, both of Donovan's managers and his record label, Pye, had lost him forever. 'Did I steal him from Pye? I stole him from Pye,' Klein admits. 'But at that time, he didn't even have a contract with them – or with Hickory in America.'

The British Invasion thus ceased to originate in London but became, as it were, short-circuited back to New York, into a lofty office suite in the Time-Life building, and a chunky thirty-two-year-old who smoked a statesmanlike pipe and quaffed incessant Coca-Cola, and who backed up his prodigious feats of mental arithmetic with portable file-cabinets, hauled incessantly back and forth across the Atlantic; whose hair was dressed with heavy oil, in defiance of all current fashions, and whose favourite casual wear was woollen cardigans with mock leather facings.

The Rolling Stones met Allen Klein just a day or so after he had promised Andrew Loog Oldham a Rolls Royce with darkened windows, exactly like the one owned by John Lennon. 'We all went down with Andrew to the Hilton to meet him,' Keith says. 'In walks this little fat American geezer, smoking a pipe, wearing the most *diabolical* clothes. But we liked him. He made us laugh. And at least he was under fifty.'

Klein, at that one short meeting, managed to activate all the vague dissatisfaction the Stones felt over an income that remained so little commensurate with their success. It was Keith Richard who largely persuaded the others to go along with the deal that Oldham obviously wanted to do with Klein. 'I said we ought to try to turn everything around – to get right out of the cheapo English scene. Klein was big – he had the Animals and Herman's Hermits, who were monster then. I said, "Let's go along with someone who could turn everything round or fuck things up once and for all."'

According to Keith's biographer Barbara Charone, the deal was mostly worked out in the high-priced darkness of Scotch of St James's. At one point, Klein barked across at Andrew Loog Oldham, 'Which one makes the records?' Oldham pointed at Keith and said, 'That one.'

The arrangement was that Klein should act as Andrew Loog Oldham's business manager, leaving Oldham free for creative activities, as he put it. Oldham would retain responsibility for the Stones' recorded output and for the more outrageous of their publicity stunts. Contracts, tour schedules, all the mundane details connected with the millions he promised to reap, would be in the charge of Allen Klein.

The flaw in this strategy was Eric Easton, Oldham's managerial partner, who had largely financed the Stones as a professional act and whose office in Argyll Street, W.1, was their London base and mailing address for their official fan club. Allen Klein had brusquely intimated that Eric Easton had no part in the deal.

Easton was informed, with all the cavalierness available to his twenty-one-year-old partner, that the Stones no longer wanted him, and that Oldham and a new associate were prepared to buy out his contractual interest. Easton's response was to start legal proceedings against Oldham for breach of their original management agreement, and against Klein for bringing about that breach. His first attempt to serve court papers on his young opponent was thwarted – Oldham simply turned and bolted like a rabbit. 'You'll have to accept them sooner or later, you naughty boy . . .' Eric Easton called after him chidingly.

Klein's approach to Oldham had been made with his customary impeccable timing. The Stones' two-year contract with Decca had expired in July 1965 and by mid-August was still not fully renegotiated. The new royalty deal, about to be concluded by Easton and Oldham, would have given the Stones 24 per cent of the wholesale price, or about ten old pence per disc sold. The situation gave scope for a classic Klein move – the 'let me prove myself before I take a cent' ploy. He offered to intervene in the Decca deal before Oldham and the Stones had officially hired him, to show what infinitely better terms he could get for them.

Decca's executives were amazed, at what they presumed to be the final discussion of the new contract with Eric Easton, to behold instead Allen Klein's squat figure leading all five Stones into the conference room. Klein's tactic on that occasion was Olympian hauteur. He flatly refused to discuss anything with anyone but Decca's chairman, Sir Edward Lewis.

The subsequent encounter between Klein and Sir Edward by all accounts presented the distressing spectacle of an elderly English greyhound trying to dislodge a mongrel terrier from its jugular vein. The upshot was that Lewis, in return for keeping the Stones, agreed to part with $1.25 million in advance royalties. The money was to be paid via Decca's US subsidiary into the Stones' collective company, Nanker Phelge Music.

To fill Eric Easton's former role of booking agent for the Stones in Europe Oldham nominated Tito Burns, a former dance-band leader whose organisation was best known for handling the saintly Cliff Richard. Tito Burns, in fact, knew Andrew Loog Oldham in days long before he became a teenage tycoon. 'I'd met him around 1960, when I was on holiday in Juan-les-Pins,' Tito Burns says. 'We always used to go to an English cafe called Butler's Tea Rooms. Andrew used to be a waiter there.'

Tito Burns was in California when he received the call to meet Oldham and Allen Klein in New York. 'I'd first run across Allen a few years earlier when, right out of the blue, he offered me $25,000 for a little music-publishing company I'd started. I could never understand why he'd wanted it so much. He told me it was just to get *any* sort of foothold in the English scene.

'I was in two minds whether to go up to New York and meet him, but eventually I did. As soon as I walked into the room, Allen barked across at me, "Howdya like to be the Rolling Stones' agent?" "Not particularly," I said.'

On August 28, the London *Evening Standard* reported that the

Rolling Stones had a new manager, Allen Klein, and a new agent, Tito Burns. The story added that, under Mr Klein's supervision, the Stones were to make five feature films over a three-year period, mainly financed by their record company, Decca, whose chairman had outbid 'two overseas companies' for the privilege. The first of these films, provisionally entitled *Only Lovers Left Alive*, was said to be already at the scripting stage.

To Fleet Street's pop music writers, the story made perfect sense. The Stones propelled by their new American mentor, clearly were about to follow the Beatles' path from Top Twenty to cinema box-office smash. Scarcely anyone bothered to report Decca's subsequent indignant denial that they had agreed to finance five Rolling Stones films (although rights to a film and sound track album were included in the £1.25 million advance). Nor did anyone notice, as the months passed, that *Only Lovers Left Alive* – which was to have portrayed a devastated world, inhabited only by teenagers – seemed to hover at the scripting stage indefinitely.

The Stones accepted their destiny as film stars as they had accepted their two new protectors: without serious murmur or dissent. Tito Burns they remembered with vague goodwill for having said encouraging things to them after an early Albert Hall concert. 'None of them ever gave me the slightest problem,' Burns says. 'It was all "'Ello, Teat," or "See you later, Teat," or "Sure, Teat, we won't let you down." And I can honestly say they never did. Charlie Watts, of course, used to sit and talk to me for hours about jazz and my days with the big bands.'

Only one feature of the new arrangement slightly puzzled Tito Burns. On the Stones' next European tour he had strict instructions from Allen Klein to receive all concert earnings in person and pay them directly not into the Stones' English bank account but into a company in Delaware, USA.

The first that New York heard of Allen Klein's takeover was a hundred-feet-high Times Square billboard showing David Bailey's album-sleeve portrait of the Stones in a blow-up 60 feet by 40 and bearing an inscription whose author could easily be guessed even before he himself appeared below it, staring up proudly through tinted glasses, along with numerous baffled Broadway citizens.

'The sound, face and mind of today,' ran Andrew Loog

Oldham's message to New York, 'is more relative to the hope of tomorrow and the reality of destruction than the blind who cannot see their children for fear and division. Something that grew and related. Five reflections of today's children. The Rolling Stones.'

Oldham's new partner had insisted that a Stones album be rush-released in America only to absorb all possible benefit from the lingering aftershock of Satisfaction. The Times Square billboard was an Allen Klein device already employed on behalf of the late Sam Cooke. The album, *December's Children*, was much less spectacular: a cobbled-together set of earlier LP tracks and studio out-takes which – as Keith was heard to mutter discontentedly – they would never have dared foist on their British public. With Klein at the helm, it quickly became clear, quality must defer to quantity.

All their Music Press poll awards and Gold and Silver discs had not lessened the pressure to stay ahead of other groups in the ceaseless scramble for the next Top Twenty hit. Their third British album, *Out of Our Heads*, though a vivid enough sample of the Stones' developing fondness for Soul Music (most notably in a version of Sam Cooke's Good Times), contained nothing as strong as Satisfaction. It was thus dismissed as 'samey and boring' by music papers like *Disc* whose lofty teenage pronouncements even Mick Jagger took as gospel. *Disc* insinuated, so it must be true, that the Rolling Stones were starting to slip.

'It's difficult to realize what pressure we were under to keep on turning out hits.' Keith says. 'Each single you made in those days had to be better *and* do better. If the next one didn't do as well as the last one, everyone told you you were sliding out. After Satisfaction, we all thought, "Wow – lucky us. Now for a good rest . . ." and then in comes Andrew Oldham, saying, "Right, where's the next one?" It got to be a state of mind. Every eight weeks, you had to come up with a red-hot song that said it all in two minutes, thirty seconds.'

The new single, Get Off My Cloud, was an upbeat dancer, with chords cribbed unashamedly from Twist and Shout, and a lyric – bawled by Jagger purposely in double time – which must represent the earliest attempt to infiltrate the British Top Ten with marijuana smoke. The vision of sitting 'on the 99th floor . . . imagining the world had stopped' and of a little flying man 'dressed up like a Union Jack' evoked all the apparently hilarious and harmless sensations of 'highs' as they were in 1966. One could write and sing about such things in absolute safety in a time when, to most English people, 'stoned' still meant tipsy; and even the starchy panellists on *Juke Box Jury* could be seen jigging up and down in delighted agreement with Bob Dylan's exhortation, in Rainy Day Woman, that 'everybody must get stoned . . .'

Allen Klein's influence was powerfully evident throughout the American tour that began on October 29 with the now customary warm-up shows in Canada. That same week, Klein's office announced an expected gross of $1.5 million, the largest box-office sum in pop touring history. Only the Beatles, in 1964, had touched a million dollars (and in the process caused such alarm to the US Internal Revenue that much of the money remained frozen in a protracted wrangle over the Anglo-American tax treaty).

Klein himself was present at most of the tour dates, dressed in a button-up cardigan with leather facings that caused Andrew Loog Oldham much feline amusement behind his chubby back. In Klein's absence, tour business was administered by his nephew, Ronnie Schneider, a young accountant whom all the Stones liked for his volatile humour and squeaky, excitable voice. Obedient to Uncle Allen's instructions, Ronnie Schneider received each night's box-office percentage in person and put it for safe-keeping under his bed.

Also present on the tour was Klein's personal promotion man, Pete Bennett – an individual whose immaculately Mafia-like aspect undoubtedly played a part in his legendary powers of persuasion over radio disc jockeys and producers. It was Pete Bennett who had implanted Get Off My Cloud in the American Top Ten within a fortnight of its release. That much could already be said for Allen Klein's management. There was also the benefit – most keenly enjoyed by Andrew Loog Oldham – of being escorted in public by a gigantic, Sicilian-looking man in a black sharkskin suit who would, from time to time, reflectively pat what seemed to be a bulge under his left armpit.

The English photographer Gered Mankowitz – whose play-wright father had written Oldham's seminal fantasy, *Expresso Bongo* – travelled across America with the tour, adding to an

173

excellent portfolio that had begun with the sleeve photograph for *Out of Your Heads*. Mankowitz shared a hotel room with Pete Bennett, whom he remembers sitting on the toilet with the door wide open, in old-fashioned sock suspenders, describing what trouble he had getting shoes hand-made for his oddly paddle-shaped feet.

'A lot of that tour was quite depressing,' Gered Mankowitz says. 'Mick was very down – he seemed to be missing Chrissie Shrimpton a lot. Charlie Watts missed his wife, Shirley. He'd be on the phone to her in Sussex every night, and hang up practically in tears.'

During their stay in New York, girls constantly invaded their hotel, the Sheraton City Square, bribing bellboys and floor waiters for access by giving 'head' in stairwells and service elevators. Shortly after the hotel management insisted that the Stones transfer to the Sheraton Lincoln Square, New York was plunged into a total blackout. At the height of this, Bob Dylan arrived to pay Brian Jones a visit, accompanied by members of the 'electric' band with which he had lately outraged his pure folk fans. Brian, Dylan and his guitarist Robbie Robertson drank, smoked and played together by candlelight, until someone knocked a candle over and set fire to one of the beds.

'Brian saw a lot of Dylan in New York,' Gered Mankowitz says. 'Where the other Stones were concerned, he seemed to be getting more and more remote. I remember a terrible scene with Brian one day when we'd all stopped on the road to eat. Brian said he wasn't hungry, and just sat in the car. When everyone else came out of the restaurant, Brian decided he *was* hungry and marched inside by himself. "Come on, Brian," the others were saying. "We're running late. We've got to go." Brian just sat there, taking no notice.

'Finally, someone – I think it was that huge guy, Pete Bennett – just picked him up by the scruff of the neck and the seat of his pants, carried him out to the car and dumped him in.'

Outwardly, at least, Brian continued to personify what gave the Stones their dangerous, irrepressible glamour. Brian had been first to adopt the new London fashion of frock coats, flowing scarves and floppy-brimmed hats such as were previously seen on the heads of Society women at Ascot. Cameras zoomed in avidly on this exotic figure, like a character in a Grimms' fairy tale, who seemed bent on extending the Stones' decadence to actual transvestism, with his wild white fedora and pressed-down gold fringe, his capes and furs, striped trews and high-stacked alligator boots. Brian made news again in Los Angeles when he appeared in public with a stunningly long-legged girl of exactly matching blondeness, just arrived from London to join him. Her name, the press discovered, was Anita Pallenberg: she was a German film actress and fashion model. According to some reports, Brian had already announced their engagement.

America's revulsion, although it remained strong in the faces of individual policemen, had been somewhat moderated on a civic level by respect for the Stones' dollar-earning power. Denver, Colorado, thus commemorated their coming with an official 'Rolling Stones Day'. Even Boston, that sepulchre of East Coast conservatism, was moved to present them with the Freedom of the City.

These blandishments did nothing to soften the truculence with which the Stones continued to delight their American audiences. In America, even more than Britain, they had become the perfect antidote to the Beatles' impish good manners. 'The Beatles want to hold your hand,' wrote Tom Wolfe in a famous epigram, 'but the Stones want to burn your town.' Though Wolfe had swallowed not one but two PR myths, his judgment confirmed the Stones' appeal to an audience for whom pop music was very far from a question of simply having fun. This second 1965 tour took place against a background of increasing turbulence throughout America's formerly peaceful schools and university campuses, and increasing student protest against the now palpable horrors of America's 'limited war' in Vietnam. It was a revolt fuelled by pop music – by the bitter, tongue-twisting polemics of Bob Dylan, the sweet-voiced reproaches of Joan Baez. To the American establishment, long hair, Mod clothes and guitars ceased to be merely absurd and became quite possibly, subversive. Nor could there be any doubt who the ringleaders were. Find an anti-war demonstration, a march or sit-in, and you would find a Rolling Stones song somewhere near. The fact that the Stones themselves, through Mick Jagger's cautious tongue, abstained from all political comment, could hardly be accounted

175

relevant. Their music was the missile: with every play of Satisfaction or Get Off My Cloud, another life of steady dates, early nights, short hair and fraternity meetings, went up in flames.

The final concert, before an audience of 14,000 at Los Angeles Sports Arena, went ahead despite real fears that only four Stones might be available to take the stage. On December 4, onstage at Sacramento, Keith had idly touched a live microphone with his metal-inlaid guitar neck and received an electric shock which left him unconscious for seven minutes.

Later that night in Los Angeles, Keith and Brian underwent further initiation from the new species of Rolling Stones fans, attending the second 'Acid Test' party given by the Acid writer Ken Kesey and his followers, 'The Merry Pranksters'. Keith and Brian both passed the test required, which was to sample a man-made drug so new it had not yet been declared illegal: lysergic acid diethylamide, known for short as LSD.

In the fifteenth century, the Pallenbergs were Swedish, a wealthy clan whose most notable member was painted by Holbein, seated among bags of gold. Anita's great-great-grandfather, Arnold Böcklin, a German Swiss, emigrated to Florence to become a painter renowned in the nineteenth-century neoclassical school. Her grandfather and father were painters also, based in Rome but with family and social contacts in Germany, Spain and France. Anita and her sister grew up fluent in four languages and accustomed to the company of painters, writers and musicians.

As a teenager, she studied picture restoration, medicine and graphic design. In 1963, aged 21, she went from Rome to New York by boat, travelling with her boyfriend, an Italian photographer named Mario Schifano. She had meant to continue studying art, and spent some time in Jasper Johns's studio, observing the great man and washing his paintbrushes. She also helped Schifano and other fashion photographers by standing in for models who were late or indisposed. Pictures began to appear in top fashion magazines of the girl with the cropped hair, the lean thoroughbred body and the snub-nosed, unsettling smile.

By 1965, Anita Pallenberg was accepting magazine assignments in all the major European capitals and had appeared in several films made by the young West German director Volker Schlöndorff. Her main social sphere, however, continued to be the art world. In London, she knew Robert Fraser and, through Fraser, met the antique dealer Christopher Gibbs. 'Anita in those days was absolutely electrifying,' Gibbs says. 'Whenever she came into a room, every head would turn to look at her. There was something kittenish about her, a sense of mischief – of naughtiness. When I talked to her, I discovered she was highly intelligent and extremely well read. She'd read obscure German Romantic novelists like Hoffmann as well as all the usual Hermann Hessery.'

In September 1965, Anita had gone to West Germany on a fashion job. She was in Munich on the night of a Rolling Stones concert and, on an impulse, decided to try to meet them. After the show, she persuaded a Swedish photographer to smuggle her backstage. 'That's how I met Brian. He was the only one of the Stones who really bothered to talk to me. He could even speak a little German. There had been some kind of disagreement within the Stones, Brian against the others, and he was crying.

'He said, "Come and spend the night with me! I don't want to be alone." So I went with him. Almost that whole night he spent crying. Whatever had happened with the other Stones had absolutely devastated him.'

She saw Brian again in Paris, when the Stones played the Olympia, and in London on her fashion-modelling trips. Their one-night stand in Munich became a love affair, even though Brian then had a steady girlfriend – a French model named Zou Zou – and Anita was constantly on the move around Europe. 'I fell in love with Brian – in love all the way. He was a great guy, you know. Talented, funny and with that instant quality of "Let's do it. Let's try anything."'

In those early days, she was conscious that the other Stones regarded her with suspicion. 'You could see them exchanging looks like "Who is this weird bird?" Mick, especially, was very hostile. But he could never make me feel uncomfortable. Even today, I can squash him with just one word. But he was the one most against my seeing Brian and being around the Stones. He told Chrissie Shrimpton she wasn't to have anything to do with me.'

Brian returned from Los Angeles apparently on top of the world, carrying an antique mountain dulcimer and an immense lump of 'California Gold' hashish presented to him by an American well-wisher. Anita had gone back to Munich on a modelling job, but was to rejoin him in a few weeks and live with him at his new mews house, behind the ABC Cinema, Fulham Road.

Even in Brian's absence, this house tended to be somewhat crowded. The spare bedroom was occupied by a young Scots film student named Dave Thomson, whom Brian had befriended the previous year in Glasgow. Frequently, too, there would be visits by Brian's French model girlfriend, Zou Zou. When Anita passed through London en route to join the Stones in Los Angeles, Brian had arranged with Thomson that she should stay for a few days while applying for a British work permit. Shortly before Anita's arrival, Zou Zou had flown in unexpectedly from Paris, intending to use Brian's room as usual. Dave Thomson had managed to get rid of her in the nick of time.

A few days after the Stones' return, Thomson was astonished to find himself taken on one side by the normally taciturn Charlie Watts. According to Charlie, Brian had been so full of pills and drink in America that he'd missed playing on several studio sessions, including the one for Satisfaction. In Chicago he had been admitted to hospital – where only Charlie and Bill Wyman had troubled to visit him. An American doctor had afterwards told Charlie that if Brian continued to drink at his present rate, he could kill himself within a year.

Even before the tour, as Dave Thomson well knew, Brian would routinely drink two bottles of whisky a day, and swallow handfuls of pills, mostly the 'uppers' that were indispensable to any pop star's all-night life. A doctor he used was among London's most bountiful providers of drugs on prescription, the model for the Beatles' in-joking song Doctor Robert. 'And there was hash and grass,' Thomson says, 'just lying on tables all over the house.'

Dave Thomson's regard for Brian was something exceptional in the Stones' retinue of hangers-on and 'gofers'. And he had good reason to believe that Brian's insecurity came from definite, as well as wildly indefinite, sources. He remembers, after their first meeting in Glasgow, going back to see Brian at the Central Hotel, and finding him listening at the door of a room where Andrew Loog Oldham and the other Stones were talking. 'They're all in there,' Brian had whispered. 'They're trying to get rid of me.'

'I thought he was just being paranoid,' Dave Thomson says. 'Then, one time, I got a lift down to London in a car with Andrew, Mick and Keith. All the way down, Andrew was talking about how they could sack Brian from the Stones, and making catty remarks about him.'

Thomson was also privy to Brian's frequent, and futile, attempts at writing the original songs which, he believed, would give him back equality in the Stones with Mick and Keith. The knack eluded Brian, even when Oldham tried shock therapy on him as with the other two, locking him in a hotel room with Gene Pitney and a piano. All Brian's musical intuition, his natural command of half a dozen instruments, could not conjure up the requisite facile pattern of chords and rhymes. Under Dave Thomson's influence he began to think, instead, about composing for films. The two were now collaborating on a surrealist scenario, to be shot in Scandinavia and the French Camargue.

Brian and the Stones power axis were not entirely estranged. There would still be times when, for inscrutable reasons, Keith would go off Mick and swing back to his old partner in bedsitter guitar duets. Keith still had no steady girlfriend or settled home, and would stay for lengthy periods in Brian's spare room relegating Dave Thomson to the living-room couch. Thomson remembers that Keith was there, and at his most mischievous, during a surprise visit by Brian's ex-girl-friend Linda Lawrence, infuriated by his involvement with Zou Zou and his failure to provide for his third son, the second Julian.

'Linda suddenly marched past me into the house. Brian was upstairs, hissing, "Get rid of her, man!" Keith just thought the whole thing was a laugh. He kept teasing Brian about how ugly the kid was and what a big head it had.'

If Brian could remain indifferent to his three illegitimate offspring, he was nonetheless haunted by terror that their existence might be discovered and exposed in some newspaper like the *News of the World*. 'Brian really wasn't that much worse than other people in the music business,' Dave Thomson says. 'All the groups had the same attitude to the girls who ran after them. They were just pieces of meat.

'Brian was always terrified that the girls he went with on the

179

tours might be under age. After every tour, he used to worry about being hit by paternity suits. Remember, there was no Pill in those days. The girls just used to tell the guys to pull out at the last moment. I remember Brian telling me how he'd come all over some girl's hair.'

At times, there seemed to be something else gnawing at Brian – an anxiety deeper even than what was happening to him in the Stones. At the Fulham mews house, for several months, he would not go out of doors until after dark. A ring of the telephone late at night would make him deeply agitated. 'I remember once,' Thomson says, 'when Bob Dylan rang through from the States at about three in the morning. Brian wouldn't believe it was Dylan until Albert Grossman [Dylan's then manager] came on the line to say it was.

'Brian once said to me, "They're out to get me, Dave – someone in America and someone over here. I don't know who they are, but they're out to get me."'

With Anita Pallenberg's arrival in London to be his live-in girl-friend, Brian seemed to recover his old, arrogant spirits. 'He took me with him to meet her at Heathrow,' Dave Thomson says. 'We drove out there in the Rolls-Royce Silver Cloud Brian had just bought from George Harrison. The idea was that we'd go straight on down to see his parents in Cheltenham, to show them the car. Brian had to prove to his father that there *was* a future in being a musician. I got the impression that he still desperately wanted his family's good opinion.'

As Brian led Anita from the Heathrow arrivals building, an airport photographer stepped forward. That picture, of the gold-haired, wide-eyed pop star and his stunning new possession in her fun fur coat, flowered miniskirt and long, suede-booted legs, nestling submissively against him, would seem to be the very essence of a young man's blessed good luck. 'We didn't drive down to Cheltenham after all,' Dave Thomson says. 'We drove straight back to the mews, so that Brian and Anita could go to bed.'

Brian's transformation continued in the weeks that followed. The morose outsider whom Dave Thomson had seen slumped in an armchair, playing endless Nina Simone albums, now sat demurely upstairs before a multifaceted mirror while Anita tinted his hair to a pallor indistinguishable from hers. To her, as to some sympathetic nurse, he confessed his many neuroses about the way he looked. Did it matter that his legs were so short? Could one see the caps he had on his teeth?

Anita meant more than beauty to Brian: she meant restoration of power. She was an instant boost to his sagging morale within the Stones. For not even Mick Jagger could show off a 'bird' like this. Brian had seen Mick's unease in Anita's company; his wariness of her ability to deflate him with a single sultry look or offhand phrase. Mick might not like Anita, but he could not help but be impressed with her standing with people like Robert Fraser and Christopher Gibbs, and Tara Browne, the young heir to the Guinness millions, and almost everyone on that high social level where he himself still felt so very far from comfortable.

Formerly, Brian's closest friends had been musicians, like Spencer Davis, Pete Townshend and George Harrison. Now, with Anita, he, too, was swept into the world of art galleries and dinner parties in tapestried Chelsea rooms. Anita found most pop musicians boring and their wives crushed almost into inaudibility by northern male chauvinism. 'When John Lennon used to come to the house, he'd bring his wife, Cynthia. As soon as they arrived, Cyn would go upstairs, lock herself in the bog and not come out for the rest of the evening.'

As well as a stunningly beautiful girl, Brian had found an accomplice whose penchant for mischief was more than a match for his own. Ronnie Schneider remembers what havoc the two of them caused in California when the Stones were having a day out at the beach, and everyone hired miniature power boats. 'Anita in that power boat was *deadly* – she'd ram anyone into splinters. After a while, Brian turned his boat around and just headed out to sea. The lifeguards were ringing bells – the Coast Guard was about to be alerted. Brian just kept on going and going.

'I said to him later, "Why did you *do* that, Brian?" He just grinned and said, "I was following the seagulls."'

As one unwilling eavesdropper can testify, Anita's was the dominant role in the sex sessions that could last for days at a time. Dave Thomson, still occupying Brian's spare room, heard noises which suggested Anita was initiating him into the more arcane

181

sexual pleasures. 'I actually saw her one night going into their room with a bloody great whip. I could hear her whipping Brian.'

Brian, for his part, had one deviant taste which surprised even Anita. He enjoyed setting fire to Dinky model cars and toy trains. The train-spotting craze of his boyhood was perpetuated by an elaborate miniature track layout, with which he would cover the entire living-room floor. Anita would photograph him as he crawled around, dousing miniature locomotives in lighter fluid and setting fire to them.

Anita was the instigator of a more exotic masquerade. When *Stern*, the West German magazine, wanted to feature Brian on its cover, Anita persuaded him to be photographed in Nazi SS uniform, grinding a doll beneath one jack-booted heel. *Stern* rejected the cover and a furore broke out in the British press which Brian could not much appease by claiming he had meant to make an 'anti-Nazi protest'. 'It was all my idea,' Anita says. 'It *was* naughty, but what the hell . . . He looked *good* in SS uniform.'

Anita evidently brought out in Brian the latent femininity he had suppressed in relentless sexual buccaneering and his almost wilful fathering of children. 'There was a legend that he broke out once, and jumped into bed with Mick. And one night, he got me to do him up in drag. You remember Françoise Hardy, the French singer? Brian said, "Can you do me up like Françoise Hardy?" So I gave him the full thing with makeup, clothes, a wig . . .'

Anita would still go away on fashion jobs in France or Germany, arousing Brian to transports of jealousy – either devastated tears, such as he had wept to her in Munich, or the sudden peevish rage that could seize him. Like other girls before her, Anita suffered physical attacks, with his fists or any weapon that came to hand. 'He would pick up anything – a tray of sandwiches, a whole table – and just throw it.' When Anita accepted a film part with Volker Schlöndorff, Brian grabbed the script from her and tore it to shreds. She calmed him that time by suggesting he should compose the film's musical score.

To this inherent emotional instability was now added the effect of the LSD which Brian had regularly 'dropped' since his initiation in late 1965. The drug was already known to have a Russian-roulette quality, offering the entirely unpredictable alternatives of a 'good trip', when the world could summer like crystal, or a 'bad trip', containing all the horrors of purgatory. For Brian – as some snapshots taken in a Soho basement show – a good trip meant grinning and cavorting like a little blond leprechaun. A bad trip brought hallucinations which left him crumpled up and whimpering with fear. 'He'd see monsters,' Anita Pallenberg says. '"Can't you see them?" he'd ask me. "They're all coming out of the wardrobe! They're horrible!"' At the album session, he refused to go into the studio where the other Stones were waiting. In his dazzled,horrified mind, the whole place was swarming with black beetles.

# 7

# 'It's down to me; the change has come . . .'

The place is a busy roundabout in West London, opposite that Sixties landmark, the Cherry Blossom boot polish factory. A black Rolls-Royce detaches itself from the traffic and sweeps to a stop on the forecourt of the Talgarth service station. Half a dozen pairs of eyes idly settle on the figure that alights from it and walks, with tentative, tripping steps towards the air-supply pump. '. . . Mick Jagger, isn't it?' someone whispers. His companions stare incredulously at the meagre body, festooned with fashionable scarves and bangles like a hurriedly dressed doll; at the mounds of hair combed down around cautious eyes and drawn-in lips; at the spindly legs on too-high boot heels, almost stumbling. Can it be only *this* which threatens their daughters, girl-friends and young wives? The notion is so confusing that Jagger is not molested, shouted at or even overtly recognized. The moment passes in embarrassed conspiracy not to see or be seen.

Not since Ancient Greece had gods formed so visible and numerous a class as in Britain in 1966 under the pullulating Olympus of the pop music industry. And, as in those mythical times, the gods came in every shape and size. There were tall ones, fat ones and skinny ones. There were some with fresh faces, and others afflicted with scrofulous acne. There were even those in the mop-top multitude with thinning hair or clumsily positioned toupees. There were those who received the rites of worship accorded all under 25, despite having the raddled and debauched appearance of middle-aged child molesters.

Fan adoration made allowance for these varieties, oddities and mutations. Behind the screams lay remembrance that the hitmakers of the moment were, after all, only quartets of lads from Liverpool, Manchester, Birmingham or Stoke Poges. Screams were emitted as much on principle as anything: they stopped as suddenly as they began, leaving only drenched mascara behind.

Doctors and psychologists who analysed them – usually for a fat fee in a Sunday tabloid newspaper – were unanimous in pronouncing them fundamentally harmless.

The only point concerning Mick Jagger's influence over 'young people' that doctors and psychologists agreed on was that it wasn't, under any circumstances, fundamentally harmless. Elvis Presley at his most scandalous had not exerted a power so wholly and disturbingly physical. Presley, while he made girls scream, did not have Jagger's ability to make men feel uncomfortable. The effect was more akin to a male ballet dancer with his conflicting and colliding sexuality: the swan's neck and smeared harlot eyes allied to an overstuffed and straining cod-piece. Small wonder that lorry drivers at the Talgarth service station, that day in 1966, stared uncomfortably off towards the boot polish factory.

*Combo*, the male pop fan magazine, expressed the prevailing confusion as early as 1964 with a story 'categorically denying' rumours that Mick Jagger was about to go to Sweden and have a sex-change operation.

That conundrum continued throughout the personality which Jagger offered to his public. On the one hand, there was the loutishness, assiduously cultivated: the Christian name cut down to its curt proletarian root; the surname, so befitting jagged doings, derived – or so he liked to claim – from an old English word for 'knifer' or footpad. On the other hand were the teasing intimations of sensitivity, intelligence, even intellect; the sense that, even as he climbed the hit parade, Mick Jagger was also steadily scaling the ladder of Society.

No one better illustrated how the ancient redoubts of the British class system had dissolved under pressure both from without and within. The 'trendy' magazines, *Nova*, *Queen* and *London Life*, teemed with stories about youthful peers and baronets, prised from a stately heritage, democratized in Carnaby Street and launched into the King's Road as hustling impresarios, gentlemen's outfitters or restaurateurs. Just at potent were the tales of working-class boys, propelled upward by fashion or photography to mingle, unabashed, with the international jet set. The word of the moment was 'classless', applied without discrimination to the clothes and hairdos and, above all, the curious, teeth-clenching accents common to those whom hopes of cashing in on the seemingly endless youth boom had moved upwards or downwards. Classlessness was simply degrees of affectation and, as such, produced snobbery more rigid and hierarchical than any it claimed to replace. Mick Jagger, alternately slurring Cockney and lispingly public school – with both incarnations clearly directed as social betterment – was classlessness apotheosized.

Jagger's face seemed to express the sensation, common to so many, of finding oneself young, beautiful and rich in an era increasingly inclined to worship youth, beauty and spending power. What made his expression so piquant was that it responded to such idolatry, not acquiescently, as young gods and Beatles should, but with indifference, even hostility – a smouldering ill-will which silk clothes, fine food, wine, women and every conceivable physical pampering somehow aggravated. The real pleasure of being Mick Jagger, one felt, was in having everything but being tempted by nothing: a drained and languorous, exquisitely photogenic ennui.

It was an attitude richly conveyed by the Stones' new single, 19th Nervous Breakdown. The song was a lampoon of upper-class girls at upper-class parties – 'dismal, dull affairs' – and, by implication, their foolish efforts to insinuate themselves into the queue trying to catch Mick Jagger's eye. 'It seems to me that you have seen too much in too few years,' he sang, doubtless with the same mock psychoanalysis he used in real life to deflate some luckless, pushy deb.

Glimpses of the other Jagger, sensitive, poetic and vulnerable, were positioned among the Stones' recorded output with tripwire delicacy. The B-side of 19th Nervous Breakdown was As Tears Go By, the song originally written for Marianne Faithfull, now scored for strings – in obvious imitation of Paul McCartney's Yesterday – and wimped by Jagger with all the pathos of Tiny Tim in his chimney corner. Choirboy innocence featured also on Lady Jane, a mini-madrigal written by Jagger for the Stones' next album, even though the title had been inspired by *Lady Chatterley's Lover* (it was Mellors's word for Connie's vagina) and the chorister in question seems to be addressing various members of an Elizabethan seraglio.

The fourth Rolling Stones album, *Aftermath* – released in April 1966 – confirmed Jagger's new individual eminence while apparently preserving the Stones' interior democracy. The difference was that all fourteen tracks were Jagger-Richards songs, with lyrics written almost entirely by Jagger. Even Andrew Loog Oldham's presence was diminished, owing to sudden spirit on Decca Records' part. Decca had refused to accept the album's original title, *Could You Walk on the Water?*, and the accompanying sleeve photograph of the Stones immersed up to their necks in an urban reservoir. Oldham's customary sleeve-note extravaganza was dropped also, in favour of straightforward commentary by Dave Hassinger, the RCA studio engineer. Oldham's credits were limited to 'producer' and, under his old alias 'Sandy Beach', designer of a substitute cover, tinted sickly sherbet pink.

On *Aftermath*, Jagger's shifting poses of scornful misogyny and little-boy winsomeness mingled with virtuoso playing by Brian Jones on a range of instruments seldom seen before in a pop record studio. The opening track, Mother's Little Helper – mockery of a pill-addicted housewife – featured Brian on Indian sitar, an instrument also adopted by George Harrison, but played here with a feel for its strange, hot, jangling dissonance that Harrison could not bring to the Beatles' Norwegian Wood. On two tracks, Lady Jane and Waiting, Brian played dulcimer, a tiny stringed instrument, half-mandolin, half-harp, given to him by the American folk singer Richard Farina. On two more, Out of Time and Under My Thumb, he played marimba, the African xylophone.

Brian's intros and solos and inter-verse embroidery gave *Aftermath* a visual quality that no Stones album would ever quite recapture. Through Brian, Jagger's songs of callow male triumph took on the chameleon colours of 'Swinging London' six months in advance of the Beatles' *Revolver*. Most evocative of all was – and still is – Under My Thumb, with its marimba notes circling downward to a strange pot-pourri of electric keyboard, asymmetric drum brushes and offkey guitar. One can almost see the King's Road, the white Courrèges boots, the bistros and bric-à-brac.

Under My Thumb, with its crowing victory over a recalcitrant female ego, was not a song likely to gladden the heart of Chrissie Shrimpton. Still less, Out of Time, insistently taunting, 'You're obsolete, my baby. My poor old-fashioned baby . . .' Now that

187

Mick was so famous and fashionable, he felt he should be seen with a girl more famous and fashionable than Jean Shrimpton's younger sister. Jagger the pop star wanted no part now of the commitment which Jagger the less cautious LSE student had made eighteen months before, and which Chrissie regarded as still binding. Even in its happiest phase, their relationship had been stormy. Now the battles went on continually, often before an audience uncomfortably aware, as she was not, that Chrissie Shrimpton's time was running out.

Their lives were intertwined in a way that Jagger still shrank from trying to unravel. They had lived together for almost a year, first in a cramped basement in Bryanston Mews, subsequently in Jagger's much smarter £50 per week flat at Harley House, a Marylebone Road mansion block. Chrissie had even left her secretarial job at Decca to work for Andrew Loog Oldham. As Mick Jagger's girl-friend, she was herself something of a personality. *Mod*, the latest American fan magazine, ran a regular column by Chrissie, 'From London With Luv', describing the Stones-Beatles social circle in terms of cosy domesticity. 'Mick and I went down to visit George and Pattie Harrison last week . . . We sat in John's private cinema, had hot chocolate and watched a film called *Citizen Kane* . . . I think Stevie Winwood is the best singer we have. (Ouch! Mick has just hit me.) . . . Recently I had my 21st birthday. Mick gave me a huge rocking horse which I named Petunia . . .'

A picture spread of Jagger in another American teen mag tells a somewhat different story. We see Jagger variously seated before a gilded Victorian mirror, lounging against a G-Plan shelf unit (on which a claret bottle basket is deliberately visible) and at breakfast, surrounded by 'outsize cups of Cantonese design'. The scene is worthy of one of those Edwardian young men about town whose only domestic companion would be a discreetly gliding gentleman's gentleman.

The monocled young rakes who would leave their Mayfair eyries to sport in the mire of Soho or Seven Dials had not enjoyed female flesh in as much quantity, and with such small regard, as this pale London lordling in his Harley House 'pad'. The fastidious sneer to be seen on Jagger's face in almost any female company hinted at how easily sex presented itself to him, and how little he esteemed the girls who offered their bodies, in any position, for however brief a proprietorial grip on his arm. It was part of his peculiar appeal, that aura of sexual surfeit so intense as to produce a kind of exhausted virginity.

On tour, Chrissie could not help but guess, Mick was as active as any of the Stones in the plethoric screwing that filled out time between one concert and the next. Their latter American tours had witnessed the advent of the 'groupie': a type of girl who would tenaciously follow this or that English group, intent on bedding one of them, or all of them (or, in some spectacular cases, all simultaneously). Brian Jones told the story of going into another group's hotel suite to find its four members occupied with a single groupie. 'Come on, Brian,' one of them had shouted. 'There's room for you as well . . .'

Mick hid such things from Chrissie as he hid them from the world – behind the impenetrable mask of his 'cool'. Journalists who interviewed him noticed his growing adeptness at side-stepping questions, or else answering them with an open-faced candour which only later revealed itself as the vehicle for no information whatever. This convenient amnesia blanketed his home and school background and all specifics of his time at LSE. As far as the world could gather, Mick Jagger had been born and bred a star and, under the closest scrutiny, remained just as bright, remote and featureless.

The mask could slip – as when, in a fit of rage against Sir Edward Lewis, he called the Decca chairman 'a fuckin' old idiot'; or when, on the Stones' 1965 European tour, he outraged the West German press by goose-stepping around the stage in time to Satisfaction. There were also the moments when his cautious and self-conscious nature gave way to something altogether different, feline and outrageous – in the recently revived stage word, 'camp'. He had once let himself be photographed in a BBC make-up department, sitting under the dryer with his hair in a net like some middle-aged housewife. When the Stones took over a whole edition of *Ready, Steady, Go* as hosts, Mick appeared with Andrew Loog Oldham, miming to Sonny and Cher's I Got You Babe, exchanging fond smiles and stroking one another's hair.

His closest friend outside the Stones was David Bailey, the young East End photographer, now almost as famous – and outrageous – as a pop star. When Bailey shocked Britain by getting married in a pullover, Mick Jagger was his equally untailcoated best man. Bailey's photographs in American *Vogue* had long since taken him to the heart of the, rather older, New York in-crowd ruled by Andy Warhol and Baby Jane Holzer. The Stones played for Baby Jane's birthday party at the New York Academy of Music, prompting Tom Wolfe to an early effusion of New Journalism on the subject of Jagger's mouth ('labial', 'concupiscent', 'giblet-red', etc.). Warhol remembers the style Jagger could get with ordinary cheap Carnaby clothes, 'putting together pants and jackets that no one else would think of doing.'

There was another side to Jagger's cautious nature, seen only by those select few friends he would agree to meet in pubs and restaurants. He hated, in almost any circumstances, to part with money. His extreme thrift was all the more noticeable in a milieu where wild spending, on clothes and cars and country estates, was part of the glamour passed on to fans. 'The Mojos shared out £100 to go shopping,' ran a typical fan mag piece, ' – and that's not peanuts!' Mick Jagger's income already equalled all the Mojos' combined, yet he remained studentishly frugal, offering a sort of quasi-Marxist indifference to money as his alibi for always letting others pick up the tab. Apart from Paul McCartney, he was the only frugal star visible on the entire pop scene. Even in this outwardly affluent post-Klein period, when all the Stones were following Beatle precedent and investing in country houses, Mick remained primarily the sort of person who would call round at David Bailey's studio and ask if he could sleep on the couch.

Charlie Watts had already bought a sixteenth-century house in Sussex, originally designed as a hunting lodge for the first Archbishop of Canterbury, and latterly occupied by a one-time Attorney General, Lord Shawcross. (Establishment figures, though they might officially deplore the Stones, never objected to selling them houses.) It proved the perfect hideaway for Charlie's deeply private marriage to Shirley Ann Shepherd; for her sculpture studio and horses and his collections of silver, jazz records, model soldiers and American Civil War memorabilia. His father, the former parcel deliveryman, approved of the property, though Mrs Watts wished he could have chosen something 'a bit more modern'.

Keith decided next, showing what a vein of English romanticism lay under his gipsy exterior by choosing 'Redlands', a fifteenth-century moated cottage in the Sussex village of West Wittering. A fan magazine journalist, paying the first of several unexpected visits to the property, found the front door wide open, all five half-timbered bedrooms still unfurnished, the kitchen a sea of dirty dishes and a burnt sausage in the frying pan.

Mick, however, stayed on at the same London mansion flat, half living with the same unsatisfactory girl-friend. Brian Jones's affair with Anita Pallenberg had increased his discontent with Chrissie. Anita was exactly the kind of 'classy bird' he had picked out for himself a hundred times from glossy magazines and films. And Anita, though she affected to despise him, seems to have given him more than one lingering glance, over Brian's golden head. 'I always got the feeling with Anita that Mick was the one she *really* wanted,' Dave Thomson says. 'I felt she was working her way through the Stones to get to Mick.'

There was, of course, another girl in the Stones' circle who more than measured up to Mick's ideals of beauty and class. She had always seemed out of his reach and, with her marriage, seemed now more so than ever. Just the same, through that hot, hectic summer of 1966, as the rows with Chrissie increased in violence, and as he couldn't get a date with his first choice, Julie Christie, Mick Jagger began to see more – and think more and more – of Marianne Faithfull.

Swinging London had reached Cambridge University early in 1965, when assorted Fleet Street journalists laid siege to Churchill College, waiting until its most envied undergraduate, John Dunbar, should attempt to enter or leave the Fine Arts faculty. After several days on the run, Dunbar wearily threw up his hands and gave the story to the *Cambridge Daily News*'s Paul Buttle. MARIANNE FAITHFULL WEDS CAMBRIDGE STUDENT ran the newsbills posted that night among freewheeling throngs in Petty Cury and Trinity Street.

For Marianne, it was a time of almost schizophrenic contrasts. On the one hand, she was still the seventeen-year-old convent girl, intent on marrying the first boy who had ever made love to her. On the other hand, she was a famous pop star whose virginal beauty made her the target of seduction attempts from almost every man she met. Gene Pitney, the American star, had already made determined attempts to persuade her to run away with him. Then, a week before her wedding, Bob Dylan inveigled Marianne into his suite at the Savoy Hotel and tried to win her in a way that only Bob Dylan would. 'He sat down in front of me and started to write songs at terrific speed. He asked who John was, and when I said, "He's a student," Dylan was terribly contemptuous.

'All the time, he was writing these songs – covering sheet after sheet with them. Finally, when it was clear I wouldn't let him come on to me, he picked up every bit of paper and put them all away. I never even saw what he'd written. I only wish I'd had the chance to nick some of it.'

The public approved of Marianne's wedding and, when a baby son, Nicholas, was born rather soon afterwards, forbore even to count fingers backward through the months of pregnancy. Her life continued, then, in its continual paradox – on the one hand, the genteel young wife and mother, given increasingly to musicians' slang; on the other hand, the package-show star, seated at the back of the tour bus with her nose buried in a Jane Austen novel.

For John Dunbar, the future seemed to hold comparable brilliance. In 1966, with two young partners, he founded the Indica Gallery in Mason's Yard, W.1. The gallery, small but chastely elegant, was to be devoted to the work of new 'swinging' painters and sculptors, while its adjacent bookshop would specialize in off-beat, radical literature from sources already known to some as the Underground.

Dunbar's partners in the venture were Peter Asher, brother of Paul McCartney's girl-friend, and a wispy boy known only as Miles who had grown up with Brian Jones in Cheltenham. The support of pop music's brahmin class was assured from the start when Paul McCartney helped to paint the gallery white before its official opening. Later that year, at an Indica exhibition entitled Unfinished Paintings and Objects, John Dunbar was to introduce the Japanese performance artist Yoko Ono to the renegade Beatle and painter manqué John Lennon.

At first, Marianne had been shocked by the Stones – by their scruffiness and spottiness and surly indifference to the gifts life was heaping upon them. Marianne remembered only too well what it

Mick (back row, right) at Wentworth County Primary, 1954

'English schooldays at their apotheosis.' Mick is on far right

The Glimmer Twins (front row, right) meet at Wentworth, circa 1954

Mick (back row, right) in Dartford Grammar School basketball club

Original 'Rollin'
Stones' with Ian
Stewart (left) already
looking much too
normal

Playing in front of the
Trad Jazz mural, Eel
Pie Island, 1962

Package tour
days, '63

Competing with other Battersea Park attractions, 1963

Andrew Loog Oldham. 'I'd made up my mind to be a little teenage tycoon shit'

The first trial of strength with original — and much ill treated — co-manager Eric Easton

Belle Vue, Manchester, 1964 (note fainting policewoman)

Bedsitter days, 1965

Marianne Faithfull, 1964. 'I lived in a Renoir'

One more British Transport hotel, 1966

Brian, photographed at Gleneagles by his friend Dave Thomson

Allen Klein makes his mark on the product

Mick and Keith at Redlands, as storm clouds gather

Brian, Anita and Keith, the fateful threesome, en route to Morocco, 1967

Mick and Keith with Les Perrin
at their committal proceedings,
June 1967

*Below left:* Mick, a free man, at
his Granada TV press conference

Mick and Marianne before the
summit conference with the
Establishment

Brian, trying to smile,
with Anita at the 1967
Cannes Film Festival

Brian, already fading,
lines up with happier
clowns in the Rock 'n'
Roll Circus

Les Perrin forgets himself at the
Beggars Banquet launch

Mick, when he liked nothing better than a sunny day
with Marianne and Nicholas

The last original lineup, 1968. Brian is just holding on

The party dress is unveiled

Vignette from Brian's memorial,
1969

St Tropez, 1971: Bianca watches her
marriage end on her wedding day

'Don't be *silly*'

'75 tour: preparation

'75 tour: 'Security'

'75 tour: Backstage glamou

'75 tour: for Mick a makeup artist, for Keith a kid's paintbox

The Glimmer Twins, 1975

The husky look, with parents Joe and Eva and younger brother Chris

Mick and Jerry. He likes the fact she has money of her own

had been like to ask for credit at the Reading shops. Part of the Stones' new stardom was unlimited credit, offered by boutiques whose trendiness would increase a hundredfold if a Rolling Stone shopped there. 'All the Stones had piles of clothes on credit, and never paid for any of them. I used to tell Mick off about that. It was something I'd been taught by Eva from childhood – however hard up you are, your credit must always be good.'

Of all the Stones, she was initially drawn to Brian; not so much for his looks as for the insouciant malice that still sparkled under his platinum fringe. 'I knew there was a psychic trial of strength going on between Brian and the others, and that Brian was losing it. And there were all these mothers of his illegitimate children in the background. We were all round at Brian and Anita's place in Courtfield Road one day and suddenly this ex-girlfriend of his, Linda, appeared in the street outside with Julian, their child, in her arms. She was standing right under the window, holding the baby up as if to say "What are you going to do about *this*?" Brian just looked down at them and laughed.'

The ex-convent girl had by now herself been initiated into all the pleasures of smart young London Society. By 1966, she was habituated to 'grass' and 'hash' and the varicoloured pills with which her new friends propped their eyes open through each night's peripatetic pleasure. Then one day at a party, Robert Fraser, the art dealer, beckoned her into another room, pointed to a small white pile of cocaine on the mantelpiece and told her to take a sniff. 'I didn't know what you had to do; I just snorted up the whole lot in one go. Robert was *very* offended.'

The domestic idyll with John Dunbar and baby Nicholas was to be short-lived. Dunbar, though brilliant and imaginative, could not keep up with the free-spending pop world Marianne now inhabited, nor maintain herself and Nicholas in the grand style of her hit parade friends. With a nanny to take care of Nicholas, she began to forsake Dunbar's art gallery circle for the houses, shut in by Moroccan drapes and heavy with camouflaging incense, where Rolling Stones and their courtiers were to be found.

Marianne claims that, before her affair with Mick Jagger, she had slept with two other Stones – by obvious implication, Keith and Brian. The subject is one upon which Keith chooses to remain gallantly silent. In Brian's case, his friend Dave Thomson believes, matters went no further than some exploratory groping. 'Brian told me he'd once been shut in a cupboard with Marianne. But all he did was give her a good feel-up.'

By mid-1966, the pressure of her too-hasty marriage and motherhood was propelling her, almost without her knowledge, into the arms of a person she thought she disliked – a person whose outward crudeness and cockiness, she found, held surprising depths of sensitivity and sympathy. 'I went to Mick because I needed a friend. Mick was a friend who also happened to be a millionaire.'

Her young assistant, Jo Bergman – a future power in the life of the Stones – puts it rather more simply. 'Marianne was living in this freezing cold flat. When Mick started to come and see her, suddenly there were electric heaters everywhere.'

Jagger, at the time, was said to be suffering from 'complete exhaustion', due mainly to a schedule that had brought the Stones back to Australia and New Zealand in February, and then packed them off again with barely a respite on a new European tour more chaotic and violent than any yet. At their Paris Olympia show, police used batons and tear gas against the 3,000 rioters. Twelve gendarmes were hurt, including one suffering from bites. At the Musicorama in Marseilles, a chair sailed out of the audience, opening a two-inch cut above Jagger's right eye.

Hardly a month elapsed before yet another US and Canadian tour. Jagger began it still in a state of manifest exhaustion, descending the aircraft steps, as one reporter noted, 'smiling lamely, supported by the brassbound epaulets on his shoulders.' He seemed to be living out the neurosis of the Stones' current single, Paint It Black, in which the singer was portrayed as a palpitant wreck, turning his head away from pretty girls, like Joyce's Stephen Daedalus, 'until my darkness goes . . .'

The tour began on a note of high fashion with the Stones featured among back-combed American debutantes on the cover of *Town and Country* magazine, and a press reception thrown by Allen Klein on a yacht in New York harbour, when fan magazines were excluded in favour of journalistic gentry (like *Town and Country*'s own Linda Eastman). The Stones were noticeably more stand-offish, as one disgruntled guest wrote. 'There's a feeling of

"Don't touch me, I'm a Rolling Stone." Even that manager of theirs is so hung up on himself, it's unbelievable . . . Mick is a hippie in the true sense of the word. When someone says something honest, he goes blank . . .'

Allen Klein's litigation-loving style was detectable in the stunt with which Andrew Loog Oldham launched the Stones on this fifth transcontinental journey. Oldham announced he had filed a five million dollar lawsuit against fourteen New York hotels for refusing the Stones as customers and so casting aspersions on their good name. It was all pure fiction and, as events proved, rather unnecessary. Headlines after Oldham's heart were already burning the Stones' progress across the American map like one of those old movie sequences symbolizing a country given over to fire and plunder.

The opening concert, in Lynn, Massachusetts, was stopped by the police after only minutes, and the audience dispersed with a ferocity that turned mere high spirits into orgiastic mob rage. As the Stones drove away from Lynn Bowl auditorium, their car windows were belaboured with wooden planks torn up from the walkways. In Montreal, the Stones stopped playing to boo the stage-front bouncers for punching and judo-chopping at girls who tried to join Mick Jagger at the microphone. In Syracuse, they were said to have insulted an American flag by dragging it along the floor of the War Memorial Hall. (Brian Jones had merely been trying to take the flag as a souvenir.) In Vancouver, the 36 concert casualties included ushers kicked in the groin, women policemen suffering from exhaustion, bouncers with alleged concussion and fans nursing assorted broken bones. In Montreal, where the police had subdued fans by ramming them head-first into a wood fence, the Stones came offstage through an aisle of 50 prostrate bodies.

The last American concert – for longer than anyone realized then – was in Hawaii on July 25. The Stones then dispersed for brief holidays before starting a new British tour late in September. Brian Jones, in Morocco with Anita Pallenberg, was reported to have broken his right hand in a climbing accident.

The British tour coincided with yet another single, Have You Seen Your Mother, Baby, Standing in the Shadow? whose involved (and quite meaningless) title was but one symptom of the pressure on Jagger and Richard to dash off another three-minute

195

smash while simultaneously ducking chairs and being attacked by wooden planks. On this song, tour chaos followed them even into the studio, upsetting the malign tautness they had achieved on Satisfaction, causing Jagger to gabble the obscure lyric breathlessly as if eyeing up exits, and everyone else to pound and scrub their instruments towards the same quick getaway. Brass and cathedral-like echo were added in a too hurried mix, to get it all finished for unveiling on the next Ed Sullivan TV show.

In America, the single was issued inside a picture sleeve that struck new horror into conservative hearts. The Stones were photographed as a group of ageing transvestites, each one adopting a 'drag' role to which his character seemed only too well suited. Brian Jones ('Flossie') pouted smoke rings in a WAAF uniform and peroxide wig. Keith ('Molly') in befrogged costume and cameo brooch, looked like an archdeacon's wife turned to drink. Jagger, his lips reddened to the size of chipolata sausages, wore a dog-eared tea-dance hat, next to Charlie ('Millicent'), grimly hatted and furred. The centrepiece was a wheel-chair in which Bill Wyman ('Sarah') sat, a sullen WAC, with skinny spinster legs almost tied in a knot.

The British tour began on September 29, amid lengthy music press post mortems as to why Have You Seen Your Mother, Baby? had not reached number one in America or Britain. If it was 'over the kids' heads', as luminaries like Eric Clapton and Mike D'Abo agreed, no more perfect theme song could have been found for concerts which eclipsed even Vancouver and Montreal in uproar and violence. British fans, deprived of the Stones for almost a year, were intent on making up for lost time. The final slow, at the Royal Albert Hall, was halted after three minutes when Jagger was attacked by three girls simultaneously, and the arbitrary collaring, punching and tossing back of half a dozen more still manifestly could not stem the screaming tidal wave.

A film sequence shot that night shows the Stones at their most goadingly indifferent – Mick Jagger in Mod crop and flowered shirt: Keith in sunglasses, collar and tie, like a blinded mafioso; Brian Jones, in velvet frock coat and heavy sideburns, laughing hysterically as the power fails, the house lights rise, loose drums roll underfoot, Charlie hastily exits to the rear, and Brian himself is turned round and shepherded away by large official hands.

*    *    *

196

Swinging London swung to its zenith through that summer season when girls went bare-thighed in wasp-striped mini-dresses and boys, buttoned up in Beau Brummell coats, swaggered down King's Road closely followed by camera crews from *Life* magazine, recording anthropomorphic data for what its sister publication *Time* had momentously – and a year late – dubbed The Style Capital of Europe. The effect of *Time* and *Life* between them had been an American tourist boom not seen since London's last royal coronation. The 'in' subculture was now a subcontinent, of boutiques, bistros, bric-a-brac markets, purveying solid versions of the parody Britishness which pop music had made the rage across America. It was a time when fortunes could be made from naming a shop I Was Lord Kitchener's Valet; when the British saw their national colours profitably transferred from imperial flagstaff to Carnaby Street plastic bag. Mass-produced jingoism led inevitably to a resurgence of the genuine article, blossoming still further in weeks of unaccustomed summer sun. When, in August, England beat West Germany to win the 1966 World Cup, it truly did seem as if Britannia was back in business.

The Beatles continued to be Swinging London's foremost citizens. They had ceased live performances in August, withdrawing, shell-shocked, into lives of individual plutocracy, reuniting only to make albums that would chart their ascent into the same iconographic firmament as Portobello Road market and I Was Lord Kitchener's Valet. The Beatles' *Revolver* is held to be the first thematic pop LP, capturing as it does, by random images, the sun-soaked euphoria of London in 1966. The Stones' *Aftermath* can make an equal claim – a better one, even, in its more constant blend of metropolitan arrogance with strange, eastern-sounding noise. But the Stones were too notorious to be regarded as heralds of an era.

The era which the Beatles officially announced – and which Brian Jones had subtly prophesied four months earlier – took shape in the odour of joss sticks, smouldering among twilit tumbles of embroidered caftans, tapestried slippers, prayer beads, leather footstools and beaten-brass trays. The Beatles' (and Stones') experiments with sitars set off a fascination with all things eastern, passed from Britain to America via the mutually reacting pop industry. In Britain, the effect was merely commercial; in

197

America, it was massively cerebral. Rumours began to reach London of young people in California who had thrown off all convention to practise Hinduism, in precept or in spirit, with shoulder-length hair and flowing beards and robes and sandals and flower garlands, barring all activity but Buddha-like goodwill and consumption of those substances with which eastern sages were said to have attained their wisdom and maintained their repose.

It was, ironically, the Tory London *Evening Standard* which published earliest details of the new 'hippie' communities in San Francisco and on the North California coast, and transmitted their apostate slogan: 'Turn on, tune in, drop out.' The *Sunday Times* soon afterwards introduced Britain to the hippie movement's first leader – or guru – one Timothy Leary, a Harvard academic who had sacrificed his career to explore the 'psychedelic' (literally, mind-expanding) properties of the man-made drug lysergic acid diethylamide. Even the *Sunday Times* did not know, however, that in Pont Street, Knightsbridge, there was already an establishment called the World Psychedelic Centre where liquid LSD was available free to anyone who wanted it, sprinkled on little fingers of bread.


Andrew Loog Oldham was also swinging to a zenith as the youth-obsessed capital's latest big businessman under 24. Oldham, in mid-1966, joined forces with his old PR confederate Tony Calder to form an independent record label, Immediate. The idea had come, inevitably, from Phil Spector's Philles label, with additional inspiration from Berry Gordy's Motown. Like Motown, Immediate was conceived as a team of song-writers, arrangers and producers, kept in harness to service artists selected by the power of one Diaghilev eye. Like Motown, Immediate would have its own distinctive style, an aura of success that headed its product to the charts before the customers had heard a word. Its grandiosely stated aim was to be 'Part Of The Industry Of Human Happiness'.

Immediate's chief in-house asset was the song-writing team of Mick Jagger and Keith Richard. To stimulate this all-important commodity, Oldham encouraged both Mick and Keith to make their first essays as record producers. Jagger's debut was with Chris Farlowe, a bulky young R & B shouter, singing Out of Time from *Aftermath*. Farlowe's version, laden with more scornful pity than even Jagger's, became the new label's first number one in August 1966. Keith's first production was the 'Arandbee' (R & B) Orchestra, playing a medley of past Stones hits grandiosely entitled Today's Pop Symphony. The aim was to prove that Jagger-Richard songs made melodies as durable as Lennon and McCartney's.

Immediate Records operated from the same small flat in Iver Court, Marylebone, where Oldham both lived and managed the Stones' personal and creative affairs. With Tony Calder established here too, in an office comparably luxurious, the only space available for employees like Shirley Arnold was corners and cubby-holes. 'It was terrible, really,' Shirley says, 'but we put up with it. The worst part of any office job is boredom. With Andrew, at least you knew you'd never be bored.'

Since fainting at Ken Colyer's club and awakening to find herself secretary of the Rolling Stones Fan Club, Shirley Arnold had become indispensable within the Oldham empire. The Stones all liked her for her Cockney good sense, her obligingness and a concern for them far beyond the call of secretarial duty. While they were on tour, Shirley would keep in touch with their parents, relaying messages, delivering assurance that this or that new press scandal was no cause for maternal alarm. 'I never really did much care for Mrs Jagger. She was always complaining. But Doris Richards was great. She was so game and ready for anything. She'd even smoked a joint with Keith, just to see what it was all about.

'The funny thing was, the Stones did everything they could to stop me ever taking any drugs. Especially Keith – even at the time when he was pouring *everything* into himself. Someone offered me something in the office once, and Keith forbade me to touch it.'

Shirley had been fond of Eric Easton and had regretted his brutal dumping when Oldham teamed with Allen Klein. Her first sight of Klein was not reassuring. 'I saw him in the office in a T-shirt, swigging from a bottle of whisky. When I got to know him, though, I liked him. He was always nice to the girls in the office, and never missed buying us presents at Christmas. Once, I remember, he gave each of us a rather dainty little china pomander.'

199

Oldham's new status as music mogul, on theoretically equal terms with Decca's Sir Edward Lewis, had prompted him to change his ferociously casual Mod malchick look for boardroom suits and pebble-lensed spectacles and a downward-turning moustache, such as Mexican bandits had sported in the Saturday morning movies of his boyhood. He had also dismissed Reg the Butcher as his chauffeur-bodyguard in favour of a more decorous guardian named Eddie.

Behind the Zapata moustache and the shawl-like jacket lapels, he was still – as Eric Easton had sorrowfully remarked – a very naughty boy. One of his favourite pastimes while being driven by Eddie in his Rolls was to invite a fellow passenger to open a door, hang out of the speeding vehicle and peep underneath it at Oldham, hanging from the door on the other side. He was playing that game one night with the stage designer Sean Kenny, unaware that a police car was close on Eddie's tail. 'When the cops eventually stopped us, they thumped both of us,' Oldham remembers. 'I suppose I *had* been a bit cheeky to them as well.'

In addition to the full-size Rolls, he acquired a miniature version, grafted on to a Mini Minor chassis, the ultimate expensive and pointless Sixties toy. 'There were only two of them in the country,' Shirley Arnold says. 'John Lennon had the first one, so Andrew couldn't be happy until he'd got one, too. It had stereo music speakers on the *outside*. Andrew took a couple of us out for a ride in it one lunch time. I'll never forget zooming round the West End in that little tiny Rolls with the speakers pounding and people leaping out of Andrew's way.'

The Immediate office thronged with youths whose potential as singers and songwriters seemed to matter less than their personal prettiness. 'We never thought Andrew was actually gay,' Shirley Arnold says. 'But he *did* like to have pretty boys working for him.'

As an employer, Shirley remembers, he could veer wildly from outrageous indulgence to almost psychopathic cruelty. 'He came in one day, wearing this beautiful brand-new suede coat. A boy in the office admired it, and Andrew just took it off and gave it to him. "Suede never did suit me," he said. Another time, there was someone in the company he'd decided to get rid of. Andrew waited until this person was out and then went in and wrecked his office.'

Oldham's executive roles as label boss and film tycoon led him increasingly to delegate and dissipate the Stones' management. With Allen Klein booking them in America and Tito Burns handling European tours, there was no longer any need to travel with them. Over the past two years, an entirely separate 'road' organization had grown up around the Stones, responsible for transporting their equipment and, more crucially, preventing their being torn limb from limb. The faithful Ian Stewart was reinforced by Tom Keylock, a hulking Cockney whose eyes swam mistily behind thick bifocal glasses. Keylock's one-man car hire company provided the Stones with the Austin Princess limousine they used for travelling between engagements. From chauffeur, he had progressed to bodyguard, using muscles, and combat techniques, acquired in the army paratroopers.

By late 1966, Andrew Loog Oldham found himself too busy even to go on devising the publicity stunts with which he had maintained the Stones' notoriety in the British press. That fictitious five million dollar lawsuit was his PE swansong. Thereafter, he gave the Stones' media image into the charge of Les Perrin, a middle-aged, thoroughly conventional Fleet Street publicist, whose hiring was to prove one of the best things Oldham ever did for the Stones.

His own dealings with the Stones now tended to be exclusively in record studios, at those unpredictable moments when they could break from touring to work on tracks for a new album. Here, even he began to notice the influence of the bodyguard Tom Keylock, especially over Keith, who had an incurable weakness for tough guys, and Brian, who was pathetically grateful even for so changeable an ally. There was also 'Spanish Tony', a Soho narcotics dealer who was Brian's and Keith's chief supplier of hashish and 'speed'.

'I got impatient with all that courtier stuff, the chauffeurs and the bodyguards,' Oldham says. 'It was like being back at public school. You had to be in Mick's house or Keith's house or Brian's house. It all started when they got involved with the so-called Society people – the Frasers, the Donald Cammells. And I didn't like the drug thing, because it got in the way. It interfered with business.'

Oldham claims that his quick thinking saved the Stones from a drugs bust somewhat in advance of their famous one, when they had met at Olympic Studios in Barnes to work on a track that eventually became Let's Spend the Night Together.

'Everyone was up in the control room, smoking away. You could look out from there, down the whole length of the studio, which was a pretty big, long room. Suddenly, at the far end, I saw about eight policemen come through a door and across the studio towards us.

'I ran out of the control room and stopped the first two. "Quick," I said. "Have you got truncheons?" Both of them brought out their truncheons. "Right," I said, "now hit them together." The coppers hit their truncheons together. "That's perfect," I said. "Just what we need on the track. Could you sit down here and do it when we record?" They all sat down, dead chuffed – forgetting all about trying to bust us – and we recorded two of them, hitting their truncheons together. It even stayed on the finished track, I think.'

It was Christopher Gibbs who first introduced Brian and Anita to Morocco. They would accompany the young antiques dealer when he visited Tangier or Marrakesh to buy carpets, fabrics and curios for his Chelsea shop. In Tangier, they would stay at the exquisite Hotel Minzah and spend days with Gibbs in the Grand Socco bazaar, wandering through the noisy labyrinths striped over by a latticework of sun. At night, they ate kebabs and couscous, and watched the acrobats and silver-hung belly dancers, taking turns to draw on a bubbling hookah of dunglike tobacco mingled with the more fragrant ancient eastern substance which Moroccans were only just learning to call 'shit'.

Morocco in the 1940s was to American literary men what Paris had been in the 1920s. The great William Burroughs, panjandrum of New York's avant-garde, lived in Tangier, ruling over a court of artist-expatriates that included Paul Bowles the novelist and Brion Gysin the painter. The Sixties brought a further influx from America and Europe to sample Morocco's now half-admissible delights of kif and male prostitutes. On the Tangier seafront, you might see Joe Orton, the British 'black' playwright, sunning himself with his future killer Kenneth Halliwell. In the High Atlas, you might well come across Truman Capote, escaping – or pursuing – his latest drama-ridden love. At the Minzah, you might see Cecil Beaton, breakfasting alone beside the fountain.

Morocco affected Brian Jones more profoundly than anything since he had first heard Elmore James. It was not just the hashish, jetted up through a hookah or smouldering in the bowl of an intricately carved pipe. It was not just the clothes, caftans, djellabahs, cloaks and waistcoats, beaded with glass or silver, which Anita and he bought by the trunkful, along with cushions, footstools, copperware, gold and beaten metal lamps for their new studio apartment. In Morocco, Brian found a country whose daily life, both spiritual and secular, is indivisible from music. He was fascinated to see, in Tangier's Grand Socco, in the green and white ceramic city of Fez, especially in the great red clay marketplace at Marrakesh, musicians playing subtle and delicate thousand-year-old Berber melodies on pipes and drums that were the natural descant to trade, conversation, worship and argument. From Brion Gysin he heard of the master musicians of Jajouka, in the foothills of the Rif mountains, whose pipe music, dating from before Islam, had so affected Gysin he swore he could not let even a day pass without hearing it again. Brian had begged Gysin to take him to Jajouka to hear the master musicians and, possibly, learn something from them about making records with the Rolling Stones.

Christopher Gibbs remembers that summer 1966 trip chiefly for the constant bickering between Brian and Anita. 'They fought about everything – cars, prices, restaurant menus. Brian could never win an argument with Anita, although he always made the mistake of trying. There would be terrible scenes with both of them screaming at each other. The difference was that Brian didn't know what he was doing. Anita *did* know what she was doing. I think that in a more gracious age, Anita would have been called a witch.'

Gibbs was with them in Tangier when Brian was said by the Stones' London office to have broken his hand while mountain climbing. In fact, he had gone to hit Anita but, instead, had hit a metal window frame.

Mick Jagger's love affair with Marianne Faithfull began late that summer, by such cautious and slow degrees that Marianne herself was for some time hardly aware of it. For Mick, even so decisive an act was necessarily hedged about with ambiguity and equivocation. Most of his friends believed that when he broke away from Chrissie Shrimpton, it would be for another girl-friend named Tish. Even when he took the plunge at last and asked Marianne to meet him secretly in Paris, he seemed to be keeping his options still open. Donald Cammell the film producer remembers, at a party there, how Mick strove part of the time to keep up a pretence that he and Marianne were together only by coincidence.

Soon afterwards, he nerved himself to tell Chrissie, at last, that it was all over between them. Chrissie took it badly, at one point trying to kill herself at Harley House while Mick was out. It would not be the last time that attempted suicide thwarted his desire, at all times, to keep up appearances.

He declared his involvement with Marianne in the most oblique way possible, taking her on an extended cruise in a hired yacht along the French Riviera. At night, they would come ashore and dance, unnoticed, in the seafront discotheques. 'We got very friendly with this particular disc jockey,' Marianne says. 'One night, I asked him if he'd got any speed.' The disc jockey poured a stream of Italian-made amphetamines into her hands.

By the time she returned to London, to move in with Jagger at Harley House, Marianne thought she had finished all the uppers the French deejay had given her. So she had – all but four, which remained where she had hidden the supply, in the pocket of a green velvet jacket of Mick's.

# 8

## 'Nobody knowing what to do, or when . . .'

The *News of the World* occupies a unique place in the mean City of London thoroughfare and gloomy side alleys collectively known as Fleet Street. Actually, the *News of the World* is in Bouverie Street, a tributary it shares with the humorous magazine *Punch*. From time to time over the years, *Punch* has attempted parodies of its neighbour publication but has invariably been forced to acknowledge its efforts totally eclipsed by the next edition of the real thing. The *News of the World* is something beyond parody.

It is unique, firstly, for the sheer, stupendous size of its readership. With a weekly circulation of six million copies, it is challenged only by Tokyo's *Asahi Shimbun* as the biggest-selling newspaper on earth. Calculating readership as three people per copy bought, one must concede that some 18 million Britons each Sunday settle down in after-lunch torpor, open the big, old-fashioned broadsheet and immerse themselves in that unmistakable half-world where scandal and prurient smut co-exist with moral indignation reminiscent of the age of Gladstone.

For three-quarters of a century, the *News of the World* has regaled its vast readership with a scarcely changing diet of vicars exposed as sex fiends, scout-masters revealed to be homosexuals, milkmen with seraglios on suburban housing estates and Methodist lay preachers surprized in love nests in Streatham. Crucifying these unfortunates under an alibi of concern for public morals is done with a voyeuristic relish closer to true pornography than anything the Soho back streets can provide. The same is true of the paper's periodic 'investigations' into larger social evils, which have a monotonous tendency to centre on organized prostitution, conducted by 'undercover' teams using all the apparatus of the agent provocateur. No such inquiry is deemed truly successful unless a *News of the World* reporter can record that, offered some forbidden favour, he 'made an excuse and left', and unless the tireless champion of Sabbath rectitude can publish its findings under its time-honoured banner headline WE NAME THESE GUILTY MEN.

Though the formula worked as well in 1967 as in 1907, the *News of the World* was always prepared to extend its righteous wrath to more current objects of suspicion, disapproval and envy. In January 1966, Brian Jones's worst fears were realized when his Cheltenham girl-friend Pat Andrews applied to South-West London Magistrates Court for maintenance payments to their four-year-old son Julian. Next Sunday, the *News of the World* ran a full-page story, THE GIRL WHO LOVED A ROLLING STONE, about Pat in her present straitened circumstances as an eleven pounds per week shop assistant. This prompted the paper's chief muck-raking competitor, *The People,* to a follow-up story (enigmatically headed BRIAN JONES HAS ANOTHER BABY) about Linda Lawrence and the out-of-court settlement Brian had recently been compelled to make to her for support of his second son named Julian.

It had been borne only gradually on the not very powerful minds in Bouverie Street that pop music offered the ingredient of lurid showbiz scandal and sententious moral crusading in one irresistible package. Pop music, to the Sunday newspaper reading public, increasingly meant drugs. It meant a perversion suddenly resurrected from Victorian novelettes to something one could practically hear issuing from one's child's transistor radio. Drugs and their increasing use by 'young people', with pop music's manifest encouragement, had become a common Fleet Street obsession. But as yet the menace remained vague. No specific pop star stood condemned. So in February 1967, in its inimitable way, the *News of the World* set out to name the guilty men.

If the Stones had wanted to set themselves up as number one target, they could hardly have gone about it better. In January, uproar swept through the British popular press over the title of their new single, Let's Spend the Night Together. A suggestive title certainly, but no more so than a dozen other songs proposing nocturnal activity, from Bing Crosby's Blue of the Night to Elvis Presley's One Night With You. The Stones were merely repeating what young boys nowadays found easy to say to girls – and vice versa. One could not, of course, expect Fleet Street to comprehend anything so simple. In America, the outrage was proportionately greater. Performing the song for Ed Sullivan, Mick Jagger had to amend the words to 'Let's spend some time together'.

An infinitely more serious thing occurred on January 22 when the Stones appeared on Britain's most popular television variety show, *Sunday Night at the London Palladium*. Something like ten million people each week watched this hour-long spectacular of jugglers and trampolinists and concluding star 'spot' that might be filled one Sunday by Frank Sinatra and the next by Dame Margot Fonteyn. The show was a weekend tradition with its visible proscenium, its live audience, its 'Beat the Clock' interlude, and that final, climactic moment when the top of the bill star mounted a circular stage among his fellow performers and high-plumed show-girls, interspersed among giant letters spelling out SUNDAY NIGHT AT THE LONDON PALLADIUM. The stage, with its cargo of artistes and giant letters, then slowly revolved, amid swelling violins and cheery waves of farewell.

Since the Beatles' famous appearance in 1963, the most major pop acts of the moment had done the Palladium show and waved goodbye from the revolving stage. It was therefore on a simple head-hunting basis that Lew Grade, boss of the ATV network, pressured his old friend Tito Burns to persuade the Stones to appear. 'I had to talk them into it,' Burns says. 'They weren't very keen. But it *was* the biggest show on television. Lew Grade was supposed to be grateful to me for evermore.'

Two hours before the show went out, Tito Burns received an anguished telephone call from the London Palladium. At rehearsals, the Stones had flatly refused to stand on the revolving stage and wave goodbye to the audience. Burns hurried to the Palladium to find Mick Jagger in a floral shirt, engaged in furious argument with Andrew Loog Oldham, the Stones' studio engineer Glyn Johns, and the show's producer Albert Locke. It transpired that Jagger was the one who would not revolve and wave. In his own words, he refused to let the Stones become 'part of a circus'.

'I did my best to persuade him,' Tito Burns says. 'I said it was part of a tradition, it couldn't do any harm.' But Jagger remained adamant. Albert Locke stamped off to devise an alternative finale with the Stones walking offstage while everyone else revolved and waved. Oldham, meanwhile, had disappeared from the theatre. 'He went off to his clinic, I think,' Tito Burns says. 'He used to go to this clinic every so often and get himself put to sleep for three days.'

The story of the Stones' 'insult' to the London Palladium, their fellow artistes and Lew Grade's revolving stage was prolonged well into the following week. On Thursday, the *Mail* still had enough angry readers' letters to fill a whole extra page. 'Who do they think they are?' wrote a typical correspondent, (Mrs) E. M. Smith of Clive Yale, Hastings, Sussex. 'I have never seen such a repulsive turn.' (Mrs) E. M. Smith would be more astounded still ere long.

On February 5, the *News of the World* published a full page exposé headlined THE SECRETS OF THE POP STARS' HIDEAWAY, and couched in the dramatic, staccato prose of reporters working under cover like ace detectives to penetrate a difficult and dangerous underworld.

The underworld in this case, somewhat surprisingly, was Roehampton, a London suburb best known for a hospital specialising in artificial limbs. According to the *News of the World*, wild LSD parties had taken place in Roehampton at a house rented to a fairly famous pop group, the Moody Blues, but frequented by a much more famous figure, Mick Jagger of the Rolling Stones.

On learning this, the *NoW* sleuths had naturally wished to seek out Mick Jagger and confront him with his heinous crime. They described their long vigil at a club he was said to frequent – Blases, in Kensington – and their triumph when the familiar Rolling Stone came into the club, consented to be interviewed and freely admitted everything they put to him – a confession made all the more spectacular by the *News of the World* team's tendency to confuse LSD with hashish.

'I don't go much on it now the cats have taken it up,' they quoted their – very talkative – interviewee as saying. 'It'll just get a dirty name. I remember the first time I took it. It was on our first tour with Bo Diddley and Little Richard . . .'

'During the time we were at Blases,' the investigators continued, 'Jagger took about six benzedrine tablets. "I just wouldn't stay

208

awake at places like this if I didn't have them," he said . . . Later at Blases, Jagger showed a companion and two girls a piece of hash and invited them to his flat for a "smoke".'

Confusing LSD with hashish was not, alas, the *News of the World* sleuths' only blunder that night. All the time they thought they were talking to Mick Jagger, they were actually talking to Brian Jones.

Anyone with the remotest knowledge of the real Jagger could have told the luckless hacks how impossible it would have been for him to swallow 'bennies' publicly and pull out lumps of hashish, let alone indulge in the matey confessions quoted. Anyone who knew Jagger knew that his attitude to drugs was as coy and cautious as to women, hairdressers, clothes and the colour of his cars. Though he certainly smoked hash, it was always with the utmost discretion. The real joke was that Jagger himself felt uneasy about Brian's and Keith's reckless use of LSD, its effect on them as people as well as the obvious risk of a police bust. Just a week earlier, he had left Keith's house in Sussex, muttering dark forebodings to Donald Cammell. 'This is all getting out of hand,' Cammell remembers him saying. 'I don't know where it's all going to end.'

On Sunday mornings at Harley House, it was his lordly habit to cover his and Marianne's bed with all the newspapers, both heavy and pop. The *News of the World* was the first thing he read, in mild amusement first, then stupefaction and finally outrage so intense as to scatter his usual caution to the winds. That Sunday evening, he was due to appear on Eamonn Andrews television talk show. When Andrews cautiously touched on the drugs question, Jagger announced that the whole story was a lie and he would shortly issue a libel writ against the *News of the World*.

It was, in Robert Fraser's phrase, 'the Oscar Wilde mistake' – rushing to law to refute a particular allegation of sins one had committed in general. An equal mistake was to imagine the *News of the World*, taxed with a claim that could cost it punitive damages, would simply pay up and apologize.

What the *News of the World* very naturally did was immediately commit even more of its peculiar resources to establish that, even if Jagger had not taken LSD in Roehampton and swallowed 'bennies' at Blases, he nonetheless took drugs and was as such a menace to society. If that could be proved, his libel action would not stand a chance. The sub judice law now prevented the *News of the World* from publishing further revelations before the libel case came to court. If however the police should discover any of the same pop stars to be taking drugs, there would be nothing to stop a fair and accurate report of the subsequent proceedings. Nor could any libel jury in Britain convict any newspaper for revealing what was proved, however tardily, to be true.

Jagger accepted an invitation from Keith to go down to Redlands with Marianne the next weekend and join a house party that was to include Robert Fraser, Christopher Gibbs, the photographer Michael Cooper, George and Pattie Harrison and new friend, Acid King David Schneidermann. He had materialized from California only three weeks earlier but had already won complete acceptance into the circle of the Stones' most intimate courtiers. For Acid King David peddled LSD. With him, in a leather attaché case, he carried quantities of the sought-after brand called Sunshine, compounded by a famous San Francisco chemist and dispensed in pellets of psychedelic orange. His aura was part wizard, part butler. He would officiate at weekend house parties, visiting each guest's bedroom in turn with early-morning tea and a Sunshine capsule. 'I can picture him now,' Christopher Gibbs says. 'He was, I suppose, a sort of up-market flower child. He knew more about drugs than anyone the Stones had ever met. "What!" he'd say. "You mean you've never heard of dimethyl tryptomine!"'

The upshot was that Mick Jagger agreed to go with Marianne to Redlands and let Acid King David give him his first dose of LSD.

Eleven guests in all followed Keith's Bentley down to West Wittering the next Saturday night for what was intended to be a pleasant Sunday's rest and relaxation. It was in effect Jagger's inner circle of Marianne, Robert Fraser, Christopher Gibbs and Michael Cooper, plus George and Pattie Harrison and Fraser's Moroccan servant, Ali. Only two of the company did not qualify as close, trusted friends. One was Acid King David Schneidermann. The other was Nicky Cramer, a King's Road 'flower person' whom Keith could not quite remember inviting but accepted nonetheless as part of his life's eternal quota of hangers-on.

For the next twelve hours at Redlands, the principal occupation was sleep. Until late next morning, everyone was still submerged but Acid King David, making his butlerine rounds of the five bedrooms with tea and enough 'Sunshine' to send each guest on a languuruous trip without so much as sitting up.

It was not until early afternoon that people began drifting down to Keith's long, high-raftered living room, relaxed and exhilarated by the visions which Acid King David had provided. The winter day being mild and sunny, it was decided to go in their assorted limousines on a mystery tour of the Sussex countryside, stopping off at a house once occupied by the surrealist art collector Edward James, and rumoured to contain a sofa in the shape of Mae West's lips.

They did not find Edward James's house, but still spent a pleasant couple of hours driving round the empty lanes and running through the woods around Keith's estate, down to a small shingle beach. Michael Cooper photographed Keith, in sunglasses and Afghan fur coat, gambolling over the pebbles, seemingly without a care in the world.

The cars came back to Redlands at about 6 p.m. Shortly afterwards, George Harrison decided he was bored, and he and Pattie drove off to their psychedelic bungalow in Surrey. With George gone, it now seems, a lucky talisman was removed from the house. Keith for one is still convinced that subsequent events could not have happened with a Beatle, almost sacredly immune to official persecution, still on the premises.

The eight males in the party were assembled in the living room that was part Olde England, part joss-scented Marrakesh bazaar. Marianne Faithfull had gone upstairs for a bath. She had brought only one set of clothes with her, and these were now muddy and crumpled after the day's country ramblings. So, rather than get dressed again, she came downstairs wrapped in a fur rug taken from one of the beds. After supper – a Moroccan buffet, prepared by Robert Fraser's Ali – the company gathered round the TV set, listening to Bob Dylan music while they waited for the Sunday-night film, Jack Webb in *Pete Kelly's Blues*. It was, in Christopher

Gibbs's words, 'a scene of pure domesticity'.

At about 7.30 p.m., a force of nineteen police officers in assorted vehicles made its way up the long wooded drive that separates Redlands from the main Chichester road. The tip-off they had received had left ample time for the raid to be plotted at West Sussex Regional Police Headquarters and a search warrant to be obtained at a special sitting of Chichester magistrates. The force included three policewomen for the searching of women suspects. (Three women, Marianne, Pattie Harrison and Anita Pallenberg, were supposed to have been in the Redlands party.) The cohorts were commanded by Chief Inspector Gordon Dineley of the West Sussex Constabulary, in full uniform and white-braided cap.

No one inside Redlands heard the police convoy arrive. The first sign of intruders was a single face, flashing briefly at one leaded window-pane. 'Keith looked up and said there seemed to be some little old lady outside,' Marianne remembers. 'He thought it must be some fan, trying to get autographs.'

A thunderous knocking at the front door then began. Keith got up reluctantly from his cushion to answer it. The others, in their gentle, slightly hilarious stupor, looked up a moment later at what seemed to Marianne to be another, this time wholly ludicrous, LSD vision. Chief Inspector Gordon Dineley stood in their midst, sombrely magnificent, like some galactic commissionaire, announcing that, pursuant to the Dangerous Drugs Act, 1964, he had a warrant to search the premises.

There ensued a brief pause while the victims gaped up at the police, now pouring in through every crevice, and the police looked upon a scene that was to be described later, under oath, as one of scarcely believable decadence. They looked at the half-timbered walls, hung with Moroccan drapes; at the huge tapestried cushions underfoot; at the TV set, mutely flickering while Bob Dylan's voice wailed and sneered out of twin stereo speakers; at the small, almost child-like figures in embroidered robes, disposed among pillows and wine bottles; at the hair tangled around chalk-white faces turned up to them, still not quite seriously; at the particular face, engraved like a Wanted poster on so many policemen's minds. 'Poor Mick – he could hardly believe his bad luck,' Marianne says. 'The first day he ever dares take an LSD trip, eighteen policemen come pouring

212

in through the door.'

Marianne, a girl alone with eight men, wearing only a fur rug, was the detail which gave the scene its immortality. The rug was, in fact, extremely large; it could – as Keith says – have covered three girls Marianne's size. Nevertheless Detective Sergeant Stanley Cudmore testified later that, as he studied her closer, trying to detect the usual symptoms of cannabis smoking, she made a deliberate attempt to provoke him by letting the rug slip, 'disclosing parts of her nude body'.

Chief Inspector Dineley, meanwhile, was inquiring formally if Keith Richard was the owner of the invaded premises. Keith – whose dignity remained unimpaired throughout – agreed that he was and requested the Chief Inspector politely not to let his raiders walk all over the valuable cushions under their feet.

Most of those present, including Mick Jagger, believed at this stage they had no real cause for alarm. Though all had taken LSD, no one possessed any. The entire supply remained in Acid King David's attaché case – which, as it happened, lay in full view in the centre of the living room.

Only Robert Fraser had cause to fear the outcome of the impending body search. In one trouser pocket, Fraser carried a carved wooden box containing 24 heroin 'jacks', supplied to him by Keith's favourite pusher, 'Spanish Tony' Sanchez. In another pocket, he had a lump of hashish and some amphetamine uppers. Despite his muzzy state, Fraser knew he must, if possible, hide the heroin jacks at least. Casually he slipped a hand into his trouser pocket to open the box, and began to shake the small white tablets out into the lining.

Police officers were now all over Redlands, opening cupboards, turning out drawers, peering darkly into book matches and plastic sachets of in-flight mustard and mayonnaise which Keith had collected on various foreign tours. In the bedroom she shared with Mick, a giggling Marianne was being searched – or rather, since she was naked, scanned – by Detective Constable Rosemary Slade. A male detective had already taken charge of the green velvet jacket Mick had been wearing since that pre-Christmas cruise with Marianne along the French Riviera.

Down in the living room, Jagger, Richard, Michael Cooper, Acid King David, Nicky Cramer, Ali the Moroccan, Robert

213

Fraser and Christopher Gibbs stood in line to be frisked. The police had by now distinguished between their quarry and the 'gentlemen' present, and indeed treated both Gibbs and Fraser almost apologetically. The first find was on Acid King David – a small tin and envelope full of cannabis, and what the policeman concerned entered in his notebook as 'a ball of brown substance'. When a policeman put out a tentative hand to Acid King David's brief case, he shouted, 'Please don't open that case. It's full of exposed film.'

By the time the young officer assigned to search him was patting his pockets, Robert Fraser had managed to shake all 24 heroin tablets free of their carved pillbox. The policeman found the box, examined it and asked what the traces of white powder in it were. Fraser replied that he was diabetic; the box contained his insulin supply. The tablets were then retrieved from his pocket lining and shown to a senior officer, who seemed ready to accept Fraser's story that they contained only insulin. 'He handed them back to me. Then he said, "I'd better keep just one back for analysis." At that moment, I knew I'd had it.'

Jagger was then shown the green velvet jacket and the small glass phial, discovered in one of his pockets. The phial contained the final four of the amphetamine uppers given to Marianne Faithfull three months earlier by her French disc jockey friend.

Jagger, in that instant, decided he must take the blame on Marianne's behalf. He agreed that the jacket belonged to him, and, when asked if the tablets were his also, replied, 'Yes. My doctor prescribed them for me.' He even named a doctor – Dr Dixon Firth – in Wilton Crescent, Knightsbridge. Asked why he needed tablets, he said, 'To stay awake and work.'

The phial was added to the raid's other spoils – two carved pipes, a pudding basin that had been used for a bedside ashtray, Robert Fraser's heroin jack and Keith's American book matches and mustard sachets. Keith was then formally cautioned that if any of these items contained unlawful drugs, he could face additional prosecution for allowing their use on his property. 'I see,' Keith said drily. 'You pin it all on me.' And with mutual farewells – for neither side ever complained of discourtesy on the other's part – Chief Inspector Gordon Dineley, his white-braided uniform and his euphoric task force left the house and disappeared into the wooded Sussex night.

A moment or so later, the telephone rang. It was Brian Jones, calling from London to say that he'd stopped work on the music for Anita's new film, and they could join the party within a couple of hours. 'Don't bother,' Keith told him. 'We've all just been busted.'

The atmosphere among Keith's house party was curiously calm. Christopher Gibbs remembers 'a rather philosophical feeling – like "It had to happen and it's happened."' They supposed the raid to have come from no other source but the British policemen, wishing to collar a Rolling Stone on any pretext whatever. If anything, they felt they had come off rather lightly. The failure to find Acid King David's LSD store was no more than astounding good luck. Whatever charges might follow the analysis of Marianne's pep pills and the Moroccan hash pipes had to be relatively trivial.

Thus reassured, the party stayed on at Redlands – all but three. Robert Fraser needed to get back to London urgently. With him and Ali in their van rode Acid King David Schneidermann, clutching his attaché case of undisclosed Sunshine.

Fraser *was* in a panic – and with good reason. To be caught in possession of heroin, the deadliest of all illegal drugs, meant almost certain imprisonment. There was, however, one chance based on the anomalous fact that the drug was legal if prescribed by a doctor to a registered addict. Fraser's only hope was to persuade some doctor to give him a backdated prescription.

Acid King David, too, was deeply agitated, as well as incredulous that the police had not hauled everyone straight off for interrogation and charging. 'I advised him to get out of the country right away,' Robert Fraser says. Acid King David did so that very night, disappearing with a completeness worthy of Houdini or, – as was later frequently said – a man who had been using an alias.

When Fraser reached home, he sent an immediate SOS to Spanish Tony Sanchez, the Soho dealer who had sold him the heroin jacks – and had himself very nearly joined the Redlands party. Spanish Tony advised bribing the police analysts to say that the confiscated jack contained only glucose. He offered to

215

sound out the various 'bent coppers' he knew in the West End division to see if the right man would accept what corrupt London policeman call 'a drink'.

Spanish Tony's inquiries proved fruitful. All the substances taken from Redlands could be 'lost', he was told, for a bribe of £7,000. The news was conveyed to Mick and Keith with a promptness for once short-circuiting all normal protocol. Andrew Loog Oldham, in California on other business, still knew nothing of the bust. The two chief Stones, for the very first time, were acting on their own initiative. Together they eagerly shelled out £5,000, and Robert Fraser managed to scrape up the residue. The money was put into a carrier bag and paid over by Spanish Tony to the police contact in a pub in Kilburn.

The following Sunday, February 19, in addition to its continuing series 'Pop Stars and Drugs', the *News of the World* ran a front-page story confirming that insidious social evil with fresh, exclusive evidence. The Redlands raid was then described, without a single name (to observe the sub judice law) but otherwise in the most intimate detail. The story said that one 'nationally known star' had had pep pills taken from him; that 'bottles and an ashtray' had also been seized for analysis; that, as well as the two 'nationally famous names' likely to face drug charges, a third had left the raided house just in time; and that 'a foreign national' was being watched for at air and seaports in case he should try to leave the country.

Every line in the piece reeked of quid pro quo. It was plain that the *News of the World* had got the story exclusively in return for tipping off the police that the party was to take place. How had the moralists at Bouverie Street possibly got hold of details supposedly known only to Keith Richard, Mick Jagger and the others invited to join them at Redlands?

The immediate conclusion was that one of the house party was a traitor. Excluding the staunch friends of the Stones, Christopher Gibbs, Robert Fraser, Michael Cooper and Moroccan Ali, suspicion naturally fell on the two who had come merely as hangers-on: Nicky Cramer, the Chelsea flower person, and Acid King David Schneidermann.

Nicky Cramer's innocence was established in a manner demonstrating what sheer thuggery now made up much of the

Rolling Stones' retinue. A mutual friend of Mick and Keith named David Litvinoff visited the unfortunate flower child and beat him up systematically. When Cramer still did not confess, he was pronounced in the clear.

That left only Acid King David, the up-market flower child who had become a Stones friend so very quickly, by stages that no one now could quite remember or explain. Elaborated by many theories suited to the drama of the moment, his persona became increasingly bizarre. Michael Cooper remembered looking into Acid King David's luggage for hashish, and seeing he possessed a second passport in the name of 'David English'. Cooper also remembered a strange talk with the American about firearms and espionage . . . 'like he was into the James Bond thing, you know . . . the whole CIA bit.'

With the story of the raid in print, there plainly was little hope that the police could be bribed to forget it. In the event, there was no suggestion that any officer involved with the raid was ever approached with a bribe. Probably there had been no hope even before Spanish Tony paid his police contact the £7,000, since there was no evidence that the money ever made its way to anyone in the West Sussex Constabulary. Even so, when a further week had passed and still nothing came of the matter, it seemed as if the money might have found its mark.

The wisest thing meanwhile was to get as far away from Britain, and probable further notoriety, as possible. In this at least Mick and Keith were fortunate, finding themselves in a rare professional lull. The Stones had just released an album, *Between the Buttons,* and had no further group commitment until their European tour, beginning on March 25.

Morocco was the obvious choice of sanctuary. To lessen the risk of harassment en route, they agreed to travel separately, meeting up, with Robert Fraser, Michael Cooper and other friends, in Marrakesh. Mick and Marianne would fly from Paris while Keith would drive down, accompanied by Brian Jones and Anita Pallenberg.

A rapprochement between Keith and Brian had lately occurred, thanks mainly to Mick's absorption in his affair with Marianne. Keith still felt it keenly that he had no steady girl-friend, and had, paradoxically, turned back to Brian for the kind of bachelor companionship they used to enjoy at Edith Grove. For some weeks past, indeed, he had been staying with Brian and Anita in their big, galleried studio apartment in Courtfield Road.

Brian welcomed him, delighted to have Keith back in his gang again, with that implied rejection of Mick; scarcely less pleased at the obvious mutual affinity between Keith and Anita. These weeks before his world disintegrated were a good time for Brian, with Keith and Anita as a new power axis, and his prestige as a musician higher than ever. To allay his first frenzied jealousy, Anita had arranged for him to write a soundtrack score for the film she was to make with Volker Schlöndorff. The film, entitled *A Degree of Murder*, featured Anita as a female assassin. Brian had thrown himself enthusiastically into the project, hiring Glyn Johns to recruit notable young freelance session men like pianist Nicky Hopkins and guitarist Jimmy Page. His finished score, using an eclectic range of instruments – with eerily atmospheric passages played by Brian himself on dulcimer, sitar and autoharp – was pronounced brilliant by Volker Schlöndorff, Glyn Johns and everyone else who heard it.

In the general Moroccan exodus, therefore, Brian, Anita and Keith travelled as a natural threesome. Keith had a hankering to make the entire trip in The Blue Lena, as he called his sky-coloured Bentley Continental. With Tom Keylock along to share the driving and handle frontier formalities, the 2,000-mile journey down through France and Spain promised fun, relaxation and harmony.

The Blue Lena crossed the English Channel without incident, stopping in Paris to pick up a fifth passenger, Donald Cammell's girl-friend Deborah. They continued southward then, with France faintly detectable beyond the in-car stereo, Brian and Anita lounging in the back like fur-wrapped, blond Borgias, and Keith up front, laughing indulgently at Tom Keylock's Cockney patter. The chauffeur claimed, while in the Paratroops, to have suffered wounds necessitating a skin graft from his bottom to his nose – as he frequently boasted, 'Most of my arse is on my face.' (A quick-witted girl in the Stones' office was once inspired to retort, 'That must be why so much shit comes out of your mouth, Tom.')

All went smoothly until the Bentley reached Toulon. Brian,

218

who had been showing signs of asthmatic unease on the mountainous route, suddenly developed a high fever and was admitted to hospital with pneumonia. He insisted, however, that Anita should go on into Spain with Keith and the other two. When he felt better, he would fly straight to Tangier to meet them at the Hotel Minzah.

It was clear to Tom Keylock, even from the evidence of his rear-view mirror, as the Blue Lena passed Montpelier, Béziers, then Perpignan, that Keith and Anita were becoming something more than friends. Keith by now realized the inevitable, though he tried to avoid it with vague plans for getting off with the other female passenger, Deborah. At Valencia, he and Anita spent the night together but next morning tacitly agreed to treat it as a pleasant interlude. 'I was still very wary,' Keith says, 'and trying hard not to fuck up the new thing I had going with Brian.'

No journey with Keith Richard could be entirely devoid of drama, as Anita discovered when they stopped in Barcelona and went to a night club. Keith got into a furious row with some waiters who would not accept his Diner's Club card without seeing his passport. While Keylock fetched the passport, Keith, Anita and Deborah were taken to police headquarters and interrogated until six o'clock the next morning. Back at their hotel there was a message from Brian, ordering Anita to return to Toulon and fetch him. She decided to pretend the message hadn't reached her.

They crossed by ferry from Malaga to Tangier a few days later, and checked into the Hotel Minzah. The desk clerk handed Anita a sheaf of Brian's frantic telegrams and telephone messages. Keith – still trying valiantly to play a straight bat – urged Anita to fly back to Toulon with Deborah to collect Brian while he and Tom Keylock went on to Marrakesh.

Mick was already at the appointed hotel, with Robert Fraser and Michael Cooper, waiting for Marianne to join him from Naples. Two days later, Brian and Anita arrived from the airport. Brian had recovered form his pneumonia but looked haggard with fatigue and suspicion. He clearly guessed something had happened between Anita and Keith, but would not – could not – accuse Keith outright. He took out his insecurity in the usual way – by beating Anita up in the privacy of their suite. The death-white, kohl-black Sixties make-up, fortunately, hid the worst of the bruises.

The week that followed put everyone else, as hoped, into a more relaxed frame of mind. The party shopped in the casbah and the big central square, drank mint tea and Scotch and Coke, smoked grass and Gauloises, dropped acid and lounged like ordinary tourists round the hotel pool. To that chlorine-scented court came Brion Gysin, the avant-garde painter and Cecil Beaton, photographer of more conventional Royalty, who coveted Mick Jagger as a subject, if nothing else, and whose famous diaries record the scene with penetrating unworldliness.

On the Tuesday evening I came down to dinner very late and, to my surprise, sitting in the hotel lobby, discovered Mick Jagger and a sleepy-looking band of gipsies. Robert Fraser, one of their company, wearing a huge, black felt hat, was coughing by the swimming pool . . . It was a strange group. The three 'Stones': Brian Jones with his girl-friend Anita Pallenberg – dirty white face, dirty blackened eyes, dirty canary drops of hair, barbaric jewellery – Keith Richard in eighteenth century suit, long black velvet coat and the tightest pants; and of course, Mick Jagger . . .

I didn't want to give the impression that I was only interested in Mick, but it happened that we sat next to one another as he drank a Vodka Collins and smoked with pointed finger held high. His skin is chicken-breast white and of a fine quality. He has an inborn elegance.

. . . By degrees the shy aloofness of the gang broke down. We got into two cars . . . [My] car was filled with pop art cushions, scarlet fur rugs and sex magazines. Immediately the most tremendous volume of pop music boomed in the region of the back of my neck. Mick and Brian responded rhythmically and the girl leant forward and screamed in whispers that she had just played a murderess in a film that was to be shown at the Cannes Festival.

. . . We went to a Moroccan restaurant. Mick . . . is very gentle and with perfect manners. He has much appreciation and his small, albino-fringed eyes notice everything. He has an analytical slant and compares everything he is seeing here with earlier impressions in other countries.

. . . He asked: 'Have you ever taken LSD? Oh, I should. It would mean so much to you: you'd never forget the colours. For a painter it is a great experience. One's brain works not on four cylinders but on four thousand.'

. . . By the time we reached the hotel, it was three o'clock . . . Mick listened to pop records for a couple of hours, and was then so tired that he went to sleep without taking off his clothes . . .

At eleven o'clock, he appeared at the swimming pool. I could not believe it was the same person walking towards us. The very strong sun, reflected from the white ground, made his face look a white, podgy, shapeless mess; eyes very small, nose very pink, hair sandy dark. His figure, his hands and arms were incredibly feminine.

None of them was willing to talk, except in spasms. No one could make up their minds what to do, or when.

I took Mick through the trees to photograph him in the midday sun . . . He is sexy, yet completely sexless. He could nearly be a eunuch. As a model he is a natural.

Their wardrobe is extensive. Mick showed me the rows of brocade coats. Everything is shoddy, poorly made, the seams burst. Keith himself had sewn his trousers, lavender and dull rose, with a band of badly stitched leather dividing the two colours.

Brian, at the pool, appears in white pants with a huge black square applied on the back. It is very smart in spite of the fact that the seams are giving way. But with such marvellously flat, tight, compact figures as they have, with no buttocks or stomach, almost anything looks well on them.

The Stones' party occupied the hotel's entire tenth floor. Brion Gysin remembers a collective LSD trip in one or another suite, with Elmore James music wailing, Keith strumming along on guitar, Mick pirouetting dementedly round the room and Brian Jones – 'like a little celluloid kewpie doll' – with Tom Keylock murmuring intrigue into his ear. When trays of food were brought in, everyone rode them round the floor like toboggans.

As the evening wore on and the trip wore off, Brian and Anita began squabbling again. Anita grabbed some sleeping pills and locked herself in their bedroom. Brian beckoned to Tom Keylock and asked the chauffeur to go out and find him a local whore. The others left him to it, racing off in various cars for an all-night trip into the Atlas mountains.

Next morning around the pool, the atmosphere was charged with imminent drama. Brian, the night before, had gone into town, returned with two tattooed Berber whores, and tried to force Anita into a group sex orgy. When she refused, he had beaten her up so severely she thought he meant to kill her.

Anita now sat in a poolside chair, locked in a passionate stare with Keith, ducking up and down in the water. Even Mick Jagger could not detach himself, as he would have much preferred, from the mounting tension. 'It's getting fuckin' heavy,' he kept saying to Robert Fraser in the intervals of packing and complaining about his hotel bill. Then Tom Keylock came in to report that a posse of British journalists was about to fly in from London. The obvious risk was that they would collar Brian and get him to blurt out something scandalous about the case pending against Mick and Keith. So Tom Keylock deputed Brion Gysin to take Brian out into the Djemaa el Fna, the big central square, to record Moroccan music, drink mint tea, buy souvenirs and get lost.

While Brian was away, Keith Richard came to a decision. 'I was so disgusted with the way Brian had treated Anita, I just threw her in the back of the car and split.' Anita tells the same story – not of being stolen but rescued. 'I was in fear of my life. I was hysterical. Keith saved me.'

Tom Keylock drove them back to Tangier, where they boarded the ferry for Malaga. There, the Spanish Customs almost put paid to their escape. Searching for drugs, half a dozen officers stripped the Blue Lena down to the chassis. The small piece of hash Keith had on him was hidden by Keylock in the most obvious place – under the flap to the petrol tank.

Two nights later in Paris, Donald Cammell was awakened by a frantic knocking on his apartment door. It was Brian, without luggage, babbling, 'They left me. They just went off and left me . . . ' Mixed up in the story he poured out to Cammell was something about a carved wooden pipe he'd bought, that afternoon with Brion Gysin in Marrakesh. He'd come back with the pipe to find Anita, Keith, Tom Keylock and the Bentley all gone.

The fugitives, meanwhile, had driven back as far as Madrid, then caught a plane for London, leaving Keylock to bring home the Blue Lena at his leisure. They were now at a small flat Keith maintained in St John's Wood, hiding out until Anita could pluck up nerve to go back to Courtfield Road for her clothes.

The hope that Spanish Tony had managed to buy off the police was dashed, virtually at the moment Keith re-entered Britain. On March 18, the *Daily Mirror* splashed the story that Mick Jagger and Keith Richard were to be summonsed on drugs charges arising from a raid on the latter's country house. Once more, through hand-in-glove co-operation with Scotland Yard, Fleet Street could pre-empt the process of the law. Four days later, as the *Mirror* had promised, the summonses came. Jagger was accused, with Robert Fraser and the vanished Acid King David Schneidermann, of possessing substances unlawful under the Dangerous Drugs Act, 1964. Keith was accused of 'knowingly permitting' his house to be used for those drugs' consumption. The case was set down to be heard by Chichester magistrates on May 10, with the option of summary trial or referral to the next West Sussex Quarter Sessions.

An aggrieved Spanish Tony later sought out his police contact and asked what had happened to the £7,000 which Jagger, Richard and Fraser had paid as a bribe. Of the £7,000 there was naturally now no trace whatever. All he could elicit was that the money had not got to 'the right man' before revelation of the bust in the *News of the World* and other papers had made a cover-up impossible.

'That's what I feel most bitter about,' Keith says. 'In America, you pay off the cops as a matter of course. It's business.'

Brian Jones was now back in London also, recovered from his hysterics and determined to regain Anita with a bravura display of masculinity. Discovering she was at Keith's 'crash pad', he drove there and hammered on the door, which Keith then suddenly opened. Brian came hurtling in and sprawled on the front hall carpet. There followed the first of many anguished scenes with Anita, with Keith hovering uneasily in other rooms.

Anita would not go back to Brian – nor was she yet ready to move in with Keith. Another film part – in Roger Vadim's space fantasy, *Barbarella* – was about to take her to Spain on location. Keith had to tour Europe with the Stones, sharing a stage for the next three weeks with Brian and his smouldering reproach.

The tour had been planned as the Stones' farewell to concert performance for the foreseeable future. Like the Beatles, they were weary of incessant touring and the necessity of making records always on the run. Exhaustion had clearly shown in their last album, *Between the Buttons*, in which lack of ideas combined with over-production to produce a curious, limply echoing effect, like a Vaudeville show in an almost empty hall. The album offered such aberrant Stones items as Back Street Girl, a French *valse musette* complete with accordions, and Something Happened To Me, gasped out by Keith's nicotine-roughened voice in a ludicrous setting of pithead brass bands. The play-out groove featured Jagger giving facetious road-safety advice. 'Remember . . . if you're going out on your bike tonight . . . wear white!'

It was not a good time to be travelling abroad. The summonses against Mick and Keith in Britain put them automatically on the Red List of suspected drug-traffickers, circulated among all European customs authorities. In France, Sweden, West Germany, Austria and Greece, going through customs meant the same ordeal for all five Stones – even drug-free, innocent Charlie Watts – of ransacked cases and, often, rough strip-searches. Brian, before each airport touch-down, would be terrorized by Tom Keylock into flushing his pills and hashish down the aircraft toilet. 'It was the only way to be safe,' Keylock says. 'I used to tell him, if he said he was clean and he wasn't, I'd chin him.'

The British press was determined there should be trouble – any kind. On April 8, the *Daily Express* reported the controversy between Mick Jagger and the Olympic long-jump champion Lynn Davies about the Stones' alleged bad behaviour at a hotel in Dortmund, West Germany. According to Davies, the hotel's breakfast room had quailed under the stream of obscenities to be heard from the Stones' table. 'I felt sick and ashamed to be British,' the sensitive athlete declared. ' . . . They are tarnishing their country's name in a foreign land . . . ' The allegations were put to Jagger in Paris, at a press conference called to complain of his continuing harassment by customs officers. 'We deny that we were badly behaved,' he retorted. 'We hardly ever used the public rooms at that hotel. They were crammed with athletes, behaving very badly.'

From Paris, the Stones travelled to Poland to make their first, and last, appearance behind the Iron Curtain. The first of two concerts at the Warsaw Palace of Culture took place before 2,000 hand-picked Communist Party officials and their children, while a mass of ordinary teenagers, who had been unable to buy tickets, waited outside, guarded by units of the Polish army. The Stones, to their great bewilderment, could elicit no audience response beyond polite congressional clapping. Halfway through the first show, Mick Jagger had a brilliant idea. Tom Keylock was deputed to drive round the Palace of Culture, scattering Rolling Stones singles just beyond the army cordons. The entire crowd at once broke through to pick up the precious discs, and were driven back by clubs, tear gas and water-cannon fire. It was only by a miracle that troops stationed on the front steps did not actually open fire with their levelled machine guns.

That night, as the running battles still continued, a Polish photographer handed Tom Keylock several rolls of film, shot as the army prepared to counter-attack. Keylock persuaded Don Short, a *Daily Mirror* reporter, to smuggle the film out when they left Poland the following day. Short, in consternation, hid the film down his underpants; then, at Warsaw airport, he lost his nerve and passed it back to Keylock, who successfully jettisoned it. The Polish customs' only victim was Les Perrin, the Stones' publicist, for neglecting to declare the currency he was exporting. Perrin could not leave until he had gone into the airport shop and spent his surplus Polish money on a full-length bearskin coat.

Things were hardly less ugly in Athens, when the Stones gave what would be their final performance for more than two years. Greece's new regime of Fascist army colonels had not yet got round to banning Rock concerts, but they showed their disapproval with hundreds of armed police, pinning the stadium crowd so far back that Jagger could not hope to perform his final, climactic trick of dancing to the stage edge and tossing out roses from a bowl.

Instead, he handed the basket to Tom Keylock and said, 'Okay, baby – run!' As Keylock sprinted towards the police perimeter, several officers at once made ready to receive him. Keylock swung the basket at them, 'chinning' two or three, then hurled it into the air and, as the roses cascaded down, ran for his life.

# 9

## 'A Mars bar fills that gap'

On May 10, Mick Jagger and Keith Richard sat with Robert Fraser in the small police court at Chichester, waiting for their names to be called among the minor larcenies and traffic peccadilloes that are the normal diet of English provincial magistrates. Both accused Stones wore sober dark suits and the expressions of downcast meekness in which their publicist, Les Perrin, had painstakingly rehearsed them. 'We were all squeezed up together on these little benches – the lawyers, the national press and us,' Keith remembers. 'It was a bit like being back at school. I don't think even at that point we expected anything much worse than a cuff on the side of the head or a ruler across the knuckles.'

Jagger had maintained that optimistic view to Marianne each time she begged him to let her confess that the tablets the police found in his jacket at Redlands really belonged to her. 'Mick kept saying that his career could stand a drug-bust but mine couldn't,' Marianne says. 'I could tell it pleased him to think he was playing the English gentleman – that he wouldn't let me be thrown to the wolves.'

Robert Fraser, alone of the trio, was prey to deep gloom and pessimism. Fraser had realized at the outset how prejudicial it must be to his own very serious drug offence to appear in harness with two such notorious co-defendants. The court's refusal to grant him a separate trial had condemned the Old Etonian to forced association with all the Stones accumulated outrage and ill-will. It was, moreover, just a few weeks since Fraser had undergone prosecution over the alleged indecency of some Jim Dine paintings exhibited at his Mount Street gallery. Robert Fraser suspected, if Mick and Keith did not, what a wave was preparing to break in that dusty, sunshiny little courtroom.

The court clerk read out the formal indictments. Michael Philip Jagger – using Les Perrin's office address of 'New Oxford

Street, London, W.1.' - stood accused of possessing four tablets containing amphetamine sulphate and methylamphetamine hydrochloride, contrary to the Dangerous Drugs (Prevention of Misuse) Act, 1964. Robert Hugh Fraser of Mount Street, London, W.1., was accused of possessing heroin and eight amphetamine capsules similar to those found in Jagger's possession. Keith Richard - charged in his real surname, 'Richards' - of Redlands Lane, West Wittering, was accused of alllowing his house to be used for the smoking of cannabis.

All three pleaded 'Not Guilty'. Mr Geoffrey Leach, counsel for Jagger and Richard, said he wished 'to deny most strongly these allegations and to challenge the interpretation thought to be placed by the Prosecution on the evidence in its possession.' Mr William Denny, for Robert Fraser, said his client 'would welcome the earliest opportunity to make answer to the charges against him.'

The three, having elected trial by jury in a higher court, claimed the right to reserve their defence until their reappearance at West Sussex Quarter Session in June. The committal proceedings, even so, allowed a lengthy précis of the Police case to be given by prosecuting solicitor Anthony McCowan. Magistrates in 1967 had no power to impose reporting restrictions if the committal evidence seemed likely to engender prejudice before the main trial. The story of Chief Inspector Dineley's swoop could therefore run at length in every national newspaper five weeks before any of the accused had uttered a word in his own defence.

The Law, however, went out of its way to protect a fourth - but vehemently absent - figure in the case. Since Acid King David Schneidermann had failed to appear to answer charges of possessing cannabis, the Bench ruled it would be unfair for his name to appear in the newspaper reports.

Half an hour later, Mick, Keith and Robert Fraser left the court on bail of £250 each, emerging into brilliant sunshine and the scrum of Fleet Street photographers, amid screams, cheers and scattered boos, escorted by Les Perrin, who could be observed at ticklish moments actually holding Mick Jagger's hand. Nearby in the crowd was a familiar and, as of now, deeply anxious, podgy face. Allen Klein had flown in from New York to attend court today and remain on hand throughout the trial to come.

\* \* \*

At four o'clock that same afternoon, the Scotland Yard Drug Squad raided Brian Jones's flat in Courtfield Road. They found Brian dressed in a Japanese kimono and bleary-eyed, sitting among the debris of an all-night party. The only remaining guest was 24-year-old Prince Stanislas Klossowski de Rola, a Swiss nobleman and would-be pop singer, known within the Stones' circle as 'Stash'.

This was the easiest Stone of all to put into the bag. The entire flat was littered with evidence of drug-taking revelry which Brian had made no attempt to conceal, even though he had received at least two anonymous phone calls warning him that the Police were on their way.

A few minutes' work by the Drug Squad among the divans and outsize cushions were enough to produce eleven different items for chemical analysis. They included a pile of hashish, some methedrine and a glass phial containing traces of cocaine. When asked if the cocaine was his, Brian recoiled in horror. 'No, man – not cocaine,' he stammered. 'That's not my scene. I smoke hash but I'm not a junkie.'

In some uncanny way, the whole of London seems to have known in advance that Brian Jones was to be busted. When he and Stash were brought out, to be questioned further at Chelsea Police Station, crowds of reporters and onlookers were already gathered in Courtfield Road. By 5 p.m., Brian had been formally charged with possession of cocaine, methedrine and cannabis resin. Stash was charged with possessing cannabis, even though no trace of the drug had been found either on his person or on the divan where he had been sleeping.

Next morning, the blond-haired, haggard Stone and the Swiss princeling made a ten-minute appearance before Great Marlborough Street Court's stipendiary magistrate. Both elected trial by jury at Inner London Sessions and were released on bail of £250 each. Brian's first act was to send a telegram to his parents in Cheltenham. 'Please don't worry. Don't jump to nasty conclusions and don't judge me too harshly. All my love . . . '

The exquisitely neat alignment of Brian's bust with Mick and Keith's committal for trial, proved beyond any doubt that the Rolling Stones, through their three most prominent and notorious members, were now under systematic attack by the Establishment whose sensibilites they had so long carelessly flouted. Not for their own misdemeanours only, but for all the pampered, nonchalant arrogance of Britain's pop generation, they had been marked down for a retribution which, in the ensuing weeks, despite all its judicial pomp and deliberateness, bore marked similarities to the medieval hue-and-cry.

The first hard lesson, for young men cocooned in flattery as much as luxury, was to realize how very few among their immense social circle had the ability, intelligence – or, for that matter, the inclination – to give them the help they now desperately needed.

There would be little help from Decca Records for musicians who had largely secured the company its current multi-million-pound annual profit. Sir Edward Lewis, though he expressed himself 'concerned' at the Stones' plight, and its possible repercussions on Decca shares, remained carefully dissociated from all strategy being prepared for their defence. 'The Stones weren't an in-house Decca act, the way the Beatles were at EMI,' Andrew Loog Oldham says. 'That's why, when the Beatles got into drug busts later, Sir Joseph Lockwood gave them all that support. To Decca, the Stones were just freelances. They had to look after themselves.'

Oldham himself played a curiously small part in the developing drama. As many remarked, it seemed that Allen Klein had taken over completely as the Stones' manager. But for Oldham, however, there would have been no Les Perrin to choreograph the manners and subdue the wardrobes of his two charges, and in every way reconstruct the prejudicial aura they would take with them into Court. Perrin also used his extensive contacts in the borderland between Fleet Street and Parliament to enlist the sympathy of liberal-minded MPs like Tom Driberg – already a social conquest of Mick Jagger's – and the Home Office junior minister, Dick Taverne. On May 19, speaking in Wales, Taverne cited the Jagger-Richard case as one where the reporting of committal proceedings must inevitably create prejudice against the accused who had not yet spoken in their own defence.

Before Mick and Keith even came to trial, most of the papers had agreed this must be the end for the Rolling Stones. So it could easily have been but for Mick Jagger, a wholly unexpected tower of strength in this period, both in marshalling his and Keith's defence and, simultaneously, motivating Bill and Charlie, those deeply bemused, innocent bystanders, to get back into the studio and begin work on an album to redeem the failure of *Between the Buttons*. An additional spur was provided, in early June, by the Beatles' psychedelic folk master-piece *Sergeant Pepper's Lonely Hearts Club Band*, combining drug-sparkled mysticism with matey Toytown humour, and packaged in an historic sleeve showing the four Beatles as sateen hussars, set about by Pop Art effigies, marijuana plants and a rag doll printed with the legend 'Welcome Rolling Stones'.

The first tentative studio sessions made clear to everyone that Brian Jones was on the edge of complete disintegration. The bust at Courtfield Road had come only days after his return from the Cannes Film Festival and an anguished week of enforced propinquity with Anita Pallenberg, as musical director and star of the West German entry, *A Degree of Murder*. Brian had stayed in the same hotel as Anita and Keith, and accompanied them on the round of parties and receptions, waiting for a chance to renew his pleas to Anita to return to him. But all that happened when he did get her alone was that old, uncontrollable urge to abuse and hit her.

Since losing Anita, he had travelled through half a dozen girls from the scores who offered themselves. His old Cheltenham schoolfriend Peter Watson remembers meeting him in Tottenham Court Road, bejewelled and bangled, a smut-eyed 'dolly bird' clinging to each arm. At the end of their conversation, Brian proffered the girls to Watson, as one might a packet of cigarettes, and said, 'Here – do you want one?'

He had subsequently acquired a steady girl-friend in Suki Poitier, a fashion model whose blonde hair and facial bone-structure were the nearest to Anita's he could find. Suki had survived the car crash that killed Tara Browne, heir to the Guinness fortune and subject of John Lennon's finest song, A Day in the Life. She moved in with Brian shortly after the Courtfield Road bust, and for the next eighteen months bravely endured the ordeal of being a living replica.

Brian was now a haunted and a haunting sight. The face, under its gold fringe, was puffy and sick-pale; the eyes, when not glazed over, wavered back and forth, bleakly corroborating the chaos inside his head. He would sometimes arrive at Olympic Studios so drunk, he could do nothing but sit among his guitars and music-stands, and sink into comatose sleep. When he could pick up a guitar, he would sometimes play it without tuning it, or so badly that the whole take was unusable. In time, the others found it simplest to have his amplifier lead quietly disconnected.

The bust and his impending trial had stopped him using hashish – and, indeed, made him paranoiacally fearful that someone else might leave some at Courtfield Road where the police could find it. He continued, none the less, to dose himself with barbiturates washed down with brandy or Scotch and, in safe houses, to carry on experimenting with new varieties of LSD. His closest friend in this period was Jimi Hendrix, the stunning young Blues guitarist who had become the earliest idol of the English Underground. In June, Brian flew to America to see Hendrix play at the first-ever Rock festival, at Monterey, California. Though present only as a spectator, warmly interested in the new generation of American Blues stars like Hendrix and Janis Joplin, he became a festival attraction in his own right, wandering round the hippy bivouacs in his silks and Berber jewellery. 'Brian and Jimi took STP together at Monterey,' Anita Pallenberg says. 'That's the acid which can give you a 72-hour trip.'

Barely noticed in the glare surrounding the Jagger-Richard trial, Brian began paying regular visits to a Harley Street psychiatrist, Dr Leonard Henry. Dr Henry considered his condition serious enough to warrant residential treatment, and arranged with a Harley Street colleague, Dr Anthony Flood, for Brian to spend three weeks at Flood's private clinic at Roehampton. The beginning of this analysis-cum-rest cure was not auspicious. Brian arrived in full regalia, accompanied by Tom Keylock and Suki Poitier, and demanded a double-bedded room for Suki and himself during his treatment. 'It's not on,' Dr Flood said tersely. 'In any case, the first thing I'm going to do is put you to sleep for two days.'

The psychiatrist's initial diagnosis had much to do with this infantile urge to exhibit sexual bravado, even in a state of manifest desperation. Brian, he noted, was 'anxious, considerably depressed, perhaps even suicidal . . . He is easily depresssed and easily thwarted. He cannot sort out his problems satisfactorily because he becomes so anxious and depressed . . . He has not a great deal of confidence in himself . . . He is still trying to grow up in many ways.'

Dr Flood was struck, at the same time, by the intelligence and perceptiveness that could shine through Brian's superstar conceits and tantrums. Psychiatrist and patient became something like friends in hours of conversation ranging from Brian's hypochondriac obsession with all forms of artificial stimulant, through his interest in railway locomotives and London buses, to quite advanced questions of history, philosophy and ethics. At one point, he told Dr Flood he had always regretted not going to university. When told that 25 was not too late an age to do so, he seemed to give the matter serious consideration.

The treatment seemed to be working until a day when Brian begged Dr Flood to let him out for the evening, because, he insisted, the other Stones needed him at Olympic Studios. The doctor agreed, on condition he was back in bed by midnight at the latest. Brian appeared at seven the next morning, so full of alcohol and pills that he could hardly walk. Dr Flood had no alternative but to put him to bed and start again from the beginning.

Trial at a regional quarter sessions, under the Old English court structure, was nowhere near as ridden with legal pomp and circumstances as the yearly Assizes. This lower court – named for its traditional convening each 'quarter day' – featured no grey-wigged judge, walking in state to the courthouse, preceded by mace-bearer and chamberlain. At quarter sessions it was sufficient for a senior lawyer – a 'Recorder', sitting alone, or Chairman, sitting with lay magistrates – to administer the case, sum up the evidence and give legal directions to the jury. The Jagger-Richard-Fraser trial was unusual in that the Chairman of West Sussex Quarter Sessions happened also to be a judge, 61-year-old ex-Naval Commander Leslie Kenneth Allen Block.

It was not in his metropolitan capacity in the Mayor's and City of London Court, but as a Sussex landowner, dairy farmer and Justice of the Peace that Judge Block found himself charged with conduct of Britain's most scandal-ridden trial since the age of Christine Keeler. He was to rise to the occasion, even so, as a classic British judge, combining unworldly and fastidious remoteness from the matter he was trying with an intermittent desire to crack jokes for the amusement of the assembled barristers.

The three-day trial, from June 27–29, turned Chichester from a quiet yachtsmen's haven into a scrimmage to glimpse the main defendants that was by no means confined to hysterical little girls. Extra police by the hundred were drafted in to control the mêlée around the court buildings, of fans, reporters, TV crews and what the press invariably describes as 'housewives – some carrying shopping baskets'. Bright sunshine and abundant hot dog and ice cream stalls lent almost a carnival atmosphere. One quick-witted huckster brought a van with silk screen printing equipment to run off T-shirts inscribed 'Free the Stones' and 'Mick is Innocent'.

Counsel for the defence of both Mick and Keith was 44-year-old Michael Havers QC, a future Attorney General, at that time one of the most eminent, and costly, 'silks' at the criminal Bar. Havers had been retained not for his eminence only but for his genuine indignation that Jagger should have been prosecuted so ruthlessly for what seemed a technicality and Keith, on such apparently circumstantial evidence. It was disconcerting, none the less, for the two Stones, after fighting their way from their limousine into the court precincts to observe Havers and the prosecuting counsel, Malcolm Morris QC, talking together as amiably as members of the same club, fraternity and family.

Mick Jagger was first to be called from the well of the old-fashioned courtroom into its elevated wooden dock. As the familiar doll-like figure appeared, dressed in a light green jacket, olive trousers, frilled shirt and multi-striped tie, an involuntary gasp came from the 80-odd girls who threatened to overbalance the narrow public gallery. The police usher bellowed for silence but could not – and would never – still an undercurrent of female anguish like the constant soft rustle of tissue paper or chocolate box wrappings.

The task before Michael Havers that morning was comparatively simple. Jagger's plea of Not Guilty to illegal possession of amphetamines left only one possible defence. Havers must convince the jury – as he had himself been convinced – that Jagger had got the four tablets on prescription from a doctor, even though no written prescription could be produced in evidence.

The secondary part of Havers's strategy was to emphasize the extremely marginal nature of the alleged offence. The tablets, though illegal in Britain, were sold openly in other European countries – were, indeed, recommended by their makers, Lepetit of Milan, as a remedy for mundane ailments like travel sickness. A law designed to curb criminal and habitual drug-pushers was being mobilized against someone whose offence, according to the evidence, was purely accidental, and could be repeated by any respectable citizen who bought travel sickness pills abroad and forgot to dispose of them before returning to Britain.

In the quick verbal brush-strokes of what he clearly considered an open-and-shut case, Michael Morris QC outlined the circumstances of the police swoop on Redlands, the search of the upstairs bedrooms and the discovery of the four tablets in Jagger's green velvet jacket. Detective Sergeant Stanley Cudmore then took the stand with his official notebook to testify that Jagger had admitted the tablets were his, and claimed they were a doctor's prescription to help him 'stay awake and work'. Sergeant Cudmore, under cross-examination, agreed that Jagger's conduct throughout the raid had been 'thoroughly adult and co-operative'.

The only witness for the Defence was Dr Raymond Dixon Firth of Wilton Crescent, Knightsbridge, Jagger's doctor since 1965. Dr Dixon Firth testified that 'some time before February', Jagger had rung up to ask about some tablets he said he'd bought on his way back from the San Remo Pop Festival, and had been taking to help him cope with a period of intense personal strain. The doctor realized the pills were amphetamines and gave Jagger permission to go on taking them, provided he did so only in an emergency. This, in Dr Dixon Firth's opinion, was a valid prescription which put Jagger in absolutely legal possession of the amphetamines. He added that if Jagger had come to his surgery for something to enable him to 'stay awake and work', the doctor would have prescribed exactly that same drug.

Judge Block turned and conferred briefly with his three fellow magistrates – two more Sussex farmers and a newsagent from Worthing. Then he addressed the jury of eleven men and one woman.

'These [Dr Dixon Firth's] remarks cannot be regarded as a prescription,' he said. 'I therefore direct you that there is no defence to this charge.' The jury retired for a token six minutes before declaring its obligatory verdict of Guilty. Judge Block turned back to Jagger, now standing and gripping the edge of the dock. 'I propose to defer sentencing you until after the trial of your two friends,' the judge continued. 'In the meantime, you will be remanded in custody.' The police warder who had appeared beside him took Jagger's arm and steered him to a police cell below the courtroom, to await the end of the day's proceedings.

The trial of Robert Fraser lasted an even shorter time. Fraser, on the advice of his counsel, William Denny, had changed his plea to Guilty. All that could be done, therefore, was to plead the mitigating circumstances of Fraser's distinguished military career in Kenya during the Mau Mau emergency and the hard work and flair by which he had afterwards founded his London art gallery. Knowing the layman's view of drug addicts as helpless and spineless beings, Mr Denny took pains to stress how desperately Fraser had wrestled wth his heroin addiction – how, after one traumatic cure, he had lapsed back into the habit but had, none the less, found courage and resolution enough to telephone his doctor for help. He was now 'completely cured', his counsel said. 'There is no reason why he should ever go back on to heroin again.'

Fraser's sentence also was deferred until the end of Keith Richard's trial. He, too, was remanded in custody and removed to a police cell, pending his and Jagger's departure to spend that night in prison. A brief period was allowed for each to confer with his solicitor. Keith, still on committal bail, had meanwhile driven at top speed back to West Wittering where Jagger had spent the previous night, to fetch him some clean clothes, a book (on Tibetan philosophy) and a 184-piece jigsaw puzzle.

Jagger and Robert Fraser were then each handcuffed to a prison officer, bundled rapidly into a grey police van with other remand prisoners and driven, through the crowd of distraught girls and craning camera-lenses, to begin the 38-mile journey to the Victorian prison at Lewes. It was a brutally drastic measure to adopt with individuals who, despite their shocked bewilderment, were never other than peaceful and co-operative.

At Lewes Prison, the two were placed together in a room in the prison hospital. Jagger, as he later admitted, was 'deathly scared and in tears'. Before Lights Out – at an hour when a Rolling Stone customarily thought of getting up – two visitors were brought in to see him. One was Marianne Faithfull, bringing him 60 cigarettes, a draughts board, newspapers and fresh fruit. The other was Michael Cooper, carrying a miniature camera in the hope of photographing Mick Jagger behind bars. A prison officer spotted the camera as he was leaving and confiscated the film inside.

Next morning, June 28, Jagger and Robert Fraser were awakened before seven, given a meagre breakfast, then handcuffed again for their return to Chichester. Some of the more sympathetic newspapermen were already asking whether the two really had to be led to and from court, manacled like murderers or psychopaths. A prison spokesman eventually replied it had been done because their guards 'had no instructions to do otherwise.'

At Chichester, they were put back into a cell under the courtroom, waiting to be brought up and sentenced if Keith Richard's trial should be concluded today. Though uncomfortable and boring, their eight-hour wait was not devoid of fleshly comforts. Permission was given for a local hotelier to bring in their lunch – roast lamb for Jagger and, for Fraser, cold salmon salad. Both finished their meal, in the drab little brickwork cubicle, with a dish of strawberries and cream.

Above them, Keith Richard now sat in the dock, wearing a black Beau Brummell suit and white polo-neck shirt, his well-worn 24-year-old face expressionless under a heaped black pompadour as ragged as if he, too, had spent the night on a prison bench. Now there was no tissuey rustling from the girls in the public gallery. The court was plunged into spellbound silence, broken only by the voice of Malcolm Morris QC, and the sound of frantic scribbling in the packed press bench. Even the dignified man from *The Times* could let none of this get away.

For the first time today, the jury received a full account of the raid on Redlands, the discovery of eight men and 'a young woman' listening to pop music while watching television, and the 'strong, sweet, unusual smell' which the police had at once detected. ' . . . In the drawing room where Richard was entertaining his guests, one of them had a large supply of cannabis resin,'

237

Malcolm Morris continued. 'The behaviour of one of the guests may suggest she was under the influence of cannabis in a way that Richard could not fail to notice . . . You cannot have any doubt at all that he was permitting his house to be used for the purpose of smoking cannabis.'

The source of 'that large supply of cannabis resin' seemed to bear a charmed life. 'He is a man not before the court, and, indeed, not now in the country,' Malcolm Morris told the jury firmly. 'You are not concerned with the name or identity of anyone at that party other than Keith Richard.' Only after pressure from Michael Havers – and a little vernacular joke from Judge Block, who observed that the man had 'done a bunk' – was Acid King David Schneidermann's name finally heard in court. Even then, it was his surname only, and rendered phonetically in most reports as 'Snidermann'.

Resuming his major theme, Malcolm Morris told the jury they would hear from a Scotland Yard Drug Squad officer, Detective Inspector John Lynch, that the effect of smoking cannabis was tranquillity, happiness and 'a tendency to dispel inhibitions'.

'You may think it could have had exactly that effect on one of Richard's guests. This was the young lady sitting on the settee. All she was wearing was a light-coloured fur rug which, from time to time, she allowed to fall, disclosing her nude body. She was unperturbed and apparently enjoying the situation. Although she was taken upstairs, where her clothes were, to be searched, she returned wearing only the fur rug and, in the words of the woman detective looking after her, in merry mood – one apparently of vague unconcern.

'*We are not concerned,*' continued the QC, not batting an eyelid, 'with who that young lady was or may have been. But was she someone who had lost her inhibitions, and had she lost them because of smoking Indian hemp?'

One can only marvel at this attempt to condemn Keith Richard on a drugs charge by implying he had simultaneously been holding a sex orgy. In doing so, Malcolm Morris was handing the press an already die-stamped banner headline – one of those scraps of smutty innuendo which, once lodged in a million or so tabloid minds, make questions of guilt and innocence scarcely relevant. Not even the Christine Keeler case had given

Fleet Street what Malcolm Morris QC gave it on June 28, 1967. At the mention of 'nudity' there had been excitement enough among the journalists present. At the mention of 'a fur rug', there was something close to collective orgasm.

No doubt could exist as to the nude girl's identity. Marianne Faithfull had been in court throughout the proceedings, sitting next to Allen Klein and Les Perrin. Though both sides in the case had agreed she should not be named, every newspaper could use her photograph in quite legal juxtaposition with its story of the raid, the rug-wrapped girl and her shameless attempts to arouse policemen in the course of their duty. Already, by some mysterious means, a rumour was travelling the length and breadth of England that, when the police entered Keith Richard's sitting room, they had interrupted an orgy of cunnilingus in which Jagger had been licking a Mars bar pushed into Marianne's vagina. The Mars bar was a detail of such sheer madness as to make the story believed, then and for ever after. No one needed any explanation of the line that appeared gnomically on *Private Eye* magazine's next front cover: 'A Mars bar fills that gap.'

Four police witnesses for the Prosecution gave evidence to support the idea that, in addition to being high on cannabis, Marianne was also a shameless nymphomaniac. Woman Detective Constable Rosemary Slade, indeed, testified that when the search party arrived, 'Miss X' – as Marianne was futilely described – had been 'completely naked'. Woman Detective Constable Evelyn Fuller described her 'merry mood' and 'apparent unconcern' when taken upstairs to be searched, and how, once alone with Miss Fuller, she had 'deliberately let the rug fall'.

The rug itself made a dramatic appearance in Michael Havers's cross-examination of Detective Sergeant Stanley Cudmore, after Sergeant Cudmore's assertion that 'one could see she had nothing on underneath it.'

'Was it a large rug?' Havers inquired.

'Quite large,' Sergeant Cudmore said.

'Was it bigger than a fur coat?'

'Yes.'

'But it's a bed-cover, isn't it?' Havers said. 'Six foot square. Here – take a look.' With help of his junior counsel, the QC then stretched the brown and white mottled rug with its garish orange lining across the barristers' bench.

'It's enormous,' Michael Havers said. 'You can see – it's about eight-and-a-half feet by five.'

Havers opened Keith's defence with an address to the jury, complaining bitterly of his opponent's smear tactics against a person who, being accused of no crime, had no chance to speak in her own defence. 'She remains technically anonymous, but the effect of all this is that she has been decribed as a drug-taking nymphomaniac. How would you [members of the jury] feel if, in another place, witnesses were going into the box and discussing your behaviour, and you could do nothing about it?

'Do you expect me to let that girl go into the witness box? I am not going to allow her to. I am not going to tear that blanket of anonymity aside and let the world laugh of scorn, as it will. This is a girl whose name has not yet been dragged into the mud. If I cannot call her into this court, I propose to call no one who was at that house.'

Havers's next point of attack was the means by which Scotland Yard had received the original tip-off to raid Keith Richard's house. After this, Judge Block adjourned the court for the afternoon. Keith was released on continuance of his £250 bail. Jagger and Fraser were put back into handcuffs and removed for their second night in custody. An agency photographer took what would become a celebrated picture of Jagger, dishevelled and scruffy, raising his and his police guard's joined arms to shield his face from flash bulbs. Society had got him where it wanted him at last – manacled, in an open tumbril, receiving the curses, boos and catcalls of the mob.

Next morning, it was time for Keith Richard to go into the witness-box. An almost audible shudder greeted this least prepossessing defendant, with his fancy clothes and the pale, sickly, wolfish face that seemed living testament to all the depraved goings-on the Prosecution had described. The very last thing expected from such an apparently self-incriminating figure was articulateness and candour, and a wit which, several times, left even a cross-examining QC outmanoeuvred.

Michael Havers's first line of questioning was designed to show the jury how little direct control a Rolling Stone had over what went on around him – and how commensurately little responsibility he ought to bear for the behaviour of those in his retinue. This necessitated a brief history of the Stones, from Keith's and Mick's first meeting at the age of six to the 'complete lack of privacy, and constant work' which, for all of them, had lasted since 1963.

'Do you need any sort of protection from your fans?' Havers asked.

'Oh yes,' Keith replied. 'I need an army.'

'And why do you need that protection?'

'I've been strangled,' Keith said, touching his neck reminiscently. 'They just get hold of your tie or scarf, and pull . . . My clothes have disappeared,' he went on, grinning apologetically as a rustle of laughter came from the court.

'And in the course of your travels you have to go to parties and are always meeting people?'

'Yes, I meet *thousands* of people.'

This led neatly to the subject of Acid King David Schneidermann, whom Keith said he had met only twice, briefly, before Acid King David had been invited to Redlands. In any case, he added, the whole idea for a weekend party had been someone else's. Keith himself had only heard on the previous day that it was going ahead. The point was well made that if pop stars did not organize their own parties, they could hardly be expected to know everyone they subsequently found enjoying their hospitality.

At Michael Havers's prompting, Keith gave his account of what now sounded an altogether normal country weekend – the cars arriving late on Saturday, the bacon and egg supper, the next morning's late lie-in (excluding Acid King David's dispensation of LSD) and the afternoon mystery tour, which had ended just before the Drug Squad's arrival. At that point, Keith said he had been upstairs, bathing and changing, and had no idea what his guests were doing.

'Do you use incense in your house?'

'Sometimes.'

'Why?'

'Well, I picked up on it from fans who used to send me joss sticks . . . I quite like the smell of them.'

'Is there anything sinister in that?' Havers asked. 'Is it done to

241

conceal the smell of cannabis?'

'No, sir,' Keith said firmly.

He was then shown the briar pipe which police analysis had proved to contain traces of cannabis resin. 'That came from Los Angeles,' he said. 'It was given to me.'

'By whom?'

'An American – a group's road manager.'

'On a trip like that, you could get a lot of stuff . . . a mountain of stuff,' Havers suggested.

'Yeah – always. When I get back to England, my suitcases are full up with rubbish.'

'Did you have any idea that anyone at your house was smoking cannabis that weekend?'

'No, sir.'

'Would you have allowed such a thing to happen?'

'No, sir.'

To counteract the manifestly good impression Keith had made so far, Malcolm Morris began his cross-examination with a well-tried device of British barristers when pitted against their social inferiors – the 'let me see if I've got this right' or 'let us establish if you are wholly or just partially cretinous' approach.

'You heard the opening address to this Court by your counsel, did you not?'

'Yes, sir.'

'It was given on your instructions?'

'Yes, sir.'

'He [your counsel] spoke of various things and in the course of that opening speech made it quite clear that your defence was that Schneidermann had been planted in your weekend party as part of a wicked conspiracy by the *News of the World*. Is that part of your defence or not?'

'Yes it is, sir,' Keith replied.

'Is your defence that Schneidermann was planted by the *News of the World* in an attempt to get Mick Jagger convicted of smoking hashish? Is that the suggestion?'

'That is the suggestion,' Keith agreed.

'. . . so, if you are seriously suggesting that this was part of a plot, it is a curious plot in that nothing, in fact, was done to

242

associate Jagger with Indian hemp.'

'He was associated with the whole raid, which is enough, I'm sure,' Keith answered.

'Is this what you are saying – and the jury will want to know – that, because the *News of the World* did not want to pay libel damages to Mick Jagger, it was arranged to have Indian hemp planted in your house.'

'Yes,' Keith said.

'There was, as we know,' Malcolm Morris proceeded, 'a young woman sitting on a settee, wearing only a fur rug. Would you agree that, in the ordinary course of events you would expect a young woman to be embarrassed if she had nothing on but a fur rug in the presence of eight men, two of whom were hangers-on and another a Moroccan servant?'

'Not at all,' Keith replied.

'You regard that, do you, as quite normal?'

Here, finally, Keith let show a flicker of his contempt for the proceedings.

'We are not old men,' was his retort. 'We're not worried about petty morals.'

Judge Block's summing up, after the lunch-recess, began with an irritated reference to the view, expressed four weeks earlier by Dick Taverne MP, that unrestricted reporting of Jagger and Richard's committal proceedings might have created prejudice in the jury's minds. 'That gentleman,' Judge Block observed, 'did not know the quality of a Sussex jury such as you are here now.' Since the quality of a Sussex jury is in general no different from that of a Surrey or Hampshire jury, it can only be concluded that the judge was buttering up the jury, as judges very often do, to make it more receptive to his own view of the evidence. The peroration that followed contained several strong indications that Judge Block, in court usher phraseology, was 'summing up for a conviction'.

That much was clear in his sedulous direction to the jury to 'put out of your minds [i.e. do not in any circumstances overlook] any prejudice you may feel about the way Richard dresses, or his observations about petty morals . . . The issue you have to try is a comparatively simple one. You have to be satisfied that cannabis resin was being smoked in the house when the police went there, and you have to be satisfied that Richard knew of it.

'. . . You must exclude from your mind,' Judge Block continued, 'anything you may have read in the papers about two of the house party either admitting or being convicted of being in possession of certain drugs . . . Finally, I would ask you to disregard the evidence as to the lady who was alleged by the police to have been in some condition of undress, and not let that prejudice your minds in any way.'

With this amazing directive added as an afterthought to the hours of unforgettably lurid detail concerning 'the young lady' which Judge Block had not thought proper to curtail, the jury rose and filed from the courtroom. They were absent just a little more than one hour. At 3:45 p.m., the foreman rose and announced they had reached a unanimous verdict of Guilty.

Amid gasps and cries of 'No!' from the girls in the gallery, Mick Jagger and Robert Fraser were put up into the dock and ranged next to Keith for sentencing.

'Keith Richards,' Judge Block began. 'The offence for which you have, very properly, been convicted carries a maximum sentence, imposed by Parliament of up to ten years.' When the cries of horror from the gallery had abated, he continued:

'That is a view of the seriousness of the offence . . . As it is, you will go to prison for one year. You will also pay £500 towards the costs of the Prosecution.'

He turned to Robert Fraser.

'Robert Hugh Fraser – you have pleaded Guilty to possessing a highly dangerous and harmful drug . . . You will go to prison for six months. You will also pay £200 towards the costs of the Prosecution.'

Lastly, he turned to Mick Jagger.

'Michael Philip Jagger – you have been found Guilty of possessing a potentially dangerous and harmful drug . . . You will go to prison for three months. You will pay £200 towards the costs of the Prosecution.'

Jagger, as the words hit him, crumpled up and clutched his forehead with his hand. Keith remained, white-faced and stiff-backed, staring in front of him. Robert Fraser blew out his cheeks as if in a blast of icy air. As they left the dock together, amid an uproar of shouts and weeping from the gallery, Mick Jagger was visibly crying.

News of Judge Block's justice had already reached the crowd outside the court building. As the three were led downstairs, they could already hear chants of 'Shame!' and 'Let them go!'

At the court building's front entrance, a crowd of 600 surged against the big metal gates, struggling for the best view of Mick and Keith when they were brought out to their prison van. A shout went up as Keith Richard's blue Bentley appeared, carrying Tom Keylock and Marianne Faithfull. Marianne, too, was crying as Keylock ushered her inside for a fifteen-minute meeting with Jagger before he left to begin his sentence.

Half-an-hour later, while a decoy van fought to get through the spectators outside the rear gate, Jagger, Richard and Fraser were hurried through the front vestibule and into a police squad car. Just outside Chichester, they were transferred to a police van with a seven-man crew. The van then headed for London – or seemed to as far as its passengers could tell. They were, they realized, in the grip of arrangements more inflexibly certain then the best-organized tour schedule.

The first stop was Brixton Prison, the gaunt Victorian fortress, in the hardly more cheerful South London ghetto, where, Authority had decided, Mick Jagger would serve his sentence well separated from his colleague in crime. Keith and Robert Fraser, handcuffed together, deduced they were bound for a common destination. Forty minutes later, the van stopped again, at the end of a long, dreary cul-de-sac, before the Gothic main gate of Wormwood Scrubs.

The events of the next 24 hours raise the interesting possibility that Authority's main purpose in bagging the two Stones was to inflict ritual bathing, delousing and barbering, and then leave them to the mercy of prisoners who would know even better than Judge Leslie Block the proper treatment for prissy and perverted pop stars.

If that was the idea, it failed most miserably. Though Jagger and Richard both underwent full induction as prisoners, exchanging their Carnaby clothes for regulation blue denim overalls and black shoes, no attempt was made to cut their hair or otherwise abuse them. Jagger, at Brixton, was taken to a single cell which – he afterwards said – 'wasn't so much worse than a hotel room in Minnesota.' At 'The Scrubs', as Keith – now prisoner number 7855 – was escorted to his cell, other prisoners shouted out 'Hard luck, mate,' threw him cigarettes – and asked him if he wanted any hash.

Authority seemed to be taking its cue from a feeling manifest in the highest official echelons, even before the subsequent outbursts of popular protest, that Judge Leslie Block had gone preposterously over the top. Directly after the sentences were pronounced, Michael Havers had asked for, and been granted, a certificate of leave for Jagger and Richard to appeal against both their convictions and sentences. The matter was set down for preliminary hearing in the Court of Appeal on the very next day, June 30. Since the full appeal, involving transcripts of the Chichester trial, could not be made ready before the current legal term ended, it was obvious that Jagger and Richard must languish in prison for the next two months or be granted bail. Before going into court next afternoon, Michael Havers was seen by the Prosecution counsel, Malcolm Morris, and told that Morris had 'direct instructions' not to oppose his application for bail.

The intervening night had seen demonstrations of protest by Rolling Stones fans that, for once, seemed devoted to a purpose other than simple mayhem. In Piccadilly Circus, 300 teenagers in kaftans and bells held an all-night vigil around the Eros statue. Others, more pertinently, collected in Bouverie Street to shout insults at the *News of the World*. In clubs and discotheques up and down Britain, disc jockeys called for symbolic moments of silence, or played non-stop Stones records. In New York, when the news came through, groups of American hippies mounted angry pickets outside the British Consulate. It was reported that other British pop groups had volunteered to play in a gigantic 'free-the-Stones' concert whose proceeds would be spent on an avalanche of flowers with which to engulf Judge Block. The most spontaneously generous demonstration of professional solidarity came from The Who – a cover version of It's All Over Now and Under My Thumb, recorded in a morning and put out over pirate radio that same afternoon, with a large press announcement that, until Jagger and Richard were released, The Who would do everything possible to keep their work before the public.

Nor was the protest confined to the sphere of pop only. Letters to *The Times* – from playwright John Osborne among others – deplored the harshness of the sentences and the many inconsistencies, to put it no worse, which seemed to have governed the trial. A newspaper interview with Christopher Gibbs did something to counteract the rampaging rumour about sex orgies with Mars bars. It carried much weight that this hitherto undisclosed Redlands guest, who swore Keith's party had been 'thoroughly decorous', was an Old Etonian and a nephew of the Governor of Rhodesia.

On June 30, Michael Havers QC rose to his feet in the Court of Appeal to request the bail for Mick Jagger and Keith Richard that some inscrutable mechanism within the British Establishment had already decided should be given. Havers, in the 25-minute hearing, barely needed to develop his argument that Mick Jagger was no drug addict or pusher, that he had verbal permission from a doctor to possess amphetamines, and that insufficient and unfair evidence had been used to convict Keith Richard of allowing his house to be used for cannabis-smoking. Lord Justice Diplock, speaking for his two fellow appeal judges, granted each bail of £5,000 with further sureties totalling £2,000 each, until their full appeal hearing when the new law term opened in September. The Court, however, refused Havers's request that Jagger and Richard should be allowed to leave Britain in the meantime, and ordered them to surrender their passports.

Robert Fraser's counsel, William Denny, asked for Fraser to receive bail pending his appeal against sentence. Mr Denny argued that Fraser was no longer a heroin addict and, in addition, felt 'a sense of grievance' that his case had been tried under the same unnatural spotlight as the two Stones'. His application for bail was refused, but with a proviso that his appeal should be squeezed in before the end of the present law term.

By 4:30 p.m., Mick Jagger was free. He sat alone in the back of Keith's Bentley, smiling wanly at a group of schoolgirls which, somehow, had collected outside Brixton Prison to see Tom Keylock drive him away. At 5:10, the Bentley arrived at

Wormwood Scrubs to pick up Keith. Keylock then drove straight to a Fleet Street pub, The Feathers, where Les Perrin had convened a rush press conference. Both Stones looked weary, crumpled, but impressively composed. Jagger told reporters he had spent some of his time in Brixton 'writing poetry'. Asked how he had been treated, he said, 'Everyone was very kind and helpful.' Keith – who had, at one point, launched into furious kicking of his cell-door – confined himself to denying the Stones had ever contemplated a break-up. Jagger drank a vodka and lime, and Keith a 'whisky Mac', for which the pub landlord refused to accept any payment.

Next morning, Jagger sat in bed once more beside Marianne, with every national newspaper spread round him on the coverlet. Fleet Street had performed a complete volte-face, greeting his liberation with almost audible church bells and cannon fire. Even the Beatles had never drawn so comprehensive a crop of banner headlines and editorial comment. Among the latter was an item whose unlikely source – and still more unlikely author – added all the more weight to words that, with hindsight, fix the precise moment when everyone stopped going barmy.

William Rees-Mogg, until that day, had seemed to have little in common with his great predecessors as editor of *The Times*. He was a man of schoolmasterly mien, slightly bookish and dusty, whose avowed passions were for the Classics and Somerset, and whose apparent remoteness from mundane editorial matters, like hard news, seemed calculated to maintain his newspaper in its least worthwhile incarnation, as a mere bulletin-board for the British Establishment.

William Rees-Mogg was at the furthest posssible extreme from Mick Jagger, the Rolling Stones, pop music or teenagers. His instincts, none the less, proved to be those of a courageous as well as deeply moral-minded journalist. On Saturday, July 1, *The Times*' first leader was given over entirely to the Jagger case. Rees-Mogg had written it himself, headlining it – as perhaps only Rees-Mogg would – with a quotation from William Blake: WHO BREAKS A BUTTERFLY ON A WHEEL.

'. . . Judge Block directed the jury that the approval of a doctor was not a defence in law to the charge of possessing drugs without a prescription, and the jury convicted. Mr Jagger was not charged with complicity in any other drug offence that occurred in the same house. They were separate cases, and no evidence was produced to suggest that he knew that Mr Fraser had heroin tablets or that the vanishing Mr Sneidermann [sic] had cannabis resin. It is indeed no offence to be in the same building or the same company as people possessing or even using drugs, nor could it reasonably be made an offence . . .

'One has to ask, therefore, how it is that this technical offence, divorced as it must be from other people's offences, was thought to deserve the penalty of imprisonment. In the courts at large it is most uncommon for imprisonment to be imposed on first offenders where the drugs are not major drugs of addiction and there is no question of drug traffic. The normal penalty is probation, and the purpose of probation is to encourage the offender to develop his career and to avoid the drug risks in future. It is surprising, therefore, that Judge Block should have decided to sentence Mr Jagger to imprisonment, and particularly surprising as Mr Jagger's is about as mild a drug case as can ever have been brought before the Courts.

'It would be wrong to speculate on the judge's reasons, which we do not know. It is, however, possible to consider the public reaction. There are many people who take a primitive view of the matter. They consider that Mr Jagger has "got what was coming to him". They resent the anarchic quality of the Rolling Stones' performances, dislike their songs, dislike their influence on teenagers and broadly suspect them of decadence.

'As a sociological concern this may be reasonable enough, and at an emotional level it is very understandable, but it has nothing at all to do with the case. One has to ask a different question: has Mr Jagger received the same treatment as he would have received if he had not been a famous figure, with all the criticism and resentment his celebrity has aroused. If a promising undergraduate had come back from a summer visit to Italy with four pep pills in his pocket, would it have been thought right to ruin his career by sending him to prison for three months? Would it also have been thought necessary to display him handcuffed to the public?

'There are cases in which a single figure becomes the focus for public concern about some aspects of public morality. The

Stephen Ward case, with its dubious evidence and questionable verdict, was one of them, and that verdict killed Stephen Ward. There are elements of the same emotions in the reactions to this case. If we are going to make any case a symbol of the conflict between the sound traditional values of Britain and the new hedonism, then we must be sure that the sound traditional values include those of tolerance and equity. It should be the particular quality of British justice to ensure that Mr Jagger is treated exactly the same as anyone else, no better and no worse. There must remain a suspicion in this case that Mr Jagger received a more severe sentence than would have been thought proper for any purely anonymous young man.'

In commenting on a case which still had to go to appeal, William Rees-Mogg was technically in contempt of court and, as such, liable to both a heavy fine and imprisonment. That no attempt was made to prosecute, or even admonish, him testifies not only to the manifest humanity and moral soundness of his editorial but also the new official line that Jagger was now to be let off the hook. The *Sunday Times*, next day, made the same points, and ran the same risk, in a quietly outraged piece by Hugo Young, mentioning the ironic fact that new drug legislation even now before Parliament would transfer the prescribing of hard drugs from private doctors to community 'treatment centres'. Jagger, wrote Hugo Young, had been convicted 'to appease the lust for social revenge.'

The *News of the World* published a front page editorial, rebutting the monstrous charge that they had planted Acid King David Schneidermann in the Redlands party to kill off Mick Jagger's libel action: 'It was a charge made without a shred of evidence to support it . . . It was a charge made within the privilege of a court of law . . . which denied us the opportunity of answering back at the time . . . These outrageous allegations are of course totally unfounded. We have had no connection whatsoever with Mr Schneidermann directly or indirectly, before, during or after this case.' The paper admitted that it had tipped off the police about Keith's house party and said that the information had come from a reader. The allegations of following and spying on Mick Jagger, and that they had done this to influence the libel, were also totally untrue.

The heavy cash recognisances extracted from Jagger and Richard had presupposed their remaining on bail until at least early September. But on July 4, Michael Havers received news which indicated further amends were being offered for their treatment at Chichester. The Lord Chief Justice, Lord Parker, had personally intervened to bring their two appeal hearings forward to the last day of the present law term, July 31.

That summer's climactic moment of pinching oneself, and finding oneself still awake, had its origins in a 23-year-old television researcher named John Birt, recently recruited to Granada TV's *World In Action* programme. A Merseysider by birth and allegiance, Birt had previously felt no special love for the Stones or their music. He none the less shared the outrage of all pop fans at what was now revealed as a concerted attack, through the Stones, by one generation on another. The subject, in John Birt's view, was one which should concern a hard-nosed investigative programme like *World In Action*. His executive producer, David Plowright, agreed, and John Birt, for his first major TV documentary project, was assigned to set up a half-hour special about drugs, the Establishment and Mick Jagger.

Whatever form the programme took, it clearly could not be broadcast until after the hearing of Jagger's and Richard's appeals on July 31. 'Funnily enough,' John Birt – now Programme Controller of London Weekend Television – says, 'it never entered our heads that the appeal would be anything but successful. Our whole format was predicated on the idea that Jagger *must* get off.' Birt's confidence remained even after a poll conducted among that larger mulitude which derived its views from such papers as the *News of the World*, revealed that 46 per cent felt Mick Jagger had deserved his prison sentence.

The format approved by John Birt's editors was hazardously simple – a 'live' television confrontation between Jagger, fresh from the Appeal Court, and members of the Establishment which had lately been so intent on crucifying him: a summit-conference, as it were, between the generations in conflict. Birt got in touch with the Stones' office and, after the usual ritual runaround, managed to see Jagger and put the idea to him. Jagger agreed in principle, but contact was then broken while the Stones worked on the new album that Judge Block had all but terminated. At last, in desperation, John Birt managed to telephone Mick Jagger at home. Jagger answered the phone himself and, without further persuasion, agreed to be the subject of a *World In Action* special on July 31.

To preside over the confrontation, it seemed natural to choose William Rees-Mogg, both for his position as editor of Britain's chief Establishment newspaper and his personal initiative in restoring moral perspective to the Jagger case. To speak for the Church, Granada approached Dr Mervyn Stockwood, the energetic and out-spoken Bishop of Woolwich. To speak for Parliament – in the absence of any incumbent Minister – it procured Lord Stow Hill, who, as Sir Frank Soskice, had been Home Secretary in the first Wilson Government. Rees-Mogg, a devout Catholic, agreed to take part on condition a member of his faith appeared also. A Jesuit priest, Father Thomas Corbishley, was found to restore the ecumenical balance.

July 31 was yet another day of cloudlessly brilliant weather. At dawn, a queue of girls had already begun to form outside the High Court in Fleet Street, hoping for admittance to the tiny chamber personally presided over by Britain's Lord Chief Justice. The drowsy press buildings echoed to the racket of a portable record-player on which someone was playing appropriate Stones songs like Mercy Mercy and It's All Over Now.

When Jagger and Richard arrived, disembarking from the same black Austin Princess, they were cheered into the court precincts like Royal champions. 'How does it feel to be free?' somebody shouted at Jagger. 'Lovely,' he shouted back. Wearing the same olive green double-breasted jacket he had put on for his trial, Jagger was then ushered alone into the Lord Chief Justice's court. Keith had contracted a dose of chicken pox, and received permission to wait in a separate room for fear of spreading the infection to his judges.

The mirage-like quality which the day had already assumed made it seem almost natural that the Lord Chief Justice of England, sitting in awesome conclave with two fellow Appeal judges, should appear as mild-mannered, amiable and reasonable as the little local judge had appeared hostile and ill-disposed. 'He was such a nice, kind man,' John Birt remembers. Birt was in

252

court with his Granada TV team, still not altogether certain that *World In Action* would have a programme to put out tonight.

Two hours later, as Keith waited offstage, trying hard not to scratch his spots, Lord Chief Justice Parker resoundingly squashed both his conviction and his sentence. The Appeal Court ruled that Judge Block had 'erred' in his summing-up to the Chichester jury by not emphasizing how flimsy was the evidence that 'Miss X' had been smoking cannabis. All three Appeal judges agreed that, had they tried the case, they would have disallowed that whole lurid section of the Prosecution's evidence. Keith Richard, therefore, could not possibly be convicted, on the evidence, of 'knowingly permitting' what the Prosecution had failed to prove ever happened in the first place.

Still louder gasps of delight greeted Lord Chief Justice Parker's pronouncement on the Mick Jagger case. The Court upheld Jagger's conviction, since the amphetamines clearly came within Parliament's definition of unlawful drugs. His prison sentence, however, was quashed, and a one-year conditional discharge substituted. 'That means,' Lord Parker told him, 'you will have to be of good behaviour for twelve months . . . If in that time you do commit another offence, you will not only be punished for that offence but brought back and punished for this one also.'

Jagger bowed his head as the Lord Chief Justice continued: 'You are, whether you like it or not, the idol of a large number of the young in this country. Being in that position, you have very grave responsibilities. If you do come to be punished, it is only natural that those responsibilities should carry higher penalties.'

From the High Court, Jagger was driven to a press conference at Granada TV's headquarters in Golden Square. He arrived in fresh clothes, symbolizing his release from courtroom formality – mauve watered silk trousers, a cream-coloured smock edged with maroon and green embroidery. With him was Marianne Faithfull, wearing the smallest mini-skirt most of the assembled press had ever seen.

The press conference – filmed by *World In Action* as a prelude to its later, exclusive footage – shows Jagger, flanked by Ian Stewart and Les Perrin, very far from his usual cool and sardonic self. 'He'd been given a lot of Valium beforehand,' Marianne says.

'And he still seemed very scared. You got the feeling he only had to say one word out of place and he'd have been taken straight back to Brixton Prison.'

All questions relating to his drug offence, or drugs in general, have obviously been vetoed in advance by Les Perrin, though Jagger, in his slightly bewildered state, seems willing to answer almost anything. The camera settles on an elderly journalist with sideburns like white ear-muffs. 'Do you think you *do* have a responsibility to the young in this country, as Lord Parker said?' Jagger shakes his shaggy head as if to clear it. 'I've been *given* responsibility . . . pushed into the limelight. I don't try to impose my views on people. I don't propagate religious views, such as some pop stars do. I don't propagate drug views, such as some pop stars do . . .' 'Do you resent the way you've been treated?' another voice asks. Here, Les Perrin interrupts yet again. 'Look – I'm going to have to cut this. We agreed in advance what was on and what wasn't . . .'

The conference over, Jagger and Marianne, accompanied by John Birt, were put into a white Jaguar with a professional stunt driver behind the wheel, and driven at wild speed across the Thames to the helicopter port at Battersea. A hired helicopter then lifted them away, down river to the place selected by *World In Action* for Jagger's summit-meeting with the Establishment. John Birt has two recollections of the journey. One is the shimmering softness of London, spread out below them as they flew eastward. The other is his own acute embarrassment, wedged on the same small seat as Jagger and Marianne when they began to kiss and touch each other passionately.

Their destination, successfully kept secret from all press and television rivals, was a Georgian country house owned by the Lord Lieutenant of Essex, Sir John Ruggles-Brise. Jagger's one stipulation – prompted, no doubt, by recent indoor experiences – was that the debate should take place in the open air. Accordingly, *World In Acion* cameras were already set up facing a rustic seat at the end of Sir John Ruggles-Brise's conservatory. While the other participants were chauffeured down from London, Mick and Marianne were taken into the house and shown to a bedroom to 'rest'.

'We thought they'd have at least an hour to themselves before we started filming,' John Birt says. 'Then, all of a sudden, I was told Jagger was needed right away. I had to go up and knock on the bedroom door and call him. There was a long silence, when it was very obvious what I was interrupting. Then Jagger's voice said "Okay."'

It looked, in William Rees-Mogg's words, like something Max Beerbohm might have drawn. Certainly, an element of some old-fashioned allegorical cartoon was present in the outdoor scene, the rustic bench, the four-man tribunal from Traditional British Life, pooling their collective intellect in an attempt to comprehend the alien being in their midst. The fact that all four Establishment members were hot and crumpled while Jagger, in his open-neck smock, seemed cool and comfortable, only heightened the sense of elderly emissaries, fidgeting before some boy potentate. On a level of pure symbolism – disregarding the fact it had been deliberately set up for the TV cameras – this was Mick Jagger's moment of supreme triumph. The Society which had mocked, abused and finally tried to destroy him, now cast itself down before him with all the apologetic reverence due to a misjudged Messiah. The editor, the peer, the bishop and the Jesuit earnestly entreated him to reveal 'what the young people in this country *really* think.'

'Er – Mick,' William Rees-Mogg began in his sacerdotal lisp. 'We know this has been a very difficult day for you . . . Perhaps I could begin by asking you this. You are orfen taken as a symbol of – ah – rebellion. Do you – ah – feel that Society has a great deal in it today that ought to be rebelled against?'

The grainy black and white of the old telerecording is as flattering to Jagger as a Beaton or Bailey lens. His face is calm and simplified to the needs of the occasion, the great lips deflated to a gentle smile, the eyes alert and, somehow, tolerant. When he speaks, it is in a voice devoid of either Cockney or black mammy; a voice whose only accent is that of perfect reasonableness, and whose command of the polite polemical tongue is a match for any of his inquisitors'.

'I didn't think my knowledge was enough to start pontificating on the subject. I didn't ever set myself up as a leader in Society. It's Society that's pushed one into that position.'

Lord Stow Hill, the former Home Secretary, with his strange

255

little boyish skull and heavy blue chin, takes up the questioning.

'In your approach to music – rhythm and so on – what is the way in which you yourself would wish to be understood?'

'For my music,' Jagger replies. 'Just for playing music. That's what I want to do. And, like anyone else, to have as good a time as possible.'

So it continues in the blurred, unreal twilight, the bishop and the Jesuit putting their points in turn, and the pop star replying, quietly, lucidly, while a breeze ruffles the curls around his face. Jagger, we realize, has reached a consummation of his talent for speaking with all voices simultaneously. On one level, he seems to be speaking for disaffected youth, of Society's 'corruption', of media bias and how the Law protects only majorities. Yet he is speaking for the Establishment also, in the Establishment's own comforting sociological formulae. 'Our parents went through two world wars and a depression. We've had none of that . . . I'm sure you do your best. It may be, for *your* generation . . . ' Debating for its own sake clearly becomes more and more enjoyable. 'You've just given a textbook definition of the English Constitution,' he tells Lord Stow Hill. 'It really doesn't work that way at all.'

'. . . But wouldn't you say that some drugs – heroin for example – represent a crime against Society?'

'It's a crime against a law,' Jagger says. 'I can't see it's any more crime against Society than jumping out of a window.'

'But surely,' Stow Hill persists, 'a real crime against Society ought to be punished to suit the case.'

'People should be punished for crimes,' Jagger says. 'Not for the *fears* of Society, which may be groundless.' Game, set and match to the infinitely subtle being who has made himself living proof of his own point.

A few weeks later, the *News of the World* published a small paragraph – the kind written by lawyers rather than journalists – announcing that Mick Jagger's libel action against the paper had been dropped. No more was ever heard of Acid King David Schneidermann, alias English, the only person able to prove whether he was, indeed, an LSD wizard, a CIA agent or – as now seems most likely – the purest figment of that unreal summer when sunshine, joss sticks and tinkling Eastern bells coexisted so

256

strangely with journalistic grubbiness, official vindictiveness and temporary insanity on the part of the British legal system.

The *News of the World*, according to its lights, had been vindicated as completely as Jagger and Richard. There was only one real loser in the whole affair.

Robert Fraser's appeal against his six-month sentence, heard without publicity, was dismissed without popular outcry. He was returned to Wormwood Scrubs as prisoner 7854. With remission, he served four of the six months, working mainly in the prison kitchen. Mick and Keith each wrote to him – letters of unusual sympathy and supportiveness. Mick said it would be 'beautiful' when he was free again; Keith signed his note 'love from 7855'.

# PART THREE

## 10

## 'Sing this all together – see what happens'

The man with whom Marianne Faithfull began living at the end of 1966 might easily have exchanged his flowered shirts and Cecil Gee jackets for the frock coat and heavy watch-chain of the Victorian paterfamilias. Social revolution might be going on on every level, but it had yet to disturb the age-old idea of male superiority and the role of women as objects for decorative and domestic use. Boy pop stars almost all came from the class whose men still called themselves 'masters' in their own homes. In the aristocracy of new-found wealth and money, each 23-year-old was an encrusted male chauvinist, demanding total female subservience, total fidelity (which need not be reciprocated), and the silently efficient management of meals and servants.

There were times, just after moving in with Jagger at Harley House, when his behaviour goaded Marianne to such despair, she would simply bolt out of the flat and down the stairs. 'Somehow, I always used to grab up the same things – a five pound note and a lump of hash. I really did try to run away several times. But Mick would always catch up with me on the stairs and bring me back again.'

As monstrous as the Redlands drug case was, it had a cementing effect on that early erratic relationship. It allowed Marianne to discover the Jagger whose innate chivalry put her career before his own and tried, in vain, to prevent her reputation from being dragged through the gutter. It allowed her to see how Jagger's outward, disdainful 'cool' masked an inward need for domestic stability and happiness, and how, divorced from his audience and courtiers, he was the most normal and natural of people. She had also discovered, visiting him on the first traumatic evening in Lewes Prison, how instantly and helplessly he could dissolve into tears.

There were those, of course, who whispered that Jagger's main fondness was for the social cachet Marianne conferred – that he was 'chuffed' beyond words to be living with the daughter of a real baroness. 'You could see it on Mick's face every time they were at a party together,' Donald Cammell says. 'It was pure possession. "Look what I've got, isn't it fantastic!" '

The end of the drug case was the start of a new life together, in the house that Jagger had eventually chosen. Deciding he could not bury himself in the country like Keith, Bill and Charlie, he had opted, instead, for one of Chelsea's most desirable locations, paying £40,000 for number 48 Cheyne Walk, by the Thames near Albert Bridge. The house was of the tall, narrow, asymmetrically elegant Queen Anne type, modestly squeezed in among 'The Walk's' many more showy and forbidding residences.

Nicholas, Marianne's three-year-old son by John Dunbar, would live with them at Cheyne Walk, Jagger insisted. He had, from the beginning, shown a fatherly fondness for Nicholas, and was determined to give the little boy as stable and secure a home as possible. 'Mick always thought it was terrible that John Lennon would never let Cynthia have a nanny for their son, Julian,' Marianne says. 'In fact, he could do everything for Nicholas that a nanny could – but he still insisted we had to have one. He interviewed all the applicants himself. You'd have thought he'd been dealing with servants all his life.'

Christopher Gibbs designed the interior of the house and supplied tasteful – and very costly – antique furniture from his Chelsea shop. Marianne made additional purchases, sometimes on a scale more suited to her Sacher Masoch ancestors' salons in Vienna. For one sumptuous crystal chandelier she paid £6,000 – a sum which Jagger, under normal circumstances, would have parted with only in direst agony. 'Look at that!' he kept saying to their first visitors, staring upwards. 'Six thousand quid for a fuckin' *light*!'

It was only when they flew into Heathrow Airport together from Ireland, and were unable to find a taxi-driver in the entire rank willing to drive them to Chelsea, that Marianne realized what notoriety now attached to them as a couple. Though the British Establishment had pardoned Jagger his drug offence, the British public at large continued to thrill with voyeuristic relish at stories of sex orgies and misapplied Mars bars. For Marianne, whose chaste career and suitable marriage had been almost public

262

property, living with Jagger was in every sense a fall from grace. 'I know that, even to this day, people in Britain bear me a grudge. They think I let them down in some way – that they put their trust in me, and I betrayed them.'

Notorious they might be – but fashionable, too, in a way that Jagger on his own could never quite accomplish. 'Mick prided himself on being so cool, but he realized he'd got nothing on the *real* upper class for coolness,' Marianne says. 'The cool they had was centuries old. They were the most restful people to be with because nothing we did ever seemed to shock them. Especially the older ones, like Tom Driberg or Diana Cooper. Everything we were doing they'd see before, in the Twenties. "Cocaine!" they'd say. "My dear, I was at dinner parties in the Twenties when every silver salt cellar was *full* of cocaine!"'

By far the most revealing portrait of Mick and Marianne together at Cheyne Walk is a profile written for the *Sunday Telegraph* magazine by Gina Richardson, a gifted young journalist who died tragically soon afterwards in a road accident. She describes the elegant house shut in at midday by heavy drapes; the carpet, tapestries and smouldering joss sticks, and the two central figures whose doll-like smallness give them 'the air of children left in charge while grown-ups are away'. She confesses to finding Jagger physically mesmeric, but feels the effect is rather spoiled by his habit of slopping round the house in slip-on mules, 'like a housewife'.

From Gina Richardson we learn that Marianne has taken Mick's cultural education in hand, with visits to the theatre, opera and, especially, the ballet. He was always saying how much he wished he could have been Nureyev. The most lasting impression of all was produced by the Royal Ballet's *Paradise Lost*, in which the principal dancers appeared through an outsize pair of lips, uncannily like Jagger's own. 'Mick thought that set, by Kenneth Macmillan, was absolutely fantastic,' Marianne says. 'It was like seeing himself there on the stage.' Almost the same design would turn up, five years later, as the logo of the Rolling Stones' own record-label.

He had always been a glutton for books. Nowadays, in the prevailing fashion, his reading tended towards the philosophical, the spiritual and mystical. He would send regular orders to his friend Miles at the Indica Bookshop, for such required 'underground' classics as *The Secret of the Golden Bough* or Charles Henry Fort's *Book of the Damned*. He was particularly interested, Miles remembers, in books about fairies, goblins and elves. Like every other pop celebrity that summer, he and Marianne based their whole lives on astrological data, and used the Chinese *I Ching Book of Changes* to make even quite mundane decisions, casting the hexagram for reference points within the volume which – its hippy devotees said raptly – had baffled even the intelligence of Confucius.

Both of them were swept up in the Beatles' brief flirtation with Transcendental Meditation and its founding guru, the Maharishi Mahesh Yogi. On August Bank Holiday Weekend, 1967, Mick and Marianne joined the Beatles' famous pilgrimage with the Maharishi to undergo initiation at a teacher training college in Bangor, North Wales. They did so against the advice of better informed underground figures like Miles, who had heard from friends in India that the Maharishi might be a little less than divine. The weekend was cut short, however. On Bank Holiday Monday, news came that the Beatles' manager, Brian Epstein, had been found dead of a barbiturates overdose in London.

Britain's two ruling pop groups had hardly been closer, even in their far-off package tour days. Hippydom had much to do with it: in kaftans and beads, the Beatles seemed no longer such naive provincials, the Stones no longer such metropolitan sophisticates. Now they were brothers, with a common enemy. The viciousness with which Mick and Keith had been prosecuted was a portent of times when even Beatles would lose their talismanic charm and be busted like anybody else. The Beatles and Brian Epstein had been among several heavyweight signatories of a letter to *The Times*, calling for the legalisation of marijuana and, by implication, protesting against the two Stones' punishment.

Bitter Top Twenty rivals as the Beatles and Stones remained, they nowadays even helped one another secretly in the record-studio. Mick had been present with Marianne at the indoor carnival that culminated in John Lennon's *Sergeant Pepper* masterpiece, A Day In the Life, and had joined in the background chorus on All You Need Is Love. In August, Lennon and McCartney lent their voices anonymously to We Love You, the

264

Stones single whose title was Mick and Keith's ironic afterword to Chief Inspector Gordon Dineley, Malcolm Morris QC, Judge Block and the *News of the World*.

The Beatles' growing discontent with Brian Epstein had, to a large extent, stemmed from the seemingly more effective performance of the Stones' manager, Allen Klein. In 1965, indeed, Paul McCartney had proposed employing Klein in a consultative capacity, to maul EMI Records on the Beatles' behalf as he had mauled Decca for the Stones. Though Brian Epstein successfully fought off that scheme, he was never able fully to recapture his protégés' confidence. They had heard too many stories from Mick Jagger about the miracles Allen Klein could do.

For a brief time after Epstein's death, serious discussions took place between the Beatles and Stones about some kind of joint investment in a studio and management office, both to be run by the Beatles' social secretary, Peter Brown. The latter idea, for some reason, caused Klein acute heartburn, and he flew to London instantly to warn Peter Brown off. On the same visit, he made yet another clumsy lunge at his true heart's desire, turning to Brian Epstein's brother Clive and growling, 'How much d'ya want for the Beatles?'

Merger discussions went as far as finding a site for the prospective studio – a tumbledown brewery in Camden Town, next to Regent's Park Canal. It became clear, however, that the Beatles' plans were founded on a magic wand fantasy, artfully encouraged by their pet electronics wizard, 'Magic' Alex Mardas. 'We'll need a hotel as well,' Paul McCartney said. '. . . So that the groups will have somewhere to stay when they're recording. And we'll build a heliport, so that foreign groups can land at Heathrow and be brought straight here . . .' When Mick Jagger interjected a word about cost, John Lennon looked at him in surprise. 'Oh – *we* won't pay for it,' he said. 'We'll get someone else to pay for it . . . Like that computer,' he said, turning to McCartney. 'Whatever *did* happen to that computer they gave us?'

'I think it's still in Ringo's garage,' McCartney said vaguely.

For Jagger, this entente with the Beatles was not without ulterior purpose. His conversion to flower power had engendered a burning desire to turn the Rolling Stones into a psychedelic band such as the Beatles had effortlessly become. The Stones'

265

inordinate delay in finishing their album in progress stemmed mainly from Jagger's insistence that it must touch all the same mystical chords as *Sergeant Pepper's Lonely Hearts Club Band*.

It was an obsession which led the Stones rapidly to their artistic nadir. We Love You is a single that loses all ironic point in its feeble attempt to echo the Beatles' summer anthem All You Need Is Love. Even the cell-door that slams midway in the song seems like a direct crib from the coffin-lid crashing down on the final chord of A Day In the Life.

To promote We Love You, the Stones borrowed another device pioneered by the Beatles – a short film sequence whose screening on BBC-TV's *Top of the Pops* show saved the musicians themselves the bother of appearing. The film employed even heavier-handed irony, featuring Mick Jagger as the persecuted Oscar Wilde, with Marianne as Lord Alfred Douglas and Keith Richard as a highly unlikely Marquess of Queensberry. Naturally, *Top of the Pops* would have nothing to do with it.

To be fair, no other recored album ever has suffered the handicap of having its three main musicians variously on trial and in prison, nor involved simultaneous internecine strife between musicians and manager, nor had to contend with the thousand-and-one incidental conflicts and vexations which beset the Stones during their ten-month labour to produce music betokening love, peace and flower-garlanded happiness. That any finished album at all emerged seems miraculous. As in an amateur dramatic production in which actors forget their lines, the scenery falls down and the producer has a heart attack, one must try to consider the positive aspects.

The Stones themselves, to this day, consider *Their Satanic Majesties Request* the lowest of low points in their career. 'It was one of the three times we came really close to splitting up,' Bill Wyman says. Though Keith likes the album better than he once did, it still mainly evokes indecision, compromise and almost terminal boredom. 'It ended up as a real patchwork. Half of it was "Let's give people what we think they want." The other half was "Let's get out of here as quickly as possible."'

*Sergeant Pepper* was the all-powerful, ultimately suffocating influence. The Beatles had covered their retreat from concert performance with a studio show whose myriad technical effects only heightened the atmosphere of live circus or vaudeville. The Stones' – at least Mick Jagger's – intention was the same, touched with some native belligerence, of course, in place of Beatle whimsy, but having no greater overall ambition than to muscle in on their friends' enchanted island.

So Mick and Keith, when they were not in court or detained at Her Majesty's pleasure, cudgelled their brains for incandescent imagery and riffs that would have the mesmeric power of Hindu mantras; with half an eye still lingering on Maharishi Mahesh Yogi, Mick Jagger set about developing a vocal style as tuneless and abstracted as if he had a clothes-peg attached to his nose. And when inspiration failed – which it did, almost continuously – there was always the same recourse to divine help. They turned the stereo needle back to A Day In the Life, Within You Without You or Lucy in the Sky With Diamonds.

By early July, when Jagger and Richard were on bail pending appeal and Brian Jones had begun undergoing residential psychiatric treatment, scarcely anything on the – still untitled – album was in a satisfactory finished state. The Beatles, for all their carte blanche at Abbey Road studios, worked in harness with a producer, George Martin, whose musicianship they still respected as a formative and disciplining force. Gifted engineer as Glyn Johns was, he remained, in the Stones' eyes, little more than a knob-twiddling functionary. Johns would frequently arrive at Olympic Studios no more certain than the girls on the doorstep that the session would take place as scheduled.

The delays were not wholly due to outside influences. Glyn Johns could see through his control-room window how deliberate the Stones' vacillation and tinkering often was, and what a combustible effect it had on Glyn's companion at the control-desk. To external pressures, the Stones added their own barely-concealed wish to do it badly, and thus defy, provoke and alienate their manager, Andrew Loog Oldham.

The year-long coolness between Oldham and the Stones had intensified in the era of drug-busts which Oldham privately considered merely stupid and time-wasting. His distance from Mick and Keith in their legal ordeal – and the growing resentment all the Stones felt against him – made all the more galling Oldham's appearance at Olympic Studios, early in 1967, ready to work his Svengali magic on behalf of his boys yet again.

His boys showed their resentment by keeping Oldham waiting for hours, sometimes days, on end, or by going into the studio for no other purpose than to play old Blues numbers, exultantly off-key. 'I put up with it for about seven weeks,' Oldham says. 'Then one day, I just walked out. "From here on," I told them, "you can deal with everything directly through Allen."'

Further time away from the studio was spent in planning an album-sleeve which Jagger insisted, must be even more elaborate and costly than *Sergeant Pepper's*. Michael Cooper – who had photographed the Beatles in Peter Blake's Pop Art hall of fame – was commissioned to surpass himself with a portrait showing the Stones as medieval troubadors, kneeling around Jagger in starred robes and a conical wizard's cap. The Stones helped Cooper build his studio-set and carry in the baskets of flowers and fruit he had ordered as props. More time passed while Michael Cooper photographed Jagger in his wizard robes, sitting alone, hugging his knees, on a bed of crushed silver foil.

Cooper's photograph was then processed into an opaque plastic square which the finished album-sleeve had stuck to it like a table place-mat: the Stones in multi-coloured 3D, against a background of mountains, planets and minaret-spires, banked up with blurry patterns, flowers and fruit. £15,000 were spent on this device, meant to give the effect of peering into a crystal ball but actually worrying the eyes into a sensation more like mild airsickness.

As autumn wore on, and a December release-date became inevitable, they at last agreed on a title: *The Rolling Stones' Cosmic Christmas*. Jagger then found a better idea inside the front cover of the passport he had so recently almost forfeited. That opening calligraphic extravagance announces that 'Her Britannic Majesty's Principal Secretary of State for Foreign Affairs Requests and Requires' that the bearer be allowed passage without let or hindrance. Jagger's title – touched by lingering anti-Establishment rancour – was *Her Satanic Majesty Requests and Requires*. When Decca refused to sanction so blatant a slur on the Monarch, the line was altered to *Their Satanic Majesties Request*, giving the far more appropriate sense of being formally invited to some diabolical garden fête.

On October 30, Brian Jones appeared for trial before Inner London Sessions on the drugs charge which had hung over him since the previous June. He arrived in his silver Rolls, dressed with almost excessive formality in a pinstripe suit, white shirt and spotted tie. But the tie was pulled too tight, as if in desperation at his image in the mirror that morning.

Brian's willingness to plead Guilty to cannabis-possession had persuaded the police to offer no evidence concerning the cocaine and methedrine found at his flat. He further admitted responsibility for any cannabis smoked earlier by his party guests, thereby disposing of the flimsy possession charge against his companion in the dock, Prince Stanislas Klossowski de Rola. 'Stash' was immediately discharged with a paltry award of 75 guineas towards his legal costs.

In Brian's case, all his counsel, James Comyn QC, could do was plead for mercy, offering the mitigating circumstances that Brian had never taken hard drugs, apart from LSD, and had vowed he would never touch cannabis again. His psychiatrist, Dr Leonard Henry, was called to testify to Brian's disturbed mental state at the time of his arrest, and to support Comyn's plea that he shouldn't be sent to prison. 'It would completely destroy his mental health,' Dr Henry said. 'He would go into a psychotic depression . . . he might even attempt to injure himself . . .'

Brian's performance in the witness-box seemed only to corroborate James Comyn's description of 'a young man with a brilliant future . . . who very much wants to go on with his composing.'

'Is it your intention to have nothing more to do with drugs?' Comyn asked him.

'That is precisely my intention,' Brian answered, almost in a whisper. 'They've only brought trouble and disrupted my career. I hope this will be an example to anyone who's tempted to try.'

None of this deterred the court Chairman, Mr R. E. Seaton, from his resolution to combat what he called 'a growing canker in this country at the moment'. After a 90-minute adjournment, Brian was sentenced to concurrent prison terms of nine months and three months, and ordered to pay 250 guineas in costs. As a tumult broke out from the girls in the public gallery, James

Comyn gave notice of appeal and asked whether, in the meantime, Brian could have bail. 'No,' Mr Seaton replied.

The silver Rolls-Royce remained where he had parked it as Brian was brought out, loaded into a grey van with the day's other prison fodder and driven away to begin his term at Wormwood Scrubs.

For him, there would be no night vigil by hippies around Eros – no public protest at all, barring the slight scuffle which occurred later that day in King's Road between police and a group of impromptu demonstrators, including Mick Jagger's younger brother, Chris. The prison staff, deprived of their earlier quarry, were jubilant at finding another 'bloody longhair' in their midst, and began loudly discussing how Brian's gold thatch would soon be planed to the scalp. The other prisoners, thinking him 'queer', remained coldly hostile. That night, on his rough prison blanket, he must have known all the horrors of total abandonment.

His psychiatrist contacted the Wormwood Scrubs medical officer and, at least, succeeded in excusing him the regulation prison haircut. Next day, the doctor appeared with James Comyn before a High Court judge in chambers to plead for Brian to receive bail on medical grounds. It was granted, for sureties of £750 and on condition that Brian agreed to undergo the independent examination of a psychiatrist appointed by the Court. An hour later, the Wormwood Scrubs 'screws' handed Brian his crumpled Savile Row suit and told him he was free to go.

At this point, six months after his brief celebrity as pop music's cleansing fire, the magisterial and facetious voice of Judge Leslie Block was heard again in the land. Speaking at the annual dinner of the Horsham Ploughing and Agricultural Society, Judge Block amused his rural audience by a punning reference to Brutus's outburst against the mob in *Julius Caesar*, 'You blocks, you stones, you worse than senseless things . . . ' 'We did our best, your countrymen, I and my fellow magistrates, to cut these Stones down to size,' Judge Block continued. 'But it was not to be. The Court of Criminal Appeal let them roll free . . . '

Private function as the dinner was, a senior magistrate should have known better than to make jokes about past victims of his judgment, especially now that another Rolling Stone was on bail pending appeal against a prison sentence. A Labour MP, William Wilson, announced he was referring the matter to the Lord Chancellor. Les Perrin, the Stones' publicist – who had picked up Judge Block's speech from a Sussex local paper – issued a press release that was more like a protest pamphlet. 'Is this the kind of justice Britain expects? Is this man typical of those who hold the title, the high and esteemed office to try and sentence people? How can the public believe, in the light of this utterance by Judge Block, that the Rolling Stones can get an unbiased hearing? His statement smacks of pre-judgement – a getting-together to "cut the Stones down to size". It is a pity he did not observe the ethics of sub judice to Mr Jagger, Mr Richard and Mr Jones by remaining silent.'

On December 12, the finished album, with its Delft blue and white border and Technicolor plastic griddle finally went on sale in the British and American shops. The long interval since *Between the Buttons*, and the garish events of the past summer, had created the largest-ever public for a Rolling Stones LP. Advance orders in the US alone totalled almost $2,000,000. Probably no pop record, before or since, was so eagerly awaited, for so stunning a disappointment. All but the most besotted Stones fans recognized *Their Satanic Majesties* for what it was – an attempt to impersonate *Sergeant Pepper*, lacking all the qualities of the Beatles' master work and simultaneously reflecting all the delay, conflict and compromise which had bedevilled it.

The Beatles had used their free run of Abbey Road studios to create a song cycle as rounded as a symphony, yet with all the intimacy of a puppet or Punch and Judy show. The best the Stones could do in reply was a rather lame singalong chant (Sing This All Together – See What Happens), opening and closing Side One in a cacophony of massed bells, rattles and gongs. Where the Beatles had used comic sound effects to express the joy of playing on top form, the Stones used them merely as infilling for many obvious, yawning gaps. So, interspersed at random, there were excerpts from a street market, a striptease club, some giggling, snoring, a voice saying – rather too audibly – 'Where's that joint?'

One song only, She's a Rainbow, found Jagger and Richard on form in the brusquely wistful manner of Ruby Tuesday or Lady

Jane. The rest, like the cover, was a blur from which the real Stones emerged in only wavering glimpses – Keith's throaty guitar, for instance, on Bill Wyman's nervous debut composition, In Another Land. Here and there, too, were flashes of the virtuosity still able to ignite in Brian Jones. Though Brian, when coherent, had bitterly opposed the psychedelic approach, it was his Moroccan drums and percussion which gave the album whatever mysticism can be divined in it. Brian also played Mellotron on 2,000 Light Years From Home, the song written by Jagger during his night in Brixton Prison – a non-starter, according to Glyn Johns, until Brian sat down and improvised its eerie electronic descant.

The release-date of *Their Satanic Majesties* happened also to be the day Brian's case came before Lord Chief Justice Parker in the Court of Criminal Appeal. Here, in addition to his two regular psychiatrists' testimony, the judges considered a file prepared on Brian by the Court-appointed psychiatric expert, Dr Walter Neustatter. This referred to Brian's 'extremely precarious state of emotional adjustment' and 'fragile grasp of reality', arising from sexual anxieties which, in Dr Neustatter's opinion, verged on an Oedipus complex. The doctor had been struck, however, by Brian's considerable personal resources and 'capacity for insight to contain his anxiety'. Dr Neustatter confirmed Dr Henry's view, that imprisonment would drive him to a complete mental breakdown, possibly even to suicide.

Once again, the Lord Chief Justice showed a degree of mercy which smaller judges had not. Brian's nine-month prison sentence was set aside: he was instead fined one thousand pounds and put on probation for three years. A further proviso was that he should continue receiving psychiatric treatment.

One other Stone, Mick Jagger, was in court to hear Lord Parker's verdict. Afterwards, Brian paused only long enough to mumble to reporters, 'I want to be left alone to get on with my life,' before disappearing into the back of his silver Rolls. The darkened rear window showed a daguerreotype of anguish, its face buried in its flamboyantly shirt-cuffed hands.

He celebrated his release with an orgy of drink and pills that, within two days, put him back into hospital again. He had collapsed at Courtfield Road after going out to a club and playing double bass on stage with the resident band. As he slapped at the bass, he also began kicking it, softly at first but with greater and greater ferocity until he'd splintered it to matchwood. Even when the bass was gone, Brian continued to play it, his fingers shaping, pinching the air, his face inclined earnestly down towards notes which only he could hear.

It was a change as sudden, as chemically mysterious, as sunlight turning rancid. At one moment, it seemed, all the young of America and Europe were proffering flowers and making signs of peace. At the next, they had taken to the streets and were smashing windows and wrenching up paving stones. Instead of beads and kaftans, all at once there were badges, slogans and military fatigues; instead of gurus, angry-faced student activists; instead of 'happenings' and 'love-ins', ferocious street battles for which many a one time beautiful person had thoughtfully forearmed himself or herself with a knitting needle to jab police horses in the belly or testicles.

It was a wave seemingly from nowhere that broke, almost completely, on the year 1968: beginning with student riots in Paris that spring, continuing through the summer in Berlin, Amsterdam, London, Washington, Detroit, Los Angeles – riots, burnings, marches and demo's, enacted against the shadowy sub-plots of Vietnam and Czechoslovakia, by chanting, angry battalions of the young. It was a revolution whose motives no one fully understood, least of all its participants; whose leaders enjoyed only the briefest heyday; whose armies had no sooner mustered than they dispersed to fresh amusements. It was a cloud of irritant pollen soon blown away, all but for one or two fatal seeds which, planted in particular minds, would become the means of holding the next decade to ransom. The German Baader-Meinhof, the Italian Red Brigades, the Irish Provo's – all terrorism carried on in shoulder-length hair and patched blue denim traces a common lineage back to this splitting open of the Age of Aquarius.

The era, like all others, needed anthems. And for once, the chief anthem-givers were found wanting. 'You say you want a revolution,' wrote John Lennon. '. . . Well, you can count me out.' He who was the new, angry order's chief hope preferred to make his protest by spending a week publicly in bed beside his

Japanese paramour. The rest of pop still sang about San Francisco and flowers. There was only one source where the elixir of anarchy – background battle-music, a sound-track for eddying tear gas – might conceivably be found.

Oddly enough it was not Keith but Bill Wyman who first picked out the restoring riff on a rehearsal-room piano while waiting for the others to arrive. 'Brian and Charlie came in next. I played them this riff and we messed around with it for about twenty minutes. When Mick and Keith walked in, they both said "Hey – what's that? Sounds good." Mick went away and wrote a great lyric for it and we recorded it straight off.'

The result was Jumpin' Jack Flash, undisputedly the Stones' best performance on record, a two-minute masterpiece whose malign energy lives on in it like some sexual poltergeist. If Jagger and Richard ever received divine guidance, it was here in their abandonment of woolly psychedelics to return to unashamed, two-fisted Rock. As partners, they had never – have never since – worked better. Jagger, at last, had written the proper litany for Keith's chord-shapes, a Grimms' fairy tale ('I was raised by a toothless, bearded hag . . .'), each verse a small nightmare, dissolving its bathetically sardonic refrain. The guitar, likewise, matched Jagger's body almost visibly, its insolent bass his jumps and struts, its tinkling treble the drawn-out lips grimacing 'It's a-a-a-aw right . . .' He has never come clearer than in the sound of that half-evil, half-playful, spring-heeled silhouette.

On May 12, 1968, the *New Musical Express* Poll-Winners' Concert at Wembley Empire Pool featured one unscheduled attraction. The Rolling Stones walked onstage and without preamble launched into their first public performance of Jumpin' Jack Flash. Even on that audience primed to hysteria, its effect was an instantaneous jolt let in through one collective vein: before the intro chords had finished, thousands were on their feet, stamping and strutting like the voodoo-possessed.

With the single, on May 24, came a promotional film sequence like none seen before in pop or Rock. The Stones, in robes that could have belonged equally to hippy mandarins or a wizards' coven, their eyes elongated by gold warpaint, performed at levitating camera-angles, as remote from their own actions as Inca priests brooding over temple-rites. Jagger was a wraith conjured up between them, an enormous head and still more enormous mouth, bowing and leering 'It's a-a-a-aw right . . .' like a pageboy at the very entrance to Purgatory.

The wild response to their *NME* concert appearance, and the speed with which Jumpin' Jack Flash flew up the British and American charts, removed any last notion among the Stones that their future lay in electronic studio masterpieces. After two years of attempted grandeur, the concert stage once more exerted its old, irresistible magnetism. Immersed as they were in a new album, with a new producer, the Stones – that is, the four fully-functioning Stones – agreed they must go out on tour again.

The road, however, was not as open as it had formerly been – especially not the gold-earning trans-America road. Two years beset by hippies, drop-outs, draft-dodgers and associated unpatriotic evils had reduced the American Establishment to the fearful belligerence of an Indian-encircled waggon-train. No one with a conviction for possessing drugs – or, as US Immigration phrased it, 'a crime of moral turpitude' – was permitted even the shortest sojourn on American soil. The previous September, when Mick and Keith had flown to New York to oversee the *Satanic Majesties* album-sleeve, they had been stopped at Kennedy Airport, questioned at length and permitted only temporary entry pending a full official review of their prosecution in England.

On May 21, the still-unscheduled '68 American tour was wiped out of existence. Les Perrin, the Stones' publicist, answered his 'phone at home in Sutton to hear a familiar lisping voice say, 'Les – they're coming in through the window.' Brian Jones was being busted again.

The Gay Hussar, in Greek Street, Soho, is a small, scarlet-painted Hungarian restaurant whose wild cherry soup, cold pike and red cabbage are, for some reason, particularly favoured by politicians, authors and newspaper editors. Among the lunch-time throng in its more fashionable downstairs, several times in 1968, could be espied a pair ill-matched even for those hallucinogenic times. One was Tom Driberg, MP for Barking, Essex, and noted radical journalist. The other – but for his expansive consumption of Gay Hussar dishes, inconspicuous almost to vanishing point – was Mick Jagger.

Since meeting Jagger socially a year or so earlier, Driberg had, twice at least, proved himself a powerful ally. It was he who first raised in Parliament the deplorable handcuffs episode at Jagger's and Robert Fraser's trial. He also had signed the famous *Times* letter, along with Graham Greene and the Beatles, calling for legalization of soft drugs, despite its possible impact on his majority among the Essex voters.

Much of Tom Driberg's interest in Mick Jagger was that of an elderly homosexual, secretly addicted to the juvenile 'rough trade'. But much was a genuine desire to understand, and perhaps find benefit in, a power which the older man was too good a journalist not to find awesome. Never in Driberg's long career among influential people had he seen influence so systematically wasted. These Gay Hussar meetings were an attempt to persuade Jagger to put his power and influence to use through the medium of conventional politics.

The thought of standing for Parliament was one which had long attracted Jagger – and would do so intermittently for some years to come. At Driberg's prompting, he would discuss it seriously, with his usual articulateness, flattered by the MP's interest in him though aware – as always – where that interest began. But even Tom Driberg, with all his oratorical skill, and bottles of Hungarian Bull's Blood, could not extract from Mick Jagger even an undertaking to read the Labour Party Manifesto.

Jagger's was not a unique malady. The same uneasy feeling had visited other pop stars in the top echelon – that fame and wealth and idolizing could become a form of deprivation; that, meanwhile, important things were passing them by. The Beatles had said as much: their years of touring had been like years in prison. To them, a convict's bread and water seemed hardly more monotonous than their own unending surfeit, the ritual extravagance and ritualistic wastefulness that reduced a superstar millionaire's habitat to the squalor of a cell with neither light nor air.

None of the other Stones faced this problem of intellectual unfulfilment. Charlie and Bill seemed quite happy to fill up the long intervals between album-sessions with hobbies like photography or collecting antique silver. Even Brian, in his quieter periods, carried on boyhood pastimes like locomotive-spotting and collecting data on types of London bus. Two double-deckers he had bought were already housed in a northern transport museum; as his mental confusion increased, so did a compulsion to buy further vintage buses and charabancs. Shirley Arnold at the Stones office frequently had to deal with the indignant vendor of yet another bus which Brian had bought when drunk or stoned and had then instantly dismissed from his mind.

As for Keith, it seemed he needed nothing outside his existence as prototype of a Rock star. In the same way that Keith onstage had inspired a whole era of guitarists to copy his wolfish silhouette, so his private life style had become the model for an entirely new human species. It was an existence characterized, above all, by gigantic inertia – by hours spent in rooms devoid of light and strewn with album-sleeves, liquor bottles and cigarette-ends; by days, and most nights, passed in the tenacious pursuit of doing nothing but lying prone on a couch, near a lamp draped with a Batik scarf, drinking, smoking and 'toking', listening to thunderous hi-fi and tinkering with an acoustic guitar.

Keith now lived with Anita Pallenberg, mostly at Redlands, the Sussex cottage whose half-timbered exterior still gave no hint of the orgiastic twilight world within. From time to time, local people would glimpse the wrecked-looking country squire and his grimly beautiful blonde, driving in 'The Blue Lena' through West Wittering or, on rare occasions, coming out of neighbourhood shops. A villager who saw them often remembers the extraordinary blackness around Keith's eyes, even before he took to wearing mascara, and how he always seemed to smoke cigarettes twice as long as normal. Lurid tales circulated about what went on behind the seven-foot boundary wall Keith had recently obtained planning consent to build – how he would zoom around his lake in a miniature Hovercraft, or hunt water rats with a shotgun, accompanied by his giant deerhound, Syphilis.

Though Jagger could live the same incubated Rock star life for weeks at a time, quite happily, he continued to feel disturbing impulses – in tune with the new mood of student militancy – that he should be doing something more with his vast reputation than just making another album. What exactly he should be doing, though, continued problematical. The avenue of conventional politics, as suggested by Tom Driberg, involved dedication and

277

self-denial that were clearly unthinkable. Far more attractive was the idea of total revolution, a concept grown so fashionable, it could be discussed even by 25-year-old millionaires, sipping wine or tequila in their Queen Anne town houses. Thus far among would be Rock star revolutionaries, only one had put forward anything like a plan for effecting social change. John Lennon suggested putting LSD into the House of Commons water-supply, to see what good might come from 'freaking out' the whole of Parliament.

The Beatles, to their eternal credit, were making one gigantic, ill-starred effort to carry through the revolutionary precepts of hippydom. Their Apple organization, founded in the summer of 1968, was an attempt to use their collective millions to help young people in every branch of the creative arts. Apple, in Paul McCartney's phrase, would be 'a kind of Western Communism' – a business without greed, run only for mutual stimulation and enjoyment, fuelled by the amity and open-heartedness that was the prerogative of everyone under 30.

Philanthropy such as the Beatles were now splashing forth, over youthful musicians, writers, film-makers, poets and Punch and Judy men, had no appeal for the calculating and practical Head Stone. Marianne Faithfull remembers that when the ex-Animal Chas Chandler first brought Jimi Hendrix from New York to London, he approached Jagger as a possible co-sponsor, and Jagger 'simply turned and ran'. Hendrix's subsequent rise to fame, and a charismatic stage presence almost rivalling Jagger's own, had, if anything, deepened his indifference towards the promotion of new recording talent. Pre-eminent as he was, he appeared insecurely jealous of Jimi Hendrix, even suspecting Hendrix of trying to steal Marianne from him late one night at a West End club.

Since the break with Andrew Loog Oldham in October 1967, the Stones' management office had been in Maddox Street, close to Piccadilly. A small, top-floor suite, formerly maids' quarters in a Georgian town house, it was far from the opulence with which the Beatles had surrounded their new business family. It had been the best the Stones' staff could do after weeks of being turned down by landlords all over the West End. They got Maddox Street only by luck, through a friend of a friend, by pretending it was to house a music publishing company, and by scrupulous avoidance, at all times, of the phrase 'Rolling Stones'.

To run the Maddox Street office, Mick Jagger approached Jo Bergman, the American girl who had worked for Brian Epstein in the Beatles' fan club and, later, as Marianne's assistant and companion. Petite and cosy, with an air of high-powered calm, she was to assume most managerial functions for the Stones in Europe, presiding over a tiny staff whose mainstay continued to be their old fan club secretary, Shirley Arnold.

Shirley remembers with what keenness Jagger took on his new role of employer and businessman. 'He loved coming in for boardroom meetings with lawyers and accountants, or when Allen Klein was in town.' At Maddox Street there would be none of the slackness and promiscuity which characterized the Beatles' Apple workforce. 'Mick was always utterly meticulous,' Jo Bergman says. 'He liked to know everyone was doing things – for him, of course – with total efficiency.' When, on rare occasions, his eye alighted on a secretary for reasons other than stenographic, the ensuing business was conducted as discreetly as a Bourbon king with a scullery-maid. Only the girl's flushed face and half-unhinged false eyelashes would give the game away.

To Maddox Street, along with the equally-apportioned Rolling Stones fan mail and hate mail, were diverted the frequent ivory-white envelopes, hand-delivered from hotels like the Connaught or Dorchester, and containing fulsome appeals to Mick Jagger to read the enclosed synopsis, treatment or full shooting script. It was a fact tantalizing to film producers on both sides of the Atlantic that, in four years as a nonpareil crowd-puller, and despite embodying female fantasy at least as potently as Rudolf Valentino, Jagger still had not starred in a feature film.

The grandiose five-picture schedule announced by Allen Klein had by now dwindled to a faintly-recurring rumour among music journalists that they might still do something with the script of *Only Lovers Left Alive*. Klein, meanwhile, blocked all outside offers, insisting that his original plan would still be carried through. There had, besides, been a little too much real life drama lately for the Stones to want to manufacture any before the camera.

It was natural that a spirit as flirtatious and procrastinating as Jagger's should enjoy the wooing of film moguls, the fancy lunches, the agreement in principle to play ambitiously unlikely roles, the enthusiasm to read scripts which, as a rule, he would close after the second or third page. Lately, however, in his restlessness and wish to extend himself, he had given the whole question of movie acting concentrated thought. It weighed with his competitive nature that Marianne was following up her pop success with a career on the legitimate stage and in films. She had appeared in Chekhov's *Three Sisters* at Chichester Festival Theatre, to unanimous critical acclaim, and was now to star in a new Roger Vadim film, *Girl on a Motorcycle*.

Towards the summer's end, Jagger did finally succeed both in finishing a script and liking it. The film was to be called *Performance*. Its writer and putative co-director was Donald Cammell, the Stones' old painter friend from Paris. It told the story of a young English gangster, on the run from members of his own protection mob, and his encounter with an eccentric and reclusive pop star. Jagger, after practically no hesitation, agreed to play the pop star, 'Turner'. The theme music was to be written by Jagger and Richard and played as a sound track by the Rolling Stones. Largely on this basis, Cammell was able to raise 1.8 million pounds in financing from the Warner Brothers corporation. To Warner Brothers it seemed a safe enough investment. They presumed they were getting a happy, zany pop music picture like the Beatles' *A Hard Day's Night*.

Marianne was considered for the part of Turner's girl friend before it finally went to Anita Pallenberg. The choice was obvious – and, in any case, the film's winter shooting schedule would have been impossible for Marianne. That summer, she had discovered she was going to have Mick Jagger's baby.

This time, the raid on Brian took place at 7:30 in the morning. He had moved from Courtfield Road and was living temporarily in a rented flat at Royal Avenue House, a King's Road mansion block. Awakened by thunderous knocking and pealing on the front door bell, he took one look through the security spy-hole, then dived for the telephone. His panic-stricken words to Les Perrin – 'They're coming in through the window, Les' – were not far short of the truth. A policeman was actually climbing into the flat via its interior rubbish-chute.

When Jo Bergman reached Royal Avenue House, shortly before 9 a.m., a smiling policeman let her into the flat. Three more hefty officers stood over Brian, in his skimpy kimono, showing him a lump of cannabis which one of them had taken from inside a ball of brown wool in the living room bureau. Brian's reaction was one of incredulous dismay. 'Oh – *no*,' he moaned. 'This can't happen again, just when we're getting on our feet.'

Later that same day, May 21, Brian returned to Great Marlborough Street Magistrates Court, charged with possessing 44 grains of cannabis resin. He was released on £2,000 bail pending trial, once again, before Inner London Sessions. He also faced punishment for breach of the probation order placed on him by the Court of Criminal Appeal.

He spent that night in the care of Allen Klein's nephew, Ronnie Schneider, sleeping in Schneider's room at the London Hilton. 'The hotel didn't want to take him,' Schneider says. 'I told them that if they wanted to throw Brian out, they'd have to throw me out, too. He went to sleep in the spare bed, crying and holding my hand. Next morning, we had a big meeting with the lawyers on Brian's case. Brian kept coming up behind me and kissing the back of my head. He told me I'd saved him.'

The second bust plunged Brian back to zero, cruelly, at the very point when his efforts to rebuild himself as a person and a musician seemed to be paying off. True to his Appeal Court undertaking, he had kept clear of drugs; he had left his psychiatrist's care and was now obliged only to make the statutory regular visits to his probation officer. He did so conscientiously though he loathed the counselling sessions in the drab little local government office.

In the studio, too, he had revived, feeling a surge of optimism in the Stones' return to their R & B roots and in the obvious quality of their new producer, Jimmy Miller. Leaving his Mellotron and flute and Moroccan pipes, he had gone back to playing bottleneck Blues guitar with an impassioned elegance already defining several tracks for the album that would become *Beggars' Banquet*. The sessions were being filmed by the French director Jean-Luc Godard as part of a polemical drama-documentary about glamour and violence in the Sixties. With Jean-Luc Godard at

Olympic studios, and cameras turning over every night, it was natural that Anita Pallenberg should frequently drop by – even that had not seemed to shake Brian's composure. He had assured several people vehemently, 'I'm not interested in Anita any more.'

Now, once more, he was the piteous, impossible Brian of four months ago, whose only defence against the horrors crowding in on him was Scotch and pills and snatching up the telephone. 'Whenever the phone went at 2 a.m., I'd always know who it was,' Jo Bergman says. 'He'd spend perhaps an hour, talking to me about some tiny thing that was on his mind. As soon as he'd rung off, he'd ring straight back and talk for another hour about the same tiny thing. Then he'd ring back *again*, horror-struck to think he'd woken me up. Next morning, I'd discover I was one of half a dozen people Brian had been ringing up through the night.'

Les Perrin's wife Janey was someone else Brian turned to constantly, for reassurance, a sympathetic ear, or just human company. 'He'd ring me about *anything*,' Janey Perrin says. 'He'd ring to say he'd got a toothache . . . a headache . . . that he couldn't turn the tap off in the kitchen. Once, he sent me an 86-word telegram. Another time, he rang me from the Dorchester and said he was going to commit suicide. I was so exasperated, I said, "All right, Brian – go into the bathroom and do it, so as not to make a mess." That brought him round a bit. Another time, he swore while he was talking to me. He rang back almost in tears, to think I'd heard him use a foul word. In the end when he rang up, he wouldn't say, "It's Brian." He'd say, "This is your other son."'

What chiefly terrified Brian between May and September, when his case came to court, was that the other Stones might secretly be planning to go on tour without him – perhaps even with a new guitarist in his place. In August, the British music press reported that Eric Clapton had been asked to join the Stones when his 'supergroup', Cream, disbanded at Christmas. It was a constant theme of Brian's late-night telephone calls to anyone who would listen: how his drug bust had given *them* the perfect excuse to get rid of him. At times, the Chelsea Police seemed only walk-on players in that longer-term conspiracy by so-called friends to steal his stardom first, then his woman, and finally to eject him from the band he had created.

In fact, despite their deeply-ingrained exasperation with Brian, and their severely limited capacity for unselfish action, Mick and Keith both genuinely sympathized with him in this new, undeserved crisis, and made intermittent efforts to show him moral support. For all they knew, indeed, Brian's busting could presage renewed police attacks on either or both of them. Their sympathy was, perhaps, too sudden for Brian to recognize it as such. Spanish Tony Sanchez remembers a summer day at Redlands when Mick Jagger took Brian into the house for a serious talk about his approaching trial. Shortly afterwards, Brian rushed through the open French windows, shouting, 'I'll kill myself' and jumped straight into Keith's water-filled moat. Jagger plunged in to rescue him before realizing that the water was only four feet deep. The two staggered out together, Brian laughing hysterically, Jagger enraged at the ruination of his new velvet trousers.

One sensible decision reached by the others on Brian's behalf was that, until his reappearance before Inner London Sessions, he had better be as far as possible from the Chelsea police, his dangerous social circle of junkies and the pressmen who would now be dogging his every move. One of his casual girl-friends, Linda Keith, had recently attempted suicide at his flat; two more had visited him simultaneously in hospital, creating an emotional tension not calculated to aid the patient's recovery. There were also insistent demands from the mother of his elder son called Julian for money to buy the lad a miniature typewriter.

It was Keith Richard's well-intentioned idea that Brian should live at Redlands with Suki Poitier, under the care of Keith's own chauffeur, Tom Keylock. There he remained from July to late September, apparently content to be surrounded by reminders of Anita. There the others would meet and try to rehearse, although Brian had lost the will for anything beyond his own desultory, and somehow secretive, acoustic strumming. He managed to keep off drugs but compensated by drinking more heavily than ever. One Sunday, when Mick and Marianne had driven down to see him, he flew into a drunken fury, lunged at Mick with his fists, then threatened him with a carving-knife. Marianne remembers his panting, bloated face – the face which, to Jo Bergman, only too clearly denoted its astrological sign. 'He was a double Pisces. His face really did seem to be turning back to water.'

The breach seemed healed on September 24, when Mick and Keith both attended Inner London Sessions to see Brian treated with wholly unlooked-for clemency. The jury found him Guilty of possessing cannabis. But the Chairman, Reginald Seaton, decided it had been 'a lapse' from previous sincere efforts to stay straight. Brian was fined £50 and a hundred guineas costs. Afterwards, Mick and Keith posed for photographs with him, their arms round his shoulders: two decolleté young gods of 1968, flanking someone who might have been an older, unwell relative.

From time to time, in his miasmic anxiety and depression, Brian would remember his plan to return to Morocco and record the ethnic music that had so excited him there – in particular, the wonderful Jajouka pipers in the foothills of the Rif. Even that bright memory seemed stained by the thought of how friends had betrayed him. To return to Morocco meant returning to the day when he had lost Anita; when he had returned from the Djemaa el Fna to find her and Keith and Tom Keylock and the Bentley, all gone.

His first trip back to Tangier, with Suki Poitier and Christopher Gibbs, brought on an almost eerie repetition of the last night he and Anita had ever spent together. 'I suddenly got this call from Brian to go down to their room,' Gibbs says. 'Suki was lying on the floor, unconscious. Brian had clearly given her the most terrible beating-up. "Can you call an ambulance, man?" he said. It was entirely in the nature of things to Brian that someone else called the ambulance to take the girl he'd beaten up to hospital. "No, Brian," I said. "You call an ambulance – and *quickly*." It was obvious that simply hadn't occurred to him.'

In the spring of 1968, he persuaded Glyn Johns to join him on an expedition to record the G'naou, a Negro – as opposed to Berber – troupe, performing on steel drums and outsize metal castanets. Brian's idea was to show the link between African and American black music by taking the G'naou tapes to New York and overdubbing layers of Jazz or Soul. In the event, he was too drunk, or stoned, even to hear the G'naou troupe properly. Glyn Johns grew understandably bored, and the taping was a fiasco.

In October, accompanied by the long-suffering Suki and a sound engineer named George Chkiantz, Brian returned to

Tangier, determined to record the Jajouka in their pre-Roman Rites of Pan festival. Brion Gysin met them at Tangier with his Moroccan partner, Hamri, and drove them up to the village that nestles in an eyrie so acoustically perfect, one can hear a dog barking on an adjacent mountain, and the waves breaking on rocks half a dozen miles below.

For almost two day and nights, Brian squatted there with Suki, smoking *kif*, apparently entranced by the soft, incessant pipe melody that – owing to the Jajouka's ability to blow out while inhaling – seems not to pause even for breath. Only a few Europeans had been to the village before; fewer still had seen this private version of the Pan rites, with children dancing, like figures from a cave mural, in brazen, unearthly light. At 4 a.m., the party bedded down in a communal hut: by noon, the festival had begun again.

Towards evening, Brion Gysin remembers, two of the musicians put down their instruments and rose to begin preparations for the meal the visitors had been asked to share. A moment later, they walked past Brian and Suki, carrying a snow white goat. As Brian looked at the goat, with its bewildered, pale-fringed eyes, a strangled noise came from him: he said in a whisper, 'That's *me*.' Suki and Brion Gysin smiled, agreeing there was some resemblance. But Brian did not smile. He continued to watch, fascinated, and to whisper, 'That's *me*,' as the two men carried the white goat into the shadow of a lean-to, and one of them drew out a long-bladed knife.

# 'There's just no room for a street-fighting man . . .'

The few close friends who knew about Marianne's pregnancy were surprised to see with what unaffected pleasure Mick looked forward to fatherhood. It was one further paradox in a character so narcissistically self-absorbed that he loved small children and enjoyed taking care of them; to a child he always granted an intimacy withheld from his closest adult friends. His happiest hours with Marianne came when he forsook his court to go off for a day in the country with just her and her three-year-old son, Nicholas. With Nicholas, he was less surrogate father than elder brother. He would play with the little boy for hours, pushing him high on swings or whirling him round by the arms in some empty Berkshire meadow.

Jagger desperately wanted this first child of his own: he also wanted Marianne to become his wife as soon as John Dunbar would divorce her. Marianne had always demurred before, afraid of such a commitment a second time – a little wary, too, of acquiring so voluble a mother-in-law. 'Somehow,' she says, 'I always felt there couldn't be *another* Mrs Jagger.' Even so, she felt her resolve weakening. For, since his discovery that she was carrying his child, he had treated her with almost maternal tenderness.

The news, when published, brought a storm of protest from people who could – and did – describe Mick and Marianne's relationship as 'living in sin'. Marianne, as the guiltier party, became the theme of pulpit orations and parish newsletters throughout the British Isles. The Archbishop of Canterbury himself spared a moment in his pulpit to ask for intercessionary prayers on her behalf. It was Marianne's pregnancy which largely provoked the backlash of so-called 'moral' people against the permissive pop world. In particular, it provided fuel for the egregious Mrs Mary Whitehouse as self-appointed defender of British morals in public figures now, as well as in a theatrical production she might or might not have seen.

Jagger, as obvious spokesman for the Permissive Society, eventually agreed to face Mrs Whitehouse on a special edition of the David Frost television show. The northern headmistress, accustomed to rolling over most opposition, did not win the easy victory she anticipated on behalf of conventional wedlock.

'The fact of the matter . . .' Mrs Whitehouse said, looking at Jagger through flyaway-rim spectacles and smiling her bright, metallic smile, ' . . . is that if you're a Christian or a person with faith, and you make that vow, when difficulties come, you have this basic thing you've accepted. You find your way through the difficulties.'

'*Your* Church accepts divorce,' Jagger replied. 'It may even accept abortion – am I right or wrong? I don't see how you can talk about this bond which is inseparable when the Christian Church itself accepts divorce . . .' It was, of course, beyond his power to confess that he wanted to marry the girl, but couldn't.

Nicholas was playing in the Cheyne Walk music room – a small garden house, smelling strongly of cats – the day Jagger sat down with Keith to try to articulate his thoughts about the insurrection he so fervently half wanted to join. 'Everywhere I hear the sound of marching, charging feet, boy,' he sang, against Keith's beating-to-quarters guitar riff. 'Summer's here and the time is right for fighting in the street, boy . . .'

To his credit, he had tried the real thing, linking arms with the anti-Vietnam War demonstrators outside the American Embassy on the day when Lady Bracknell's prophecy came true of 'acts of violence in Grosvenor Square'. The press soon spotted Jagger and chased him from the scene, well before police horses started falling down. Today, looking from his summerhouse to his Queen Anne mansion, he realized where his true allegiance must lie. The insolent battle cry tailed off into indecision; the passion curdled into even colder feet than Lennon's. ' . . . but what can a poor boy do, 'cept to sing in a Rock 'n' Roll Band . . .'

Chaos was far more efficaciously present, had he realized it, in another new song, whose recording had been observed in its entirety by Jean-Luc Godard's documentary film crew. Godard subsequently dropped the title he had meant to give his film, *One Plus One*, and instead gave it the song's name, Sympathy for the Devil.

Even before Jumping Jack Flash, there were those eager to connect the Stones' music with a darker, more deliberate paganism. They had acquired a fervent fan, and a slightly unsettling friend, in Kenneth Anger, film-maker, connoisseur of the Occult and disciple of Britain's most notorious black magician, Aleister Crowley. To Kenneth Anger, the Stones in their concerts showed the power to invoke forces not invoked since Crowley, 'The Great Beast', had gone to his sacrilegious grave. Mick Jagger, in Anger's ravished eyes, was no less than a latter-day Lucifer, with Keith as his attendant devil, Beelzebub. So he wanted to cast them in his intended masterpiece, a screen version of the black magic epic *Lucifer Rising*.

There was also Anita Pallenberg, whose knowledge of the black arts was rumoured far more than perfunctory, and whose influence over and around the chief Stones had aroused suspicions that she was actually a witch. Spanish Tony Sanchez, Keith's intermittent chauffeur-bodyguard, claims to have seen the collection of human relics allegedly used in spells against those who had incurred Anita's displeasure.

At Anita's prompting, Keith himself had grown fascinated by black magic and witchcraft and convinced – as many others had been – that Kenneth Anger possessed the powers of a 'Magus', or sorcerer. At one point, Keith and Anita even contemplated a pagan marriage ceremony, with Anger officiating: they were deterred – according to Spanish Tony – by an unmistakable warning not to meddle in realms that could become dangerous.

Jagger, too, flirted briefly with diabolism, as an extension of his interest in magic and fairies. Flattered, above all, by his elevation to Lucifer, he offered to compose theme music on his new Moog synthesizer for Kenneth Anger's film *Invocation of my Demon Brother*. His experiments with the black arts, however, did not proceed one step further than was quite prudent. For something like a year afterwards he, very noticeably, wore a large wooden crucifix.

It was not Kenneth Anger, but the eclectically-read Marianne, who gave Jagger his reference-point for a song in which Satan would make an actual, named appearance. Marianne had just read Mikhail Bulgakov's *The Master and Margarita*, a surrealist Russian novel of the 1930s, in which Satan pays a visit to contemporary Moscow to survey the effects of the Revolution. Bulgakov's is the smooth-talking Satan later epitomized by George Sanders: a figure in immaculate evening dress, with a long cigarette-holder, bowing low and purring, 'Permit me to introduce myself . . .'

The phrase launched Jagger into a lyric of daring bad taste: a soliloquy by just such an urbane and ingratiating Mephistopheles, looking back over his interventions in human affairs, from Christ's Crucifixion through the Russian Revolution to Hitler's Blitzkrieg and the Kennedy assassination. A similar irresistible impulse in the studio wrenched the song away from its original, rather folksy arrangement, into a bongo-spattered Samba beat that seemed to find a groove more compulsive than any Blues. As Jagger moved through his Devil's apology, overweening politeness rising to the glottal roar of a punk samurai, an impromptu chorus, 'Woo-woo, woo-woo,' broke out among Anita Pallenberg and her friends in the control-room. Played back, it seemed indivisible from the song: a sound-track from a coven of sarcastic witches.

Christopher Gibbs had suggested naming the new album *Beggars' Banquet* in accord with the prevailing atmosphere of wizards, hobgoblins and devilish paradox. A final mix was ready in time to be played at Mick Jagger's 26th birthday party, at Spanish Tony's Vesuvio Club, on July 26. The guests included John Lennon, Paul McCartney and other pop notables whose opinion Jagger particularly valued. Their acclaim was instant and unanimous. At the first wild Samba beat of Sympathy for the Devil, almost the whole company surged on to the dance floor to dance the whole album through. For Jagger, it was a night of triumph, marred only slightly when Paul McCartney gave the club disc jockey the Beatles' new single to play, and everyone went wild a second time, listening to Hey, Jude.

In *Beggars' Banquet*, the Stones had produced an album whose simplicity and minimal elegance seemed more marvellous, recalling the washy jingle-jangle of *Their Satanic Majesties*: an album whose daring, often dangerous themes, are hidden within the forthright, artless styles of Blues or Country music. Exhortations to riot, blaspheme or fornicate are conveyed by no more than the lilt of a hillbilly piano. Complex evils come hidden among plainly-strummed acoustic guitars. It is a work which shows the Stones simultaneously pushing into territory never charted by pop, and rediscovering the spirit of Eel Pie Island. The most arresting minor track – more so than the melancholy No Expectations or the semi-pornographic Stray Cat Blues – is Jagger's devout treatment of Prodigal Son, a Gospel classic written by the Reverend Robert Wilkins 40 years before. Even on unfamiliar and risky ground, everything went right. Salt of the Earth, a song for 'the hard-working people', makes a rather better showing nowadays than that deluded anthem, All You Need Is Love.

The original *Beggars' Banquet* sleeve, art directed jointly by Jagger and Richard, who to have depicted, simply, a lavatory wall, shot from just above pedestal-height, with song titles and studio credits scrawled as graffiti around its pipes, toilet-roll holder and evil-looking cistern, among such examples of scatological philosophy as 'God rolls his own' and 'Wot! No paper!' Not surprisingly, both Decca and the Stones' American label, London, rejected the design. The Stones – that is to say, Mick Jagger – refused to consider any alternative. The release-date, August 24, was moved back into September.

Street Fighting Man had, meanwhile, been launched on an American summer already rent by assassination and race-riots – only days, indeed, after Mayor Daley's Chicago police had systematically beaten up innocent protesters at the Democratic Party Convention. Street Fighting Man was denounced as plain incitement to further violence and banned by every radio station in the Chicago area, together with dozens more across the continent.

The battle with Decca over the lavatory wall sleeve deteriorated into a public slanging-match between Jagger and Sir Edward Lewis. Decca's Chairman was quoted as calling the sleeve 'silly' and 'offensive'. Jagger retorted that Decca had seen nothing offensive in issuing a Tom Jones album (*A-Tomic Jones*) with a cover showing an A-Bomb's mushroom cloud. Next, he challenged Decca to issue the sleeve in a plain brown paper wrapper marked 'Unfit for Children'. Sir Edward did not rise to the challenge. The release-date was moved back again, to sometime in October.

While the Stones battled with Decca, their managers, past and present, battled with each other in a wild fandango of changing partners and rebounding writs.

For more than two years, Eric Easton had been trying to obtain legal redress for his ousting from the Stones' co-management by Andrew Loog Oldham in cahoots with Allen Klein. Easton was suing Oldham for breach of contract, and suing Klein for having engineered that breach. Proceedings had been delayed initially by Oldham's nimbleness in avoiding service of the legal papers, and subsequently by Allen Klein's will o' the wisp appearances in London and equally sudden disappearances back to New York.

In November, 1967, Eric Easton finally succeeded in bringing Andrew Loog Oldham before a High Court judge. It was a bizarre occasion, of which the undoubted highlight was an attempt by each ex-partner to have the other jailed for contempt. The result was an order from Mr Justice Buckley, freezing some two million dollars in Rolling Stones royalties until Easton's claim against Oldham and Klein was resolved.

By this time, of course, Andrew Loog Oldham was no longer acting directly as the Stones' manager – was, indeed, on hostile terms with them following his walkout during the non-making of *Their Satanic Majesties*. After the Oldham-Easton High Court battle, the Stones took the opportunity to repudiate the original agreement made with their co-managers. They claimed it had been signed by only one of them – Brian Jones – and was legally invalid, anyway, since Brian had been under the age of 21.

By this time, too, Oldham and Allen Klein were no longer the cosy, conspiratorial duo which had cut up Eric Easton. The matter at issue was the $1.25 million in advance royalties which Klein had wrung from Decca in 1966 and which – Oldham then assumed – had been paid into his and the Stones' joint publishing company, Nanker Phelge Music Ltd. Instead, he discovered, the money had been placed with something called Nanker Phelge *USA*, an entirely separate company formed by Klein a week after the Decca deal, with himself as president and sole shareholder. In other words, for three years past, the $1.25 million seemed to have existed, not as capital for the Rolling Stones but as a negotiable

291

asset for Allen Klein and Company.

Oldham's response – though he was still linked to Klein in the Eric Easton case – was to file suit against him in America, claiming that Nanker Phelge USA had been used as 'a vehicle for the diversion of assets and income' from Oldham, the Rolling Stones and Nanker Phelge UK Ltd to Allen Klein 'for his own personal use and benefit'.

The suit was worth $1.5 million, and it quickly became bogged down in the litigious everglades all around Klein's portly person. Klein's injured contention was that, since his company had done the Decca deal, his company would naturally have received the proceeds; and that, since the Stones were guaranteed their royalty payments spread over a twenty-year period, the name he chose to call the handling company was irrelevant. In any case, once filed, the Oldham lawsuit had to take its place in a queue of some 50 other legal disputes involving Allen Klein.

The Oldham-Klein case dragged on for most of 1968 – a year in which Klein waxed still greater in New York, first by acquiring the nearly defunct Cameo-Parkway record label, then by 'talking up' its shares to many times their value with rumours of grandiose acquisitions and takeovers. In the event, Cameo-Parkway's only acquisition was the firm of Allen Klein and Company (whose listed assets, oddly enough, included General Motors shares to the precise value of $1.25 million.)

In October 1968, Allen Klein approached Andrew Loog Oldham with a deal. He would buy off Oldham's lawsuit, plus all his residual interests in the Rolling Stones, for one million dollars, to be paid on the instalment-plan. It was, as he well knew, an offer Oldham could not refuse.

That left only the unfortunate Eric Easton, still trying to obtain satisfaction by conventional legal means from a fat man in New York whose far more important pursuers now included the US Securities and Exchange Commission, and from a young man in London whose overwrought emotional state now led him to spend his weekends in the therapeutic care of nuns. On Monday morning, the nuns would unlock the door, and Andrew Loog Oldham would return to his life as a boy tycoon.

The Warner Brothers executive editor who had visualized

*Performance* as a film on the lines of *A Hard Day's Night* would doubtless have been spellbound by the early scene in which James Fox as Chas, the young Cockney hoodlum, ritualistically pours acid over the Rolls-Royce of a hostile barrister, then shaves the head of a bound and gagged chauffeur, whistling a cheerful barber's shop air. The scene in which Chas's gang boss, a bald, hairy-chested brute, given to sententious utterances about 'Old England', huddles in his vest under a pink satin counterpane while his half-naked catamite preens himself nearby, might also have given warning that the film starring Mick Jagger was something other than all-round family entertainment.

When Jagger came on set, early in October, Donald Cammell's production team was ensconced in the ramshackle terrace house, in Lowndes Square, chosen as the retreat of the reclusive pop idol, Turner. With Christopher Gibbs as set-designer, the house quickly assumed the appearance of a Rolling Stone habitation: vampire-dark, hung with exotic drapes and, in certain visible places, none too clean. Here, hiding out from his gang boss after an impolitic murder, Chas was to undergo initiation into drugs, wigs and other weirdness by Turner and two female companions.

The requirements of playing Turner had caused Jagger to agonize at length over whether it might not do his real life pop image irreparable harm. For most of the picture, Turner had to wear full female make-up, lipstick, powder and rouge. At the climax of the magic mushroom trip administered to Chas, Turner underwent transformation from pop star to underworld gangster, with his hair slicked back like a Fifties Teddy Boy.

But most of all, Jagger worried that the character developed in Donald Cammell's script – the morose and playful, pretentiously bookish superstar hermit – bore not the slightest resemblance to himself. Long discussions with Cammell and the film's director, Nicholas Roeg, could not find a coalescence of Turner and Mick Jagger that would hold up for a minute before the cameras. Then, as always, his mimic's gift came to his rescue. The Turner he chose to play was an amalgam of two close acquaintances. In appearance, dead black and brooding, festooned with outsize silver belts and baubles, Mick turned into Keith Richard. In manner, he turned – almost uncannily – into Brian Jones.

As Turner's girl friend, Anita Pallenberg, at least, was perfectly

293

cast. Everyone who knew her recognized the rangy blonde, dressed only in a marmalade-coloured fur, teasing the bewildered Chas with her green eyes and long, golden legs, as a perfect cinematic version of Anita's mischievous, unsettling power. Her role in the strange house, impermanent, indifferent, laughingly malevolent, was exactly her role within the Stones. Her part in disorienting the painfully 'straight' young gangster chiefly lay in confusing him – as she had apparently confused Brian – about his sexual identity. At one point in Chas's ordeal, Anita holds a mirror up to his face, reflecting it above her own bare breast. The scene was to have a lasting effect on James Fox, and make more than one bystander remember the old whispers about Anita's supposed power as a sorceress.

It began as a joke between Mick and Keith that Donald Cammell's script required Turner and his girl friend to make lingering love, together with an androgynous French girl, in the star's huge carved and canopied antique bed. After shooting had begun, however, Cammell realized that Keith was deeply uneasy about Anita's role as Mick's lover and, in particular, their simulation of sex together for the camera. 'And, of course, Anita didn't help his insecurity,' Cammell says. 'She seemed to be teasing Keith about wanting Mick, the way she'd teased Brian about wanting Keith. While we were shooting at Lowndes Square, Keith hardly ever came near the house. He'd sit outside in his car and send in messages.'

In the event, their screen encounter brought a resolution of the love-hate feeling which had so long smouldered between Anita and Mick. As the cameras turned, under a perfect alibi of fiction, the two began to make love in earnest. In its final, much-edited version, the film shows little more than Anita's lips nibbling Jagger's huge ones, and a cinematically-fashionable tumble and twist of limbs. However, the off-cuts were illicitly spliced together into a separate short feature which, a few months later, won a prize at a festival of blue movies in Amsterdam.

Keith knew what had happened, though – like Brian before him – he somehow could not bring himself to accuse Anita outright. His method of retaliation was endlessly to postpone working with Mick on the single Jagger-Richard song required for the film – a song sung to Chas by Turner, transformed to a hallucinogenic gang boss. 'Keith just *refused* to get down to it,' Cammell says. 'I kept asking Mick "Where's the goddammed song?" Mick kept saying "It's okay, it'll be ready" but he knew very well what Keith was doing, and why.'

Finally, near desperation, Cammell himself sat down with Jagger to write a song they called Memo From Turner. When the Stones met to record it, Keith's antagonism remained all-pervading. 'With Keith against it in the studio, the song sounded just awful – still and lifeless,' Donald Cammell says. 'But without the song, we couldn't end the picture. Keith knew he had the power to sabotage the whole thing.

'In the end, I got Mick alone. I took him into a pub in Berwick Street and said, "Mick, for God's sake, what about the *song*?" Standing there at the bar, he suddenly burst into tears. It was a thing he could always do for maximum effect – just like John Gielgud. "I'm sorry," he said. "I blew it." It was then that I realized he'd decided to get the song finished. From then on, after all that indecisiveness, the decisions were made like *lightning*.'

Memo From Turner was re-recorded by Jagger with a studio full of high-powered session musicians, including Stevie Winwood and Jim Capaldi from the flower power group Traffic. This left *Performance* devoid of any Stones music, since its musical director, Jack Nitzsche, used American session men – notably slide guitarist Lowell George – to play over the film's opening and closing credits.

While Jagger worked on *Performance*, Marianne spent much of her time in Ireland, at a house in County Galway, rented from Molly Cusack Smith, the Master of the local hunt, the Galway Blazers. It was a setting chosen to afford maximum peace and tranquillity during the middle and late phase of Marianne's pregnancy. She was determined to take every care, remembering how casual she had been while carrying Nicholas, and because her doctor had warned there might be complications. She thus remained unaware of the drama between Mick, Keith and Anita, engrossed by happy thoughts of what a father Mick would make. They both wanted a girl and had already chosen a name for her – Carena.

In the seventh month of pregnancy, despite all her care, Marianne lost the baby on which she and Jagger had pinned inordinate hope. Such things are never other than devastating. Like any other young couple, they cried out the cruel disappointment in each other's arms: two child-like figures, in that grown-up house, between whom the bond of love and sympathy could never be so strong again.

On December 5, *Beggars' Banquet* was released, four months late, clad in a tasteful buff-coloured sleeve adorned only with the title, the artists' name and 'R.S.V.P.' The fight over the lavatory wall sleeve had gone on well into October, with Decca continually postponing release dates until it seemed the Stones might not release an album at all in 1968. The result was inevitable: while the critics and public went wild about *Beggars' Banquet*, the Stones themselves were only bored by it.

Their attitude was made plain at the album's launch-party – a mock-ceremonial banquet at the Queensgate Hotel, attended by dignitaries such as the US Ambassador-elect Lord Harlech, and concluding in a custard pie fight which left each long-haired guest festooned with plates of artificial cream like so many Abominable Snowmen. Lord Harlech evidently enjoyed the pie-throwing. So did Les Perrin, whom one cameraman snapped, towering above the fray, oozing missile in hand, his usual circumspection quite forgotten. Another lens caught Brian Jones, slamming a pie into Mick Jagger's face with what, bystanders agreed, seemed somewhat excessive force.

This mood of sarcastic bonhomie which the Stones had made peculiarly their own continued in a Christmas 'special' Jagger had undertaken to do for BBC Television – the famous *Rolling Stones Rock and Roll Circus*. Recorded over two days, December 11 and 12, at the old *Ready, Steady, Go* studios in Wembley, it featured the Stones in live performance with superstar friends such as John Lennon, Eric Clapton, the Who and Jethro Tull as supporting acts, interspersed with jugglers, lion-tamers and clowns. A certain similarity might have been detected to *Magical Mystery Tour*, the Beatles' TV special shown almost exactly a year previously, save that where the Beatles had sadly flopped, Mick Jagger was determined to have a hit.

During 48 hours of almost continuous filming, the *Rock and Roll Circus* presented its carnival-hatted and decibel-drowned big top audience with many remarkable sights. There was John Lennon, dressed as a be-ruffed and stockinged juggler, accompanied by Yoko Ono in the all too convincing black vestments of a witch. There was the Blues musician Taj Mahal, in bewildering propinquity with the concert pianist Julius Katchen, the black fashion model Donyale Luna and the Merry Prankster Ken Kesey. There was the unprecedented novelty of seeing John Lennon play his song Yer Blues with an ad hoc group comprising Eric Clapton on lead guitar, Keith Richard on bass and Mitch Mitchell, from the Jimi Hendrix Experience, on drums, while Yoko crouched nearby, enveloped in a black bag. There was the more predictable surprise, during the Who's performance, when water spurted from Keith Moon's drums. There were the varied side-show astonishments of seeing Mick Jagger dressed as a ringmaster, posing with a quiescent tiger: Keith Richard as a vampire-faced, moustachioed stage-door johnny; Brian Jones in a top hat sprouting satyr horns – a lecherously colourful figure, divorced from the small, defeated voice which gasped out his only line of dialogue: 'Here come the clowns.'

There was, finally, the Stones' own contribution, begun so far into the second night that most of the audience had gone home: a transfixing performance which ranged from old R & B favourites like Route 66 to a Jumpin' Jack Flash set about by lights which could actually damage eyesight, and, climactically, *six* takes of Sympathy For the Devil, with Jagger wrenching off his red T-shirt to reveal Satan daubed on his chest. The superstar cast then joined the stupefied audience to sing Salt of the Earth from a prompt-board, swaying from side to side.

*Rock and Roll Circus* was not televised that Christmas – it has not been shown to this date. The veto was Mick Jagger's. He liked the film but not the way he himself looked in it. He felt that the Who had upstaged him.

On December 18, an apparently reconciled Mick and Keith took ship for Rio de Janeiro, accompanied by Anita, Marianne and three-year-old Nicholas. They were to spend a month travelling through Latin America, reportedly enlarging their knowledge of magic by hobnobbing with headhunters and pygmies in the Amazonian rain forests. 'We are very serious about this trip,'

Keith told the *Sunday Express*, maintaining an absolutely straight face. 'We are hoping to see a magician who practises both black and white magic. He has a very long and difficult name which we can't pronounce – we just call him "Banana" for short.'

It was in fact to be a perfectly normal holiday. Mick had suggested Majorca before Marianne reminded him he was now a millionaire. To Keith, the most restful part was the sea voyage from Lisbon to Rio, among middle-aged people who drank pink gin, dressed for dinner each night and regarded the Jagger-Richard party as some sort of mysterious addition to the ship's entertainment programme. 'We used to see the same couple in the bar, who kept saying to us, "Who *are* you? What's it all about? Come on, give us a clue. Just give us a glimmer." That's when Mick and I started to call ourselves The Glimmer Twins.'

Nicholas Dunbar remembers the holiday chiefly for the time he spent with his mother and Mick, living in a simple hut at the edge of a long, white beach. Every day, Mick would take him off to play or paddle, all the time gently helping him over the hurdles from babyhood to boyhood, showing him how to undo his own buttons to pee. 'I remember his voice, saying, "Mind your feet on the sharp stones. Put on your sandals."'

Their only experience with magic occurred by accident, when they blundered into a celebration of Macumba – religious rites which no outsiders were permitted to see. 'I remember when you and Mick got stoned,' Nicholas would say to Marianne in later life. 'I mean – I remember when those people started throwing stones at you.'

Back in London, at one of the parties that still happened every night, Miles, from the Indica Bookshop, caught a glimpse of his old Cheltenham friend, Brian Jones. There was the usual frock-coated finery, the gorget and flowered cravat, the wide-brimmed hat, pressing his gold fringe down around his eyes and cheeks. There was the usual girl companion, blonde like himself – or like someone he both longed and dreaded to forget. In the midst of the party, Brian and the girl had both nodded off to sleep, their big hats and weary child faces together, amid the dancers and noise, innocent as babes in the wood.

\* \* \*

Late one afternoon in January 1969, John Lennon and Yoko Ono slipped furtively from a white Rolls-Royce, into the Art Deco foyer of the Dorchester Hotel. The couple were by now almost indistinguishable, save for John's beard and Yoko Ono's manifest air of continually propelling him forward. Five minutes later, in a bedroom overlooking Hyde Park, they finally came face to face with Allen Klein.

For Klein, it was an emotional moment. His desire for the Beatles, undiminished after four years, had seemed no closer to fulfilment in the 18 months since Brian Epstein's death, notwithstanding the managerial chaos which Epstein had bequeathed: Klein had merely been one entrepreneur among many, watching the Beatles' Apple venture slide into disaster, and longing to apply drastic remedies. He had seen John Lennon with Yoko at the Stones' *Rock and Roll Circus* and, recognizing his isolation from the other Beatles, had bombarded Lennon's mansion with telephone calls, all to no avail. Then, in January 1969, Lennon had confessed to *Rolling Stone* magazine that, if Apple went on losing money at its present rate, he would be 'broke in six months'. Allen Klein's moment had come.

This short meeting with John and Yoko at the Dorchester was, despite his own nerves, a virtuoso Klein performance. At its conclusion, Yoko sat down and, at John's dictation, typed a note to Sir Joseph Lockwood, Chairman of EMI: 'Dear Sir Joe – from now on, Allen Klein handles all my stuff.'

George Harrison and Ringo Starr met Klein a few days later, and were similarly impressed. His offer seemed irresistibly sensible. He would go into Apple and clear out the spongers and spendthrifts. He would then make them richer than even they, the Beatles, had ever dreamed, by gaining them control of the companies Brian Epstein had set up around them, and by renegotiating their royalty rate with EMI. George and Ringo, too, liked Klein's blunt manner and his picturesque fiscal imagery. 'Ya shouldn't even have to *think* about money,' he told them. 'You should be able to say "F.Y.M. – Fuck you, Money!"'

Paul McCartney, however, no longer saw Allen Klein as the Beatles' only possible saviour. McCartney never liked rough diamonds; he had, moreover, almost persuaded the others to hire his prospective father-in-law, the New York lawyer Lee Eastman, to take over Apple and fight the two boardroom battles they now faced. McCartney attended only one meeting with Klein, and walked out soon after it had begun. This, apparently, mortified Klein almost to the extent of abandoning his dream. 'It was an ego thing,' his nephew, Ronnie Schneider, says. 'He wanted all *four* of them to like him. I told him that was crazy. "What the hell!" I said. "It's a majority decision."'

McCartney's dislike, and the Eastman family's contempt, merely stiffened the others' resolve to bring in Klein as their manager. It was in vain even for Lee Eastman to point out how low Klein's reputation stood in New York as a result of the Cameo-Parkway affair, and that he now faced prosecution from the US Internal Revenue Service on ten counts of failing to file income tax returns.

As with the Stones in 1966, Klein had offered his 'Let me show you what I can do before I take a cent of your money' ploy. He would work unofficially, in 'co-operation' with the Eastmans, looking into Apple's financial plight while they dealt with boardroom strategy, but taking no percentage until *all* the Beatles were ready to put their trust in him.

The news brought a curious response from Mick Jagger, who had recommended Klein to the Beatles so many times over the years, but who was now heard to tell John Lennon on the telephone: 'You're making the biggest mistake of your life.'

Jagger had returned from South America with a deep tan that faded almost as quickly as his pleasure in the unpretentious life. Plans were now under way to re-shoot *Rock and Roll Circus* in circumstances guaranteeing that the Stones would not be upstaged again. The circus-ring this time was to be the Coliseum in Rome. Ronnie Schneider, at Klein's office, had actually booked that immortal ruin as a backdrop for Mick's second take. 'I went to Michael Lindsay-Hogg [the director] and told him "Okay, you got the Coliseum." But he said he wouldn't know what to shoot there.'

Problems were reported, too, from the Warner Brothers Corporation, whose executives had now seen *Performance* and realized it was no happy-go-lucky pop farce. At an early screening, the wife of one WB man was so overcome with nausea, she actually vomited. Despite angry representations, that included a telegram jointly from Donald Cammell and Jagger, Warner Brothers refused to consider releasing *Performance* until it had been extensively cut and re-edited.

Early in 1969, Jagger was offered a second film – a starring role this time, and one so bizarrely out of character, he could not help be both flattered and challenged. He agreed to play Ned Kelly, in a film about the nineteenth century Australian bandit and folk hero. The director was to be Tony Richardson, whose Woodfall Film company had made, among other things, the excellent *Charge of the Light Brigade*. As an extra inducement, Marianne Faithfull was given the supporting part of Kelly's girl friend. Shooting was to begin in Australia, the following July.

The necessity of planning the year ahead – and, in particular, the American tour that was becoming ever more crucial – raised yet again a problem Jagger, no less than the other Stones, had long shrunk from facing. By May 1969, the decision could no longer be postponed. Some way would have to be found of firing Brian Jones.

It was not, even now, a decision taken lightly. All Brian's infuriating haplessness over the past three years could not cancel out the bonds of their early friendship – the realization that, without Brian, none of them might be where they were today. Even last year, confident of what seemed a bottomless income, the Stones could afford to keep on carrying Brian. This year, in an atmosphere of worsening financial anxiety, they couldn't afford *not* to ditch him.

With two drug busts on his record, Brian hadn't a hope of getting the work permit necessary for a major American tour. The fact that he had appealed successfully against his second conviction – on January 13 – could scarcely be accounted helpful. Immigration authorities read only headlines.

Brian was living out of London now – in surroundings as unlike his former ones as only Brian could have contrived. In November, 1968, he had paid £32,000 for Cotchford Farm, near Hartfield, Sussex, the former home of A. A. Milne. The garden was still maintained as a shrine to childhood, with rights of access in perpetuity by the Winnie-the-Pooh Society. It was strange – or was it entirely fitting? – that Brian's journey through the Sixties should have brought him finally to rest at The House at Pooh Corner.

Jagger had special reason to feel a resurgence of sympathy for Brian. Since Brian's departure from Chelsea, the local police had been obliged to find an alternative Stone to harass and pursue. Recently, as Jagger was riding along King's Road with his new young chauffeur, Alan Dunn, a patrol car had flagged down his Rolls, and two officers had demanded to search both Jagger and the car. Jagger had refused, ordering Dunn to lock the car and then telephone for his solicitor to come straight there.

On May 28 – the day his film role as Ned Kelly was announced – Jagger opened the door at Cheyne Walk to behold the very CID man who had busted Brian, accompanied by half a dozen other officers. 'I didn't get the chance to say anything,' Jagger commented later. 'One of them stuck his foot in the door and the rest came barging in. They put me in the dining-room while they searched the place.' Within a few minutes, the squad had unearthed a small wooden box containing approximately one quarter-ounce of cannabis.

Jagger and Marianne were taken to Chelsea Police Station and charged under the usual Act. Next day, they appeared together at Great Marlborough Street court, to plead Not Guilty to possessing cannabis. The Magistrate adjourned the case until June 23, remanding each on £50 bail.

Finding himself in Brian Jones's place as the Chelsea drug squad's favourite target was a salutary lesson to Jagger that Brian's catastrophes had not all been self-induced. Though Brian must be sacked if the Stones were to survive, Jagger now agreed it must be on terms as tactful and generous as possible. The offer, worked out in consultation with Allen Klein, was that Brian be asked to leave primarily to allow the Stones to go on tour in America. As far as the press and the fans were concerned, it would be only a temporary absence, to allow him to work on solo projects like his *Jajouka* album. As well as his royalty-share from past Stones albums, a settlement of £100,000 would acknowledge the Stones' debt to his musicianship and personality.

Tact and consideration were evident in the method chosen by Jagger to prepare Brian for the approaching shock. He and Keith separately got in touch with Alexis Korner, the Stones' –

especially Brian's – old Blues mentor. 'Mick and Keith told me Brian was sick and they were worried about him,' Korner remembered. 'Because he wouldn't talk to them, or didn't trust them, they asked me if I'd go down to his place and see him.' Remembering the boy who had parachute-rolled through the kitchen window at Moscow Road – his neat Italian suit, and 'beautiful mixture of good manners and rudeness' – Korner agreed to try to do what he could.

# 12

# 'He hath awakened from the dream of life'

Mary Hallett knew Cotchford Farm better than did either of its two famous owners, the author and the pop star. She was born there, in the great, secure age when Sussex was a remote county, and the sixteenth century house served merely as adjunct to hard-working land, shared by two farm labourers and their large Edwardian families. Mary was one of eight children who helped their father with the haymaking and milking, and rescued lambs from winter snowdrifts before the crows could peck out their eyes.

When A. A. Milne owned Cotchford in the Twenties, Mary Hallett lived still only a few minutes' walk away. She remembers the author's shiny motor car, and the national adulation for 'Christopher Robin', the fictional boy whose prototype could be seen every day out in the village with his nurse. 'He *was* a dear little chap – but he was a mischief, too. He used to like my brother, who worked at the stables, to shut him up inside the horses' feed-bins.'

Forty years later, after her birthplace had changed from labourer's cottage to rich man's country mansion, with trim lawns, topiary bushes – even a swimming-pool – Mary Hallett got to know Cotchford Farm all over again. Its present owner, an American named Taylor, needed help in the house because his wife had fallen ill. It was arranged that Mary Hallett should go in every day for the Taylors to clean and keep house.

The news that the Taylors were moving from Cotchford, in November, 1968, and that it had been bought by a Rolling Stone, who intended to live there permanently, caused Mrs Hallett understandable dismay. Though not specially prejudiced against the Rolling Stones – being of a generation unable to tell one pop group from another – she had read and heard enough about such people to know she probably would not get on with them. At the new owner's request, however, she agreed to continue coming in on a trial basis. So, with many misgivings, Mary Hallett made the acquaintance of Brian Jones.

It was an experience which caused her to revise all her preconceptions of pop stars as ruffianly, inconsiderate young men. 'You couldn't have wished for a nicer, more polite boy. In all the months I worked for him, he was kindness itself to me. And always so well-mannered. With Brian, it was never "I want . . ." or "Do this . . ." It was always "Please, Mrs Hallett, would you mind . . ."

'Nobody could have been more generous. After I'd started working for him, he discovered I wasn't on the telephone. Straight away, he had a 'phone installed for me – and the bill was always paid. Whenever it rang, I'd always half expect to hear Brian's voice. "Oh, Mrs Hallett . . ." he'd say, so woebegone. "I *can't* get this fire started. *Do* you think you could come over?"

'It was a pleasure to work for him – he was so appreciative of every little thing. We had a long talk together one day while I was cleaning and he was sitting at the kitchen table. I'd seen him reading this big, old-fashioned family Bible, like the one we used to have when I was a girl. I discovered he knew his Bible very well – better than I did. I always had the feeling he was a very lonely boy. After I'd been out shopping, I often used to come home and find Brian sitting and waiting for me on my front door step.'

It was at Cotchford Farm, surrounded by relics of Winnie-the-Pooh, Piglet and Christopher Robin, that Brian Jones, one evening late in May, finally ceased to be a Rolling Stone. Mick Jagger and Keith Richard drove down together from London to do the job they had postponed for more than a year, accompanied – as a further instrument of clemency – by Charlie Watts. Even Charlie, kind-hearted as he was, realized there was no other way.

The moment was not as traumatic as everyone had expected. Mick and Keith pretended not to be firing Brian for ever; he, in turn, pretended he was glad to go. They agreed the press should be told he was leaving voluntarily, because of musical differences with the others. Brian undertook to say nothing of the matter until Mick and Keith could find someone to replace him. The four broke up on friendly terms. Then Brian went into his kitchen, laid his head on the scrubbed wooden table, and wept.

305

Despite his promise of secrecy, he could not resist telephoning the Stones office next day and confiding in his great ally, Jo Bergman. 'He said, "You will go on doing things for me, won't you, even when I'm not in the Stones?" I said, "Oh, of *course*, Brian, for goodness sake . . ."' Peter Jones, the music journalist, met him in London that same week, wearing a look that was half-shamefaced, half-triumphant, as if he had done something very silly but couldn't help feeling pleased.

Alexis Korner, on visits to Cotchford, found Brian excited by the challenge of starting again in what was, after all, the prevailing fashion among top musicians. Eric Clapton had disbanded the hugely successful Cream, to link up with Stevie Winwood, from Traffic, in the experimental heavy metal group Blind Faith. Graham Nash had left the Hollies, uniting with Steven Stills of Buffalo Springfield and Dave Crosby of the Byrds, to form Crosby, Stills and Nash. With Brian's reputation and his circle of virtuoso friends like Lennon, Townshend and Hendrix – so Korner reasoned – he would not long want for company.

He was talking already about starting a pure Blues band, on the model of Korner's Blues Incorporated but with the cutting-edge of new American groups like the Allman Brothers and Creedence Clearwater Revival. It was the time of Creedence's first great 'swamp-rock' hit, Proud Mary. John Fogarty's voice, rasping against the lazy paddle-wheel beat, echoed repeatedly through Cotchford Farm as Brian poured out his plans to Alexis Korner. 'He was excited in a vague way,' Korner remembered later. 'He'd start to talk, then he'd stop and put on another Creedence record, slurring the needle across it. Then he'd have a different idea. He and I would form a new band together and take it on the road. At that point, I had to say, "Now, hold *on*, Brian . . ."'

On his first trip down to Cotchford to pave the way for Mick and Keith, Korner had been shocked by the change in Brian's appearance – by his haggard face, his developing paunch, in particular his complexion, bloated white and glistening, 'like old, cold fat'.

He had greatly improved since then, helped by the country air, the constant, restful quiet and, not a little, by Cotchford Farm's powerful association with a tranquil, rosily secure world of childhood. Knowing the Winnie-the-Pooh stories almost by heart

as he did, it gave him special delight to show Alexis the sundial –
under which Milne's original manuscripts are reputedly buried –
and the bridge over the little stream where Pooh and Christopher
Robin invented their Pooh-sticks game. He felt proud to be the
guardian of such a shrine, as if the money he paid for the house
had brought him an extra gift of responsibility and trust.

He had managed to stay off drugs, he told Alexis – was, indeed,
so terrified of being busted again that he would not allow so much
as a joint to be rolled under his roof. He was drinking less, too,
forsaking whisky and brandy for beer and white wine. But for his
asthma – the recurrent problem that caused him to keep a small
inhaler always with him in summer time – he could be believed
when he said he hadn't felt so good in years.

He was insistent that Alexis should spend regular weekends at
Cotchford with his wife, Bobbie, and their daughter, Sappho. The
Korners both remembered Brian's excitement, one weekend, at
having persuaded his parents to come from Cheltenham soon and
stay a whole week. 'He wanted to show them he lived in a *real*
house,' Alexis Korner said. 'That seemed important – proving to
his father that his music had brought him to a quite conventional
end.'

Happily excited as he was, there still remained fears and
anxieties that Brian would confide to Alexis as they sat in the
ingle-nooked living-room or – as summer drew on – outside, next
to the swimming-pool.

Chief among his anxieties was a gnawing suspicion that Mick
and Keith's latter consideration might be no more than some
elaborate game; that, having persuaded him to leave the Stones,
they might now be plotting to renege on the terms of the
agreement. The promised £100,000 had not yet been paid. Brian
needed money, both to support his heedless superstar lifestyle and
to satisfy the heavy demands of so large and old a property.

To renovate the farmhouse he had employed a builder named
Frank Thorogood, a school friend of Tom Keylock whom Keylock
had first brought in to do extensive work for Keith Richards at
Redlands. On top of the £32,000 Brian had paid for Cotchford
Farm, he was committed to £10,000-worth of improvements by
Thorogood and a four-man gang hired in Chichester. The work
ranged from restoring antique beams in the kitchen and making

new stone floors upstairs, to draining and levelling a large field behind the house.

Unofficially, Frank Thorogood's job was to keep an eye on Brian during Tom Keylock's frequent absences on service for the other Stones. Keylock gave him the power to draw money from the Stones' London office to pay incidental expenses. He even moved into Cotchford Farm, living through the week in a flatlet above the garage, where he would be joined intermittently by a female friend, a young local nurse named Janet Lawson.

Brian's soft-heartedness and love of any company made not only Thorogood, but also the most temporary workmen, free of his home, his food and wine. Mary Hallett, his housekeeper, remembers that Thorogood spent much of the time sitting around the house with Brian, sunning himself in the garden or swimming in the pool.

Sometimes even Brian would complain about Frank Thorogood. Then his mood would change again: he would put on Proud Mary, and talk further about Blues bands yet unformed. The Korners would leave him in his Winnie-the-Pooh garden, stretched out along the diving-board of his bright blue swimming-pool, staring up into a sky almost as blue as it used to be in Morocco.

Mick Taylor was eight years old when he saw his first guitar. His parents – themselves young enough to be Rock 'n' Roll fans – and taken him to a Bill Haley concert at the Golders Green Hippodrome. Between the baby-faced small boy and the glinting, amber silhouette on Haley's chest there passed a charge which was to give the boy's life thereafter a wonderful simplicity. All he thought of was getting a guitar, learning to play it, then playing it better and better. By the age of twelve, he was sought after by every amateur group in Hatfield, Hertfordshire, the drab aero-engineering suburb where his father worked as a fitter for de Havilland Ltd.

Shy and quiet as he usually was, the guitar gave Mick Taylor nerve enough for anything. At fourteen, he went to see a concert by John Mayall's Bluesbreakers, featuring Eric Clapton, in nearby Welwyn Garden City. He talked his way backstage, only to find that Eric Clapton hadn't turned up that night. The

308

fourteen-year-old schoolboy persuaded John Mayall to let him play lead guitar in Eric Clapton's place.

He was still only seventeen when John Mayall asked him to become the Bluesbreakers' lead guitarist as a replacement for yet another graduate from that seminary of British Rock. Peter Green, who had succeeded Clapton, was now leaving, with bass-player John McVie, to form the prototype Fleetwood Mac. One day, Mick Taylor was at school in Hatfield. The next, he was on the road as star instrumentalist in Britain's best, as well as busiest, pure Blues band.

He remained with John Mayall for four years, playing almost every night, refining his technique and also strengthening his nerves under the autocratic leader who would train up such brilliant pupils only for so long as they threatened no direct rivalry to himself. 'John was a great eccentric,' Taylor says. 'He'd lived in a tree once – somewhere near Manchester. He collected erotica and wore all his harmonicas on a belt round his waist. And every conversation you had with him, he'd record on a tiny little tape.'

In May 1969, when John Mayall announced yet another reshuffle of the Bluesbreakers, Mick Taylor realized he had become too good for Mayall's peace of mind, and had better find employment elsewhere. Then, one night, John Mayall rang him up in Paddington and asked if he fancied becoming lead guitarist in the Rolling Stones. Mick Jagger had asked Mayall, along with many other people, to nominate a successor to Brian Jones. Mayall had recommended his ex-pupil as the best young virtuoso in contemporary Rock. It was arranged that Taylor should meet the Stones at Olympic Studios, during sessions for the album that would become *Let It Bleed*.

He went along, very nervous, thinking the Stones needed someone only for temporary session work. 'I'd never met any of them before. The only one I'd ever seen was Mick Jagger, sprinting down the King's Road one day with a pack of photographers after him.

'I met their producer, Jimmy Miller, first. Then the Stones themselves started drifting in. Keith, I remember, arrived about three hours late. It was all very easy and friendly. The track they were working on was Live With Me. I gave them a riff – it seemed to work in well. I still thought I was being auditioned to play just on the one album. It wasn't until the end of the session that I realized they were asking me to join them.'

The deal offered by Jagger was not instant enfranchisement. Mick Taylor would join the Stones initially as an employee, for a salary of £150 per week. Only if things proved satisfactory would he receive his full one-fifth share of concert fees and record royalties.

On June 9, Les Perrin's office was finally allowed to give the prearranged story to the press that Brian Jones had 'resigned' from the Rolling Stones because of disagreements over musical policy. His replacement would be a twenty-year-old unknown whom first newspaper pictures revealed to be so angelically boyish, with his round, clear face and thick, wavy hair, there was even some speculation that the Stones might be turning into middle-aged pederasts. It was further noted of this apparently willing sacrifice to decadence incarnate that he neither drank nor smoked, and was 'into' macrobiotic food.

To reporters who reached him on the telephone at Cotchford, Brian dutifully gave the same story of a regretful decision to quit the Stones 'because I no longer see eye-to-eye with the others over the discs we are cutting . . . I have a desire to play my own brand of music . . . We have agreed that an amicable termination of our relationship is the only answer.'

The plan to induct Mick Taylor into the Stones slowly, by way of album-sessions, was thrown suddenly into reverse, however, when Mick Jagger accepted an invitation from Eric Clapton to the debut performance of his new 'supergroup', Blind Faith. The concert took place in Hyde Park and – extraordinary innovation! – was free of charge to its audience. The result exceeded all expectations. A crowd of 150,000 carpeted the greensward, from Marble Arch, back to the Serpentine. They could hear the metal thunder, that afternoon, in boroughs as distant as Fulham and Notting Hill.

Jagger was astonished by the size – and benevolent spirit – of the Blind Faith audience. Being Jagger, too, he could not help but wonder how much larger an impromptu audience he himself might be capable of attracting. There and then, with Keith, he sought out a representative of the concert-organizers, Blackhill

310

Enterprises, and offered to appear at a similar event with the Stones, on the very earliest date it could be arranged. Within literally hours, an announcement went forth which seemed to confirm this new mood of generosity among Rock stars. The Rolling Stones, with their new guitarist Mick Taylor, would give a free concert in Hyde Park on Saturday, July 5.

They never intended it to inaugurate the era after Brian. Jagger had even rung Shirley Arnold at the Stones' office, and asked her to try to persuade Brian to come.

Her name was Helen Spittal – though, in the ordinary course of events, no one would have bothered to know it. Her face was pointed and pale, her hair regulation madonna-length; round her neck, in the same state of readiness as a gunslinger's Colt 45, she carried a 50 shilling Instamatic camera. She was sixteen years old and, despite the fierce-elbowing competition all around her, was recognizably Brian Jones's greatest fan.

She had begun as merely a Stones fan, willing to get up at 5 a.m. and walk from her parents' home in Hampton across to Barnes, in the faint hope of seeing the Stones emerge from Olympic Studios after recording all night. Albums full of Instamatic prints, taken in bad light, showed the invariable friendliness of these encounters – mostly with Mick Jagger. 'I never used to see Brian at Olympic that much. Once when he was there, he came across and blew me up for being out so early in the morning by myself, and worrying my parents.'

To Helen, Brian was never other than friendly, considerate – in a strange way, even fatherly. He would usually chide her for being out so early, or so late, and for neglecting her school work. With this, his greatest idolator, he, paradoxically, lost all pretence, posing for her Instamatic with a resigned and hangdog, 'God I look awful' grin. In one blurred London street shot, taken by someone else, the little girl he cuddles close to him could be his daughter or niece. His notoriety as a sexual buccaneer is something which, to this day, Helen Spittal refuses to believe.

Knowing Brian's fondness for Helen, and vaguely perceiving her beneficial effect on him, the Stones' office gave her privileges allowed no other fan. Tom Keylock would tell her when they were next recording at Olympic. Shirley Arnold would relay her messages to Brian, and his back to her.

'He'd often said he'd invite me down to Sussex, to see Cotchford Farm. A few days after he'd left the Stones, I got a message from Shirley that Brian wanted me to ring him. While we were talking, he suddenly asked me if I'd like to go down there and spend the day.'

Every minute of that day remains vivid in Helen's mind. She went by train to Haywards Heath, telephoned Brian from the station, and he sent a local mini-cab to collect her. She arrived at Cotchford Farm in dazzling sunshine. Brian was waiting for her in the driveway, with his two dogs. He wore the striped matelot shirt she always pictured him in, with red and black striped trousers and an old, scuffed pair of canvas shoes.

Even Helen's uncritical eye could not help but notice his poor physical state – in particular, the sagging paunch under the matelot stripes. Brian himself was painfully conscious of this. Walking with her round the garden, proudly pointing out the sundial and Christopher Robin statue, he agreed to be photographed only on condition the prints never left her private album.

With him at Cotchford Farm was Anna Wohlin, a 23-year-old Swedish girl who had moved in – despite opposition from Tom Keylock – some three weeks previously. Helen noted Anna's strong resemblance to Suki Poitier, and each of the other blonde girl friends with whom Brian had tried to re-create Anita Pallenberg. Helen and Anna took to each other and, as the day progressed, talked on fairly intimate terms. Anna mentioned how afraid Brian was of anyone bringing drugs into the house. On her own arrival, she said, he had ransacked her luggage, to be sure it contained nothing that might bring the police down on him again.

For most of the afternoon, the three sat beside the swimming-pool, drinking wine and talking while Frank Thorogood moved around in the distance on what seemed to Helen to be somewhat indecisive building work. She asked whether Brian was going to the Stones' free concert in Hyde Park, two Saturdays from now. He said he didn't think so. 'The way the Stones feel about me now,' he added, 'I'd probably be the only one they charged to go in.'

He talked a lot about Creedence Clearwater Revival, saying

312

*that* was the kind of music he wanted to play from now on. He insisted on taking Helen into the house to hear Proud Mary on the stereo system he kept in his bedroom. While it was playing, she remembers, Brian looked out of the window and saw Frank Thorogood down in the garden. 'He suddenly went all strange. He said something like "That man's not doing what he's *supposed* to be doing . . ."'

Later, Helen sat downstairs on Brian's lime green velvet sofa while he talked about his plans for a new group and meditatively strummed a Gibson 'Firebird' guitar. 'He was asking me about my exams at school. I told him I'd got an English exam the very next day. He got quite annoyed – he told me I ought to be at home, revising for it. Then he insisted I ring my parents, to let them know I was all right.'

In the evening, the girls watched *Top of the Pops* on television. Anna cooked a chicken for dinner, which was served in the dining room. Brian didn't eat, but wandered back and forth, under the low beams, drinking from the bottle of red wine in his hand. He kept saying how much he loved being at Cotchford – how, when he died, he wanted to be buried there.

Wednesday July 2 was an uneventful day at Cotchford Farm – hot, sunny and silent but for the mumuring of bees. It was a day on which the high pollen count brought suffering to asthma and hay fever victims all over Britain. In rural Sussex, naturally, the pollen count reached its maximum. Mrs Hallett, at her work around the house, could hear Brian wheezing in agony, and the frequent hiss of the decongestant 'puffer' which, in this long hot spell, he had seldom let out of his sight.

That afternoon, Mrs Hallett remembers, Brian received a telephone call that put him in a state of high euphoria. 'He came *running* in and said, "My money's coming through from America, at *last*. We're going to be all right!"'

Three or four of Frank Thorogood's builders were at work with Thorogood during the day. They drove off at about 6 pm, all but Thorogood, who retired to the flat over the garage with his companion, the young nurse Janet Lawson.

Brian and Anna spent the early part of the evening drinking and watching Rowan and Martin's *Laugh-In* show on television.

At about 10.30, Brian walked across to the garage flatlet and asked Frank Thorogood and his girl friend to come down and join Anna and him beside the swimming-pool. Thorogood was later to testify that Brian already seemed fairly drunk, staggering in his gait and not fully articulate.

Frank Thorogood and Janet Lawson made their way to the wooden garden seat at the pool's shallow end where Brian and Anna were already established with bottles of brandy, whisky and vodka. Two spotlights, which Thorogood's men had just installed, shone down with unearthly brilliance on the blue-tiled, motionless water.

The four between them almost finished the bottle of brandy and of vodka, and drank about half the bottle of whisky. From time to time, Brian would swallow a black pill, a legally-prescribed 'downer' of the sort he was accustomed to take at night, to calm his nerves, and ease him towards sleep on the mingling streams of music and alcohol.

At about midnight, the opposite seemed to have happened. Brian suddenly awoke from his torpor and announced that he was going in for a swim. Janet Lawson – a qualified nurse – told him he was in no condition to be in the water. Anna, too, objected, saying she wanted to go to bed. Brian ignored them both and went into the house to change. Frank Thorogood, though himself fairly drunk by now, volunteered to accompany him. Thorogood, in fact, had to help Brian mount the springboard over the ten-foot deep end. The water presented minimal shock, since Brian had turned the thermostat up to almost 80 degrees. Both of them as they swam looked 'sluggish' to Janet Lawson, she later said, but they seemed to be feeling no ill-effects.

Anna swam briefly, then came out, complaining of the cold, and went into the house to dress. Janet, a non-swimmer, followed her, while Brian and Frank Thorogood still moved round in the overheated water, talking desultorily. A few moments later, Thorogood emerged from the pool, saying he was going into the house for cigarettes. In the spotlit water, in the centre of the dark, breathless garden, Brian Jones was now alone.

As Thorogood entered the back door, Janet Lawson was on her way outside again. He remembers that, as he reached the living-room, the telephone began to ring. Anna came downstairs to

314

answer it, saying it was for her. At that moment, both of them heard Janet Lawson shout for help.

Thorogood, followed by Anna, rushed to the pool-edge. The spotlights showed Brian at the deep end, lying face down on the bottom, his hair floating round him like a spread fan.

Shirley Arnold's parents in South London had just acquired their very first telephone. It rang for the first time sometime after midnight on July 3. Shirley herself picked up the receiver.

'It was Tom Keylock's wife. She said something like, "Brian went into the swimming-pool but he didn't come out again." I thought she meant he'd wandered off into the woods or something, and they couldn't find him. Even when I put down the receiver, I still thought she was saying Brian had got lost.

'I rang her back a few moments later and said "Have they found him?" "No," she said. "You don't understand. He's dead."'

Frank Thorogood had initially tried to contact Tom Keylock, but had found Keylock neither at home nor with his alternative masters. Earlier in the day, he had driven down from London to West Wittering to pick up two guitars which Keith Richard needed for that night's recording session. Though the journey took Keylock quite close to Cotchford Farm, he saw no reason to call in there. Since the Stones' session would not begin until very late, Keylock took his time on the journey, stopping to have a meal at a place he can remember now only as 'some sort of country club'.

By the time he reached Olympic Studios with Keith's two guitars, the Stones had been contacted, and were sitting round in an incredulous daze. 'We think Brian's dead,' Mick Jagger told him.

Keylock and Les Perrin arrived at Cotchford Farm together, shortly after 3.30 a.m. They found the garden overrun with police. Brian's body had already been removed. At the pool-side there remained only the towel on which, apparently, his companions had rested his head while trying to revive him.

The size of the police contingent, and their overtly sceptical attitude, clearly indicated suspicion that drugs were involved somewhere. As Les Perrin walked round the pool-edge, he spotted Brian's asthma-inhaler lying on the grass. 'Very clever, Mr

Perrin,' was the sarcastic reply of the officer to whom he pointed this out. 'You're working like a good PR man. What did you do – drop it down your trouser leg?'

Keylock, meanwhile, drove off to collect Frank Thorogood from East Grinstead police station and hear the stricken – now very sober – builder's account of how Brian Jones had died. Thorogood said he had made three attempts to reach Brian before getting a grip on his hair strong enough to raise him to the surface. Thorogood and Anna Wohlin had together lifted him from the pool, and Janet Lawson, with her nurse's training, had attempted artificial respiration, pumping water from Brian's mouth and massaging his chest. When this had no effect, Anna had tried the 'kiss of life' method. At one point as she knelt over him, she had felt Brian's hand grip hers. There was no other movement.

The story broke in that morning's *Daily Mirror* – a brief stop press item, under a '3.30 a.m., latest' sticker, by Les Perrin's old Fleet Street crony, Don Short. London's two evening newspapers, the *News* and *Standard*, confirmed it at midday in identical one inch banner headlines, BRIAN JONES DEAD IN POOL TRAGEDY.

It was a story to delight the simplistic heart of every mass-circulation feature writer. The following day's *Mail, Mirror, Express* and *Sketch*, in addition to front-page follow-ups on Brian's death, all carried lengthy inside spreads, chronicling his boyhood in Cheltenham, his rise to fame as a Stone, his illegitimate children, his drug busts, the bizarre coincidence of his having died at the House at Pooh Corner. The *Express* story took its headline from Alexis Korner's assertion that, since Brian split from the Stones, 'he had never been happier.' The *Mail* ended by quoting portentously from Winnie-the-Pooh's search for his hidden treasure trove. ' "That's funny – I know I had a jar of honey there . . ." Brian Jones had the honey, labelled for all to see. But when he reached for it, it never seemed to be there . . .'

Of the many pop celebrities asked to comment on Brian's death, only two managed anything memorable. George Harrison said, 'I don't think he had enough love or understanding.' Pete Townshend of the Who, with somewhat greater insight, said, 'It's a normal day for Brian . . . like, he died every day, you know.'

The Stones themselves, taxed with that perennial newshound's question, 'How do you feel?', could only mumble that they felt devastated, and try to carry on with the day's business, an appearance on BBC-TV's *Top of the Pops* show to launch their new single, Honky Tonk Women.

Afterwards, all of them drifted back to the Maddox Street office as if reluctant to lose the solace of being together. 'They were all in a terrible state,' Shirley Arnold says. 'Charlie was crying. Mick kept wandering to and fro and tripping over a dog's bowl that was on the floor.' Shirley herself had spoken to Brian by telephone on the day of his death, and had afterwards written him a long letter saying she'd always do anything she could to help him. Mick Taylor – who had never met Brian – could only sit there, inwardly noting 'a sense of inevitability, as if everyone had been half-expecting it to happen.'

The immediate question was whether they should go ahead with the Hyde Park free concert in two days' time. Jagger said it was too late to cancel an event on which thousands were depending – and for which he, personally, had already accepted some considerable inconvenience. The day after the concert, he was due to fly to Australia to start work on *Ned Kelly*. The film's producers, in a state of agitation since Jagger's cannabis bust, had only just learned that his bail from Great Marlborough Street Court would allow him to travel abroad. They now feared that the free concert on July 5 would give him an excuse not to be on set, as promised, on July 9. They had even intimated that, if he sang in Hyde Park on Saturday and didn't appear in Australia the following Monday, they'd sue him.

It was Charlie Watts, sitting dejectedly in his corner, who first mumbled the notion that would save, not only the fans' treat but also the special souvenir number of the *Evening Standard* already in preparation, the six Granada TV crews already in transit, the stage outfit already chosen by Jagger at the Mr Fish boutique, and the expenditure already incurred from hiring such disparate items as potted palm trees, African tribal dancers and a military armoured personnel-carrier.

'Couldn't we do it as . . . sort of a memorial to Brian?'

Cavalry officers from Knightsbridge Barracks, cantering in pairs round the outer stand track, were not, as usual, Hyde Park's

317

earliest visitors that summer Saturday morning. As the sun climbed over feathery horse chestnut trees and the dew glittered dry on new-cut grass, a few figures had already begun to stir in the encampment of sleeping-bags, strewn for several hundred yards all around a flimsy, low-lying wooden stage. Cavalry officers trotted on with averted eyes. Ducks, coots and black-faced Canada geese swooped in from their island colony and massed along the Serpentine-edge, as if sensing better than usual pickings today.

By mid-morning, every quarter of Swinging London had registered a noticeable drop in population. The Portobello Road antique fair, the boutiques and hypermarkets along Kensington High Street, the pubs of Chelsea, Fulham and Bayswater, all seemed unaccountably quiet. For the present, only taxi-drivers knew where the Saturday crowd had gone. Taxi-drivers, spinning along Bayswater Road, had seen what appeared, by midday, to be a great rug of semi-clad humanity, gathered on the park's north-eastern peninsula and stretching back as far as the Knightsbridge treetops.

The six Granada TV film crews were also at work early, filming the first awakening of those who had slept in the park overnight to ensure favourable vantage-points, and the diverse activities with which they beguiled the hours before the first warm-up band took the stage. Since Hyde Park numbers among its amenities a substantial police station with adjacent dog-kennels, those activities were of the most bucolic, innocent nature. Wild-haired, bare-midriffed figures of both sexes could be seen sitting in deckchairs, blowing soap bubbles, rowing in skiffs like Edwardian apprentices, feeding the ducks or strolling along the rim of the Serpentine in a palpably intensifying heat haze. If love had perforce been confined to damp groundsheets in the pre-dawn hours, the peace was unquestionable and, amazingly, remained so as the human rug spread down the Park Lane boundary and outward, through glades and hollows, lapping round the park-keeper's lodge and the ornamental band-stand. It would be estimated by police surveillance helicopters and other, unseen, crowd-monitoring devices that something like quarter of a million people were in Hyde Park, waiting for the Rolling Stones and, meanwhile, doing no damage whatever.

Random interviews conducted by Granada among the 250,000 showed what a fund of goodwill had been created by the Stones' gesture. '. . . They make you feel you can have a good time and not worry . . .' 'They're not like the Beatles, spending seven days in bed . . .'

Another camera alighted on Tom Keylock, in pebble lenses and cherry-red cardigan, briefing the auxiliary stewards hired to protect the stage and its environs during the Stones' performance. The stewards were Hell's Angels, English imitators of California's motorcycle terrorist-gangs, uniformed in black leather, chin-strapped Nazi helmets, spiked belts and steel-toed boots, their backs metal-studded with ceremonial names such as 'Rocky X', 'Wild Child' and 'Wild Little Willie'. Keylock's instructions – not fully audible – concerned the handling of that sworn Angel foe, the ''ippy'.

The addition of hard Rock to already combustible elements, hot sun, melting ice cream, sweltered hot dog onions, shirtsleeved policemen and scowling Hell's Angels, could not discompose the prevailing atmosphere and conventions of an English garden fête. It was a mood perfectly expressed by the day's compere, Sam Cutler, speaking to the horizonless masses, for all his love-and-peace accent and worried Mexican moustachio, like some minor curate, patiently exhorting forbearance and co-operation for the common benefit, interspersing performances by King Crimson, Screw, the Battered Ornaments and Alexis Korner's New Church Band, with advice concerning cramp and heat stroke, appeals to respect the trees, and the names of lost children awaiting their parents at the Serpentine boat-house.

The very Hell's Angels – as their blank suburban faces and freshly-shampooed hair might have indicated – bore as much similarity to their Californian cousins as tapioca does to paraquat. At one point, the stage-front press enclosure became over-full of supernumerary females – among them Suzy Creamcheese and the 'Hair' star Marsha Hunt, fetchingly outfitted in white buckskin. 'Clear 'em out,' the chief Angel, 'Wild Child', ordered a swastika-capped lieutenant. 'Do you want me to use *force* or something?' the swastika cap queried nervously.

Yet another camera crew was in position to film Mick Jagger emerging from 48 Cheyne Walk and then join him in the

319

limousine, with Marianne and Nicholas, as they drove a roundabout way from Chelsea to Mayfair and up a deserted back-double to the east of Hyde Park Corner. Jagger wore an apricot blouse split to the waist, and seemed excited in the way schoolboys are before a sports day or swimming gala. 'Fantastic day, innit? Yeah . . . what, Nicholas? Is Charlie going to wave to you, Nicholas?'

The others had made their separate ways to a first base rendezvous, not at the obvious Park Lane Hilton hotel but at its much less smart neighbour, the Londonderry. From their tenth floor suite, they could see the outer perimeter of their audience and hear the vague thunder echoing over the tree-tops. Among the party was Allen Klein, apparently still persona grata, perched on his hands on a gimcrack table-top wearing – as always on such occasions – an expression of almost child-like wonderment.

Shortly before 3 p.m. from the direction of Speakers' Corner, a military armoured personnel-carrier, such as had recently come into use in earnest in Northern Ireland, could be seen, moving through the half-naked crowd and flattened deck chairs as cautiously as if this were the Belfast Falls Road. Inside, sprawled on mattresses, were the five Stones and their two 'official' photographers, Michael Cooper and Spanish Tony Sanchez. On the day they needed it least, the Stones' pre-performance security had never been better.

From the armoured personnel-carrier they were decanted into a caravan trailer behind the stage, though still in view of several hundred fans whom the Hell's Angels had given up trying to intimidate. From time to time, Charlie Watts's arm would appear from a window to pass out an apple or orange from the plentiful supplies within. The stage, meanwhile, had been cleared of all inferior equipment and personages, built up with the Stones' own giant amplifiers and embellished with a huge blow-up colour photograph of Brian Jones. Tom Keylock and his helpers set down several brown cardboard boxes, from which one telltale white butterfly floated free. Those near the stage-front, versed in such portents, saw its palm-leafy wings suddenly infiltrated by celebrities and their unreprovable children.

Whatever the 250,000 people in Hyde Park expected of Mick Jagger that afternoon, none could have expected him to take the stage in lipstick, rouge and eye-shadow, and wearing a white, frilly garment which, for all the white vest and bell-bottoms visible beneath, still resembled nothing so much as a little girl's party dress. Round his neck was a tight, brass-studded leather collar. On the place where his bust ought to have been there hung – interestingly – a stout wooden crucifix.

Folding his hands in an Eastern sign of *namaste*, then blowing kisses from his fingertips, he greeted the quarter of a million in that now familiar drawl, lodged indeterminately between Dartford and Memphis.

'We're gonna have a good time – awright?'

As the sound of agreement washed back like a slow wave, out to the distant archipelago of Kensington and Knightsbridge, Jagger brought his face close to the microphone, flipping back his chin-length wings of hair.

'Now listen . . . cool it for a minute. I really would like to say something about Brian . . . about how we feel about him just goin' when we didn't expect it . . .'

From behind his back, like a little girl hiding a present, Jagger took a small calf-bound book. Holding it up in both hands, tossing back his hair once more, against the unreal backcloth of TV gantries and potted palms, he began to read what perhaps half a dozen among his quarter of a million listeners recognized as a stanza from Shelley's *Adonais*.

Peace, peace! He is not dead, he doth not sleep—
He hath awakened from the dream of life—
'Tis we who, lost in stormy visions, keep
With phantoms an unprofitable strife,
And in mad trance strike with our spirit's knife.
Invulnerable nothings! We decay
Like corpses in a charnel. Fear and grief
Convulse us and consume us day by day
And cold hopes swarm like worms within our living clay.

Out over the huge, restive expanse, the whole of Stanza 39 echoed through the Rock stage PA, in a voice as empty of artifice as it could remember to be and as close to public sincerity as it knew how. Jagger's frills billowed gently in the breeze as he turned to a

321

new page, marked by his fingers, and Stanza 39 continued into
Stanza 52:

> The One remains, the many change and pass.
> Heaven's light forever shines, earth's shadows fly.
> Time, like a dome of many-coloured glass
> Stains the white radiance of Eternity
> Until Death tramples it to fragments – Die!
> If thou would be that which thou doest seek.

As Shelley's words died away in genuine silence, Tom Keylock
and his helpers picked up the cardboard boxes and shook them
outward, releasing several hundred white butterflies. It was
afterwards claimed that most of the butterflies had been killed by
confinement without an adequate air-supply. Enough survived to
crowd the air above the crowded grass – and, later, to devastate
gardens and allotments for several square miles around.

The tribute to Brian had been grand, even gracious – but it was
over. The last white butterfly unclipped the microphone. On the
first chord of Honky Tonk Woman, Jagger's frilly wings jackknifed
into their own special kind of flight.

For Mick Taylor, the next hour passed in a blur of heat and faces
and bodies and their manifold odours; of noise both stupendously
near and unreally distant, like sea-echoes in the ear of a shell. 'I'm
always asked if I was nervous, coming out to play with the Stones
for the first time in front of 250,000 people. The honest answer is, I
don't know. I can't remember. It was all over too quickly.'

Granada film crews, shooting from the stage-front pit and from
the crowded plantation, in the wings, preserved for posterity what
is, possibly, the Stones' worst musical performance ever. They had
not played together publicly for more than a year and, what with
the trauma over Brian, had managed only one brief limbering-up
session in the basement of the Beatles' Apple house. It was, in
short, one of those times when Keith Richard walked on stage
looking as if he had just got out of bed, and when half, if not more,
of every chord he played seemed still resolutely drugged to the
eyeballs.

Within the clumsy, ramshackle playing, visible only to a few thousand on the grass, and a few dozen more on the branches of surrounding trees, Mick Jagger gave a performance which aroused even those nearly comatose with sun and grass and patchouli oil to a state of lascivious agony. The figure that doffed its frilly frock, and continued singing in white vest and trousers, still had not become definitely male. Its shoulder-length hair and bulging biceps, its schoolgirl waist and flaunting crotch, conjured up before all eyes the same indeterminate mirage of lust. Its behaviour throughout was closer to strip-tease than anything Rock had known. At one astonishing moment, it dropped to its knees and spread its hair forward over a hand-mike supported between its thighs, closing its lips over the bulbous head. There in broad daylight, before 250,000 people and six TV crews, Mick Jagger seemed to be sucking himself off.

The finale was literally mesmerizing: a version of Sympathy for the Devil almost twenty minutes long in which the Stones were joined, as if spontaneously, by African tom-tom players and, climactically, by a troupe of native dancers whose plumed and grey-daubed leader thrust a burning torch about him to spell out the doom that would not be unleashed today . . .

Today was peace, even hours after the Stones had gone, and volunteers moved around, collecting rubbish in sackfuls by the hundred, and the African tribesmen, restored to their everyday suits, packed their drums and assegais in the backs of their Ford Cortinas and drove off towards Brixton.

The simplest death cannot be disposed of in clouds of white butterflies. This was not a simple death; nor would it ever be allowed to become so. Even in his coffin, it seemed, the world could not leave Brian Jones alone.

On Monday July 7, when Mick Jagger was half-way to Australia, and the last vestiges of rubbish were being cleared from Hyde Park, the inquest on Brian's death opened at East Grinstead Coroner's court. In the front row sat his father, the small, stiffly correct aeronautical engineer from Cheltenham. Only the deep grooves frozen into Lewis Jones's cheeks throughout that week's events betrayed his grief, and continuing bewilderment.

Frank Thorogood, Anna Wohlin and Janet Lawson each repeated their account of the midnight scene around the

323

swimming pool and why each of them had gone into the house a few seconds before Brian sank to the bottom. Each described their subsequent combined efforts at artificial respiration which, in the flat, formalized press reports, would appear coolly scientific rather than – probably – panic stricken and clumsy. Truly, it must have seemed to Lewis Jones that his son had died at the hands of guardian angels with life-saving certificates.

Dr Albert Sachs, Consultant Pathologist at Queen Victoria Hospital, East Grinstead, gave the results of the post mortem examination which any sudden death in unusual circumstances automatically entails. Dr Sachs had found Brian's liver to be twice the normal size and 'in an advanced state of fatty degeneration'. His heart, too, was distended well beyond normal proportions. Blood and urine tests had revealed large quantities of alcohol and 'an amphetamine substance', though there was no trace of barbiturates. In Dr Sachs' opinion, death was due to drowning 'associated with alcohol, drugs and severe liver degeneration.'

Dr Sachs' evidence might have been expected to dispel a belief already held by most of Britain's newspaper-reading public, that Brian's death had been suicide, brought on by excess of fame, money, sex and privilege. There was also the testament of Lewis Jones that, when his parents visited him on May 18 and throughout their week-long stay at Cotchford Farm, Brian seemed happier than they had seen him in years.

The only clue to whatever sudden spasm had plunged a better than average swimmer face down in the heated water, was the asthma Brian had suffered from since childhood. Anna Wohlin said he often needed the 'squirter' to help him breathe while swimming but claimed that, in six weeks of living with Brian, she had never seen him have a serious attack. His father said he had been acutely asthmatic as a child but 'seemed to have grown out of it.' Only his housekeeper, Mrs Hallett – not called at the inquest – seems to have heard the wheezing fit come over him on the morning of his last day alive.

The verdict of the Coroner, Dr Angus Summerville, was Death by Misadventure. When inquest evidence points to something more complex than an accident, yet finds no discernible culprit or culprits, the only recourse is to commiserate with the deceased's ill luck.

The question of Brian's death was therefore not closed but left open to speculation which, fourteen years later, still regularly exercises the Fleet Street gossip mills. The speculation is that Brian did not die by accident, neglect or suicide, but was murdered – drowned in his own swimming pool by an assassin never brought to book, for a reason concealed somewhere back among the chaos of his 27 years alive.

The matter has not been helped by the pall of discomfort, embarrassment, guilt – and, it must be said, genuine unhappiness – which Brian's death was to cast over the Rolling Stones, for ever. As they are today, demigods above the ordinary run of human affairs, it is practically as embarrassing to reflect that they did their best for Brian as to live with the mythical notion that, in their pent-up exasperation with him, they somehow conspired to hound him into his grave.

Keith, in particular, had serious misgivings about the circumstances surrounding Brian's death, though engrained Rock star indolence prevented him from making serious inquiries. 'It's the same feeling with who killed Kennedy.' He added enigmatically, 'You never get to the bottom of it.'

In recent years, the murder theories have grown more elaborate. A purported close friend of Brian, Nicholas Fitzgerald, claims to possess evidence of foul play. *Sun Day* magazine, colour supplement to (surprise, surprise!) the *News of the World*, devoted large space in March, 1983, to an article headlined WHO MURDERED A ROLLING STONE?, incorporating Fitzgerald's claims into an 'investigation' of predictable journalistic standard. *Sun Day*'s theory – offered in the classic con-artist's form of questions rather than answers – was that Brian had been killed by 'revengeful drug-pushers', who hid in the pool-side bushes until he was alone, then plunged his head into a bucket of water, drowning him that way before tossing him into the deep end.

Nicholas Fitzgerald was quoted as saying that two hours had elapsed between Brian's submersion in the pool and the ambulance's arrival – two hours, it was suggested, in which Brian was left to expire while others, at Cotchford Farm for whatever reasons, made good their escape. *Sun Day*'s investigation, however, did not extend to the London telephone book, where Frank Thorogood is still listed, nor to reading the inquest report confirming Thorogood's story: that police and ambulance were on the scene within fifteen minutes.

All this, and much more, can be dismissed as mere mud-stirring by journalists with a vested interest in keeping the Brian Jones 'riddle' alive. The same may be true of two people close to the Stones in 1969, who, when interviewed for this book, not only expressed their firm conviction that Brian *was* murdered, but also showed deep, and apparently genuine, unease about the matter, desiring not to be quoted or even named.

Just the same, as Keith Richard put it to *Rolling Stone*, in the aftermath of Brian's death, some 'very weird things' undoubtedly did happen.

There is a less satisfactory explanation for the subsequent flurry of comings and goings at Cotchford Farm, and the unseasonably autumnal smell of bonfire smoke wafted towards Mary Hallett's house, nearby. A local man who had sometimes worked in the garden at Cotchford told her that more than one bonfire had been lit, and that someone was burning Brian's clothes.

Further mystery surrounds the mass of Brian's pop star finery that clearly *was* valuable, the expensive furniture, Moroccan antiques and numerous musical instruments that were cleared from Cotchford Farm prior to its sale to realize Brian's estate. Shirley Arnold, who visited Mr and Mrs Jones regularly in the months that followed, believes that many things were missing. 'Brian's parents had everything they'd been sent from Cotchford spread out in their garage,' Shirley says. 'There were only a few of Brian's clothes. They hadn't got all his guitars, or his Mellotron.'

Strangest of all was the revelation, a year later, that Brian had died almost broke, with debts of nearly £200,000. His estate was calculated at £33,784 – a sum largely reached by selling Cotchford Farm, for which he had paid £32,000. At his death, he could have had only a few hundred pounds in the bank. Even his payoff from the Stones would have covered no more than half his debts. A Rolling Stone with such liabilities and no immediate chance of settling them might well have believed – as Brian apparently did – that someone was out to 'get' him.

The funeral was on July 10, at the Parish Church a few steps away from Brian's parents' house in Hatherley Road, Cheltenham. The face of Lewis Jones remained immobile, like one carved in granite, as he supported his distraught wife through a nightmare scrimmage of fans, photographers and floral tributes that would have done credit to some dead gangster chief. Behind the Joneses, Brian's younger sister Barbara and the officiating clergy, Canon Hugh Hopkins, walked Tom Keylock, in his role as funeral director, and Suki Poitier, dressed in the wild scarves and bangles of a grieving gipsy queen. Then came Bill Wyman, Charlie Watts, Michael Cooper – garlanded with Nikons, Spanish Tony Sanchez, Les Perrin and Linda Lawrence, most persistent among Brian's ex-girl friends, carrying one of the two illegitimate sons he had mischievously named Julian.

It was a spectacle which inspired Canon Hopkins in his address to deliver a vigorous attack on twentieth century godlessness and materialism, implicitly directed at most of his overswollen, attentive congregation. Intercessionary prayers were offered, too, for Marianne Faithfull, that godless world's most recently-gazetted victim. For Brian's epitaph, Canon Hopkins quoted first from the New Testament parable of the Prodigal Son, then from a telegram which Brian had sent his parents at the height of his troubles in 1968. 'This, my son, was lost and is found again . . .' 'Please don't judge me too harshly . . .'

Later, as the hearse entered the gates of Priory Road cemetery, a policeman, instinctively and with no sense of irony, brought his hand up in a salute.

One other memory would stay with Lewis and Louisa Jones of their inexplicably famous and infamous son. It was a moment during their visit to Cotchford Farm in May, 1969, when Brian, sorting through a drawer, came across a photograph that stopped him in his tracks. His father remembers how he stared at the girl in the photograph – at her straw-blonde hair and double-daring smile – and murmured softly to himself, 'Anita . . . Anita . . .'

327

# 13

## 'We're gonna kiss you goodbye'

On July 8, while Mick Jagger slept away his jet lag in their Sydney hotel suite, Marianne had slipped out of bed, across the twilit room to the dressing-table mirror. What she saw reflected there gave her the final impetus to end her life. She picked up the telephone, dialled room service and asked for a cup of hot chocolate. Then she took a bottle of 150 Tuinal sleeping pills and began methodically swallowing them, forcing each mouthful down with sips of chocolate. Having taken enough barbiturates to kill three people, the girl from the Renoir painting that had become a nightmare by Bruegel, settled down beside her Rock star lover and waited for death.

The experience of almost dying is one that Marianne – like others accidentally recalled to life – can describe in vivid, almost nostalgic detail.

'I remember finding myself in this big, grey, still place where there was no climate at all – no wind or cold or sun, no weather of any kind. And Brian Jones was there. I remember talking to Brian, who was *terribly* pleased to see me. He said he'd woken up cold and frightened, not knowing where he was. He'd been looking and looking for a familiar face. "Oh, I'm so glad—" he kept saying. "I'm so glad that you're here."

'We started walking along together through this great big, weatherless place, Brian and I – not so much walking as jogging with long, slow strides. Brian was talking in just the way Brian would, hopeless but funny as well. "Hey man – what a drag . . . Woke up this morning, reached out for the pill bottle and realized I was dead . . ."

'We jogged along like this, right up to a place where the land stopped – like the edge of a plane. Brian turned to me and said, "I've got to go on from here alone." Then, far away behind me, I could hear three voices calling to me. One was my mother's. One was Nicholas's. And the other was Mick's.'

\*  \*  \*

Jagger had awoken, found her unconscious and summoned help in the nick of time, not only to save her life but also prevent the brain damage that so massive an overdose could have caused. Of all sad mementoes to the Rolling Stones saga, none is more harrowing than the picture an Australian photographer snatched as Marianne was brought out of the hotel on a stretcher. The face under the rough blanket could be some dead child's, preserved in a Victorian locket.

She remained in a coma for six days as Brian Jones was buried, across the world, and Canon Hugh Hopkins asked extra prayers on her behalf. For most of the time Jagger stayed at her bedside – at this moment, ironically, more her protector than he had ever been. When a British journalist bluffed his way into St Stephen's Hospital and actually got into Marianne's room, Jagger had to be restrained by Les Perrin from physical assault. 'I'll get him . . .' he kept babbling to Perrin. 'I'll *get* him.'

The despair that had engulfed her was not wholly Marianne's own. For six weeks, up to Brian's death and the Hyde Park concert, she had been playing Ophelia in *Hamlet* at the Royal Court Theatre. 'I'd willed myself into a suicidal state of mind, quite apart from what was going on around me. And I'd cut my hair very short. All the business about Brian and Ophelia seemed to get mixed up in my mind. When I woke up in that hotel suite and looked into the mirror, I thought it was Brian's face looking back at me.'

She tried to explain it to Jagger after she had returned to consciousness and found him beside her, holding her hand. What she could not explain – nor he begin to comprehend – was that dying, after Ophelia's and Brian Jones's fashion, seemed the only remedy for living with Mick Jagger.

Marianne convalesced in Sydney throughout the two months that Jagger spent in Australia, trying to portray the country's principal folk hero on film while simultaneously making plans to save the Rolling Stones from imminent financial catastrophe.

It was already clear that *Ned Kelly* was an ill-omened project, conceived on free-spending Sixties euphoria and nurtured largely by the publicity around its unlikely star. Jagger did his best with the role, working at his Irish accent and bush-ranger's scowl, completely in the dark – as all film actors are – over the shape or

329

quality of the finished picture. The production was hampered by the outrage of many Australians at seeing their nation's Robin Hood portrayed – as some put it – by 'a limey pantie-waist'. There were even threats from a present-day outlaw gang to kidnap Jagger and cut off his hair. Out at the location, conditions were often chaotic, with Jagger protesting to Tony Richardson about the embarrassing script he had to learn and Marianne's understudy, Diane Craig, forced to go before the camera without having learned her lines. In one scene a prop pistol exploded, badly gashing Jagger's left hand. When he visited Marianne, he pretended the bandage was part of his Ned Kelly costume.

In September, after filming had ended, they flew to Indonesia together for a holiday intended to repair the ravages of the summer. It worked – as long as they were left alone together. Back in London, Jagger was plunged into fresh preoccupations. And Marianne found her predicament to be as desperate as ever.

Once again, her warmly and chaotically passionate nature found itself trapped in the congealing gold of a public image as hard and bland and all-protecting as if Jagger's personality truly were encased in amber. 'The worst thing of all about being with Mick was this rule he laid down that you must *never* show emotion, in case people realized you weren't cool. Over the months, everything used to get bottled up inside me. I remember, on one of those holidays with everyone in Morocco, being in the middle of the Atlas Mountains and suddenly just bursting into tears.'

In three years, inevitably, the physical fascination between them had dwindled. Marianne could resign herself to the fact that, when Jagger lay beside her in their Moroccan-draped four-poster at Cheyne Walk, it was usually just to pore over the latest book she'd got him to read. She could resign herself to the knowledge that, as his desire for her decreased, he more and more frequently exercised the *droit-de-seigneur* he held over half the women of the western world. 'Mick's other affairs *did* bother me. But that wasn't as bad as the feeling of being pinned against the wall by the whole superstar thing. I sometimes think it might have helped if there had been more drink around instead of just dope. If Mick and I had got drunk together a few times, we might have stood a chance.'

He could still be an artfully persuasive lover, wooing her back

330

from fury or estrangement with gifts and flowers. One of Marianne's minor complaints was against his extreme stinginess. To keep up the Cheyne Walk house – as a woman *must* keep house for her lord and master – he allowed her only £25 a week. Yet he had bought a country cottage for her mother, Baroness Erisso. And he continued to be kindness and generosity personified to her son, Nicholas.

The disintegration of their love was reflected by the country house they had planned to live in together, in those far off days, eighteen months ago, when Jagger's greatest joy seemed to be whirling Nicholas round by the arms or pushing his swing higher and higher towards the sun.

Christopher Gibbs, the antique-dealer, had been commissioned to find a property which – it was implicitly stated – must be no whit less grand than Bill Wyman's new Suffolk mansion, Gedding Hall. 'The whole process took an *extremely* long time,' Gibbs says. 'As Mick, Marianne and I were setting off to look at a house I'd found, Marianne would say, "Let's have lunch in Henley on the way." "But Marianne," I'd say. "Henley isn't on the way. We're going to Shropshire." "But it *could* be on the way," she'd say. The result was that a two-hour journey would take six or seven hours.'

Gibb's most promising find was 'Stargroves', a mock-Gothic folly, near Newbury, Berkshire, which had belonged to the eccentric Sir Henry Cardon and was now on the market for the extremely small sum of £20,000. 'Mick and Marianne drove down to look at it in pitch darkness, with a great carload of people that included Terry Southern. Anyway, dark or not, the *chemistry* was right.'

Elaborate plans were put in hand for the restoration of 'Stargroves', both inside and out. An elderly groundsman, acquired with the property, shuffled round with Marianne, listening dazedly to her schemes for making mazes and medieval herb gardens. Jagger, however, seemed to lose interest in the place almost as soon as he'd bought it. Months later, the renovations were still not complete. The Gothic mansion floated in a sphere of embarrassment and indecision more powerful than any of its purported Victorian ghosts.

For Jagger, too, this was a time of great depression and anxiety. Even his talent for self-abstraction could not blind him to the high level of Marianne's drug-intake, nor his famous 'cool' restrain him from furious anger when her *grande dame* carelessness with hash or pills opened up the road to Brixton Prison all over again. Already, thanks to Marianne, one bust for marijuana hung over their heads, jeopardizing the whole strategy Jagger had worked out to save the Stones from ruin. Worst of all, the hash and 'speed' and 'coke' had begun to affect Marianne's looks. The brimmingly lovely face had grown haggard, the great, liquid eyes vague and foggy, the voice hoarse and noticeably deeper. To someone who measured life in looks and profit, it must have hurt to see such a prize become such a liability.

Matters were only made worse by the arrival of Keith Richard and Anita Pallenberg to live at number 3 Cheyne Walk, a couple of hundred yards to the east. The move had been intended to facilitate Mick and Keith's song-writing partnership as well as to liberate Anita from the restraints of country life. For £50,000, the undead king and queen of Rock acquired the Queen Anne residence of a former Tory government minister, Anthony Nutting. They moved in in August, 1969, the month that Anita gave birth to their first child, Marlon.

Marlon Richard opened his eyes to eighteenth century wood-panelled rooms, transformed by Anita into replicas of Moroccan hashish-dens, their elegantly-wrought ceilings supporting beaten metal lamps inlaid with fake rubies and emeralds. The second-floor drawing-room, where Tory ladies had once sipped tea, was now devoted to tripping – or, possibly, more exotic rites – before an altar formed by the fireplace and two giant candlesticks. From the ceiling hung a ball of multi-faceted mirror glass that could be made to turn slowly, drenching the walls and moulded cornices, and whatever figures lay below, in specks and spermatozoa of eerie, wriggling light.

Keith and Anita, in their secret black and midnight hours, had long since ridden the 'speedball' roller coaster to the seeming shelter and level headedness of pure heroin. Like all before them, they had no thought of becoming addicts. 'Heroin is like a slow process of seduction,' Keith says. 'You try it, and you stop. You find you don't feel any worse than after a dose of flu. You say "Hey – they've been lying to me. I'm not hooked!" That's when you *are* hooked. Your body needs it and you'll do anything to get it.'

Keith and Anita were the last encouragement Marianne needed to throw caution to the winds. By late 1969 she, too, had begun taking heroin, believing she could stop whenever she chose. 'People always assume I was already a junkie when I was with Mick – but I wasn't. At that stage it was still an experiment. I went into it with my eyes wide open.'

The end of the decade, looming unreally beyond September, added fresh urgency to the manoeuvre that Mick Jagger had long been secretly plotting and preparing. It was a manoeuvre compared with which Sinbad's unseating of the Old Man of the Sea from his back seemed relatively straightforward. The Rolling Stones wanted to break away from Allen Klein.

Keith, Bill and Charlie now believed, as Jagger long had, that ditching Klein was the essential first step in correcting a situation so farcical that no one would have believed it. The Stones, at the apogee of their career as performers and recording artists, were almost broke. Their one chance of making it into the Seventies was the plan Mick had hatched for starting again almost from the beginning.

Allen Klein, in 1966, had promised he could earn them greater sums than pop stars had ever earned before. That promise Klein indubitably had kept. At an initial rough estimate by Mick Jagger's parallel accounting system, something between ten and seventeen million dollars in record royalties and tour grosses had been collected by Allen Klein's company on the Stones' behalf. Where they had erred was in believing those earnings, like the jackpot cash prizes in certain primitive TV quiz shows, would instantly be poured over them where they stood. That, of course, formed no part of Klein's undertaking.

His handling of the $1.25 million Decca royalty advance in 1966 was but a foretaste of Klein's ability to tie up the earnings he generated for his clients in financial structures whose labyrinthine ingenuity the clients themselves did not always fully appreciate. He could claim that such devices operated for the clients' good, freeing them from the tiresomeness of managing their millions, ensuring them regular long term dividend payments, so much better than untidy, inconvenient capital. Without Klein's fiscal rhetoric, however, the same provoking fact reasserted itself. The

333

Stones had earned seventeen million dollars. But the money wasn't in their bank accounts.

What they had received – a trifling million or two – they had spent in the blithe Sixties belief that there was plenty more where that came from. It was an attitude positively encouraged by Klein with his 'Whaddaya want?' and 'Ya got it' routine. The Stones, between them, had frittered away fortunes, but that was not the worst part: they also had spent as if each disregarded pound and dollar wholly belonged to them. By mid-1969, the day of reckoning was at hand for careless living right back to 1966. The Inland Revenue had begun to take an active interest in their affairs.

The appointment of Prince Rupert Loewenstein as Mick Jagger's personal financial adviser eighteen months previously, further underscored Jagger's mood of disenchantment with Klein. Loewenstein it was who gave the party at which Jagger first wore his Hyde Park dolly dress; in subsequent conversation he had proved himself a man of business infinitely more to Jagger's socially conscious taste than an uncouth accountant from New Jersey. Prince Rupert was an authentic sprig of Austrian royalty whose Savile Row suit, but for history's accident, might have been a gold-braided uniform and his *pince-nez* a haughty Hapsburg monocle. History having decreed that Prince Rupert should manage empires rather than possess them, he had wisely developed certain useful plebeian attributes, principally a voice with the swift, calculating click of an abacus, and eyes in which visions of imperial glory had been replaced by the less subtle colours of a Las Vegas fruit machine.

Prince Rupert Loewenstein waited, with some little patrician embarrassment, to assume the reins of business manager for all the Stones at that unspecified future date when Allen Klein could be persuaded to release them. The moment for such a change could hardly have been less opportune. In a few months – mid-1970 to be exact – the Stones would reach the end of their contract with Decca Records. Since, as was well known, they would rather commit hari-kiri than re-sign with Decca, there was bound to be spectacular competition among other record companies to acquire them. Klein, on visits to London, was already to be heard boasting about the deal he intended to do. At the same time,

Prince Rupert looked into the possibilities offered by the anti-Klein methods of courtly correspondence and mandarin politeness.

Klein in normal circumstances would bitterly have resented – and taken rapid steps to counteract – any such subtle erosion of his power. But Klein was deeply preoccupied elsewhere. Since the previous May, his attention had been concentrated on four individuals who, even at this point of dissolution, managed yet again to throw the Stones into general eclipse. Three of the four Beatles had now ratified Klein as their manager, allowing him to move into the Apple house and begin his great work of recouping their mislaid millions. All summer the British press had teemed with stories of the carnage wrought by Klein among Apple's defenceless hippies, and of his boardroom skirmishes with Beatle stakeholders like EMI, Sir Lew Grade and the Triumph Investment Trust. Few of these stories even mentioned that Klein managed the Rolling Stones also. The exception appeared in the *Sunday Times*, whose formidable Insight team compiled a lengthy examination of Allen Klein's business methods based on his relationship with Andrew Loog Oldham, Eric Easton and the $1.25 million Decca advance. 'The Toughest Wheeler Dealer in the Pop Jungle', as Insight dubbed him, issued a writ for libel forthwith.

The Stones might want no further part of Klein. But they still bitterly resented his treating them as also-rans to the Beatles. By August, relations between Klein and them were, to put it mildly, distant. When Keith Richard exchanged contracts for 3 Cheyne Walk, he needed £20,000 to make up the purchase price. Tom Keylock was sent to see Klein in New York with instructions not to come back without the money. 'I just kept on walking until I was in Allen's office,' Keylock says. 'He was so amazed I'd managed to get to him, he agreed to give me the money for Keith.'

This was the problem which had preoccupied Jagger in Australia, while mouthing his awful *Ned Kelly* lines. The only way the Stones could raise the wind on a scale sufficient to their vast personal outgoings was to undertake the American tour they had been discussing, and aborting, since mid-1968. All were agreed, firstly that they must get back on the road; secondly, that under no circumstances did they want Allen Klein to be involved in the arrangements. Care must be taken, however, not to alienate Klein to the point of actual legal dispute since that would allow him, as a matter of course, to freeze the accumulated royalties pending a court decision that could take years.

Jagger's skilful solution was to approach Ronnie Schneider, Klein's nephew and principal adjutant in the bloody 'reorganization' at Apple. Schneider had always been fraternally fond of the Stones, particularly Brian and Keith; he also had become disaffected by his uncle's apparent emotional fixation on the Beatles, and was looking for a chance to break into solo management. Klein, still deep in Beatle boardroom conflict, consented to let Schneider handle the Stones' tour, provided he did so from the Klein office. When this proved unworkable – as it did almost immediately – arrangements were too far forward to cancel. Ronnie Schneider was in charge of the Rolling Stones.

The news that the Stones were to tour again caused a momentary diversion from Fleet Street's running saga of the Beatles, Apple and Allen Klein. One radio interviewer even asked George Harrison why he thought Jagger and Co. were going back on the road again. 'I think they need the money,' was George's spot-on reply. '. . . and that new guitarist of theirs is fantastic.' Keith Richard, too, spoke of the new dimension and subtlety Mick Taylor had brought to the band. 'It's taken a bit of time to weave him in . . .' ('*Right!*' the interviewer agrees fervently.) 'But the band's really together now.' ('*Right!*') 'We're really looking forward to getting back out there . . .'

In fact, all of them were jittery at the prospect of returning to a milieu barely recognizable as the one in which their reputation had been made. When they had last toured, in 1967, it was still basically as a pop group, obliged to do little more than fill a theatre with screams. These past two years had seen the evolution of pop into Rock – a simple excess of sound and spirits into a culture: *a consciousness*. Rock was not only a thousand watts louder; it was also a thousand times more serious. Seriousness devolved equally on the bands (not groups any more), playing songs as huge and difficult to stop as ocean liners, and on the audiences, listening with an intentness that implied almost comparable virtuosity. Few enough ex-pop groups had dared chance their arm in the Rock subcontinent. The Beatles themselves would ultimately perish, not so much from the financial coils enmeshing them as from fear that if they played in public again – as Paul McCartney wanted – people might actually listen to them.

Jagger, of course, had tested the water of the new consciousness in Hyde Park, and found its welcome positive. He also presciently recognized the importance of a new San Francisco-based rock paper in determining key figures for the new music's hall of fame. It was no small help that the paper was called *Rolling Stone*, in tribute to the Stones' early impact on its founder and editor, Jann Wenner. As well as an inspired editor, Wenner was a determined socialite for whom friendship with stars was the sine qua non of success. He even persuaded Jagger to part with money to launch a British *Rolling Stone* edition, with the implied promise that Jagger would enjoy some editorial control. The project languished however when its London staff proved hippyishly inept and indolent. Wenner – whose guiding ethos was already closer to Lord Beaverbrook than to Buddha – cut off financing, fired the staff and closed the office down.

Since putting on a Rock tour in 1969 was a process understood by no one in the Stones' employment, Jagger besought help from his old friends the Who, already expert travellers in the modern manner. The Who lent the Stones their road operations manager, Peter Rudge, who had begun his career booking pop groups for the Cambridge May balls. Rudge's brief from Jagger – inspired by past dissatisfaction with American promoters – was to assemble a road show independent of all outside interference or bungling. The Stones would travel with their own maintenance, publicity and security staff and their own compere, Sam Cutler. Removing the last perquisite of concert promoters, they would even book their own supporting acts. Their choice was the husband and wife Soul duo, Ike and Tina Turner, and their old Blues idol, B. B King. Keith reacted strongly to suggestions that the supporting acts might be a little too good. 'I *want* a strong opening act,' he insisted. 'If they're good, it's going to make me work that much harder.'

The crucial factor, as everyone knew, would be Jagger's own performance. In a world where the long haired Rock star had grown commonplace, a head-tossing cliché, how could Jagger re-create his old, unchallengeable spectacle and shock? He pondered the matter at length, with frequent reference to an earlier figure whose leaps could bring the heart of an audience into its mouth. At one point, he called Jo Bergman and said, 'Find me a Diaghilev.'

Any idea that the Stones had lost power as a concert attraction was dismissed by the instant reaction of promoters across America. Ronnie Schneider, in London, was inundated with transatlantic calls, offering them virtually any price or guarantee they cared to name. For a concert relayed on closed-circuit TV in the current style of world title prize fights, one overwrought showman was prepared to pay four million dollars. Schneider, for all his excitability, was prudent enough to divide the itinerary between established promoters and top prestige venues like the Los Angeles Forum and New York's Madison Square Garden. The advances that rolled in gave the tour its sorely needed financial float – especially since Ronnie Schneider ordered the cheques to be made out, not to its overall booking agency, William Morris Inc., but to the Stones' own ad hoc company, Stone Tours.

America's ears were simultaneously to be assaulted by no less than three new Rolling Stones albums. The first was a collection of golden oldies entitled *Through The Past Darkly* and dedicated to Brian Jones – whose presence, indeed, permeated every track. Then there was a fourteen-cut promotional disc, issued to 200 radio stations in the hope of its being broadcast complete as a history of the Stones from Route 66 to Love In Vain, a sneak preview track from their new album *Let it Bleed.*

*Let It Bleed*, now in final mixing stage, was scheduled for release in early December, when the tour would be reaching its climax. Just how large a climax, no one, of course, imagined – nor how horribly apt an album-title could be.


'Are you,' a laconic woman journalist asks Mick Jagger, 'any more *satisfied* now than when you last came over here?'

The question is so uncharacteristically witty for an American Press Conference that even Jagger deigns to show a flicker of amusement.

'D'you mean financially?' he banters, craning to see her in the media crush. 'Sexually? Philosophically?'

'Financially and philosophically satisfied.'

The place is New York's ultra-smart Rainbow Room, perched

on the 30th floor of Rockefeller Center. The date is November 25, two days before the Stones' appearance at Madison Square Garden. The mood is euphoric – an upswing nothing now can spoil. Around the white-suited Jagger, Nikon shutters snap and buzz. Protective arms endlessly reposition the microphone into which, smiling broadly, he delivers a slightly more expansive non-reply than usual.

'Financially . . . just sa'isfied. Sexually sa'isfied . . . y'know. Philosophically . . . tryin' . . .'

'Don't expect them to scream,' someone whispered as a last warning to Jagger before he went onstage at Los Angeles Forum on November 7. And certainly, the 18,000-strong audience, traversed by Zeppelin searchlight-beams, bore out in their murmurous restraint everything the Stones had heard about the bromide effect of 'serious' Rock.

It lasted until the searchlights cut off, plunging the miniature universe into a more dizzying dark, and a voice of giant, unapologetic Englishness said, ''Ere they are, ladies and gentlemen, after three years . . . the greatest Rock 'n' Roll band in the world . . .' Before Sam Cutler could say 'Rolling Stones', the entire darkness was on its feet, screaming to the full force of its lungs.

On a stage drenched with psychedelia's painful blue-white light – discovered there, somehow, in mid-leap – was a figure whom no Diaghilev had dressed in its gamine black off-the-shoulder jersey and split-flared gaucho trousers, pinched together by a broad, heavily-studded belt. Round its bare neck was a knee-length scarf, of the type that throttled Isadora Duncan. On its head was a red, white and blue striped top hat. Attentiveness and Woodstock dignity melted against a voice so hardly on key, it seemed not quite human, bawling out the fable of its sub-human genesis:

'Aah was bawn in a cross-fire hurri-caayne . . .'

Keith Richard, in spangled orange and earrings, a gipsy dipped in ketchup, played an almost indecent-looking see-through guitar. Charlie Watts at his drums seemed to have changed clothes at the last minute with an ordinary construction worker. Bill Wyman was in one-piece Faustian red. Only Mick Taylor conformed to West Coast type with his masking woolly hair and leg-of-mutton smock-sleeves, his virginal face angled sideways, as he followed his own playing, solemn as some thinking girl in a novel by George Eliot.

They were, in short, outlandishly different and triumphantly unreformed. Playing their old songs, about London dolly birds, or their new ones, about Hitler and Satan and riot and rape, the same vicious power was still there, plunging and re-plunging into its listeners' minds like a mainliner's needle or a vampire's fangs. For, in that time of rampaging pretentiousness, it seemed as miraculous that they bothered to play the old songs as that they dared to play the new.

For most of the large number of serious Rock critics present, Mick Jagger's new range of theatrics caused as much discomfort as a hand straying to their collective knee. The moment in Jumping Jack Flash when he took off his studded belt and whipped the stage with it was considered a detail too fraught with innuendo for most even to mention. For Albert Goldman – a middle-aged academic afflicted with the strangulating desire to write 'hip' – the conclusive moment came in Street Fighting Man, when the Forum audience stood up and beat time with upraised arms and clenched fists.

'Ja wohl!' wrote Albert Goldman in the *New York Times*. 'Mein friends, dot's right! Dot good old rock'n'role could warm the cockles of a storm trooper's heart. OK – they don't give you a torch and an armband, like in the *real* old days, and send you down the Rhine to swing with the summer solstice. But you can still squeeze in hip by haunch with thousands of good *kamerads*; still fatten ears, eyes and soul on the Leader; still plotz out while he socks it to you in stop time, and best of all, boys and girls, you can get your rocks off, no, with that good old arm action that means . . . well, you know what it means.

'No question about it, Der Fuhrer would have been gassed out of his kugel by the scene at the Forum . . .'

Even Albert Goldman (when coherent) could not deny that just the warm-up acts in the Stones '69 tour were outstanding entertainment value – first B. B. King in his grey flannel suit, bending elegant notes on his guitar, Lucille; then Ike and Tina Turner, black Soul music's most blatantly sexual performers, a laconic guitarist standing by, apparently indifferent, while his half-naked Zulu princess wife teased a hand microphone into an erect phallus, fondling it with bejewelled fingers, flicking it with her tongue as she murmured and gurgled an act of fellatio, communicable to thousands. Of all the influences on Mick Jagger's stagecraft, none was to be so great as Tina Turner. He would stand each night and watch her, his body absorbing her mannerisms like data entering an information bank.

Two sell-out shows at the Forum grossed $260,000, breaking the Beatles' record for a single night's concert-earnings – as well as roughly quintupling the Beatles' share of the box office receipts. At San Diego two nights later, the Sports Arena was stormed by 2,000 fans who had been unable to buy tickets. Forty-six were charged with offences ranging from drug-possession to throwing rocks at cars.

A new hazard of touring was the plethora of political groups, weaned from love and peace to more strident protest, and anxious to acquire the huge Rock audience as a target for their propaganda. The Black Panthers in particular dogged the Stones' tour, because black musicians were involved and because Jagger himself, in his revolutionary phase, had several times intimated sympathy for the Negro militant cause. In Oakland, the Panthers demanded that Jagger formally announce his allegiance; when he did not, death threats were issued. 'I went backstage,' Ronnie Schneider says, 'and Ike Turner shouted to me, "Hey Ron – if you're worried about the Panthers, come stand with us." All of their bodyguards – and Ike and Tina, too – were carrying 45s.'

As tour-manager, Schneider had been enjoying himself since he had been able to shout down the telephone at Bill Graham: 'Frankly, Bill – what have you ever really *done*?' Admittedly, all Graham had done was run the San Francisco Mime Troupe, organize Bob Dylan's 1964 American tour, turn the Fillmore West into Rock's only worthwhile concert-hall and, through his association with Jefferson Airplane and the Grateful Dead, become the most powerful – as well as most respected – Rock music promoter in California. He was, none the less, running only some of the Stones shows and obliged to liaise with Ronnie Schneider about matters he was accustomed to decide for himself. Disputes between the two grew ever more fierce until at Oakland, in a fight over who should and should not stand on the stage,

Ronnie Schneider hit Bill Graham with his briefcase.

The tour had reached Dallas when some news came in from London which sent Mick Jagger's courtiers into an agonized huddle outside his motel room door. British newspapers were reporting that Marianne Faithfull had left London for Rome in the company of Anita Pallenberg's one time boyfriend, Mario Schifano. Questioned by reporters, Marianne had made it clear she was leaving Jagger for Schifano, whom she described as her 'Prince Charming'.

Jagger was, as predicted, furious. Though he himself had been having a semi-public affair – with the black actress Marsha Hunt – it seems never to have occurred to him that Marianne, too, might seek solace for their atrophied relationship. To be cuckolded thus, in the very spotlight, dealt his pride a terrible blow. Out there, under the Zeppelin beams, they would know all about it. They would know there was a better lover in the world than Mick Jagger. Still, the image made its inexorable demands. He must rouge and powder himself, tie on his Isadora scarf, tip his Uncle Sam topper and leap forth like Nijinsky with his mock-Dixie yell of 'Hi y'all . . .'

Consolation came in the madness of the road, the whirl of limo' travel, wrapped in his silver cloak, the harem attentiveness of girls for whom sleeping with Rock stars had become practically a vocation. The Stones, by divine right, could avail themselves of such famous groupies as Miss Mercy, Susie Suck or, most memorably, the Plaster Casters, named for the unusual method they had devised of recording their conquests' virility. Despite the challenge implicit in rival plaster casts, there was still no doubt as to the groupies' ultimate objective. The story is told of a particular – though not very particular – girl who, upon emerging from each night's exertions with this or that Music Legend, always made the same comment: 'He was great – but he wasn't Mick Jagger.' Eventually, it is said, the day came when Jagger himself summoned her to his hotel room. Next morning, her friends gathered round avidly. 'So how was he?' someone asked. 'He was great,' the honoured one replied. 'But he wasn't Mick Jagger . . .'

Film and TV cameras saw only the usual sardonic, untouchable Jagger, born of groupie myth rather than fact, controlling the Rainbow Room press conference on November 25, and telling the lady reporter he was 'financially sa'isfied, sexually sa'isfied, philosophically tryin'.' The real Jagger, observed by no one, had been desperately ringing up Marianne in Rome and pleading tearfully with her to come back to him.

'"Philosophically *tired*" did he say?' the *New York Tribune* whispered.

'Do you,' another questioner tried, 'identify with revolutionary youth in America?'

'We're with you,' Jagger laughed. '—right be'ind you.'

'How about the war in Vietnam?'

'Just get over it as soon as you can.'

'What do you think about John Lennon returning his MBE medal to the Queen?'

'He should have done it as soon as he got it.'

'I read in the paper that you're going to be giving a free concert. Is that true?'

'We are going to do a free concert,' Jagger said. 'It's going to be on December – er – sixth in San Francisco. But it *isn't* going to be in Golden Gate Park. It's going to be somewhere adjacent to Golden Gate Park and a bit larger . . .'

The whole ghastly business had its origins in a desire to do something nice. It began because the Stones felt that rare collective impulse, a twinge of conscience.

Financially and sexually satisfied as they were by the tour's official end, they could not help but notice what a backwash of resentment it had left behind. Promoters in almost every city attacked them for the huge percentage they had taken, for their egomaniacal Rock star arrogance, their lateness in performing, their voracious consumption of buffets and wines, their petty-minded rage if B. B. King or Ike and Tina Turner received too much appreciation. The most frequently voiced criticism concerned a ticket-price allegedly 50 per cent higher than for any comparable Rock attraction. To amass their two million dollars gross, it was suggested, the Stones had systematically and callously ripped off teenagers all across America.

Most such condemnation appeared in newspapers to which the Stones paid little heed. But elements of the underground press, too, had begun to comment adversely on their rough-shod

343

triumphal progress. Most damning of all was Ralph J. Gleason, co-founder of *Rolling Stone* magazine and influential columnist for the *San Francisco Chronicle*.

'Can the Rolling Stones really need all that money?' Gleason asked in his *Chronicle* column. 'If they really dig the black musicians as much as every note they play and every syllable they utter indicate, is it possible to take out a show with Ike and Tina Turner and not let them share in the loot? How much can the Stones take back to Merrie England anyway? . . . Paying six and seven dollars for an hour of the Stones a quarter of a mile away because the artists demand such outrageous fees says a very bad thing to me about the artists' attitude to the public. It says they despise their audience.'

In fact the ticket-prices, from $4.50 to $7.50, were only marginally higher than what Rock fans were currently paying to see Blind Faith or the Doors. The Stones themselves had been horrified by the $8.50 top price at LA Forum and had publicly announced it was set by the management, not them. '*Rolling Stone* reprinted what Gleason wrote, without checking any of it,' Ronnie Schneider says. 'It was all bullshit – like claiming the Stones were conning Ike and Tina when they'd *booked* them in the first place. They were paying B. B. King, even though he'd have gone on that tour for nothing.'

None the less, the damage was done. Jagger had seen Gleason's article reprinted in *Rolling Stone*, and had been aghast at the suggestion that he was ripping off audiences. The answer was obvious, and of proven effect. The Stones would say 'thank you' to America by giving a free concert.

For such an event there could be only one possible city. San Francisco was where hippies, acid, love and Rock first coalesced: it was the home of major bands who might well participate: it was also the home of *Rolling Stone* magazine. As well as being the source of Rock consciousness, it was one of the warmest places to hold an outdoor concert in December. Jagger's idea could not have come at a more timely moment. Four months had passed since the Woodstock miracle; it was time for another great show of freaked-out togetherness. What had begun as purely a Rolling Stones project instantly became the property of San Francisco's supergroup community whose leaders were the thunderous and cerebral Grateful Dead. The Dead had already offered to play and act as co-organizers with the Stones' tour staff. Jefferson Airplane, Santana, Crosby, Stills, Nash and Young, and the Flying Burrito Brothers all volunteered to be on the bill.

The guarantee of film cameras added to this altruistic eagerness. It had been Jagger's intention all along to have the Stones' tour filmed as the cinema feature which their Hyde Park concert, mysteriously, never became. Jagger, after all, had drawn almost as many people together in one day as Woodstock's massed talents had in three. He was irked to think that the Woodstock film would shortly be released across America when *The Stones in the Park* had been seen only once on British television.

His original nominee to make a rival to *Woodstock* was the cameraman-director Haskell Wexler. Wexler accepted the job but then pulled out, leaving the tour half-finished and no footage yet shot. Not until the Stones reached New York did Jagger find an alternative in Albert and David Maysles, film-making brothers whose credits included a fascinating *cinéma vérité* chronicle of the Beatles' first visit to New York. The Maysles filmed the Stones at Madison Square Garden and in two further shows, but still had far from enough material in the can. 'Then we heard there was going to be a free concert in San Francisco,' David Maysles says. 'We couldn't decide if it was worthwhile going to that or not.'

After their final paid appearance, at the Miami Pop Festival, the Stones travelled to Muscle Shoals studios in Alabama to work on songs for the album that would become *Sticky Fingers*. Their staff, led by Jo Bergman, moved into the Grateful Dead's office in Marin County, south of San Francisco, where the new Woodstock would have to be organized in less than two weeks.

It seems incredible now that people so addicted to the study of signs and portents – people for whom 'vibes' were so important a consideration – could not see or feel the force already propelling them towards catastrophe. All summer, one fact had made itself insistently plain: that love and peace had an underside of insecurity, anger and viciousness. Two Rock festivals convened in Woodstock's triumphant name had been marred by violence, inflicted haplessly, through drug excesses, or calculatedly by hippy militant groups dubbed with eighteenth century martyrs' names like the Diggers or Weathermen. So ritualized had the battles around the Rock stage become that *Rolling Stone* was obliged to become part political broadsheet, calling this 'the year of the American revolution' and spelling its country's name with a Fascist 'k'. One episode above all expressed the change with dreadful simplicity. A bearded dropout named Charles Manson, only weeks earlier, had let his homespun 'family' loose in the Bel Air mansion of actress Sharon Tate. Four people, including the eight months pregnant Tate, had been butchered, apparently in the name of flower power.

And over all, like a sound-track to the new barbarism, floated *Let It Bleed* – the surly, smoky incantation of Gimme Shelter; the homicidal playfulness of Midnight Rambler, with additional dialogue by Albert de Salvo, the Boston Strangler. The Stones had made destruction cool and the Devil a rock star; they had sold a million copies of an exhortation to slaughter. They were the household gods of every spaced-out, subterranean screwball in America. 'Welcome Rolling Stones!' ran a typical street-corner manifesto, '– our comrades in the desperate battle against the lunatics who hold power. The revolutionary youth of the world hears your music and is inspired to even more deadly acts. We will play your music as we tear down the jails and free the prisoners, as we tear down the state schools and free the students, as we tear down the military bases, arm the poor, as we tattoo "burn, baby, burn" on the bellies of the wardens and the generals and create a new society from the ashes of our fires . . .'

Meanwhile, at the Grateful Dead's Marin County house, people living in the past four months ago told each other this would be the biggest love-in and freak-out ever. The concert had by now attracted a huge crowd of putative organizers, drawn from virtually every faction in San Francisco music, socio-politics and street-corner activism. Among the arguing daily throng could be identified Jerry Garcia and Phil Lesh of the Grateful Dead with Rock Scully, their manager; Jo Bergman and Ronnie Schneider of the Stones' staff, Sam Cutler, their compere, and John Jaymes, their security manager; Chet Helms of the Family Dog; Emmett Grogan of The Diggers; David Crosby of Crosby, Stills, Nash and Young; plus dozens of lower-caste Bay Area celebrities, propagandists, hangers-on and journalists.

There were also the Maysles brothers, filming what was still seen as the prologue to a climactic triumph. The Maysles were at San Francisco airport to record the arrival of Chip Monck, a blandly-smiling, Afro-permed youth who had built the highly successful Woodstock stage and had been commissioned to repeat his achievement here. Chip Monck vanished, still smiling, into the increasing hubbub which a *Rolling Stone* reporter drily noted. 'Meetings of two, three or ten people in every side office broke up in confusion after a few minutes . . . There was an air of frantic activity about the place. But in fact, nothing was happening.'

The problem – not foreseen until now – was finding an accessible open space whose owners would permit its occupancy by half a million-odd encamped Rock fans. Everyone had assumed that Golden Gate Park, the most obvious and suitable site, would be made available: unfortunately, however, no one contacted the San Francisco Parks department until some days after the concert had been announced. It was then learned that the Parks department required a bond of four million dollars for insurance against damage to city property and to pay for the mammoth job of clearing up afterwards. Frantic telephone calls were made to other large landowners in the San Francisco area. They, too, were imbued with visions of littering and defecating rather than love and peace, and brusquely refused to donate their open spaces, as suggested, gratis.

The difficulty seemed solved when Craig Murray, President of the Sears Point Raceway, offered his land at no charge and on minimal conditions, foremost of which was that any proceeds from the concert should benefit Vietnamese orphans. As a site, the raceway was ideal, being large, accessible to crowds and practised in dealing with their food and sanitary requirements. Craig Murray's offer was gladly accepted. Chip Monck and his stage-building and lighting crews moved out to Sears Point to begin the process of transformation.

Not until the stage was almost built, and tens of thousands of hippies were rolling up their bundles for the trek to Sears Point, did a fatal flaw reveal itself. Sears Point Raceway was owned by Filmways, a Los Angeles-based movie company whose attitude proved noticeably less philanthropic than Craig Murray's. to the terms originally offered by Murray, Filmways attached a last minute rider stipulating that they must receive exclusive distribution

347

rights to any film shot at the concert. The alternative was to pay them a million dollars in cash, with a further million dollars lodged in escrow to compensate for any damage done to their property.

It subsequently emerged that Filmways had some cause for this apparent bloody-mindedness. Another of their subsidiaries, Concert Associates, had promoted the two shows at Los Angeles Forum when the Stones had carried off three quarters of the $260,000 box-office gross, had made exorbitant demands for backstage amenities and – Concert Associates claimed – had reneged on a promise to play a return date at the Forum. With this residual bad feeling, Filmways could not be expected to show largesse to any event involving the Stones. Ronnie Schneider, on his side, flatly refused to give away the film distribution rights or pay the sums demanded. Twenty-four hours before the concert was due to start on a stage already built, Sears Point Raceway was scratched.

At this apparently hopeless juncture, with the Grateful Dead faction squabbling impotently among themselves and the Stones threatening to play, if necessary, on some empty parking lot, a striking new figure entered the entrepreneurial limelight. This was Melvin Belli, San Francisco's most famous trial lawyer, a white-haired legal showman who had been attorney to Jack Ruby, Lee Harvey Oswald's killer, and was now involved in the Charles Manson murder trial. Mick Jagger, losing faith in hippy initiative, retained Mel Belli to untangle the mess with Sears Point and Filmways, and try to find a last minute alternative concert-site.

The Maysles' cameras ran on in Belli's office as 'The King of Torts' in brown Beau Brummell suit and bright yellow shirt, diverted his powerful mind from the Charles Manson case to the dilemma of San Francisco's free Rock festival. As Ronnie Schneider remembers, Belli's initial advice was somewhat unorthodox. 'He said, "You could always just go ahead and do the show at Sears Point, and take a chance on them suing you. Maybe they'd never ever get around to it."'

The spectacle of Mel Belli cross-examining possible site-donors by telephone as Schneider and John Jaymes looked on – and Manson witnesses waited in the next room – gave the crisis a surrealistic touch. One such alternative donor had been found, but was now raising objections in a voice of increasingly passionate irritation that Belli's drawling courtroom wit seemed only to exacerbate. ' . . . You don't understand my problem. I have a *time* problem,' this unnamed individual pleaded. 'My people need more time to work on this thing . . . I see nothing but trouble . . . This whole thing is getting to be a pain in the *ass* . . . ' 'Well, I'm not a proctologist here,' the lawyer replied suavely.

Amazingly enough, in the course of that Friday morning, Mel Belli did find somewhere. A man named Dick Carter, proprietor of the Altamont Raceway, near Livermore, California, phoned in with an offer to donate his land on terms even more moderate than Sears Point's original ones. The only conditions were that the concert must be free, that its organizers guarantee $5,000 to clear up afterwards, and that a million-dollar insurance policy be taken out to protect against major damage.

The site, some 40 miles south-east of San Francisco, was a stock-car racing track carved into an 80-acre grass plot which – on paper – seemed more than adequate to contain the expected audience of 300,000. The crucial question was whether, in the twenty hours remaining, Chip Monck and his construction team could dismantle the stage they had built at Sears Point, transport it with all its ancillary towers and generators the 65 miles to Altamont Raceway, and reassemble it in time for use at noon the following day. Monck – the solitary hero this enterprise would produce – replied that it could be done, with extra volunteers, if everybody worked through the night.

By mid-afternoon, Mel Belli had concluded negotiations with the philanthropic Mr Carter, a thin-faced man wearing heavy hair-oil and a short toothbrush moustache. 'The Sheriff wants to know,' quipped Belli rotundly, 'who's going to the bathroom, and where.'

'It's on!' *Rolling Stone* announced in a jubilant stop-press. 'It will be a little Woodstock and, even more exciting, it will be an *instant* Woodstock . . . ' The same message went out all evening over scores of rock radio stations, turning the migrant tide away from Sears Point and towards Altamont. A few people did not share the general euphoria. 'They'll never do it,' said Bill Graham, the promoter, speaking from his stores of untapped experience. 'They

349

should call it off or it'll explode in their faces . . . ' Others, casting a horoscope for the event as had been done for Woodstock, were dismayed to see that on December 6, the Moon would be in Scorpio, portending a time of chaos and violence.

Exactly who first had the idea of hiring Hell's Angels as a security force, no one can remember now. Some say it was Rock Scully, the Grateful Dead's manager; others remember Emmett Grogan of the Diggers proposing that the Stones be escorted to the stage by a ceremonial guard of 'a hundred Angels on hogs . . . that way, no one will dare to go near them.'

The idea did possess a glimmering of logic. Previous Rock concerts in the San Francisco area had found it better to invite the Angels than to risk their arrival, unbidden, in a spirit of antagonism. Giving them spurious official status had proved an even better emollient. So, in the spirit of Aquarian brotherhood and devout hope that the same ruse would work again, various Hell's Angel chapters throughout north California were contacted and invited to act as 'stewards' at Altamont.

They were not hired as bodyguards for the Stones, as all subsequent reports would allege. What happened was that Stones people – notably Sam Cutler, the concert compere – went along with the plan to invite them. To Cutler, as to the Stones themselves, all the term 'Hell's Angel' probably signified were the pimply-faced boys with freshly-washed hair who had been so cosmetic and inoffensive a feature of the Hyde Park free concert, five months ago.

Californian Hell's Angels were not the same. They were highly organized, semi-outlaw gangs whose Fascist leather and insignia were all too accurate a reflection of character, and whose vicious mass reprisals against anyone suspect of slighting their brotherhood made even the police unwilling to challenge them. Heaven help anyone on the freeway not showing due respect to an Angel, his woman, his chapter emblem or, most of all, his neurotically gleaming, high handlebar 'hog'.

In latter years they had acquired a certain chic, thanks to writers like Hunter S. Thompson and Emmett Grogan, who perceived in their impenetrable brutishness and grubbiness a candour otherwise absent from modern American life. So it was politic, but also 'groovy' to set these real life urban bandits in visual counterpoint to the mythic outlaws and vagabonds of Rock.

It was now six o'clock in the evening of that confused and frenetic Friday, December 5. The weak winter sun had declined into chilly dusk. On the hills around Dick Carter's raceway, scores of figures could be seen, tramping with a peculiar dogged, fatalistic tread which, added to their beads and plaits and rolled blankets, gave them the appearance of Red Indians on the way to a new hunting ground. The first spectators were arriving at Altamont.

The end of their journey was very far from being a beauty spot. On three sides of the racetrack stretched empty slopes covered with grass whose pigment seemed burned out of it by exhaust-fumes, and dotted here and there with the wrecked shells of cars used up in the track's 'demolition derbies'. Shards of rusting auto metal and broken glass crunched under sandalled feet. It all looked bleak and uninhabited – and, indeed, it generally was. Altamont Raceway had long been teetering on the edge of bankruptcy. This was a golden opportunity, in Dick Carter's eyes, to give the place 'a new image.'

The first-comers pitched their tents and, as the night grew colder, lit fires made with palings from the wooden perimeter fence. Others squeezed in to sleep or make love behind the eviscerated dashboards of the wrecked stock cars. On the low-lying section nearest the highway, Chip Monck's volunteer crew worked under arclights to put together the stage they had transported from Sears Point. The atmosphere was good humoured, as at Boy Scout camp, with touch football under the arclamps, guitar singsongs and good trips by firelight. A ragged cheer greeted the arrival of eight ancient trucks, each loaded with a dozen portable one-person toilets that were presumed – incorrectly – to be merely the advance guard of the sanitary facilities.

At about 3 a.m., the Stones themselves arrived by limousine with Ronnie Schneider. Mick Jagger, dressed in a pink cape and bulbous pink velvet cap, inspected Chip Monck's nearly com-pleted stage, then walked among the camp fires like young King Harry visiting his troops before Agincourt. Someone democra-tically held up a joint to him and – having asked for the TV

351

cameras to be averted – Jagger took a 'hit' and passed it back. The vibes at this stage could hardly have been better. Keith Richard liked the feel of the crowd so much, he stayed the rest of the night, talking, smoking and eventually settling down to sleep on the grass.

By early Saturday morning, as the wan winter sun came up, 100,000 were already on the site, with thousands more arriving each hour, abandoning their cars eight miles away on a jammed-solid ten-mile stretch of half-finished freeway, and joining the Red Indian trek down the access road, over the hills or along the railway line. From the air, the effect was of a huge ploughed field, its furrows alternately earth brown and denim blue, moving as if by some seismic compulsion over the paler-contoured semi-desert.

For half a square mile around Chip Monck's stage, the slopes were solid with bivouacked bodies, each clinging to its precious inches of space with as much fervour as if the Earth were shortly to be turned upside-down. Here and there, stumbling among the legs and backs, could be seen one or other of the dozen film crews which Albert and David Maysles had mustered for the occasion. The Maysles wanted vignettes of hippydom, and they were not disappointed. Everywhere the camera-lens looked, it saw painted faces, tattooed bodies, babies being suckled at the breast. Ever and again, in the delight of a good trip or the anguish of a bad one, some half-clad figure would leap to its feet and demonstrate the whirling dervish ritual of freaking out. All seemed to be going exactly to plan for what the organizers had begun to call 'Woodstock West'.

The Hell's Angels began arriving at about 10 a.m. Cheers and even applause were heard as the roar of 850cc engines parted the crowd like gossamer, and the grime-black squadrons bumped and swerved their heavy steeds downhill in ceremonial order: the 'Frisco chapter, the San Bernardino, the Oakland, the San José. With them by way of commissariat the Angels had brought a yellow school bus filled with supplies of beer, cheap red wine and 'tabs' of even more dangerously cheap LSD. They had also brought, as badges of their stewards' rank, chains, knives, brass knuckles and their own special persuaders, sawn-off wooden pool cues, weighted with lead.

As the cavalcade passed through, bottles of wine and joints were offered to them and graciously accepted. One female onlooker, forced to jump aside, shouted a reproach. The Angel stopped and waited while his girl-friend dismounted, walked up to the other girl and punched her in the mouth.

By midday, the scheduled starting-time, even on the part of the site not policed by Hell's Angels, good vibes were fast melting away. Sunshine had given way to cloud and a grey, grubby light which showed Altamont Raceway in all its true depressing character. Three hundred thousand people had long since swamped the few meagre facilities provided to feed and amuse them. Queues stretched for hundreds of yards from the tiny outcrop of portable toilets. Nineteen doctors, in scattered medical centres, were already inundated by victims of the bad drugs apparently being peddled by organized syndicates. Supplies of antidote drugs like Thorazine were running low. Nothing could be done with most of the victims but to put them behind rope enclosures to jerk and writhe like plague victims not quite dead. Nothing had happened yet to indicate this was Woodstock West rather than a vast, agglomerating slum of bodies either inert with chemical horrors or comatose with boredom. Not a note of music had been played. The sound system wasn't even working properly.

Down at a stage already overburdened with roadies and Hell's Angels like a water-logged life raft, Sam Cutler, with his straggly moustache and careworn leather doublet, turned in exasperation on a black man who had climbed up to join in. Or, rather, stepped up – the stage-rim was, inexplicably, only four feet or so from the ground.

In a love and peace accent almost visibly bursting at the seams, Cutler said:

'I'd really like you to get off the stage, baby – *please.*'

'Okay, man,' his tormentor said, also in the idiom that could express only pacts between friends. 'I can dig that – you know?' A moment later, when Cutler's back was turned he stepped up on to the stage again.

'Ladies and gentlemen . . .' an only slightly less brittle version of Sam Cutler's voice eventually boomed out over the still wavering PA system. 'We give you Santana, the first band in the best party in 1969 . . .'

Santana's blend of Latin big band energy and the passionate lone guitar played by Carlos Santana himself, was the newest sensation in Rock. As the fat brass sound rolled outward, with all its suggestions of fun and fiesta, good humour very nearly won the day. Figures were up and dancing everywhere, shaking kaftan sleeves like ragged eight-armed Indian gods. 'It was almost pure ecstasy,' Sol Stern of *Ramparts* magazine later said. 'Turning round, all I could see were people back as far as the clear blue horizon. It was like being in the eye of a hurricane with energy and turmoil all around. I thought everything was going to be all right – that the power of the music would keep it all in balance.'

By half-way through Santana's set, swirls and flurries of violence, at first almost too quick for the eye to follow, were happening all along the stage-front to its scaffolded corners where massed Hell's Angels confronted the ordinary public. A blond-haired boy, trying to break through, disappeared under a hail of punches and kicking motorcycle boots. An older freak with a Mexican moustache, who had stripped to reveal pendulous breasts and a penis clenched like a button mushroom, stood, apparently in deep thought, after numerous blows from an Angel's weighted pool cue. A photographer who tried to record the incident was felled with pool cues, kicked and stomped as he lay bleeding and finally smashed in the face with his own camera.

While the stage was re-set, Sam Cutler attempted to curb the Angels' rampage, as all around him urged, by circuitous politeness and tact. Santana's performance had been punctuated also by a fusillade of full beer cans, thrown from the Angels' school bus commissariat 30 yards away. Cutler sent an emissary to the Angels in charge of the bus, offering to buy their entire beer supply for $500. The beer could thus be put *on* the stage, preventing its use as random missiles. This was the origin of one powerful Altamont legend: that the Hell's Angels were hired by Rolling Stones people for $500-worth of beer.

Next to perform were Jefferson Airplane, a band of psychedelic chamber musicians fronted by the vengefully beautiful and beady-eyed Grace Slick. The Airplane had always championed Hell's Angels, even played benefit concerts for them. Grace Slick, all crow-black hair and fitted blue satin, attempting to establish camaraderies, said, 'Will the Hell's Angels please take the stage?'

Jefferson Airplane played We Can Be Together and the violence re-erupted – quick flurries of black leather, white insignia, a face or arm upraised under flailing pool cues. 'Hey – we're cool . . .' Grace Slick's voice protested over the PA system. 'We can be cool. Hey down there – why are we *hurting* each other?'

Jefferson Airplane played Revolution, with its hopefully empathic refrain 'up against the wall, motherfucker.' More Angels closed in like soldier ants around a single black youth. Marty Balin, the Airplane's vocalist, leapt off the stage to intervene and was himself bludgeoned unconscious. Paul Kantner, the lead guitarist, said into the microphone, 'I'd like to tell you all what's happened. The Hell's Angels have just smashed Marty Balin and knocked him out for a while.'

Across the stage, a bearded Angel seized a spare hand-mike. 'Is this thing on or what?' his voice rasped gigantically. ' . . . Are you talking to *me*?'

'I'm not talking to you,' Kantner's amplified voice answered. 'I'm talking to these people.'

'Fuck you,' the Angel's voice roared back.

Hippydom could not comprehend, lacking even the vocabulary to describe what was happening.

'It's really weird up on that stage,' someone kept saying. 'Man, it's really *weird*.'

Jefferson Airplane were still onstage when the Stones' charter helicopter touched down 50 yards to the rear, on an asphalt strip meant to be a high security musicians' landing and departure area. In fact it was as crowded and chaotic as any other part of the site. No attempt was made to camouflage the Stones or steer them to the trailer dressing-room any way but straight through the crowds jostling for a sight of Mick Jagger. They had gone only a few steps when a teenage boy, half-crazed with cut price acid, lunged forward and punched Jagger in the face, crying, 'I hate you, you fucker. I want to kill you.' Bodyguards twirled the boy in one direction and Jagger, visibly pale and shaken, in the other. He managed to make light of the incident, however, and ordered that no reprisals be taken against his attacker.

The passing of the word that Jagger was here seemed to cause a lull in the stage-front violence. Things improved still further as the

Flying Burrito Brothers, featuring Keith's new friend Gram Parsons, played their sweet, anodyne country rock. The Stones, in their backstage trailer – unaware that there had been any particular trouble – went about the familiar procedures of tuning up and holding court. Jagger, fully himself again, appeared on the steps outside and began autographing the proffered books, album-sleeves and military draft cards. Later, he and Keith walked across to look at the audience and even climbed onstage for a few moments with the Burritos. It was noticed that, wherever a Stone went outside the trailer, he was accompanied by a guard of between three and six Hell's Angels, visibly armed to the teeth.

In fact – as Ronnie Schneider confirmed – the Stones placed no reliance on this grubby phalanx and had hired their own personal bodyguards for protection against the Angels as much as any demented fan. Their two principal guards, an inoffensive-looking white man and an enormous black man named Tony Fuches, both quickly ran into Hell's Angel trouble. At an access-point to the stage, the white bodyguard had a cigarette stubbed out against his hand. More Angels were rushing to join the attack when a signal from one of their leaders – the celebrated Sonny Barger – caused them suddenly to back off. According to Schneider, the man concerned was an FBI agent, a figure whom even Hell's Angels dared not challenge.

The black bodyguard, Tony Fuches, made his presence felt in a more straightforward way. Threatened by two Angels at once, he punched them in the face simultaneously, so hard that he broke both his wrists.

Crosby, Stills and Nash were onstage with their new addition, Neil Young, their choirboy harmonies barely audible over the deteriorating PA. Stills, Nash and Young had not wanted to play at all and were doing so only after strong persuasion from Dave Crosby. Their performance, nervous and desultory, was like a green light to chaos to break out again. Hell's Angels were now surrounding and beating onlookers at random – spectators, male and female, even their own camp followers and chapter novitiates. At one point, for no apparent reason, a ten-strong group charged outward into the audience, pool cues hacking to right and left. Crosby, Stills, Nash and Young finished their set, unplugged their guitars and without even troubling to learn whether they were being applauded, bolted for their escape helicopter.

There was a further lull as stretchers were passed along to pick up the fallen and those behind pressed forward to fill the vacated spaces. Sam Cutler, hemmed in at his microphone, played his final card. 'The Rolling Stones won't come out,' he said, 'until *everybody* gets off the stage.'

Cutler's words were apparently the signal for a dozen or so Angel 'officers', led by Sonny Barger, to ride their bikes through the crowd and park them in a slanted line directly below the stage. Barger would afterwards maintain that the concert-organizers had specifically asked him to provide this special barricade, augmented by gleaming, untouchable hogs. Sam Cutler and Rock Scully would be equally sure that no one ever made any such request.

To all this fast accumulating danger, the Stones now added their usual imperious and indolent disregard of the fact that people wanted to see them perform. More than ever on this tour, it had been their habit to delay and delay, piling up the tension, the expectation, the half-adoring rancour at this new demonstration that they couldn't give a damn. Round the stage, a rumour circulated that they were long since ready but that Mick Jagger wanted complete darkness so that the stage lights would show off his costume and make-up to best effect.

Darkness was falling rapidly. As the cold intensified, fires were lit from the remnants of the raceway fence, or from garbage. A pall of smoke, rancid with singed waxed paper and burning Cellophane, drifted up and settled around the still darkened stage. Doctors working in a nearby medical tent asked for extra light, but were told that might spoil the impact of Jagger's entry when it came. Backstage, the Stones' helicopter pilot told Ronnie Schneider he was too nervous for his machine to wait until the end of their performance, as arranged. Tony Fuches, the black bodyguard, said he'd hold the pilot there at gun-point if necessary.

When the Stones finally materialized, in a demon-red spotlight blaze, so did an escort of Hell's Angels so dense as to be almost obliterating. Jagger, wearing an orange and black satin cloak and his Uncle Sam topper, had literally to fight his way to the low stagefront. The Angels were no longer protecting the stage: they

357

had commandeered it for a display of their own power in which the Stones figured only as semi-captive mascots. Jumping Jack Flash found himself hobbled in a tiny recess between crimson-lit Angles, being borne in a cross-fire hurricane with barely enough space to swing his elbows. 'Fellers—' he kept saying in pretended amusement. 'Will you give me some room? Will you move back, fellers, *please*?'

Half-way through Carol, even that good tempered Rock 'n' Roll number, pool cues began flailing again among the faces close to Jagger's silver boots. Out in the darkness beyond the smoke-red arena, Keith Richard's chords were finding their mark. Boys and girls stripped naked in the dank cold, flinging themselves forward against the cracked leather cordon as puny white martyrs, almost begging to be surrounded, beaten, stomped and kicked. In the stage-front area, a dozen photographers, mindful of their colleague's earlier fate, kept their lenses resolutely blinkered. Only the Maysles' film-crews, each with an Angel 'shotgun' guard, avidly recorded all there was to see.

Now came the moment when – according to which equally possible version one prefers – Mick Jagger's intuition deserted him or his vanity became overmastering. Either way, the result was incredible stupidity. Folding his cloak around him, he stepped forward in the mincing gait he had evolved for this most presumptuous of all his masquerades. 'Please allow me to introduce myself . . .' sang Satan, in his trendy orange satin, across a landscape whose authentic hellishness he could not, or would not, see.

The effect was as sudden as if the ground had opened up. Faces down to Jagger's left collapsed sideways under the tossing assault of Hell's Angel staves. The Devil-invoking samba beat expired in a tugboat whistle of guitar feedback. Satan, cut off in mid-verse, grasped for words that would return him to the hippy plane. 'Brothers and sisters . . . brothers and sisters, come *on* now. That means *everybody* – just cool out. Just cool out now. We can cool out, everybody. Everybody be cool now, come on . . .'

The beating down of pool cues paused as if in answer to his exhortation. 'Okay,' Jagger said, evidently believing he had worked some similar miracle to that of James Brown in the race riots. 'I think we're cool now . . . we can groove.' A shaky little joke revealed his continued failure to grasp the situation below him. 'We always have something very funny happen when we start that number . . .'

Something, not very funny, *was* happening, the incidental purpose of which seemed to be to stop Sympathy for the Devil ever from getting beyond its first few bars. It had re-started but petered out again. In the mêlée below Jagger, a naked girl struggled her face, breasts and arms through a crevice to reach up entreatingly to him in the instant before her black leather shroud closed in. 'Fellers . . .' Jagger protested lamely. 'Does it take *five* of you to handle that?'

The stage now thronged with Angels like a bar at closing-time. There was also a large and extremely ugly Alsatian dog prowling round unattended, sniffing at Charlie Watts's bass drum and Bill Wyman's trousers. As Jagger stood indecisively there, an Oakland Angel with a Mormon elder chin-beard came up beside him and began to speak frowningly into his ear. If Jagger lacked resolution, Keith Richard did not. Pointing furiously across his guitar, he shouted to the stage-front Angels to stop what they were doing. Sam Cutler rushed forward to restrain him, but Keith kept pointing and shouting, 'That guy there . . . if he doesn't stop it, man . . .'

'Er – *people* . . .' Jagger began again. 'Who's fightin' and why? What are we *fightin'* for?'

'It's that guy down there,' Keith shouted, still pointing. 'If he doesn't cool it, man . . .'

'San Francisco . . . This could be the most beautiful event. Don't fuck it up . . .' It was that rare thing, Jagger's ordinary voice, accentless, wan, almost trembling. He stood there, a forlorn, flat-footed figure, wrapped in black and orange satin, punctured with the uncomprehending dismay of finding himself totally ignored by an audience.

'All I can do is ask you – *beg* you to keep it together. It's within your power.'

To underline Jagger's entreaties to everyone to sit down, Mick Taylor and Bill Wyman began to improvise a slow instrumental sequence from the chords of Under My Thumb. Behind them, on a trailer belonging to the Grateful Dead, David Maysles signalled his cameraman, Baird Bryant, to keep filming this unprecedented instance of the Stones playing calm-down Muzak. Jagger himself still stood there helplessly. Close beside him, the face of a Hell's Angel stared into his, enlarged by the unreal perspective, its eyes sightless with unpronounceable malice, its bearded lips opening and closing like a poisonous pink anemone.

Twenty feet from the stage, the crowd suddenly parted to form a broad avenue, such as might open to greet a conquering hero. Down the middle came a lanky young black man, dressed in a light green suit, and running with inspired energy. For a hypnotic second or two, this oddly lean and elegant figure, its right arm stretched up as if to touch off an Olympic flame, whirled in the half dark between a clump of Hell's Angels and a girl in a white crocheted mini-dress. Just for a trice against the crochet work, the object in his right hand showed its dark, long-barrelled silhouette. Then the dark mass surged in again to obliterate him.

The stabbing to death of 18-year-old Meredith Hunter by a Hell's Angel wearing the skull and crossbones insignia of the Oakland chapter, should by rights have been witnessed by only two or three among the thousands standing torpidly near. No one on the stage saw it, least of all the Stones, at this moment trying to collect themselves enough to begin playing again. It happened too quickly even for Baird Bryant, the stage cameraman, to see it in his own view-finder while filming it. David Maysles, acting as Bryant's sound man, was aware only of a flicker 'like a tassel . . . something you'd wave.'

Neither cameraman nor sound recordist realized what had happened even as they filmed Mick Jagger leaning forward, trying to hear something being shouted up at him. The appeal then broadcast by Jagger seemed no different from others which had preceded it. 'We need a doctor . . . now please. Look – could you let the doctor through, please? Somebody's been hurt . . .' Jagger could not see that people around Meredith Hunter were holding up hands soaked in his blood to try to show the awful extent of his injuries.

The Stones had pulled themselves together and were playing again by the time a young doctor in a green combat jacket had fought his way to the clearing where Meredith Hunter lay, and had taken over from the couple of horrified boys trying to wash away the blood with hot coffee from a paper cup. By the time the doctor had got Hunter to the backstage medical tent, the performance was on its feet again. 'Under mah thumb . . .' Mick Jagger sang. 'A Siamese cat of a girl . . .' It could have been that very girl, in her white crocheted mini-dress, who stood by the unwanted ambulance, crying, 'They can't hear his heart . . . I don't want him to die . . .'

The ambulance had been put there, in fact, to transport the Stones the 50 yards back to their helicopter. 'I was out there, searching for the driver, to help the guy who'd been hurt,' Ronnie Schneider says. 'I ran into a cop – the first one I'd seen all day. As we stood there, this cop heard over his walkie-talkie that the guy was dead.'

The Stones played on, meanwhile, vaulting from Under My Thumb to Midnight Rambler, Queenie and Brown Sugar, hitting each head-on with the kind of lucid brilliance that terror so often inspires. 'We knew that if we stopped, there really *would* have been a riot,' Mick Taylor says. They even did Street Fighting Man as per programme, with its now sickly inappropriate valediction from Jagger: 'We're gonna kiss you goodbye . . .'

As the Stones bolted from the stage, the Angels moved in on the remaining beer supply, howling that now 'the party' could really begin. Across in the asphalt pit area, fourteen people threw themselves into the Stones' eight-seater helicopter. Before the door closed, it was lifting off, its perspex bubble crammed like a cookie jar with bodies and leather lapels and boots, and Mick Jagger's sweat-smeared, frightened face.

There was none of the usual after-show drinking and carousing that night. Even Keith Richard seemed to want to do nothing but fold his tattered frame into a brocade armchair, nurse a bottle of Jack Daniels and stare glumly off into space. Mick Taylor locked himself in his hotel room and slid the chain across the door.

Shocked as they all were, they still did not realize what a piece of butchery had been enacted literally before their eyes. Next morning's *San Francisco Chronicle* reported the Altamont festival as a brilliant success only slightly marred by death. As well as Meredith Hunter, three more youths had been killed; two run over by a car as they lay in sleeping-bags, the third drowned in an irrigation-ditch. The *Chronicle* preferred to stress Sam Cutler's claim that the event had been literally life-enhancing. According to Cutler, four babies had been born during the day's events. Dick Carter, the raceway owner, was reportedly delighted with his first foray into pop promotion and was now planning an even bigger festival, headlined, he hoped, by the Beatles.

London newspapers picked up the same line of a Stones-inspired freak-out where death had been almost cosmically counterbalanced by birth. STONED! chortled the *Daily Express*, unconsciously echoing that long-forgotten B-side. Arriving back in London, all the Stones were understandably tight-lipped. Even Keith Richard told a UPI reporter that Altamont had been 'basically well-organized, but people were tired and a few tempers got frayed.'

The real story only began to emerge late that Sunday night, via an exhaustive on-air inquest by San Francisco's rock station KSAN. Numerous callers-in reiterated the grisliness of conditions at Altamont and the mindless brutality they had witnessed there. Despite obvious fear of reprisals from the Angels, even Sam Cutler was persuaded to admit, 'I didn't dig, in fact, what a lot of people did yesterday.' For editorial balance, there was the voice of Hell's Angel Sonny Barger, almost plaintive in its claim that the Angels had been the victims of Rock star vanity and vagueness. 'I didn't go there to police nuthin', man . . . They used us for dupes.' According to Sonny Barger, the trouble had started after several Angels below the stage had their bikes deliberately kicked over, and one even set on fire. 'I ain't no peace creep, man . . . Ain't nobody goin' to get my bike, man. Anyone tries that, they gonna get got. And they *got* got.'

It further emerged that no babies at all had been born during the festival. The nearest approximation was a youth who announced he was pregnant, just prior to jumping from a traffic flyover and suffering serious multiple injuries.

The most damning account of all did not appear until almost six weeks afterwards, in *Rolling Stone* magazine. A 20,000 word article by a committee of *RS* writers who had been present reconstructed the whole chaotic story with a wealth of investigative detail not previously associated with underground journalism. Among the eyewitness testimony was a description of how Meredith Hunter, an apparently law-abiding black teenager from

362

Berkeley, had had his hair yanked by a Hell's Angel and, on giving 'a mean look', had been set on by half a dozen more. Hunter, it was said, tried to escape but had been knifed in the back as he ran towards the stage. Bystanders saw him pull a gun from his coat pocket and wave it in the air. An Angel had then moved in, stabbing Hunter repeatedly with a seven-inch knife, clubbing and kicking him as he lay bleeding, even standing on the victim's head before strolling nonchalantly away. Meredith Hunter had died from massive stab wounds in the back, side and temple which the sketchy medical facilities could not begin to staunch. His only audible words had been to his attacker: 'I wasn't going to shoot you.'

*Rolling Stone*'s conclusion was unequivocal. The real blame for Altamont lay, not with Mel Belli or Dick Carter or even Sonny Barger, but with those whose name the paper bore on its own masthead. The Stones were portrayed throughout as monstrously conceited, deaf to all warning signs, careless of all the terrible consequences. It was powerful, even courageous journalism, albeit marred by inaccuracy and confusion. *Rolling Stone* still had no idea how much its own harping on inflated ticket-prices had hardened Jagger's resolve to do a free concert. Nor could its writers resist embroidering a too perfect detail: that when Meredith Hunter was stabbed, the Stones had been playing Sympathy for the Devil.

Most stinging of all was the comment on the Stones' hurried exit from San Francisco, leaving others to pick up the pieces and the corpses. '. . . Fuck Mel Belli. We don't need to hear from the Stones via a middle-aged jet set attorney. We need to hear them directly. Some display – however restrained – of compassion hardly seems too much to expect. A man died before their eyes. Do they give a shit? Yes or no?'

Bill Graham, the concert-promoter – whose expertise had been so consistently ignored – was more specific in his furious condemnation. 'I ask you what right you had, Mr Jagger . . . in going through with this free festival? And you couldn't tell me you didn't know the way it would come off. What right do you have to leave the way you did, thanking everyone for a wonderful time and the Angels for helping out? What did he leave behind throughout the country? Every gig, he was late. Every fucking gig he made the promoter and the people bleed. What right does this god have to descend on this country this way? But you know what is a great tragedy to me? That cunt is a great entertainer.'

On January 8, 1970, a 22-year-old Hell's Angel named Alan Passaro went on trial in Oakland, California, for the murder of Meredith Hunter at the Altamont free festival on December 6. Passaro admitted stabbing the black boy but stated it was in self-defence, after Hunter had actually fired the gun he was waving. He further stated that he had inflicted only slight wounds and that someone else must have made the ghastly rent in Hunter's left temple, the gouge at the top of his spine and the lungs through his tailored jacket into his abdomen.

The main prosecution evidence consisted of a feature film currently on release throughout America. It was the Maysles brothers' documentary, rush-released to cash in on the post-tour publicity, and named, after the Stones' latest incantation to chaos: *Gimme Shelter*.

The climax of the film – not even seen by the cameraman until its editing stage – formed the crux of the murder trial in Oakland. There on screen, playing three times daily coast-to-coast, was the killing of Meredith Hunter.

The Maysles' film had enabled police to identify Hunter's attacker as a prisoner serving time in a California jail for a drug offence committed a few days after the Altamont festival. Further screenings were held throughout the trial to help the jury determine whether the obese Angel striking at Hunter was Passaro, and whether his seven-inch knife, or someone else's, had struck the fatal blows.

Since Passaro's Angel brothers had already delivered Hunter's loaded gun to the California highway patrol, the jury had no choice but to acquit him.

A California court room was thus the first to see the film record of the Stones' triumphal comeback and its obscene climax. There, as the jury watched, were the good tour moments: the wild scenes at Madison Square Garden, the good mix of Wild Horses down at Muscle Shoals. There was the genial press conference, when the woman journalist said, 'Are you any more satisfied now . . . ?' There was Mick Jagger, in beret, scarf and lipstick – looking uncannily like the young Leslie Caron – watching his own repartee on the Maysles' film-editing machine.

'Financially . . . just sa'isfied. Sexually sa'isfied, y'know. Philosophically tryin',' Jagger's on-screen voice said.

'*Rubbish!*' commented his voice derisively in the editing-room.

There, at last, was the crucial moment at Altamont in the red-spotlit dark, as Mick Jagger stood, helpless among the real demons his masquerade had summoned up. There was the crowd, falling back to form a wide avenue. There was the long-legged, prancing figure in its light green tailored suit. There was the converging blur of a Hell's Angel, a death's head badge, a plunging knife, a gun silhouetted on a girl's white crocheted dress. There it was again in slowed-down replay; murder in highlight, like some great sporting moment, a man dying twice for dramatic emphasis.

There was the sequence showing the Stones again, several weeks afterwards, watching Meredith Hunter's end on the Maysles' editing-machine. There was Charlie Watts, as divorced from the unholy fable as ever, yet dominating the scene with his long, sensitive, bewildered face. 'Some o' those Angels, y'know, couldn't have been nicer . . . It was all so insane, what went on y'know . . . it was just unreal . . . Oh, dear – wha' a shame . . .'

There for all time is Mick Jagger, evidently shocked by what he had just seen, yet ruled as ever by the need to show no emotion. His reddened lips have not stirred from their photogenic pout as Altamont ends and the dejected hippy masses wander off like refugees towards a new, unsympathetic decade.

Eventually he gets up and tosses his scarf over one shoulder.

'Okay . . .' he says. 'See y'all . . .'

# 14

## 'The Stones like France tremendously'

The new decade sat there, unwanted and unwelcomed, an alien numeral instantly cancelling out fun and warm rainbows. All around lay spilled debris of the spree that had ended; carnival debris, trodden underfoot or scavenged by those whom the celebrations had not included. Suddenly, one saw Pakistanis in flowered shirts. Bus drivers sprouted side whiskers down to their collars. Peers of the realm took up with Indian gurus. Female customs officers at Moscow airport adopted the miniskirt. Palestinian terrorists crossed into Israel to dynamite some kibbutz nursery school, wearing faded blue denim patched with the sign of Aquarius or a whimsical butterfly.

The hit song of the moment was no heavy rocker or psychedelic labyrinth but a sad cypress lament called Bridge Over Troubled Water, by Simon and Garfunkel. 'When you're weary . . . feeling small,' sang Art Garfunkel, his voice riven with pity for all those who had awoken in the Seventies, rubbed their eyes, and realized they were twenty-six years old.

The draining away of magic was most powerfully expressed in the breakup of the Beatles. Still unannounced officially, it was visible to all in Let It Be, the film of their penultimate record session which Allen Klein had dumped on a public quite unprepared for the melancholy scenes it contained. No vestige of that all-powerful magic remained in the four bearded figures at their bleak, unproductive rehearsal, alternately squabbling and sulking. The Apple house, where Klein now ruled, was a chilly accounting office. Paul McCartney fulminated on his Scottish farm. George Harrison was an unhappy kerb-crawler, Ringo Starr a bit-player in bad movies. John Lennon was off with Yoko on a dozen different crazy crusades. His final act of apostasy had been to take his press arrangements away from his own people and turn them over to the Rolling Stones' publicist, Les Perrin.

That seven-year race, through charts and *Melody Maker* polls and cockpit clubs and wardrobes and millionaires' mansions, had declared a winner at last. The Beatles were breaking up. But the Stones were breaking out.

On July 30, 1970, Les Perrin's office confirmed that the Stones had terminated their relationship with Allen Klein and would henceforward be represented by Prince Rupert Loewenstein of the merchant bankers Leopold Joseph. It was further announced that the Stones had ended their relationship with Decca Records and its US subsidiary, London. The group and their merchant bankers were still undecided about whom to choose of the twenty-one different companies reportedly competing to sign them.

The break with Klein seems to have taken that prescient gentleman oddly by surprise. On June 3, *Variety* had quoted him extensively on his plan to give the Stones a business structure much like the Beatles' pared-down Apple. In particular, *Variety* said, they would have their own record label, distributed by whichever corporation was lucky enough to acquire them. Two months later, the Robin Hood of pop turned round to find an arrow in his back.

After the arrow came a full-frontal arbalest. The Stones filed suit in the New York State Supreme Court, seeking $29 million in damages from Allen Klein, and claiming he had used his position as their manager 'for his own personal profit and advantage'.

Though the break with Decca had long been on the cards, some last-minute efforts were made by Sir Edward Lewis's men to stop so gigantic an asset from walking away. Decca joined the frantic wooing of the Stones by hopeful record companies that was so marked a feature of their 1970 European tour. In Paris, Ronnie Schneider was asked if Decca could do any little thing to make them more comfortable. Schneider said it might be nice if their bill were paid at the George V hotel. Glad to, the Decca man said, not realizing that the George V still let its VIP guests order goods to be delivered from the Paris shops and have them paid for by the concierge.

The size of the bill told Decca unequivocally how things stood. Relations thereafter were terminated with malevolent politeness. Decca informed the Stones that, under their present contract, they were obliged to provide one more single. The Stones duly delivered an unusable studio doodle entitled Cocksucker Blues.

They had entered the new era, in fact, with rather too much alacrity for the taste of those still clinging to a driftwood Sixties dream. Altamont seemed in retrospect the deliberate smothering of all things beautiful, with the Stones looking on, impassive as gas-chamber guards. Britain too, had seen the *Rolling Stone* special report by now, as well as highly critical follow-up pieces in papers like the *Sunday Times*. Enormous resentment was felt throughout the Rock culture at the Stones' apparent lack of remorse and their seeming escape from all comebacks and comeuppance. (Actually, they had been threatened with indictment as accessories in the Meredith Hunter murder. They were currently being sued for $80,000 by Altamont farmers and were themselves suing Sears Point Raceway over the enforced last-minute change of venue.)

Their fourteen-city European tour, that August and September, confirmed the new decade's pattern with the almost reflexive violence and arson that followed their shows. In Paris, the street battle around L'Olympia recalled the Sorbonne riots of '68, with gendarmes launching tear-gas attacks and cars overturned and burning. In West Berlin, sixty-five policemen were injured and twenty-one vehicles damaged in attacks by ticketless fans on the city's Deutschlandhalle. It was the same – almost wearily the same – in Hamburg, Helsinki, Milan, and Gothenburg. Baton charges, falling bodies, the scamper of ambulances with quaint foreign sirens: all would blur into one image on TV screens in the Seventies, barely causing one to glance up from the meal tray on one's knees.

It is somewhat to Mick Jagger's credit that he allowed the release of a film whose climax showed him in such an appallingly unflattering light. He had commissioned the Maysles brothers to make *Gimme Shelter*; he could easily have suppressed it, or demanded removal of its more damning scenes. His decision to let it go out uncut – despite probable repercussions on the European tour – seems mostly to have been based on the $30,000 he had personally invested in it. He did, however, seek advice from his old filmmaking friend, Donald Cammell, who told him what fourteen years' showings have since confirmed: that *Gimme Shelter* is an ugly masterpiece.

368

The brickbats aimed at Jagger as revealed in *Gimme Shelter* were mild compared to those that assailed him as Ned Kelly, the Australian outlaw, when the film received its unwisely touted premiere in July 1970. Just how a director like Tony Richardson could have propagated so sorry a mess remains mysterious. All the film seemed to consist of were men in slouch hats, on horses, riding very fast to unspecific destinations while a (puzzlingly American) voice-over warbled the ballad of Kelly's exploits. There in almost every foundering scene was Mick Jagger, uncomfortably chin-bearded, railing in a feeble brogue against 'the stiff-necked English'. All the critical fury deserved by the direction was unfairly hurled at him. One newspaper reviewer wrote that Jagger was 'as lethal as last week's lettuce'; another said that, encased in Ned Kelly's home-made armour, he looked like 'a cut-price sardine'. Jagger himself affected scornful detachment. '*Ned Kelly* – that load of shit! I only made it because I had nothing else to do.' Donald Cammell's recollection is that after seeing the finished film, Jagger burst into tears.

Jean-Luc Godard's *Sympathy for the Devil*, showing the Stones at work on *Beggars' Banquet*, also appeared in 1970. So did *Performance*, the 1968 fantasy that should have been Jagger's screen debut with James Fox and Anita Pallenberg. A management shakeup at Warner Brothers, and general paranoia in Hollywood about an impending recession, finally allowed the film to be released, in a heavily truncated version. Here, at least, Mick Jagger was not a laughing-stock. His portrayal of Turner – widely interpreted as a portrayal of himself – received mild praise that, compared with *Ned Kelly*'s reception, sounded like standing ovations. For all its faults, and the heavy-handed studio interference, *Performance* seemed to belong to 1970 rather than any part of the Sixties. Still denied general release, it was to become a cult movie, drawing capacity houses in whichever cinematic backwater it chanced to resurface.

Jagger's career and his private life were in a state of flux, matching the new decade. He said as much during the European tour, his inner uncertainty producing an interview of almost unprecedented candour. 'You get to the point when you have to change everything – change your looks, change your money, change your sex, change your woman, because of the business.'

369

Changing his woman was proving a process far more painful than those casual words would suggest. He was still in love with Marianne, as well as bound to her by three years of familiarity and habit. Rather to his surprise, his love had stretched to pardoning her her fling with Mario Schifano and his own resultant worldwide humiliation. He had remained her protector the previous December, just after Altamont, when they appeared together before Great Marlborough Street Magistrates – still visibly estranged by Marianne's Italian Prince Charming – to answer the drugs charge dating from the previous June. The arresting officers' testimony unconsciously corroborated how Jagger had tried to shield and soothe Marianne during the bust, saying, 'Don't worry . . . it's all right. Nothing will happen . . .' The Bench fined him £200, but acquitted Marianne.

Back at 48 Cheyne Walk, the store of happiness continued to dwindle. Jagger was constantly absent, recording with the Stones, conferring with his new advisers – or seeing Marsha Hunt. Marianne's heroin addiction deepened, her looks deteriorated, her behaviour grew erratic and irrational. In restaurants, as she herself admits, she would sometimes pass out face down in her food.

By the time Jagger left to go on a tour in August 1970, the pressure of changes about to be made was practically ectoplasmic. Marianne, in the end, proved the decisive one. 'I knew it was the end of an era,' she says. 'I knew nothing could ever be the same again.' So one night, taking Nicholas and a few clothes from the plundered wardrobes upstairs, she left.

For a time his affair with Marsha Hunt seemed consolation enough to Jagger; a stunning black girl, circled by a cloud of Afro hair, she fascinated and amused him, yet offered no threat to his newfound bachelor independence. All she did say, quite straight-forwardly, was that she would like to have a baby and wanted him to be the father.

His other affairs were numerous and fleeting. He fell into the habit of using his unfinished country house in Berkshire as a kind of illicit one-night hotel. Two years after buying Stargroves, he still had spent only a couple of nights under its Gothic roof. As caretakers he variously installed his parents, his younger brother Chris, and a young man named Maldwin Thomas who used to cut his hair in Knightsbridge. Maldwin grew accustomed to being awakened late at night by Jagger, with some temporary companion, demanding to be let into the guest cottage.

For months he still did not accept that Marianne really had gone for good. He wrote to her and telephoned her constantly at her mother's house in Berkshire. 'In the end,' Marianne says, 'I let myself get fat. It was a conscious decision – I wanted to show I wasn't in the market anymore. When Mick walked in and saw me, his jaw dropped. I knew that really was the finish.'

The introduction was made formally, for once, after the Stones' Paris Olympia show. 'Mick – this is Bianca,' Donald Cammell said, drawing the ever evasive Rock star towards a girl who had been watching the proceedings with the slightly contemptuous detachment of an Egyptian royal cat.

'You two are going to have a great romance,' Donald was inspired to add. 'You were made for each other.'

Her name, Bianca Pérez Mora Macías, wafted the euphony of high breeding into Jagger's ears, even as her stunning and singular beauty focused in his wandering eyes. It was the stern beauty of Latin America, hawkish and head-tossing, yet softened by years in her adopted country; an Inca princess dressed like a Dior mannequin. Her elegance was something sheer, reducing all other women in the room to the level of badly dressed bookmakers' wives. There, in that instant, stood all that Mick Jagger wanted and needed, including his own perpetual reflection. Donald Cammell, melting away diplomatically, had noted the almost eerie facial resemblance between them. Narcissus looked into the pool, and was lost.

They spent that night at Donald Cammell's flat, declining the affable American's offer of a foursome with himself and his Ethiopian girlfriend, Myriam. When Cammell awoke next morning, it was as he had expected: Mick and Bianca had gone off together.

Bianca Pérez Mora Macías was the daughter of a wealthy Nicaraguan commodities dealer. Her uncle was Nicaraguan ambassador to the Batista regime in Cuba. A distant cousin of her mother had been cultural attaché at the Nicaraguan embassy in Paris and afterwards ambassador in Bonn. Throughout Bianca's childhood in Managua, Nicaragua was ruled, as it had been for forty years, by the corrupt and homicidal Somoza regime. Her father was apolitical but Bianca's mother hated Somoza passionately. Women, however, were not supposed to have political convictions, as Bianca discovered when she and her brother, Carlos, joined student demonstrations in protest at the almost annual crop of opposition figures whom Somoza had eliminated.

Her parents divorced and her mother, inadequately provided for, was reduced to running a small restaurant in Managua. Though Bianca adored her father – whom she resembled in all but his green eyes – she rebelled fiercely against the principle of male domination he represented. She vowed she would never let herself be so dominated and so thrown aside.

In 1960, at the age of seventeen, she won a scholarship from the French government to study at the Institute of Political Science in Paris. Her mother encouraged her and her brother, Carlos, to leave Nicaragua, saying that if Carlos, especially, stayed on there he would probably be killed by the Somoza regime.

In Paris Bianca was diverted into a social whirl that ultimately prevented the completion of her political science thesis. She became the girlfriend of Michael Caine, the British actor, who brought her to London, showed her off at the Dorchester, and took her shopping for clothes at Thea Porter's Soho boutique. When she met Mick Jagger, she was deeply in love with Eddie Barclay, the head of France's leading record label. Barclay was a much older man in whom, Bianca admitted, she saw a father figure. Since he was already married, she believed the affair was hopeless. She fell for Jagger not just because he was famous and fascinating and funny and clever, she later said, but also because he was young.

Her effect on him was mesmerizing. Until the Stones left Paris, he spent every possible minute of the day and night with her. She flew to join him in Rome and travelled with him for the rest of the tour. He asked her to return to England with him; she agreed. He had never made so many rapid, irrevocable decisions.

Bianca's arrival, very naturally, sent shock waves radiating through hotel bedrooms to right and left of Jagger's peripatetic Royal suite. No one close to him had ever seen him so completely – so unabashedly – smitten. Bianca herself could not but add to the whispered confusion: a creature almost wilfully remote from the business and compulsion that were Jagger's driving force. All the nuances and needlepoints of protocol within the Stones' European tour were thrown into disarray. Bianca found herself treated, like any parvenu princess, with elaborate frontal courtesy, while the envious jibes and nicknames multiplied behind her back.

Most keenly was the needle poised within the Stones' purdah compartment, where Anita Pallenberg ruled, like a blowsy begum, over Mick Taylor's wife, Rose, and Bill Wyman's Swedish girlfriend, Astrid. Anita, it was rumoured, still had her own designs on Mick. In any case, Bianca's advent as a whiff of disruptive exotica was altogether too much like Anita's own, back in the years before hell-raising, heroin, and childbirth had taken their toll. Anita, therefore, turned on Bianca with all the mischievous resource of her character. She would borrow Bianca's clothes, on the pretext that her own were still unpacked, and then leave the exquisite capes and jackets strewn about the floor. According to Spanish Tony Sanchez, Anita approached him to dig up 'any dirt' on Bianca – preferably that she was really a man who'd had a sex-change operation.

Rome has never been the ideal place for a celebrity to begin a clandestine romance. This particular celebrity knew no way of setting foot outside that would not bring a horde of paparazzi in ravening pursuit. The harassment grew so bad that Jagger ran up to one cameraman and punched him. The result was a heavy fine for assault and a house rule that, in future, paparazzi must be dealt with by Jagger's bodyguards. That was the method in Vienna, while Jagger escaped by shinning over a wall. The outcome was only to be expected. By the time he returned to London with Bianca, the story of their courtship was international news. At Heathrow Airport, Jagger took refuge in sardonic cliché, alleging they were 'just good friends'. Bianca, fixing her tormentors with a dark frown, declared, 'I have no name. I do not speak English.'

By November 1970 she was living with him at Stargroves, where the Stones had gone to try to finish their new album, *Sticky Fingers*. 'They could hardly get any work done, with Mick the way he was about Bianca,' Shirley Arnold says. 'She'd come into the studio and give him the eye . . . he'd leave the other Stones and follow her upstairs.'

That same month, in St Mary's Hospital, Paddington, Marsha Hunt gave birth to a baby daughter. Though the press suspected who the father was, Marsha – for the moment – refused all inducements to name him. 'We had a baby on purpose . . .' was all she'd say. 'Now he's no longer involved with us. At first I thought I cared for him a lot, but I found out afterwards I didn't really know him at all . . .'

In 1970, Bill Wyman discovered that he owed £118,000 in back income tax. It was doubly a shock to the most provident and sensible Stone to find himself facing the vengeance of British tax law against all high earners who do not put away half their income religiously until the day the government asks for it. Bill, with his mathematical mind, instantly grasped the hopelessness of his position. 'Once you owe £118,000 you *never* catch up. All the money you earn to pay that off, you get taxed on as well. You're working for the government forever. And it's *your* fault, even though you're not to blame. All you've ever done is take advice. You have to trust *somebody*.'

Bill's was, if anything, a modest debt compared with those of Mick and Keith, whose incomes from song copyrights had, at least, equalled their share of the Stones' collective earnings. 'I just didn't think about it,' Jagger said later. 'And no manager I ever had thought about it, even though they said they were going to make sure my taxes were paid. So, after working for eight years, I discovered nothing had been paid and I owed a fortune . . .' All the rearguard actions fought by their accountants would be likely to reduce the whopping sum by no more than a fraction. The Inland Revenue, if necessary, was going to get blood out of the Stones.

The single alternative to gritting their teeth, paying up – and wiping out all their American profits – was explained to them by Prince Rupert Loewenstein. By absenting themselves from Britain in the financial year 1971–72, they could escape all tax on their income in 1969–70. The same oracle would work, retrospectively, for every subsequent year they could prove non-residence in the United Kingdom.

The choice of France was an almost inevitable one in those days when tax exile still carried a cachet vaguely associated with W. Somerset Maugham. To Mick Jagger – especially in light of his recent experience there – Paris was the only possible substitution for London. In France, the Stones – far more than the Beatles – had always been ultra chic. There were, moreover, positive fiscal advantages for a pop group serving an international market to be domiciled in a country relatively free of restrictive exchange controls. And, on top of everything else, there was the sunshine, the food, and the booze.

In September 1970, discussions began between Prince Rupert and France's leading financial lawyer, Maître Michard-Pellissier, about the feasibility of a mass migration by the Stones to Paris the following April. Discussions continued in October when the Stones passed through on tour – and were, apparently, not jeopardized by the vehicles burning round L'Olympia. An early whiff of the plan reached the London *Evening Standard* via its wily Paris correspondent, Sam White; then – to Prince Rupert's undoubted relief – the subject was chased from the headlines by the riddle of Mick Jagger's new love.

The official announcement came in March 1971, at the start of a short British tour designed to give it maximum impact. Even the lordly *Times* and *Telegraph* sent reporters up to Newcastle-upon-Tyne to receive the news that the Stones were quitting Britain to settle together in France. Their decision, it was emphasized, had nothing to do with income tax, nor should any such unkind thing be adduced from their planned exit in April, just before the start of the new British tax year. 'It's not a case of running away from the tax man,' Les Perrin said, roughly a dozen times per day. 'The Stones like France tremendously.'

'If you know me,' Jagger added with a grin, 'you know I'll probably be back in Britain more times than I have been in the past . . .' He looked like a Frenchman already, in his floppy blue cap and grey suede maxicoat. Bianca accompanied him on this journey of valediction to Coventry, Manchester and Glasgow; they posed together, pouting identically, and conversed in French for most of the time.

Essentially rootless as he had always been, Jagger found no difficulty in shutting up his two little-loved English properties and contemplating a tax exile's disconnected life. The move was far harder for Bill and Charlie, with their settled homes – harder still for Mick Taylor, who had earned no very large sums yet but was nonetheless compelled to uproot his wife and new baby and follow the others abroad. As for Keith, he simply refused to acknowledge how quickly the days to April 5 were running out. He continued to lie prostrate beside his Batik-draped lamp at 3 Cheyne Walk, as if he had all the time in the world.

Where the Stones were to settle in France remained undecided until only a week or so before their departure. Paris was ruled out at an early stage after it was hinted that Jagger, as a convicted drug user, might be subjected to twenty-four-hour police surveillance. The search then moved to the Riviera. A task force from the Stones' office, led by Jo Bergman, travelled to Cannes and began inspecting likely properties for rent up and down the Côte d'Azur. It was rumoured that estate agents were being asked to provide bathrooms able to accommodate up to eight people for 'Roman-style orgies'. A visit by the team to Mougins, an exclusive hamlet sheltering Pablo Picasso and Prince Sihanouk of Cambodia, produced such alarm among the inhabitants that the mayor fought his next election campaign solely on a pledge that he would never permit Rolling Stones within the town limits.

By mid-March, only Charlie Watts had seen a property to his liking – a characteristically well-hidden farm in Provence. The others were to live together in Cannes while Jo Bergman continued the search for orgy-sized bathrooms. Jo had agreed to emigrate with them, leaving the London office in Shirley Arnold's charge.

The Stones' farewell to London was a concert at the Round House on March 14, followed by a televised appearance at their old haunt, the Marquee Club. Keith – by now in a state of open insurrection – sat at home in Cheyne Walk until almost the moment the cameras were set to roll. Then, furious and barefoot, he flung himself into his Bentley, drove to Soho, left the Bentley on a double yellow line, and stamped in to his place on the stage. It was unfortunate that the Marquee had the same manager, Harold Pendleton, who had annoyed Keith often in the past. It was still

376

more unfortunate that Pendleton wanted a large neon sign reading MARQUEE CLUB behind the Stones as they played. The upshot was that Keith – repeating history – swung his guitar at Harold Pendleton's head, and had to be dragged from the club backwards, his bare feet trailing on the ground.

On the day of departure, Jo Bergman's task force descended on 3 Cheyne Walk, picked up everything around Keith – furniture, bottles, half-full ashtrays, clothes, scarves, Marlon's toys – packed it all into cartons, transported it across the Channel, and rearranged it in the same pattern around Keith as he subsided into his new home in St Jean Cap Ferrat.

On April 7, two days into their official exile, the Stones signed a new recording contract with Kinney Services, American parent company of the New York-based Atlantic label. They had chosen Atlantic for its reputation in Soul music and because, of all the record-company moguls who had wooed them over the past year, Atlantic's president, Ahmet Ertegun, had created easily the most favourable impression. Armenian by birth, son of Mustafa Kemal's ambassador to Washington, Ertegun had cut a unique swathe through the music industry with his flair, imagination, and incorrigible fondness for American popular culture. Black performers from Ray Charles to Otis Redding owed much, for their expert and equitable propagation, to the little, bearded, bald-headed gentleman in his St Laurent blazer and his highly polished alligator shoes.

Ertegun, of all the competing moguls, had unblinkingly met Prince Rupert's terms for an advance on six albums to be delivered over four years. These would be released on the Stones' own label, Rolling Stones Records, but manufactured and distributed by Atlantic. The head of the new label would be Marshall Chess, whose father, Leonard, had founded the famous Chess label in Chicago. Multimillion-dollar dealing and purist sentiment seemed, in all respects, to have made the perfect match.

It was no more than natural that, for the new label's logo and visual accompaniments, Mick Jagger should employ the world's most famous and infamous artist, Andy Warhol. Warhol's design left no doubt as to whom the new deal had most gratified. Jagger's own lips sagged open in a livid red escutcheon from which his unmistakable tongue slavered forth as if to lap up the promised millions. It was – and remains – among the more brilliantly suggestive examples of corporate identification. Marianne Faithfull found it particularly evocative, remembering how much Jagger had admired a stage set like an open mouth at the Royal Ballet, years ago when she was educating him.

On April 16, the new label released its first product, a single with three tracks: Brown Sugar, Bitch, and Let It Rock. A week later came *Sticky Fingers*, an album whose packaging, no less than its contents, flaunted the new era of liberty. The sleeve, also designed by Andy Warhol, showed a denim-clad crotch, its fly a real zip fastener opening to reveal Mick Jagger's lips and tongue. The reverse of the sleeve was the backside of the jeans. Where Sir Edward Lewis would have had a heart attack, Ahmet Ertegun merely twinkled.

Brown Sugar was an instant Jagger-Richard classic, fusing Keith's indolently repetitive opening riff with Jagger's hip-shaking Dixie drawl in a paean of racist sexism that could have been about Marsha Hunt, or brown Mexican heroin, or cunnilingus on a female plantation slave with Jagger as Simon Legree wondering 'How come you taste so good?' Brown Sugar was the stickiest treat to be found on *Sticky Fingers*. But for Wild Horses – a poignant memory of loving Marianne – the rest was little more than a glossary of drug jargon. 'Cocaine eyes', 'speed freak jive', 'cousin cocaine', 'sister morphine' were smuggled into the ear, wrapped in slickly inventive guitar and sax work. The very serial number of the album was COC 59100. All of it sounded new-mintedly brilliant – yet something, somewhere, was missing. The Sixties were missing.

Decca, meanwhile, had sought to clog the market by releasing a compilation of old Stones tracks entitled *Stone Age* and packaged in a sleeve much like the one for *Beggars' Banquet* that Sir Edward Lewis had banned three years earlier. The Stones hated the compilation so much they spent £700 on press advertisements warning their fans it was substandard.

On May 11, Mick Jagger telephoned Shirley Arnold in London and told her he was marrying Bianca in two days' time in St Tropez. He then gave her a list of the seventy-odd people he had chosen as wedding guests. The list ranged from Paul McCartney to the Queen's cousin Lord Lichfield. Shirley had to contact them all within twenty-four hours and get them on a specially chartered plane from London.

His decision to marry Bianca, after only seven months of however headlong an affair, might have indicated to Jagger's friends how deeply the break with Marianne had affected him and how, rather desperately, he wanted a wife. Though Bianca was now pregnant, she herself was not particularly anxious to get married, despite her Catholic convictions. As it was, the friends and would-be friends saw nothing but a disastrous mistake. It was known that the other Stones had not taken to Bianca – that Keith, in particular, backed up by Anita, opposed the marriage bitterly. Bianca was seen as a threat to the Jagger-Richard partnership and thus to the whole future of the Stones. As Yoko Ono could have told her, marrying into a supergroup can give one several extra sets of hostile in-laws.

The wedding, on May 13, was to consist of a civil and a religious ceremony. Since Bianca was a Catholic and Jagger nominally an Anglican, he had to agree to take preparatory instruction in his new wife's faith. He did so willingly, in French, impressing the local abbé, Fr Lucien Baud, with his intelligence and receptivity. He seemed to want to do everything right. That was his reason for leaving the wedding arrangements so late – he wanted to stop it from turning into 'a circus'.

The contradiction between this wish for simplicity and mobilizing his press agent was one apparently lost on Jagger throughout an event for which 'circus' was, finally, a somewhat mild description. The need to be noticed at all times must be a disease that even its worst victims do not recognize. That is all one can conclude from Jagger's seeming compulsion, while drafting top-secret plans and lists, to have the whole world at his wedding, and reduce an important and emotional day in his life to the level of a squalid bear garden.

The world's press had been let into the secret at an early stage. Planeloads of reporters and photographers took off from Heathrow Airport on May 12 along with the chartered jet carrying Paul and Linda McCartney and their children, Ringo Starr, Eric Clapton, Keith Moon, Ossie Clark, Joe and Eva Jagger, and

379

others of The Chosen, supervised by Les Perrin's wife, Janey. 'All the musicians were smoking drugs, even on that short journey,' Janey Perrin says. 'It worried the life out of me. "Right," I said, "You, you and you – make sure you get rid of that before we land."'

The nuptial day began with a dispute between Mick and Bianca over the wedding contract they each had to sign. French law stipulates that a couple embarking on marriage must state whether their property is to be held in common or separately. A French marriage contract is a cold-blooded document listing everything of the bridegroom's that the bride may or may not share. Jagger wanted Bianca to agree to waive any right to his possessions in the event of a divorce. Bianca was upset by the calculation of it, and pleaded with Mick to call the wedding off. She would still have his child, she said, and they would live together. Mick grew angry, saying 'Are you trying to make a fool of me in front of these people?' So the contract was signed, witnessed by Mick's assistant, Alan Dunn.

Meanwhile, in the council chamber of the Hôtel de Ville, Mayor Marius Estezan waited to conduct the civil ceremony beneath a portrait of President Pompidou. In France, civil marriages are open to the public. The scrum of photographers and TV lights was only slightly less in the council chamber than in the sunshine outside.

After twenty minutes' delay, word was brought to the mayor that Jagger would not come unless the chamber was cleared of all but invited guests. The mayor replied that it was a public occasion and the public had a right to stay. Appeals to the commissioner of police produced the same answer. The mayor unhooked his official tricolour sash and said that if the couple did not appear in ten minutes the wedding would not take place.

The ultimatum was telephoned by Les Perrin to Jagger in his prewedding hidey-hole. 'Then I'm not going through with it . . . it's all off,' Jagger retorted. Janey Perrin heard her stoical husband patiently repeating: 'Don't be silly. Don't be *silly* . . .'

Fifty minutes after the appointed time, the bride and bridegroom entered the council chamber together. Bianca, wearing a gigantic-brimmed white hat and a white bodice slashed almost to the nipple edge, looked timorously beautiful. Jagger, in a pale three-piece suit and floppy-collared floral shirt, looked like almost anyone from the stag line of a Saturday-night dance. Fist fights among French photographers, jockeying for the best position, distracted attention from the fact that the bride was four months pregnant.

Jagger tried to turn back again, but was propelled by Les Perrin to the mayor's table, almost dragging Bianca behind him. The civil marriage was accomplished at last, amid a clamour of automated shutters that obliged the mayor to raise his voice to an exasperated squeak. The official witnesses – no one quite knew why – were Roger Vadim, the French director, and the film star Nathalie Delon. Behind them stood Keith, in a state of ferocious décolletage, apparently having a whispered row with Anita.

Up the whitewashed hill, Jagger's theological instructor, Abbé Baud, waited inside the pretty fishermen's chapel of St Anne, facing a congregation whose numbers Les Perrin had controlled by the simple expedient of locking the front doors. When the newlyweds emerged from their hired Bentley, hard pressed by *Paris-Match* photographers and radical student demonstrators, they had to hammer at the church door for admittance. They were heard at last and let in, and the religious part of the proceedings began. The bride was given away – again no one knew quite why – by Lord Lichfield. In his address, the abbé referred to his talks with Jagger. 'You have told me that youth seeks happiness and a certain ideal and faith. I think you are seeking it, too, and I hope it arrives today with your marriage.' At Bianca's request, the organist played Bach's wedding march and the theme from the film *Love Story*.

The reception took place in a small theatre next to the Café des Arts. Lord Lichfield, in his other capacity as Society photographer, moved around snapping the famous faces. Bianca, reappearing in a full skirt, a breast-exposing blouse, and a sequinned turban, managed to upstage even Brigitte Bardot. An awkward moment occurred when Keith Richard hurled an ashtray through a window, but it passed off when Keith passed out on the floor. Later, the bridegroom took the stage for an impromptu perform-ance with Steven Stills and Doris Troy. Bianca, seemingly upset, returned to their hotel suite alone. She would say to friends, later, that with the arguing over the bridal contract, the lawyers, and the mêlée at the ceremony, her marriage had ended on her wedding day.

The party went on all night, heedless of the various small children slumped half asleep amid the marijuana smoke. It is debatable which was the more melancholy sight: those neglected superstar children, or Joe and Eva Jagger, wandering around still trying to find an opportunity to give their son his wedding present.

Marianne heard about the wedding while on her way to Paddington to catch a train down to her mother's in Berkshire. She remembers staggering into an Indian restaurant where, some time later, she passed out into a plate of curry and was removed to spend the night at Paddington Green police station.

'Next morning, when they let me out, they realized I was famous and asked me to sign the visitors' book. It was a brand-new police station: the only other signature in the book was the Home Secretary's, after the official opening.' Marianne signed her name under the Home Secretary's and walked unsteadily out into Marylebone Road.

Before leaving England Keith and Anita had both undergone treatment for heroin addiction. Keith took his cure at Redlands with the famous 'Dr Smith', while Anita, muttering darkly, was conveyed to a clinic in far-away Middlesex. No hope existed for either unless they could be kept scrupulously apart.

Withdrawal from heroin – the 'cold turkey' of John Lennon's bleak song – has been compared to rolling naked on a bed of barbed wire while simultaneously swallowing a bottle of disinfectant. 'You sweat . . . you scream . . . you hallucinate,' Keith says, with what might seem scientific detachment. 'I can remember being *sure* that behind the wallpaper there was a needle and some smack, if only I could get to it.' Every so often, 'Dr Smith', a nurse with the cheerful manner of a district midwife, would pop another drug-substitute capsule under his tongue.

'In seventy-two hours, if you can get through it, you're clean. But that's never the problem. The problem is when you go back to your social circle – who are all drug pushers and junkies. In five minutes you can be on the stuff again.'

382

Keith's new home on the Riviera was Nellcôte, an enormous Roman-style villa, built by an eccentric English Naval officer, on a hill above Villefranche-sur-Mer. Its steep garden was full of rare and exotic plants, its balustraded terrace commanding spectacular views of the mountains and Cap Ferrat. The rent was a thousand pounds per week with an option to buy for two million pounds if its new tenant found it agreeable.

The villa's airy, elegant salons were transformed, like all his previous habitations, into the environment Keith found most comfortable – that is to say, the semblance of a motel room recently ransacked by the police. Album sleeves, wine bottles, discarded clothes, half-smoked joints settled as usual on the grand piano and the marbled mantelpiece. Baby Marlon voyaged, nappyless, along brocaded sofa rims. Nellcôte was the centre of the Stones' exile, its familiar squalor lending continuity – comfort even – to the others' more stilted expatriate lives. It was the meeting place for employees, business advisers, record-company people, fellow musicians, and all the multifarious persons whom this added distance – from London or California – seldom deterred in their supplicant eagerness to 'hang out' with Keith and the Stones. 'In all the time we were in that place, we were never by ourselves,' Anita says. 'Day after day, it was ten people for lunch . . . twenty-five for dinner . . .'

As exiles the Stones socialized, if anything, less than before leaving England. Though Bill and Charlie both lived nearby, they chose – no doubt wisely – to keep their households private and their public profile low. Jagger had rented a villa in St Tropez, but he and Bianca spent the greater part of the summer in Paris, staying at Mistinguette's favourite retreat, L'Hôtel. From June to September Keith's most steady companion was Mick Taylor, who lived with Rose in a much less grand house up the hill from Nellcôte. One weekend when the crowd of hangers-on there was particularly large, Keith and Anita knocked on Taylor's door and said, 'Can we come in for some peace and quiet?'

For the first few weeks, Keith seemed content to absorb himself in the Riviera pursuits of eating, drinking, sunbathing, swimming, and sailing his boat, *Mandrax*, with whomever he could rouse from the Nellcôte floors to act as his crew. Heroin had not killed his taste for the outdoor life – as a two-, a five-, even a ten-year junkie, he would remain physically superior to Mick at his most ostentatiously clean-living and *sportif*. 'Mick got very into tennis while we were in France. He took it *very* seriously. I hadn't bothered since the tennis-club days, when I'd go with my mum and dad in Dartford. But I could still go out on a court and beat the shit out of Jagger any time.'

He also found time for fatherhood. Two-year-old Marlon, thus far, had seen little home life outside the tumbled hotel suites where Shirley Arnold would put him to bed. Marlon learned to walk on a Rolling Stones concert stage; according to Keith's biographer, Barbara Charone, the first words Marlon ever spoke were 'room service'. In Villefranche, he was finally allowed to become a child. Keith devoted the best part of every day to him, carrying him around clamped to the skinny chest that once admitted no encumbrances but its guitar strap and dangling cocaine spoon.

By early May – as his unruly behaviour at The Wedding showed – Keith was starting to chafe against his new life, blaming it on Jagger's infatuation with Bianca and the Paris social scene. More trouble broke out in June – a fight between Keith and the Beaulieu-sur-Mer harbourmaster, who had tried to stop him hitting an Italian motorist after a minor traffic scrape. According to Spanish Tony Sanchez, a Nellcôte house guest, Keith pulled a toy gun on the harbourmaster and was very nearly shot by the official's own heavy-duty firearm.

It was inevitable, as the months passed, that he and Anita should pull each other back to the only possible cure for their shared, oversurfeited boredom. A supply of cocaine arrived with Spanish Tony, hidden in a toy piano the dealer had brought Marlon. Heroin was obtained for them by a French pusher with contacts in the Corsican underworld that ran the narcotics trade in Marseilles. Now they were 'shooting up' rather than 'snorting', buying the drug in £4,000 consignments that rarely lasted longer than a month.

All summer long, the waterfront cafés of Villefranche swarmed with drug pushers of every kind and complexion, avid to supply – and, if they were fortunate, join – the orgies rumoured to take place each night up at Nellcôte. If rumour was to be believed, these orgies did not belong to ancient Rome so much as the wilder hillbilly regions of Kentucky. One English student, hoping to peddle his mite of hashish, found himself drawn into a French conversation that made the Mars bar legend sound positively conventional. 'Zat's right . . .' his neighbour nodded. '*Les poules* . . . chickens. Zey do it with chickens . . .' He was not referring to the Nellcôte cuisine.

Keith and Anita were by no means the only notorious ones. In June, Charlie Watts's wife, Shirley, was involved in an altercation with a customs officer at Nice airport and sentenced, in absentia, to six months' imprisonment for assaulting him. The Aix-en-Provence appeal court later reduced her sentence to a suspended fifteen days, allowing her to re-enter the country. Charlie was, understandably, devastated by this first blot on his family name.

It all added weight to Keith's insistence that France was having a bad effect on them, and that the best cure was to get into a studio and start work on a new album. The Stones had been followed to France by their 'Mighty Mobile', a £65,000 trailer studio, equipped with every technological marvel, including closed-circuit television. Nellcôte, in addition, had a basement that could be converted into extra studio space.

A new album was certainly due in early 1972, when Jagger planned for the Stones to tour America again. Atlantic wanted a special blockbuster, to launch the tour and also counteract the flood of inferior compilations Decca were putting on the market (not to mention the proliferating bootleg albums recorded illegally at concerts).

Keith, therefore, turned his villa over to the Stones, their session musicians, and all the extra personnel needed to build and maintain the improvised basement studio. Anita even volunteered to cook for them. The album that was provisionally entitled *Tropical Disease*, and only later renamed *Exile on Main Street*, began late in 1971 as the biggest house party of Keith Richard's hospitable career. 'I can remember fifty people sitting down to lunch,' Mick Taylor says. 'It was like a holiday camp.'

Jagger arrived from Paris leaving Bianca ensconced in their suite at L'Hôtel. Now eight months pregnant, she had refused to endure the longueurs of a Stones recording session and renew her former acquaintance with Anita. She would say later that she was scared of everyone to do with the Stones except Bill and Charlie, and that, while not wanting to be anywhere near Anita, she was tormented by rumours that Mick was having an affair with her.

Jagger was visibly torn between his obligations to his wife and to his band, and tried to keep the peace by dashing back to be with Bianca whenever possible. 'Mick's fucked off to Paris again,' Keith would tell the others peevishly, reawakening speculation that Bianca had eclipsed a love affair far earlier than the one with Marianne.

Recording in the basement of even a palatial French villa proved hideously difficult. Space was so limited that Nicky Hopkins, the pianist, had to sit in a separate cubbyhole. The power, as usual in France, flickered and faded eccentrically. The current chef, a Frenchman named Fat Jack, interrupted artistic flow by blowing up the kitchen.

Keith and Anita were so strung out on heroin one night that they set fire to their own bed. Recording was interrupted again when a sneak thief walked into Nellcôte through an open door and stole most of Keith's treasured guitar collection.

On October 21, Bianca gave birth to a daughter at the Belvedere nursing home. Jagger announced that she would be called Jade 'because she is very precious and quite, quite perfect . . . I've always been a good father,' he added, 'and this kid makes it easy to be.' He phoned Keith to say that he would not be back in Villefranche for another three weeks. The Stones were to go on recording instrumental tracks, and he'd fill in the vocals when he had time.

There is a legend – half corroborated by Anita Pallenberg – that *Exile on Main Street* was recorded with power illicitly diverted from the French national railway system. Its more vital energy was tapped from a physique in which the most murderous of all drugs could not dull or smother the instinct to make marvellous sound. As Keith himself puts it, 'While I was a junkie, I still learned to ski and I made *Exile on Main Street*.'

On May 12, 1972, it was announced that the Stones' $29 million lawsuit against Allen Klein had been settled out of court. No details were given, other than that 'all outstanding differences' between the parties had been resolved, and both wished it made clear that Klein's company ABCKO Industries, no longer had any part of managing or representing the Rolling Stones.

The action might have continued for years longer, dragging the Stones' frozen royalties with it, but for the intervention of Klein's nephew, Ronnie Schneider, acting unofficially for Mick Jagger to procure a quick settlement. Jagger's offer, relayed through Schneider, was to drop the lawsuit if Klein would release the cash he was holding and pay token damages. Since Ronnie Schneider thoughtfully tape-recorded his talks with both his uncle and Jagger, it is possible to listen in on the transactions. '. . . we'll meet 'im if 'e likes,' Jagger's voice says. '. . . the 'ole thing's just gotten to be a drag . . .' 'The money's there,' Klein's voice says. '. . . the payments are guaranteed . . .' At one point he adds, rather plaintively, 'I believe Mick Jagger still *likes* me . . .'

Freeing the Stones' pent-up millions earned Ronnie Schneider no percentage whatever. They did, however, pay his telephone bill.

Dear Promoter

We know it doesn't happen in America, but in rather barbarous outlands [sic] of Europe we have encountered many dressing rooms which lacked towel and soap . . . It would be nice to know we do not have to worry about the same problem. A clean group is a happy group.

Amenities to be provided in backstage changing area:

Two bottles per show of Chivas Regal, Dewars or Teachers Scotch.

Two bottles per show Jack Daniels Black Label.

Two bottles per show tequila (lemon quarters and salt to accompany).

Three bottles iced Liebfraumilch.

One bottle per show Courvoisier or Hine brandy.

Fresh fruit, cheese (preferably not plastic), brown bread, butter, chicken legs, roast beef, tomatoes, pickles etc.

Alka Seltzer.

Yours sincerely, the Rolling Stones

The tongue-in-cheek humility and room-serviced arrogance concealed genuine trepidation. Two years had not distanced Altamont's horrors: in one way or another, the Seventies were turning out to be almost nonstop Altamont. The temper of the time was such as to make even Mick Jagger fear the response he might arouse, by design or accident. 'Don't say I wasn't scared, man,' he told a reporter at the end of the 1972 tour. 'I was scared shitless.'

Jagger had wanted to return to America with a show that would tacitly apologize for the Altamont shambles by confining itself to small theatres where everyone could see and nobody need get killed. Unfortunately, it was too late for the Stones to beat the economics they themselves had largely invented. In an exercise that had to yield a two million dollar gross, the chief concern could only be how best to lay hands on two million dollars. The bottom line – plangent Seventies phrase!—was an inexorable equation of cities, performing in vast spaces like the one they had barely escaped from with their lives, to audiences among whom it was now commonplace to snort cocaine and throw bottles at the band.

Rehearsals took place in Montreux, Switzerland, close to the clinic where Anita Pallenberg was undergoing treatment for heroin addiction prior to the birth of her second child by Keith Richard. A baby girl, Dandelion, entered the Rolling Stones' world on April 17, apparently unscathed by the drugs Anita had continued to absorb until the fifth month of pregnancy.

In Los Angeles, Peter Rudge, the Cambridge graduate – graduated now to first class honours in the Rock travel business – was already constructing an operation whose complexity was based on the simple premise that nothing whatever must be left to chance. The Stones were to travel this time with their own stage, built and maintained by Chip Monck: a vast white proscenium, surmounted by intertwined cartoon sea serpents, backed by a 40-by-16-foot mirror and six 1500-watt Super Trooper spotlights, and lubricated with a solution of water and 7-Up to make it more danceable. The equipment, light cables, gantries, forklift trucks, would travel overland by theatrical pantechnicon. The Stones, and the pick of their fifty-strong tour staff, would travel by private Lockheed DC-7 jet, the fuselage of which had been decorated with Mick Jagger's mouth and lapping tongue. Peter Rudge's schedules, and the multifarious and subtly graded backstage passes issued with his countersignature, bore the artless letters S.T.P. – Stones Touring Party.

By the time the Stones flew in to Los Angeles to rehearse on a sound stage at Warner Brothers studios, sales of *Exile on Main Street* were touching 800,000. The FM atmosphere seemed to carry nothing but their new single, Tumbling Dice. Money rained down to the novel clack of Ticketron computers. In Detroit, 120,000 applications had been received for the 12,000 seats at Cobo Hall. In Chicago, 34,000 tickets for the two shows at the International Amphitheatre sold out in five hours. Around Los Angeles the black-market price of a $6.50 concert ticket was $75 or its equivalent in hashish.

Two flamboyant Rock music publicists, Gary Stromberg and Bob Gibson, had been hired to blitz the nation's press with Stones stories while simultaneously making Mick Jagger the most unattainable interviewee since Greta Garbo. Every major magazine wanted to cover the tour and was vying with its competitors by nominating 'big name' writers meant to appeal to what was dimly recognized as Jagger's literary side. The *Saturday Review* offered William Burroughs (conveniently a heroin addict as well as a magisterial novelist) but were forced to substitute Terry Southern. *Rolling Stone* commissioned Truman Capote in hopes of a non-fiction drama equalling *In Cold Blood*. The tour was to be filmed by Robert Frank, whom Jagger knew from a collection of still photographs recommended to posterity by Jack Kerouac. Literary as well as social snobbery was to pervade the Stones' dressing-room, even though, in the end, the combined literary talents would contrive not one sensible or original word about the tour in print.

Six months earlier in New York, a concert for the Bangladesh refugees, organized by George Harrison (with Allen Klein) and featuring Harrison onstage with Bob Dylan, Leon Russell, Ringo Starr, and others, had given the state of Rock stardom a tenuous dignity. All that, and more, was about to be undone by the Stones Touring Party.

It was the summer when Governor George Wallace of Alabama was gunned down and crippled for life at a Maryland shopping centre; when Arab guerrillas in tracksuits penetrated the athletes' village at the Munich Olympics and annihilated two thirds of the Israeli weight-lifting team; when the sectarian slaughter in

Northern Ireland was extended to policemen, milkmen, and teenage boys. It was the summer when the Seventies suddenly focused on an age of terrorist warfare, waged in streets, department stores, restaurants and airport lounges, against bystanders whose innocent deaths were proving a better attention-getter than any UN resolution. It was a time when merely standing in a crowd seemed foolhardy enough. To stand above the crowd, in any context, was automatically to enter the rifle-sight of a hundred homicidal grievances.

The same question would be asked of Mick Jagger time and again as he stood waiting to go on in his pink-sashed purple jumpsuit and his fish-shaped mascaraed eyes: 'Mick – aren't you ever afraid of getting shot?'

'Yeah,' Jagger would answer levelly. 'Yeah – I am.'

The current terrorist craze for aircraft hijacking added further rich deposits of paranoia. On June 5, en route for the traditional Canadian warm-up concert, the Stones' private DC-7 was denied permission to land in Vancouver because of an inadequately filed flight plan. Marshall Chess managed to get a telephone call through to the Canadian prime minister, Pierre Trudeau, but to no avail: the Stones had to land in Washington state and, braving roadside customs, cross the border in a fleet of hired limousines.

That night, in Vancouver's Pacific Coliseum, a more traditional form of warfare reasserted itself. Two thousand non-ticketholders stormed the front entrance, throwing bottles and lumps of rock and iron. Thirty policemen were hurt before a relief column of Mounties reached the scene. A single backstage door dividing the Stones from the mob was held shut only by bodyguards' shoulders and piled-up metal garbage skips.

There were those who had audibly wondered if the Stones would pull it off this time, gnarled as they were in their later twenties, and beset on all sides by prepubescent phenomena like the Osmonds, the Jackson Five, and David Cassidy. In a world that did not blink at the high camp of David Bowie and Marc Bolan, nor at Elton John's outsize Lolita sunglasses, what was there left for Mick Jagger to do? Jagger had grown accustomed to questions about the date of his retirement. 'There's a time when a man has to do something else,' he admitted. 'I can't say what it'll definitely be. I don't want to be a Rock 'n' Roll singer all my life. I couldn't bear to end up like Elvis Presley and sing in Las Vegas with all those women coming in with their 'andbags . . . it's really sick.'

The Jagger of the 1972 tour was a Jagger resolved to scotch all rumour that his body had in any way deteriorated. On his order, the first dozen rows at every concert were kept free of press and VIPs, so that those who mattered, the eighteen-year-olds, could best compare him with themselves. The one-piece jumpsuit, with its dangling pink sash, clung shinily to wishbone hips and buttocks tiny as twin collar studs. It became a ritual in each night's performance for him to inch open the frontal zip, past the undeveloped nipple and the crucifix, down to the very shadow of his overstuffed codpiece – or was it a mound of Venus? There was still no one remotely able to portray that dancing paradox of athlete and stripper, that perpetual indecision between predatory satyr and timid, glitter-eyed faun.

Around Jagger's purple and pink self-ravishment, a double album's worth of fresh new material was interspersed among the expected showstoppers – Rocks Off, Rock This Joint, Shake Your Hips, Casino Boogie; the old, encrusted Sixties elixir, fizzed up with Fifties Bebop and Jamaican Reggae and the inspired sax playing of Bobby Keyes. Supreme egotists as they were, the Stones still somehow managed to reaffirm their allegiance and deference to black music at its purest and simplest. For an opening act they had chosen Stevie Wonder, the blind boy prodigy of Motown Soul. Stevie Wonder's act, a show in itself, was given full measure, even subtle precedence as the *real* article, heralding its inimitable counterfeit.

On June 4 the Stones recrossed the US border to play the Seattle Coliseum. That same day in California, Angela Davis, the black power activist, was found not guilty on patently trumped-up charges of conspiracy to murder. 'Who got free today?' Jagger asked his Coliseum audience. 'Angela Davis got free today. Fuckin' great . . .' The Stones played Sweet Black Angel, a song dedicated to Angela Davis and, for many, the pièce de résistance of *Exile on Main Street*. Radical politics were then forgotten in the tour's first party, back at an opulent hotel on Puget Sound where the traditional sport among visiting English bands was to bait lines with room-service steaks and fish for mud sharks out of the window.

391

The Stones' return to San Francisco on June 6, their first since fleeing the Altamont debris, put Peter Rudge's security arrangements to an early and conclusive test. The vital rapprochement was with Bill Graham, who had booked two Stones shows at his 5,000-capacity Winterland arena with no guarantee they would escape a tongue-lashing for their behaviour on the '69 tour. Mick Jagger took the initiative, walking up to Graham with hand outstretched and saying 'Hello, Bill, how are you?' The promoter thawed, admitting generously that he himself, in 1969, might have been 'not the nicest person around'.

To discourage any offensive acts by Hell's Angels, disillusioned flower children, or friends of Meredith Hunter, the Stones were immured in a hotel like a World War II gun emplacement. At Winterland, Bill Graham employed a special force of 75 police to ensure that no one with a motorcycle came anywhere near the auditorium. Two all-out Stones shows gave them absolution in Graham's eyes and, apparently, in San Francisco's. No hint of trouble occurred until they boarded their jet for Los Angeles and a female writ-server in hot pants managed to push a sheaf of legal papers relating to Altamont under Mick Jagger's nose. Seconds later, the writ-server stood on the tarmac, gasping 'He hit me – the sonofabitch . . .' while Keith Richard hung out of the aircraft door flinging her subpoenas after her.

In San Diego, fires made from police barricades were started during the Stones' performance. That and the heat reminded Jagger of a Scottish date, long ago, when they thought the place had caught fire – actually, steam was rising from the audience. Tucson, Arizona, had thoughtfully equipped police at the Civic Arena with tear gas. In the eddying smoke, affecting officers as much as rioters, three hundred arrests were made. One patrolman hurled a rock through a car windscreen, shattering the nose of the seventeen-year-old girl inside.

In Denver, Robert Frank filmed Keith and his friend Bobby Keyes throwing a TV set out of a tenth-floor window in their hotel. Keith mentioned other pastimes for bored musicians on Sundays, like ramming a room-service trolley through the TV screen or dropping a firecracker with a waterproof fuse down the toilet, in hopes of blowing up some other guest's toilet three floors below.

In Chicago, at least, offstage security was assured. The Stones had been invited to stay at the mansion of Hugh M. Hefner, founder and publisher of *Playboy* magazine. For three days, between shows at the International Amphitheatre, they and the Stevie Wonder band enjoyed the run of the Hefner mansion's salons and saunas and jacuzzis and private pinball arcades, the white-gloved servants, the 24-hour kitchen, and other singular amenities, which had enabled Hefner not to set foot out of doors for almost a decade. Every couch in every room – to quote a bystander – 'pulsed with women'; Bunnies from Playboy clubs or Playmates, pneumatic and glossy as the pages they adorned. Hefner himself drifted to and fro, somewhat bemused by his guests' table manners but placidly engaged in his usual pastime: watching television. The Stones were invited to join him in the private pool under his bedroom but found, to their disappointment, that it was only for a bath.

Another disappointed member of the party was Bobbie Arnstein, Hefner's one-time girlfriend, now his personal assistant, and, for coincidental reasons, a sufferer from anorexia nervosa. Reacting against several days' self-starvation, Bobbie Arnstein ate an enormous dinner, finishing with cheese and onions and a slice of Black Forest gateau, which she took with her up to her room. Shortly afterwards, she answered a knock on her door and was amazed to find Mick Jagger there, dressed in tight-fitting white leather trousers. For several uncomfortable seconds, Bobbie Arnstein tried to succumb to Jagger's advances while simultaneously trying not to let him smell her oniony breath or see the plate of Black Forest gateau reposing on a chair. Caught off balance as she turned away, Jagger stumbled back against the chair and, in his white leather trousers, sat straight down on the Black Forest gateau.

The most fun at the mansion seems to have been had by Charlie Watts, talking to Hefner's cook about his days as a driver for the Chicago mobs. 'I don't sleep on tours,' Charlie says, ''cause I got no one to sleep with. So I talk to people – and I draw.'

In Kansas City Truman Capote arrived, a piping little person in shades and a wide-brimmed fedora, accompanied by Jackie Onassis's sister, Princess Lee Radziwill. It might have occurred to *Rolling Stone*'s editors that Capote was far too much a prima donna in his own right ever to establish any rapport with Jagger, and that the result of their encounters could only be ripe bitchery. Jagger disliked Capote for 'trying to make everyone laugh'; Capote described Jagger as 'a scared little boy . . . about as sexy as a pissing toad.' Good things of that kind are apt to get around.

Nevertheless, Capote was allowed to watch the show from a no-go area onstage, taking voluminous notes for the article he would eventually abandon. Princess Lee Radziwill also played at music journalism, flitting around the breeze-blocked backstage corridors as if attending a UN reception. Keith apparently did not relish his implied elevation to the Four Hundred and, later that night, was to be observed outside the Princess's hotel room, shouting 'Princess Radish – c'mon, you old tart, there's a party goin' downstairs!' Capote having proved equally unresponsive to cries of 'Wake up, you old queen!' Keith and Gary Stromberg – dimly apprehending his fame as an investigator of mass murders – smeared the outside of his door with tomato ketchup.

Capote was also permitted to ride the 'Lapping Tongue', as the Stones' private jet was nicknamed, and to enjoy its nonstop bar and buffet and the attentions of stewardesses 'Ruby T' and 'Brown Sugar'. So were Terry Southern and Robert Frank, the latter assiduously shooting scenes for yet another Stones film destined never to see the dark of cinemas. Among Robert Frank's doomed inflight vignettes was the stripping naked of a groupie by road crew members while Mick Jagger and Keith Richard danced down the aisle playing bongoes and a tambourine. According to Capote (whose interest in such things was perforce severely limited), the so-called tour doctor then made love to the girl, strapped on his lap by safety belt. When the plane landed, the doctor still had not managed to put on his trousers again, and disembarked holding them in one hand.

In Washington, appearing on the Fourth of July, the Stones were dissuaded from giving an afternoon performance with fireworks and Jagger in Revolutionary War breeches and tricorne hat. In Indianapolis, a pet hanger-on of Keith's was found to be shaking down drug dealers for a percentage, and was scientifically beaten up by one of the black bodyguards. In Detroit, Chip Monck and Gary Stromberg hid a chicken leg in the bowl of rose petals that Jagger scattered over the audience at the end of Street

394

Fighting Man. In Philadelphia, the rose petals concealed a lump of raw liver; at the next show, it was a whole pig's foot.

In Montreal, one of the equipment trucks was dynamited by French separatists. While bomb squads searched the stage area for three other charges reportedly hidden there, 3,000 victims of forged concert tickets rioted out in the street. Disembarking at Warwick, Rhode Island, en route for Boston, Keith Richard hit a local press photographer who had been annoying Jagger. In the ensuing scuffle, Keith, Jagger, Marshall Chess, Robert Frank, and a black bodyguard named Stan Moore were all arrested. At 8 p.m. that night, as 15,000 people streamed into the Boston Garden arena, Jagger, Richard, and their companions were still locked in police cells at Warwick, sixty miles away. Boston's mayor, Kevin White, arranged for the five to be released on bail and rushed to the Garden with a police escort, five hours late. Stevie Wonder had kept the crowd happy with a two-hour set. When Stevie could sing no more, Chip Monck walked onstage and began reading aloud from *Jonathan Livingstone Seagull*.

In New York, Peter Rudge attended a secret meeting with some Hell's Angels desirous of 'straightening out' the Altamont affair, which, they claimed, had cost their brotherhood $60,000 in legal fees. When Rudge offered no recompense, there was a spate of death threats. The Stones checked into separate hotels under aliases – Mick and Bianca as Mr and Mrs Shelley, Bill and Astrid as Lord and Lady Gedding, Keith as Count Ziggenpuss. All the party were advised to order no food from room service in case it was poisoned.

The final concert was at Madison Square Garden on July 26, Mick Jagger's birthday. Custard pies were thrown about onstage, and the 17,000-strong audience sang 'Happy Birthday to You'. Afterwards there was a party at the St Regis Hotel, attended by Andy Warhol, Princess Lee Radziwill, Tennessee Williams, and other members of the new Rock elite. In the centre, at a table covered with so much luxury it approached squalor, Jagger sat with his white satin lapels flat on his meagre chest, eating voraciously while Ahmet Ertegun spoke into his ever attentive ear. He was twenty-nine – the age at which Nijinsky appeared in public for the last time.

## 15

## 'Hey, Mick – What's happening?'

The new age must have idols of its own. It found one in a family of singing, smiling Mormons, the youngest – and fiercest-adored – of whom was only eleven years old. As John Peel, an intelligent disc jockey, remarked, Seventies' music was more or less doomed from the moment Little Jimmy Osmond sang Blue Suede Shoes. Around the piping infant a dire pantheon, comprising David Cassidy, Gary Glitter and the Bay City Rollers, quickly took shape. Elton John, their presiding genius, had his talent reckoned in baldness and high-heeled shoes. Black music all but vanished under Barry White's grunting avoirdupois. Queues stretched twice round the Albert Hall to see the Carpenters.

In the Sixties not a day seemed to pass without someone somewhere writing a brand-new song. The Seventies had no need for that. Seventies songs were Sixties songs, not to mention Fifties and Forties songs, recycled with minimum effort to satisfy the prevailing nostalgia for any time even marginally better than this. Magic left the music and went into the machine. That long studio desk, serried with bulbs and buttons like the control-centre of a subway-system, needed less and less input to deliver its multi-tracked and vacuous perfection.

The superstars of the Sixties became an embattled millionaire minority clotted in fame that, while it could never diminish, remained powerless to raise them above Karen Carpenter or Donny Osmond in the modern-day charts. Some, like John Lennon, rode out the whole decade on accumulated goodwill. Others, like Paul McCartney, bravely reindentured themselves to learn the new, bland idioms. Still others – Jimi Hendrix, Janis Joplin, Jim Morrison – found a conclusive way to spare themselves the embarrassment of ageing.

Aside from the Osmonds phenomenon – the David Cassidy phenomenon, then the Bay City Rollers phenomenon – glimpses could still be obtained of what seemed, by contrast, like an old-fashioned costume drama, performed with scrupulous regard for precedent by players destined to be type-cast for ever. It mattered not what year; what new, teeny talent filled the ready-made vaults of fan uproar. The Stones were still around. The headlines still smelled dangerous.

In December, 1972, the Nice police issued a warrant for the arrest of Keith Richard and Anita Pallenberg on charges arising from the alleged use of heroin at their villa, Nellcôte. It emerged – in Sam White's *Evening Standard* column – that for the past year all the Stones had been under intense police surveillance with periodic stake-outs at their villas, even infiltration of their social circle by gendarmes posing as drug dealers. Just prior to the US tour, all five had to appear before an examining magistrate in Nice. Jagger, Wyman, Watts and Mick Taylor, after detailed questioning, were pronounced in the clear. Not so Keith, against whom damning evidence existed in the form of a dope-taking ex-chef at Nellcôte. By the time the warrant went out, however, Keith and Anita were safe in the West Indies.

That effectively put an end to the Stones' Riviera tax exile. After recording in Jamaica, for the album that would become *Goat's Head Soup*, all five returned for Christmas in 'good old England', as they were quoted as calling it. The Jaggers were at Cheyne Walk when, on Christmas Eve, an earthquake devastated Managua, Nicaragua's capital and Bianca's birthplace. Attempts to contact her mother there proved fruitless. On Boxing Day, Les Perrin received a call at home in Sutton, asking him to arrange an airlift of medical supplies to Managua. Next day Mick and Bianca flew to Jamaica, then on to Managua carrying $2,000-worth of anti-typhoid serum they had collected en route. Managua was a scene of almost total ruin: neither Bianca's mother nor her father could be found anywhere in the city. Eventually, after Jagger organized appeals over the radio, both turned up, safe, in the neighbouring town of Leon.

Bianca stayed on in Managua while Jagger returned to Los Angeles to organize a benefit concert by the Stones, on January 18, 1973, which raised $280,000 for the Managuan homeless. The problem was getting the money past President Somoza, who controlled all the relief and reconstruction agencies and was busily doubling his personal fortune at the expense of the earthquake victims. Bianca sought help from Senator Jacob Javitts while Mick and the Stones rehearsed for their Far East and Australasian tour.

Japan was removed from the itinerary after its government refused to give the Stones visas under any circumstances. Australia declared Keith Richard persona non grata because of his heroin habit, but then relented and admitted the Stones despite an awkward moment at Honolulu, en route for Hong Kong, when a syringe was found in Bobby Keyes' saxophone. The tour poster showed Australasia, putting out Jagger's tongue to welcome their Boeing jet. On the journey, Les Perrin developed hepatitis, presaging a long deterioration in his health.

In June, 1973, Marsha Hunt went to court in London, claiming that Mick Jagger was the father of her year-old daughter, Karis, and requesting a magistrate's order for maintenance. Though Jagger privately had never denied Karis was his child, he raised a smokescreen of legal prevarication, demanding an adjournment for blood tests. The story in the Stones' camp was that, willing enough to pay maintenance, he had been stung by Marsha's action in going to court. The dispute reached a private settlement: Karis would be maintained by her father.

On June 26, as Keith and Anita lay in bed at Cheyne Walk, police entered the house with a search warrant and ransacked it from top to bottom. Keith, Anita and their friend 'Stash' – the same Swiss princeling who had been busted with Brian Jones – were taken to Chelsea police station and charged with possessing cannabis, Mandrax tablets and Chinese heroin. Keith by himself was charged with illegally possessing a .38 Smith and Wesson revolver and 110 rounds of ammunition. According to Keith, the drugs had been left there by one of the succession of people they had allowed to use the house during their absence on the French Riviera. Released on a thousand pounds bail at Great Marlborough Street they adjourned to Redlands which, four days later, mysteriously burst into flames. Keith carried Marlon and Dandelion to safety, then, harangued by Anita – for some reason, wringing wet – began salvaging what furniture he could. By the time Chichester firemen had extinguished the blaze, Redlands was without its thatched roof and virtually gutted.

398

On August 31, the Caribbean-influenced *Goat's Head Soup* was released inside a sleeve showing Mick Jagger's face, seen as through the folds of a Victorian motoring-veil. The album – too slow for many people's taste – was eclipsed by its smash hit single, Angie, and by the scandal surrounding a track, called Starfucker, whose lyric mentioned vaginal deodorant, 'pussy' and 'giving head to Steve McQueen'. On Ahmet Ertegun's insistence, the title was changed to Star Star, and an assurance obtained from Steve McQueen that he would not sue Atlantic for libel. Even so, the BBC banned the song on all wavelengths. Jagger also could be heard anonymously on Carly Simon's You're So Vain, a song reputedly dedicated to him and full of pointed references like 'You had me several years ago' and 'Your scarf it was apricot'.

It was an accident, but an unfortunate one, that David Bailey's photograph of him for the *Goat's Head Soup* cover – that face softly luminous through gauze – bore an uncanny likeness to the way Marianne Faithfull used to look.

Marianne had become just another hollow-eyed scarecrow among the dozens of drug addicts who traditionally haunt Piccadilly Circus, its tributary streets and subway alleys, hoping to buy, or beg, the day's fix. Marianne's particular trysting-place with the heroin-peddlers was a stretch of wall in Great Windmill Street, close to the famous vaudeville theatre. For eighteen months in the early Seventies, she was conscious of little but that wall in Windmill Street and going there all day, every day, at the nadir of human dignity, waiting to meet the next puncture-mark in her arm.

The experience was not all horrific. 'In a way,' she says, 'I found it *fascinating*. All my life up to then, I'd been the centre of attention. I'd always been looked at. Now nobody recognized me. I was watching the world as it passed by. And I was never, ever harmed by the people I dealt with. I wasn't mugged. I wasn't raped. The whole of that underworld, for some reason, treated me with incredible gentleness.'

John Dunbar had finally divorced her on grounds of her adultery with Mick Jagger, just before Jagger and she finally parted. After Mario Schifano, she had an affair with an antique-dealer named Oliver Muskett. He was kind and supportive to her in her attempt to cure herself of heroin-addiction. She did so finally at a hospital in – of all poignant places – Dartford, Kent.

The Rock star became a male mannequin, in flared yellow suit and white pumps, lolling back against his Latin beauty dressed for the nonce like Scarlett O'Hara, complete with parasol, amid the cosmetic glades of Biba's roof garden. The photographer was Leni Riefenstahl, whose most notable previous assignment had been filming the Berlin Olympics for Adolf Hitler. Shake up the words how you will, they still spell Mick and Bianca and everything chic in London circa 1974.

Fleet Street had just re-invented the gossip column, rightly supposing fatuous tittle-tattle to be the perfect antidote for the ugly facts of Seventies life. The Jaggers were a subject of prime interest to these latter day Boswells, glimpsed after midnight at Tramp, in the members' stand at the Oval or flying from Heathrow on their incessant trips to New York or the Caribbean. With Princess Margaret, Roddy Llewellyn, Lord Hesketh and the Hon.Colin Tennant, they figured in a cast of bold type names as rigidly predictable as any soap opera whose least substitute for interesting activity was sufficient for a snatched picture or peephole paragraph.

A brief era of fashion collected around Bianca's undeniably original wardrobe – the vampish gowns and Forties pillbox hats, the collection of short swagger canes that became her especial trademark. Fashion had been searching for such a grown-up look to supersede the knock-kneed Sixties dolly bird. Girls who sat in Biba's Rainbow Room, sipping ersatz cocktails and listening to Manhattan Transfer, were all to some extent modelled on the new Mrs Jagger. And all over Britain, twenty-year-old mothers shouted at their two-year-old daughters, 'Don't do that, Bianca.'

Bianca had insisted from the beginning that Mick and she were 'separate people' and that she intended to have a personality and a career of her own. Inevitably, since the wedding, she had been deluged with offers of modelling work and film parts. Her appearances as a model were rare, highly publicized and always accompanied by drama. In a charity show for Oxfam at the Grosvenor House hotel, she wore a low-cut gown and a two-tone wig, and carried a short, silver-knobbed cane. To the fashion world she became much what Maria Callas was to Grand Opera, arriving with trunks, hatboxes, maids and shoemakers in her train. The model as prima donna is generally accepted to date from Bianca Jagger. She also began work on a feature film, *Trick or Treat*, produced by the energetic David Puttnam.

Within the Stones' organization, Bianca continued to evoke only dislike, resentment and faint derision. Janey Perrin, Les's wife, remembers her at large in London with a wad of twenty-pound notes in her handbag, phoning in to complain she was 'peesed off'. Shirley Arnold dreaded her tantrums over limousines sent to collect her; according to Shirley, she once sent a chauffeur away because he refused to tip his hat to her. 'That car-hire company had worked for us for years – but they stopped. They said they just couldn't put up with Bianca any more.'

It depressed the loyal Shirley to see how little happiness Mick's marriage seemed to have brought him. Away from the fashion cameras, he and Bianca could be heard in ever more frequent and furious rows. Bianca was seen as a gold digger, ruthlessly using the Jagger name to further her own ambitions as a model and film actress. Tales were told of her obsession with herself, the hours she spent each day before the mirror and at beauty parlours. More serious were the allegations of her shortcomings as a mother to three-year-old Jade. She seemed to resent Jade for tying her to Cheyne Walk while Mick was off enjoying himself. She would alternate between maternal obsessiveness and periods of apparent indifference when she turned the little girl over to a nanny and went off for another day at Ricci the hairdresser's. The same nanny looked after Mick Taylor's daughter, Chloe, and took vengeance for her low wages by letting the children play with their Daddies' gold discs in the bath.

Bianca may have been arrogant, proud and temperamental. She was also a deeply old-fashioned, even puritanical person, whose discontent, from 1974 onwards, stemmed largely from the inability of her marriage to produce conventional, old-fashioned things.

Since her wedding day, she had grown still more uneasy about Jagger's obsession with money, both making it and hanging on to it, which meant that they still had no settled home. They flitted constantly between America, France and England, moving on just in time to prevent Mick's qualifying as a taxpayer. For one improbable period, they had even lived 'unofficially' at Cheyne Walk, ducking down each time they passed the windows.

Bianca rebelled against her subjugation – so much worse than her mother's – under a regime which at times seemed almost as repressive as Somoza's. Her private name for the Stones' empire was 'the Nazi state'. Even as Jagger's wife, she found herself obliged to beg for admittance, like other courtiers, to his inner circle, and compete for attention and favours – the more so if that favour involved money. Staying on in Nicaragua after the earthquake, she had to ring Ahmet Ertegun in New York and get Ertegun's assistant to plead with Mick before he would send her the rent for the house she was living in.

She found herself appalled by the squalor and amorality of life around the Stones, particularly Keith and Anita. Her cold declaration that 'I have nothing to do with them' arose chiefly from fear of becoming like Anita – or Marianne. Her only point of communication with the Stones, paradoxically, was Charlie Watts. She respected Charlie for sticking to his principles, never posing. And because Charlie's wife Shirley – Bianca believed – was the only Stones wife Mick had never screwed.

When Shirley Arnold left the Stones' office, after nine years with them, Mick and Bianca turned up separately at her leaving party. Each had brought Shirley a present 'from both of us'. A furious argument broke out in front of Shirley about which the official joint present was. It seemed to bystanders that their only purpose in communicating was to try to hurt each other.

Shirley had despaired of getting the promotion she deserved with the Stones, and had accepted an offer to join Billy Gaff, noted gay manager to Rod Stewart and the Faces. Stewart, an old Sixties crony of the Stones, was by now a big star, enjoying Jagger-like notoriety for having photographed his own tour orgies with a Polaroid camera. When Stewart and the Faces played Kilburn State Theatre in London that winter, Jagger joined them backstage to get drunk and sing Cockney songs like My Old Dutch ''Ow about comin' back to my 'ouse?' he said later. 'I got some brandy, I fink.' It was not the voice of a jet-setter, nor of a man anxious to get home to his wife and child.

\* \* \*

402

In 1971, Talitha Getty, daughter-in-law of the world's richest man, died mysteriously of a heroin overdose. She had lived in Cheyne Walk, Chelsea, just a few doors away from Mick and Keith, and had entertained them at her house in Morocco. In 1972, their photographer friend Michael Cooper committed suicide after becoming so hopelessly addicted he had to use a wheelchair. In 1973, Gram Parsons, Keith's Country Rock teacher, died suddenly in California and was cremated before a post mortem could be carried out.

At each death, people said much the same thing. 'That's what comes of living too close to the Stones. In the end, you try to live like them. The Stones use people up.'

One potential victim, at least, got out while he was ahead. In December, 1974, as the Stones prepared to record a new album in Munich, Mick Taylor suddenly resigned. He had become disillusioned by Jagger's refusal to broaden the Stones' repertoire, all too evident on their glibly self-deprecating 1974 album *It's Only Rock 'n' Roll*. The angelic, non-smoking vegetarian was now a heroin addict, though, he says, not quite past the threshold to permanent enslavement. Mick Taylor, in effect, was running for his life. The official communiqué said he wanted 'a change of scene'.

Keith Richard sent him a telegram saying 'Thanks for the past five years – it's been a pleasure working with you.' Jagger, peeved by this defection at an inconvenient moment, cattily downgraded Taylor's worth to the Stones when asked what qualifications would be needed by his successor. 'No doubt we can find a brilliant six foot-three blond guitarist who can do his own makeup.'

A dozen or so famous names were variously touted to fill Taylor's place, among them Jimmy Page, Peter Frampton, Jeff Beck, Steve Marriott, Shuggie Otis and Chris Spedding. The album-sessions, in Munich first, then Rotterdam, served as an audition for the short list of Rory Gallagher, Robert A. Johnson, Wayne Perkins and Harvey Mandel. Perkins and Mandel both contributed solos to the album released, more than a year later, as *Black and Blue*.

Wayne Perkins, Keith's candidate, had practically overcome

Jagger's havering indecision when it was learned that Rod Stewart's band, the Faces, would be splitting up soon and their lead guitarist, Ronnie Wood, needed a new situation. Ronnie Wood might have played more bum notes than any guitarist in British Rock. But his hair was spiky. His wrists were bangly. His legs were spindly and knock-kneed as if he perpetually needed to pee. He made Mick laugh. He would be a sidekick for Keith. He fitted.

The arrangement was that the Stones should 'borrow' Woody from the Faces to help them out on their 1975 American tour. The diplomatic language fooled no one in the music industry, particularly since Keith Richard was known to have been 'hanging out' at Woody's house in Richmond, 'The Wick', while they established a partnership between their guitars. 'The Wick' shortly afterwards received a sudden visit from the Drug Squad, but disclosed only Woody's wife, Krissie, and a female acquaintance in bed. The friendliest Face – who had once shared a flat with Gary Glitter and whose party trick was to demonstrate Glitter's rude simulation of 'a one-eared elephant' – was already on the road with his new friends.

The main problem facing the 1975 tour was how to get Keith past immigration authorities who termed mere cannabis-smoking 'a crime of moral turpitude'. Keith had paid a heavy fine for his Riviera heroin exploits and was now technically free to re-enter France. He had paid a smaller fine for the drugs and .38 Smith and Wesson found at Cheyne Walk, half-convincing Great Marlborough Street magistrates that the stuff had been left there by his sub-tenants. He was still as unlikely to receive his H2 temporary working visa as Dracula was to gain admittance to a blood donor session.

Blood was apparently the issue when Mick Jagger approached Walter Annenberg, the US ambassador in London, seeking a quid pro quo for the donation of almost a million dollars to the Pan American Development Fund. According to Spanish Tony Sanchez, the condition for letting Keith into America was that his blood must show not one speck of heroin. The story subsequently arose that he complied by having all the blood in his body replaced. Keith himself denies it, though he did spend time at the

Swiss clinic where blood changes were given. 'I was just fooling around with some people. I came in, opened my jacket and said "Hi – do you like my blood-change?" That's all it was – a joke.'

The Stones announced their new tour to New York by an impromptu performance on the back of a flatbed truck rolling down Fifth Avenue. This time the road organization involved thirteen articulated trucks, 150 tons of lights and a stage even more costly and elaborate – a huge flower whose (allegedly bulletproof) petals unfurled to reveal the Stones inside as thunderous pollination. In Star Star (formerly Star-fucker), quick-release gear bounced forth a gigantic rubber phallus for Jagger to punch and pummel. It was also the tour on which the Stones dared play Sympathy for the Devil again. But for one exploding fire-cracker, the forces of evil remained uninvoked.

Anti-Stone outrage was by now almost as cosmetic as the colours on Mick Jagger's face. Rupert Murdoch's supermarket tabloid The Star called for the exorcism of 'this demonic influence on our children' much as it had previously warned of the approach of swarms of man-killing bees. A church minister in Florida made the significant observation that, of a thousand unmarried mothers in his parish, 984 had become pregnant while listening to Rock music.

For all that, the tour was almost devoid of headlined naughtiness. It would have been completely so but for Keith Richard, who attempted to drive from Memphis to Dallas, with Woody and the Stones' security officer, Jim Callaghan. In Fordyce, Arkansas, Keith's hire car was stopped by an unmarked police vehicle. Mistaking cocaine for tooth powder, the officer charged him with reckless driving and carrying a knife.

Bianca did not travel with Mick or visit him on the tour. She had refused to get involved again with 'the Nazi state'. He commented on her absence belittlingly. 'There's really no reason to have women on tour unless they've got a job to do. The only other reason is to screw. Otherwise they get bored. They just sit around and moan.' None the less he consented to pose in his dressing room with Liza Minnelli on one arm and Raquel Welch on the other.

Woody was a full-fledged Stone in April, 1976, when the tour reconvened for a 39-date European tour destined to keep Jagger in perpetual motion throughout that spring and summer. When *Black and Blue* was released on April 20, after eleven months in cold storage, its sleeve showed Woody's anteater countenance floating with the others' like profiles for a punk Mount Rushmore. The album disappointed many with its rather hollow attempts at black ethnic idioms, disc-funk and Salsa, and the audible one-upmanship between 'guest' guitarists competing for Mick Taylor's job. Nor could it be concluded, from Ronnie Wood's solos on Cherry Oh Baby and Hey, Negrita, that even the second-best instrumentalist had won.

Europe proved even more conclusively than America had that the Stones were no longer calculable simply as musicians or performers. They were a synonym for glamour and danger whose power far outweighed any album they could make, and instantly dominated any year in which they chose to resurface. Before May, 1976, British pop fans were believed to care for nothing but Abba and the Brotherhood of Man. For the Stones' first London concert in three years, almost a million postal applications were received. Doubling their three-concert series at Earls Court arena still satisfied barely one-tenth of the demand. Jagger impressed his British promoter, Harvey Goldsmith, by personally touring the unlovely hangar, checking on seats and audience facilities. 'He's the governor,' Goldsmith was heard to whisper reverently. As Jagger drove away from Earls Court after rehearsals, he stopped his car and handed out free tickets to boys and girls on the street. On his order, refreshments were handed out free of charge to the box-office queue.

Despite all his and Harvey Goldsmith's care, the first Earls Court show was disastrously bad, due mainly to a £500,000 sound system which *Melody Maker*'s critic compared to a railway platform tannoy. The lotus flower stage and Jagger's bouncing phallus seemed elaborate theatrical substitutes for what the Stones used to deliver, unadorned by anything but truculence. Four songs from *Black and Blue*, to quote *The Times*' reviewer, 'were accepted rather than seized on.' The audience then settled to an hour of Stones nostalgia, punctuated by confetti and water showers from a figure who – what with quadrupling oil prices, hyperinflation and encroaching Arabs – almost seemed to symbolize continuity of the British way of life.

406

Again, the tour would have passed without scandal but for Keith Richard's unpredictable and hazardous urge to take the wheel of a motor car. Driving his own Bentley from the Stafford concert back down the M1, to London, Keith nodded off for a moment: the Bentley left the motorway, smashed through a fence and came to rest in a ploughed field. Keith, Anita, Marlon and two other passengers were shaken but unhurt. Minutes later, a police car happened by and a friendly young PC leaned out with the offer of a lift to Newport Pagnell service station. Recognizing Keith Richard, his manner became less cordial. A search of the Bentley revealed a silver necklet with a 'snorting' tube containing white cocaine dust, and a scrap of paper which lab tests later found to be impregnated with LSD. Keith was charged with possession of both drugs, then released on bail to allow him to continue touring Europe.

On August 21, the Stones played their first Rock festival since Altamont, performing to 200,000 in the grounds of Knebworth House, Hertfordshire, in company with Todd Rundgren, Lynyrd Skynyrd and 10CC. The Stones' show began four hours late and was described by *The Times'*gadfly critic as 'a shambling parody'. 10CC, the hit of the afternoon, had earlier played a song containing words that the *Times* reviewer found all too apposite: 'Old men of Rock 'n' Roll come bearing music. Where are they now? They are over the hills.'

Knebworth was Les Perrin's final appearance as the Stones' press officer. The hepatitis he had contracted on the '73 Far East tour had been followed by a stroke from which he was never fully to recover. Frail as he had become, he insisted on turning out for the Knebworth festival. Seeing his determination, Jagger sent a car to collect him, with strict instructions that he mustn't work. For once in his life, the Stones were to look after Les Perrin.

Taking things easy came hard to the energetic little man in the old-fashioned suit whose promise was the same to all journalists, 'You can call me 24 hours a day', and whose uncompromising saneness had steered Mick Jagger through so many media ordeals. Unimpeachably respectable as he was, Les had shared in the Stones' notoriety, his telephone intermittently tapped, his wife Janey subject to disquieting police visits. At one point in the Sixties, impressed by his PR job for pop music's make-believe criminals, some real criminals had approached Les Perrin and asked his help in getting a better press. Reggie Kray himself, using the code name 'Mister James', would ring up Janey Perrin and ask if Les had reconsidered his decision not to take on the Kray Brothers' account.

On the European tour, one of Jagger's executive decisions was finding a successor to Les Perrin. He had someone in mind already – the ex-music journalist Keith Altham. But none of the Stones wanted Les to think he was being sacked.

His meeting with Jagger at the Knebworth festival betrayed the mutual affection that both habitually concealed within staccato offhandedness. 'You wrote me a letter . . .' Jagger said. '. . . Why didn't you answer it?' Perrin said. 'I didn't have a stamp,' Jagger said, emphasizing each answer by pulling Les's trilby a little further down over his eyes.

A BBC-TV crew, returning from Knebworth, sighted Bianca Jagger, all in white, standing by her ditched limousine and trying to thumb a ride back to London. The BBC men offered her a place in their car. Travelling back, sharing the marijuana joint she offered round, they were surprised how friendly, warm and funny Bianca turned out to be.

In 1977, Jerry Hall was just 'Jerry', a 21-year-old American model internationally in demand for her bright gold hair, her lovely, equine face and a merry mouth recognizable even when magnified 50 times for lip gloss ads on the sides of London buses. Her boyfriend was Bryan Ferry, a Rock singer several eras newer than the Stones. Though their careers meant long separations, they seemed a settled pair. 'There goes Jerry,' Ferry would say as another bus displaying her lips passed by.

When Bryan Ferry heard from America that Jerry had left him for Mick Jagger, he was in London, preparing to go on tour with his band Roxy Music. His initial response was true to his native Tyneside. He said he would fly over and punch Jagger on the nose. Friends dissuaded him by pointing out that Jagger was looking very fit these days and might give back as good as he got.

Jerry had captivated Jagger for reasons that made it hard to understand why he ever chose a wife like Bianca. There was nothing exquisite, proud or intense about Jerry Hall. She was an ebullient Texan, a truck-driver's daughter whose hobbies were horse-riding and leg-wrestling and her only social manner a series of *faux pas* at which she herself laughed uproariously. That laughter – perhaps that leg-wrestling, too – seemed the more enchanting and liberating to a man who had spent five years with a mirror-image, different from himself only in that it frowned.

At first, Jerry seemed no different from the many rather young women with whom Jagger had affairs while outwardly insisting that his marriage remained intact. Bianca corroborated this idea of a relationship deeper than mere monogamy. '[Mick] sleeps with many women, but rarely has affairs with them,' she said. 'They are all trying to use him. They are all nobodies, trying to be somebodies. Mick would say "go ahead" if I wanted an affair . . . but he knows I won't do it.'

Such friends as they had in common were long accustomed to the uncomfortable sight of Mick and Bianca trying to maintain this façade in public. At one New York dinner party, given by Halston the designer, Bianca arrived alone, in a male tuxedo; Mick did not appear until after dinner, emerging from the shadows with that unostentation which, to Bianca, represented his uttermost arrogance. She railed at him for the way he treated people who gave him social invitations. He mocked her for caring too much about 'the fuckin' jet set'.

By 1977, they were leading virtually separate lives. While Mick was seen around with Jerry Hall, Bianca was noticed in the company of Ryan O'Neal the actor, Helmut Newton the photographer, and, for a brief period, Jack Ford, son of the President of the United States. She lived mostly in New York, part of the social circle that revolved around Andy Warhol, Halston, Truman Capote and The Factory, a discotheque where queues formed each night to watch the famous, old faces arrive. A poignant snapshot of the period shows her at The Factory, sitting with William Burroughs. Bianca looks like an earnest little schoolgirl, desperate to hear something significant from the great man's lips. Unfortunately, the great man's lips are clamped tight on a straw stuck into a Coca Cola bottle.

The marriage survived for the sake of Mick Jagger's public face, and for Jade, the daughter he idolized. As things stood, Jade's life was sufficiently disconnected, shuttled between New York,

409

London and Joe and Eva Jagger in Westgate-on-Sea. Whenever he could spare the time, Jagger devoted himself to her. He would collect her from nursery school and linger there, quizzing the teachers about her progress and behaviour. Her teachers, privately, considered her trying. At one moment, she would disrupt a whole class with her tantrums; at the next, she would climb into her teacher's lap and curl up kittenishly. Often, she seemed in want of attention and affection, as – more secretly – did her mother.

In 1978, when Bianca was in California, Mick and Jerry flew into Los Angeles together, openly. Bianca had been talking to a lawyer, but only on a 'what if . . .' basis. Now she decided: she would file papers for divorce.

Keith Richard's third child by Anita Pallenberg, his longed-for second son, was born in Geneva in March, 1976. They named him Tara, after Tara Browne the Guinness heir, who had died so tragically young. Keith then left in a mood of high euphoria to tour Europe with the Stones. In Frankfurt it was announced that, after seven years together, Keith and Anita finally intended to marry. Keith maintained it was purely for convenience, to qualify Anita for a British passport that would cover their three children. The date and place of the wedding were not announced. Keith toyed briefly with the idea of having it onstage at Earls Court arena.

On June 4, the ten-week-old baby boy died. The cause of death was given officially as a flu virus. Keith heard the news in Paris, shortly before he was due to go onstage with the Stones. Stricken as he was, he insisted that the performance must go ahead. His face that night was skull-like as his arm pumped out the old infantile array of girls, flash and carelessness.

He continued the tour, drowning his desolation in mindless noise and light, the Southern Comfort bottle on his amplifier, and the company of his surviving son. At seven years old, Marlon Richard had long ago exchanged the role of child for that of friend and father confessor. He was with Keith onstage, on the next bar-stool; at whatever hour of night up in the hotel suite, playing with the video cassettes and toys and telephones they used in common, Marlon would bear his father company.

Keith's – and Anita's – engulfing love for Marlon, redoubled after their baby's death, was oddly contrasted by their apparent indifference towards their daughter, Dandelion. The little girl suffered from a speech defect and, at the age of almost four, was barely able to talk. Anita seemed to reject her, leaving her in a state of lovelessness which others in the Stones' circle – notably Mick and Bianca Jagger – did their best to assuage. When Dandelion fell ill in Paris, it was Bianca who took her to hospital and visited her there. Over-indulged as Marlon was, he too lacked the more mundane forms of child care. Bianca was putting him to bed once and found she could not take off his socks; they were literally stuck to his feet. Marlon told her he'd been wearing the same pair for almost a month.

While Marlon played underfoot, Keith and Anita faced each other like captives in a cell padded with everything that could be ordered by telephone; sharing a life-sentence of luxury from whose undistracted boredom the sole escape came via the needles they plunged into their arms. Anita almost exulted in her addiction – she called heroin 'Henry' and enjoyed initiating others, like Mick Taylor's wife, into its use. She would tease Keith mercilessly for his inability to 'handle' his habit, as when he tried to hide the syringe from servants or hotel waiters. She despised him, too, for letting it take his sex drive away. Tired of snorting cocaine and trying on clothes, she would wander into their bedroom: a moment later, her voice would begin calling Keith, querulously first, then mockingly.

Making him jealous, like Brian Jones before him, was a trick Anita could accomplish even in her present unkempt condition, with junk-dilated eyes and deteriorating teeth. In Jamaica, when the Stones were recording there, she caused such a scandal by running around with the local Rastafarians that Keith returned to London without her. She subsequently got herself arrested and was badly beaten up by the local police before staggering back to England and Keith's forgiving arms. In 1976 she was in trouble with him again for visiting clubs devoted to the new Punk Rock music, where teenage boys strapped their legs together and stuck safety pins into their cheeks. The archetypal Punk guitarist, whom many wild young bands took as their inspiration, told Anita sternly to stay away from such places.

411

The mutual tolerance that had kept the Stones together through so many trials and aberrations, showed signs of severe strain in the later Seventies as Mick Jagger rose higher into society with his new model girl-friend and Keith Richard sank lower, with Anita, into heroin. The more respectable Mick became, the greater seemed Keith's determination to remain a Sixties outlaw, crashing cars, carrying guns and knives, destroying hotel rooms and letting his teeth turn black. For the first time since the age of six, their inseparably opposite natures were in open conflict. Keith criticized Mick for social climbing reflected in the 'theatrical shit' with which he had dressed up the '75 tour. Mick was disdainful about Keith's inability to stop being busted, and the schoolboy pranks with Woody, like invading the Jagger hotel suite and bouncing on the Jagger bed, shouting that they were 'the Trampolini Twins'.

For Bill Wyman and Charlie Watts, the effect of keeping Mick and Keith simultaneously in focus had become almost schizophrenic. Bill, at least, seemed to be tiring of the effort. His first solo album – *Monkey Grip*, in 1974 – had shown him he need not stand at the back of the stage for ever, and he had almost resigned after Mick Taylor in 1975. Even stoical Charlie disliked the atmosphere of bitchiness between Mick and Keith, and was talking about going off to find some peace and quiet in a jazz band.

The first part of 1977 was already planned. In February the Stones would meet in Toronto and give a series of performances at a small club called the El Macombo. These club dates would be the basis of a live album and would also keep them in practice for the following year's North American tour.

On January 13, at Aylesbury Crown Court, Keith Richard was found guilty of possessing the cocaine-snorter discovered in his Bentley after he had crashed it in Buckinghamshire the previous September. The jury rejected his counsel's plea that the snorter wasn't his but accepted that the LSD also found in the car might have belonged to someone else. Keith was fined £750, with £250 costs, and warned that if he committed another drug offence in Britain, he would be sent to prison. During the three-day trial, Mick Jagger had flown in unexpectedly from Los Angeles to lend him moral support and give evidence if necessary. As he left the court with Mick, Keith described the verdict as 'a good old British compromise'.

Bad feeling boiled up again on February 20, when Mick arrived in Toronto as planned to rehearse for the El Macombo dates, and discovered that Keith had not yet even set off from Britain. For five more days, as the Stones awaited him in Canada, Keith dawdled on at Redlands, deaf to transatlantic calls and even a furious joint telegram from the others reading WE WANT TO PLAY. YOU WANT TO PLAY. WHERE ARE YOU?

At Toronto Airport on February 25, customs officers, searching Anita's bag, discovered a piece of hashish and a burnt spoon, later found to be encrusted with heroin. Anita was held for questioning, then released pending analysis of the spoon and a blue Tic Tac mint also confiscated from her.

Three days later, a squad of Royal Canadian Mounted Police burst into Keith's suite at the Harbor Castle Hilton hotel, bearing a warrant for Anita's arrest. Lying about the suite they found cocaine and an ounce of pure heroin worth £2,500 – enough to warrant a charge, not merely of possession but of intent to traffic. Keith was taken to Toronto police headquarters and booked for an offence which under Canadian law carries a maximum penalty of life imprisonment.

Mick Jagger had intended the Toronto visit to be a discreet, low profile affair. Instead – thanks to what seemed a continuation of Keith's perverseness into actual insanity – the Stones suddenly found themselves facing Judgment Day.

For the next 48 hours, as the world's press trumpeted their imminent dissolution, the Stones attempted to rehearse at a warehouse in downtown Toronto besieged by reporters and TV crews. As an additional handicap they had Margaret Trudeau, errant wife of the Canadian Prime Minister, who had somehow attached herself to Ronnie Wood, booked a suite at the Harbor Castle and was 'hanging out' there with Woody in blithe disregard of political consequences.

On March 2, Jagger suddenly left Toronto for New York. His excuse was that Jade had appendicitis and Bianca was not in town to look after her. Keith held the night's rehearsal without him, wearing a sheepskin coat and making pointed remarks like 'Let's

413

go back to the hotel, read all Mick's books and get ourselves properly educated.'

Jagger was back again on March 4 when the Stones began their drastically cut-down taping sessions, two nights instead of the projected five, before a live audience at the El Macombo club. Against all the odds, both performances were brilliant with Keith, seemingly unmindful of what hung over his head, pulling out Chuck Berry licks not heard since he was a boy at the Crawdaddy Club.

On March 7, he appeared in court to be told he would be additionally charged with possessing one-fifth of an ounce of cocaine. Next day, he returned to the same courtroom on the charge of intent to traffic heroin. He was remanded for a week on bail of $25,000, and had his confiscated passport returned to him.

Later that day, the Rolling Stones began visibly to disintegrate. Jagger told Keith he was leaving for New York and did so with only a curt farewell over the telephone. Woody also abandoned his friend, after much agonizing, and followed Jagger to New York. Margaret Trudeau went along too, provoking press rumours that she and Jagger had been having an affair in Toronto. It gave the drama a surreal touch to hear Prime Minister Pierre Trudeau angrily responding to charges that his wife had been seen in a bathrobe, 'partying' outside Jagger's hotel suite: for a time, indeed, the Stones seemed to have precipitated the Trudeau government's collapse as well as their own.

Bill Wyman and Charlie Watts hung on in Toronto until March 10, then they, too, left to carry on lives which, having been denied all fruits of the Jagger-Richard partnership, could not be expected to share in its terminal crisis. Shortly afterwards, Keith, Anita and Marlon visited Niagara Falls. 'Shall I jump?' Keith asked, not altogether rhetorically.

The future of the Rolling Stones hung in the balance during April and May, 1977, as Keith stayed marooned on bail in Toronto; Mick Jagger flitted in and out of gossip columns, giving fulsomely non-committal predictions of the outcome if Keith were jailed for life; and the world, with far more modern scandals to think about, wondered whether it really mattered anyway.

Keith spent his time in Toronto listening to the El Macombo

playback, taping songs for the solo album he might one day make and gazing fondly on Marlon's prodigious intake of carbohydrates. Anita decorated their hotel suite with newspaper headlines chronicling the intertwined dramas of the smack and Margaret Trudeau: STONE ON HEROIN PUSHING CHARGE. COULD THIS BE THE LAST TIME? PREMIER'S WIFE IN STONES SCANDAL. THE MAGGIE MYSTERY TOUR. MAGGIE, MICK IN NEW YORK DENY HANKY-PANKY. BREAKUP FOR STONES ON CARDS SAYS JAGGER. HEY, MICK – WHAT'S HAPPENING?

In June, Keith's lawyers succeeded in obtaining permission for him to leave Canada to 'practise his profession' during the months before his case came to trial. A special visa had been granted to admit him to America for heroin addiction treatment at the Stevens Psychiatric Centre, New York. There Anita and he received neuro-electric acupuncture, a new cure which cut the horrors of cold turkey by administering mild electric shocks. Since Keith's visa forbade him to travel outside a 30-mile radius of the clinic, tapes for the new album, *Love You Live*, had to be brought to him by Jagger. The rift between them repaired itself in a drinking bout that ended, most unusually, with Jagger passing out. The crisis was past. The subordinate Stones received word to meet in Paris, to record the album that would become *Some Girls*.

Keith's case did not come to trial until October, 1978. In return for a guilty plea, the trafficking charge had been reduced to one of mere possession. Though the prosecution asked for a jail sentence, Judge Lloyd Graburn was impressed by Keith's apparently determined efforts to cure himself for good. He was put on probation for a year and ordered to continue his drug rehabilitation programme. An extra proviso was that the Stones should compensate Toronto for the trouble they had caused there by giving a charity concert in aid of the blind.

The Canadian government appealed against the lightness of the judgment but it was upheld. Keith Richard – quoting his own phrase in a note to his mother, Doris – was no longer 'the fugitive'.

After the '78 American tour, there was little to report but the sparkle of the tiny diamond set into Mick Jagger's right-hand upper front tooth, and the unvarnished ferocity with which he set about preventing his estranged wife from laying hands on twelve and a half million dollars of his fortune.

Marsha Hunt had already felt the chill of a parsimony that seemed to increase the more millions and mansions Mick gathered unto himself. His boast that he had never given any woman anything held good also when Chrissie Shrimpton, his old girlfriend, tried to sell some of his adolescent love letters for publication in the *News of the World*. Jagger used his heavyweight British lawyers to stop Chrissie selling the letters and threatened to sue her for breach of the copyright vested in his adolescent handwriting and sentiments.

When Bianca filed for divorce, on grounds of 'irreconcilable differences', Jagger instantly cut off all her New York charge accounts. He also had the furniture removed from 48 Cheyne Walk, telling Jade it was going away to be 'repaired'. Jade could not understand why the antique wall tapestries in the dining room needed repair, and innocently asked if people had been walking on them.

Bianca wanted the case to be heard in California where, irrespective of French marriage contracts, a divorced wife automatically receives half her husband's property. To this end she retained Marvin Mitchelson, a Hollywood lawyer famed for the 'palimony' settlement he had wrung from Lee Marvin on behalf of the actor's ex-mistress. Bianca, naively, hoped that Mitchelson would not talk to the press. The press, shortly afterwards, learned from Marvin Mitchelson that Bianca was claiming twelve and a half million dollars – half of Jagger's estimated earnings during their marriage – with $13,400 per month in expenses, meantime, and a $50,000 advance against her lawyer's fee.

Bianca admitted later that she was unwise to hire so provocative a lawyer as Mitchelson, but said it was a natural reaction to the offer of $100,000 which Jagger had made to her privately.

After several months' legal manoeuvring, Jagger's lawyers managed to get the action heard by the far less alimony-conscious judges of the British High Court. There at last, late in 1980, the marriage ended: the mirror cracked. Bianca's final settlement was one million dollars.

\* \* \*

For the young of 1979, there was no long, lingering summer of hope, as for the young of 1969, that a golden age might stretch on into eternity. To be young in 1979 was to be preternaturally aged, as fashion took its ideas from fatalistic dole-queues. The heroes of Rock music were those most successful in making themselves as ugly, shabby and mundane as their audiences. The Police, the Specials, Madness, Duran Duran: their very names hurled contempt at anyone who had ever found music glamorous, they dressed like the disapproving parents of fans who had once followed the Stones.

In Cheyne Walk, Chelsea, two Queen Anne houses, deserted by their tax exile owners, joined the company of London's lesser shrines. Number 48 was irreproachably shuttered and still. At number 3, the windows were often illuminated. A series of sub-tenants lived there, on condition they did not disturb the petrified debris of Keith Richard's last hasty exit. In every room lay half-packed cartons, expensive children's toys, old Sixties finery and single ski boots. A double aircraft seat, showing signs of having been physically torn from its moorings, lay on the floor of the elegant downstairs drawing-room with its view over Albert Bridge.

Up the twisting stair, dimly-lit by jewel-studded Moroccan lamps, Keith's purple music room and psychedelic piano were just as he had abandoned them. So was the oddly bare 'tripping' room, with its medieval candlesticks and the shrine to Jimi Hendrix. The glass mirror ball could still be turned on, sending flecks of light dancing into wood-panelled corners where so many cushions and insensible beings used to lie.

For some months in 1981, Anita's friend Molly Parkin borrowed the house. Sleeping in Keith and Anita's top floor room – in the carved wooden bed used in *Performance* – she became convinced that the place was haunted. Alone there at night, she would hear scufflings on the stairs, voices and movement in the rooms below her, as if the house were helplessly re-enacting its unwanted and unbelievable past.

# EPILOGUE

# 'Something happened to me yesterday'

ALLEN KLEIN lost the core of his business empire in 1971 when Paul McCartney brought a successful action in the High Court to dissolve the Beatles' partnership. Though still in titular control of Apple and its two least accomplished founders, George Harrison and Ringo Starr, the Robin Hood of Pop seemed to have spent most arrows in his quiver. In 1979, the US Internal Revenue Service had him indicted on six charges of income tax evasion, involving $216,000 allegedly earned from selling Beatles albums that were supposed to have been given away. Thanks largely to testimony by his old associate Pete Bennett, he was convicted, fined $5,000 and sent to prison for two months. Since the late Seventies, his attention has moved from music to feature films (*The Greek Tycoon*) and productions for the Broadway stage.

ANDREW OLDHAM relinquished the 'Loog' – and much of its attendant outrage – after moving to New York in the late Sixties. He is still in record production, until recently working from a small office in the Broadway Brill Building, not far from the site of his famous Times Square billboard in 1966. He is married to a Colombian film star, and spends several months of each year in Bogotá – which, he says, is just like England in the mid-Fifties. Though all his more colourful delusions have left him, he still would like to have been Laurence Harvey, sashaying and fingersnapping round those magical, coffee-scented Soho streets. His most recent project has been to supervise a compilation of music on the old Cameo-Parkway label for – guess who – Allen Klein.

MICK TAYLOR made his bid for individual stardom with one of the most costly and self-indulgent solo albums even the mid-Seventies had seen. It was unsuccessful, and he has since opted for the quieter glories of a studio session guitarist – heard most recently on Bob Dylan's 1983 album, *Infidels*. His years with the Stones have left a lingering bitterness. He sometimes describes himself as 'the only lead guitarist ever to have left them, and lived.' However, on their 1981 American tour, he visited them backstage in Kansas City

421

and later walked on to play a couple of numbers with them, giving further proof that he was the Stones' one and only virtuoso.

ALEXIS KORNER continued to be a father figure to British Blues musicians while working with successors to Blues Incor-porated and, later, pursuing a varied career in radio and television. That whisky-warm voice, introducing an eclectic showcase of music each Sunday night on BBC Radio One, was still the best friend any Bluesman could have in a foreign land. He died suddenly in 1983.

BIANCA JAGGER lives in New York, where she is visible chiefly through her work on behalf of Nicaragua, her birthplace, and other troubled Central American countries. That work includes public fund-raising, conferences on relief and welfare and, not infrequently, visits to highly dangerous battle-zones. Opinion is growing that she may well have been misjudged.

MARIANNE FAITHFULL came back from the wall in Windmill Street to build a career as the serious musician she had always hoped to be. The voice that had been so shy was now raw and nicotine-stained, distilling the lessons of her 30-year lifetime with bitter world-weariness but still-game insouciance and trust. She has made three highly regarded albums (*Broken English*, *Dangerous Acquaintances* and *A Child's Fantasy*), has become a number one hit in Ireland and become a cult figure in West Germany. Today, despite the pop jargon and gestures she uses, her manner most strongly evokes that of an emigrée Austrian countess. 'Vere Dignum Justum Est,' she quotes, speaking of the scurrilous Stones book by their ex-drug pusher, Spanish Tony: 'Truly it is right and just.' Apart from one calculated lapse in the mid-Seventies, she has refused all offers to cash in on her life with Mick Jagger. In 1977, she married the guitarist Ben Brierley, whom she had met in the Punk Rock era, performing under the name 'Ben E. Ficial'. In 1982, she and Ben were living in Chelsea, just a few streets away from Cheyne Walk, still suffering routine harassment from police and press. They were so poor that Ben was selling off his guitars and Marianne, the pictures painted of her long ago when she herself seemed to live in a cornfield by Renoir. 'I'm always skint,' she admits. '. . . always have been always will be. But one thing I still can say. My credit is good.'

CHARLIE WATTS still catches the first plane home at every

opportunity and returns to his wife, his house, his horses, his antique silver and collection of American Civil War kepis, sabres and long-barrelled Colts. Between Stones duty, he and Ian Stewart play in an ad hoc pub Blues group called Rocket 88. Stew recruited both Charlie and Bill Wyman to join the assorted middle-aged superstars who performed in the 1983 benefit concerts for Action Research for Multiple Sclerosis.

BILL WYMAN, second class Stone for so many years, has steadily come into his own as a solo hitmaker, composer, photographer and walking encyclopedia of British pop. In 1980 he composed an original score for the film *Green Ice*; he has since had a Top 20 single, collaborated on a book of words and photographs with the nonagenarian Marc Chagall (meeting whom was, he says, 'a greater thrill than meeting Chuck Berry'); accepted a large advance to write music for a Broadway show and begun work both on an official history of the Stones and a video chronicle of his own life. As well as music, he is interested in archaeology, astronomy and Australian aboriginals, and is a member of the Royal Horticultural Society; with his food and wine and filed-away facts, he can claim, at 47, to be 'totally at peace with myself'. In 1982, thanks to easier tax laws in England, he and Astrid Lundstrom – his common law wife and energetic personal agent – came back from France to live in London, where Bill, among other things, hopes to found a Tony Hancock Appreciation Society.

ANITA PALLENBERG is not easily recognizable as the bewitching, long-legged Sixties girl whose power within the Stones seemed to verge on the supernatural. Since parting from Keith, she has put on weight massively, suffered illness and a broken hip and in general become the saddest casualty among those many whom the Stones left strewn in their wake. Lonely as her life is, it still contains almost involuntary drama and scandal. In 1980, at her house in Long Island, a teenage boy killed himself with a shotgun on her bed. In 1983, she was raided for drugs at London's Grosvenor House hotel; shortly afterwards her name cropped up in circumstantial connection with the Stephen Waldorf shooting. She is conscious that people suspect her of practising witchcraft around the Stones – she says she only wishes it *had* been true. She speaks of Keith nowadays almost maternally, playing his tapes as a proud parent might and warning him to 'watch out for those American girls'. In her handbag she carries a photograph of their eleven-year-old daughter Dandelion, whom Keith's mother has taken over (and re-named Angela) . . . 'Isn't she like Keith?' Anita says fondly. 'Keith and I still love and respect one another, you know. The trouble is, we can't live together. The people who really love Keith are all waiting for him to grow out of the kind of life he lives and the creeps he lets surround him . . . I've always been his greatest fan.'

KEITH RICHARD put the s back in his surname as proof of his wish to regain touch with the father he had not seen since he was a semi-delinquent eighteen-year-old. Bert Richards had subsequently parted from Doris and was living alone in retirement – with no thought of benefiting from his millionaire son – when Keith discovered his address in 1976 and began writing to him. They met up finally in London during the Stones' 1982 tour, Bert flinging his arms round Keith and saying, 'Wotcher, mate.' The episode was symbolic of Keith's desire to return to normal life after his ten-year heroin odyssey – a desire which, it seems, could be accomplished only through a final and irrevocable break with Anita. Since then, he has met and (in 1984) married Pattie Hansen, a breezy young American actress who tells all about her that the vampire is 'a good egg'. He still, however, likes guns, knives, long words, ugly dogs, even uglier bodyguards, big cars and – most of all – the Scotty Moore guitar solo on Elvis Presley's I'm Left, You're Right, She's Gone. He still drapes a batik scarf over the lamp in whichever hotel room he happens to be occupying. He still expects every policeman who approaches him to turn him round, with arms against the wall – though today, more often than not, all the policeman wants is an autograph.

MICK JAGGER sacked his British publicist, Keith Altham, before the Stones' '82 European tour, and instead hired 26-year-old Alan Edwards, PR for many new young British bands and as personable and pretty as Jagger insists all his retainers should be. Like others before him, Edwards was astonished at the different tones and voices Jagger offered to the press – 'a bit of sex' for the *Sun*, quiet intelligence for the *Sunday Times*, camp bitchiness for *Time Out*. Habitual snobbery showed when, after rejecting many competent press interviewers, he agreed to talk to John Mortimer, QC, playwright and adaptor of *Brideshead Revisited*, who had previously understood 'Alexis Korner' to mean a traffic junction in Birmingham. Since that tour, apart from working on the new Stones album, Jagger has done almost nothing, yet has maintained himself constantly in the international headlines. In 1983, he accepted an offer reputedly worth three million dollars from Lord Weidenfeld to write his autobiography. Interviewing almost as many ghost writers as he had interviewed lawyers for his divorce, he finally settled on John Ryle, deputy literary editor of the London *Sunday Times*, an authority on esoteric French literature. The resultant synopsis was offered by dramatically secretive means to British paperback publishers, and was turned down by most of them. In 1983, Jerry Hall enjoyed a brief adventure with the millionaire Robert Sangster, but returned to Jagger and, shortly afterwards, announced she was to have his baby. Their daughter was born in February 1984. Jagger has confirmed that they will marry but declined to name a date. He still declines to give most information. A recent *Rolling Stone* cover interview with him yielded so little, the magazine had to abandon its usual question-and-answer format. The question most frequently put – and most unanswered – is whether Jagger intends to go on leaping with the Stones through his forties. He has still shown no sign of seriously trying to do anything else. Possible film parts still float perpetually in the wind. The flavour of his personality remains as it has always been – familiarly exotic, mysteriously mundane. His ambition is, to all appearances, limitless, and he seems incurably afraid to take a chance.

THE ROLLING STONES released a new album, *Undercover*, in late 1983, accompanied by a promotional video that the BBC considered too violent to show on its *Top of the Pops* show. STONES VIDEO BANNED screamed every British tabloid front page. Even at the height of Sixties madness, that would have merited only a two-column filler somewhere inside. As long as Fleet Street suffers from Rupert Murdoch brain-death, the Stones can go on for ever. As long as a dilettante Englishman sees his truest reflection in a white-faced gipsy, and the Glimmer Twins outshine either Jagger or Richards, the Stones can go on for ever. As long as people will pay money to see a legend from a quarter of a mile and fifteen years off, the Stones can go on for ever. For what they were, and what people think they still are, the Stones do go on for ever.

# AUTHOR'S NOTE

This book could not have been written without the help of its principal characters. I am grateful to the Rolling Stones for the access they gave me during their 1981–82 tour, and for illuminating interviews with Mick Jagger, Keith Richards and Bill Wyman. I also have drawn on conversations with them, and with Charlie Watts, Ron Wood and the late Brian Jones, during my years on the *Sunday Times* and various other newspapers, back to 1965.

I owe a special debt, for their help, generosity and candour, to Andrew Oldham, Marianne Faithfull, Anita Pallenberg, Robert Fraser, Christopher Gibbs, and the late Alexis Korner.

Sincere thanks also to: Keith Altham, Shirley Arnold, David Bailey, Dr W. Bennett, Jo Bergman, John Birt, Tito Burns, Donald Cammell, Barbara Charone, Tamara Glenny, Giorgio Gomelsky, Brion Gysin, Mary Hallett, Keith Howell, Glyn Johns, Lewis Jones, Tom Keylock, Laurie Lewis, Ken Llewellyn, Lord Lichfield, Astrid Lundstrom, Gered Mankowitz, Albert Maysles, David Maysles, Miles, Molly Parkin, Janey Perrin, Dick Rowe, Ronnie Schneider, John Spinks, Helen Spittal, Ian Stewart, Dick Taylor, Dave Thomson, Frank Thorogood, Mike Turner, Keith Vyse, Robert Wallis, Peter Watson, Leslie Woodhead.

Though reliable source books on the Stones – as on all pop subjects – are extremely rare, the following have been useful and are recommended for further reading: *The Rolling Stones – the First 20 Years* by David Dalton (Thames & Hudson, 1981); *Up and Down with the Rolling Stones* by Tony Sanchez (William Morrow, 1979); *Keith Richards*, by Barbara Charone (Futura, 1979); *Stones Touring Party* by Robert Greenfield (Michael Joseph, 1974).

My special thanks, for encouragement and inspiration, to Jack Artenstein, Michael Sissons, Peter Matson, Roger Houghton, Russell Miller, Caroline Taggart and Lucy Sisman.

# Index

427

429

430

431